HEMINGWAY
in His Own Country

HEMINGWAY
in His Own Country

ROBERT E. GAJDUSEK

UNIVERSITY OF NOTRE DAME PRESS

Notre Dame, Indiana

Manufactured in the United States of America

Library of Congress Cataloging-in-Publication Data
Gajdusek, Robert E.
Hemingway in his own country / Robert E. Gajdusek.
p.   cm.
Includes bibliographical references (p.   ) and index.
ISBN 0-268-03059-6 (cloth : alk. paper)
ISBN 0-268-03060-x (pbk. : alk. paper)
  1. Hemingway, Ernest, 1899–1961—Criticism and interpretation.
I. Title.
PS3515.E37 Z59545   2002
813'.52—dc21

                                              2002012304

My love and gratitude for all those who endured my unavailability and suffered and supported my commitment to these essays—especially to Karl, who even when young carried my cameras and generously shared me with Hemingway.

Let me additionally acknowledge the reciprocal gift of scholarship, that the effort to know and discover comes flooding back as excitement, delight, moments of grace and beauty, as cities and landscapes and sea journeys, and the intimate companionship with the man I study, his sensitivity, his precision of sight, and his rare standard of truth.

It is very bad for a writer to talk about how he writes. He writes to be read by the eye and no explanations or dissertations should be necessary. You can be sure that there is much more there than will be read at any first reading and having made this it is not the writer's province to explain it or to run guided tours through the more difficult country of his work.

—Ernest Hemingway,
interview with George Plimpton
in *Paris Review* 5 (Spring 1958)

"Well, I thought, now I have them so they do not understand them. There cannot be much doubt about that. . . . And as long as they do not understand them . . . you are ahead of them. Oh sure, I thought, I'm so far ahead of them now that I can't afford to eat regularly. It would not be bad if they caught up a little."

—Ernest Hemingway,
in *A Moveable Feast*

Contents

Foreword

Ernest Hemingway often worked long and carefully before settling upon his titles, and Robert (Robin) Gajdusek may have done the same, for his title *Hemingway in His Own Country* conveys very well certain qualities of this collection of essays. It is a splendid book that meets Hemingway's writings on his own terms and brings all of Gajdusek's intelligence and instinct to bear on exploring the rich literary landscapes of Hemingway's "own country."

As critical fashions come and go, Hemingway has attracted different interpreters with varying degrees of success in helping readers understand Hemingway's art. One of the first books about Hemingway, Philip Young's *Ernest Hemingway* (1952), was groundbreaking, not in the way of an earthquake but rather in the sense of preparing a new critical edifice. It was the harbinger of many similarly psychologically and biographically oriented interpretations of Hemingway's fiction and life, generally written by literature professors with minimal credentials in psychology, and who generally cared little for aesthetics or the integrity of the stories and novels. Hemingway's works, for these critics, were means to ends and not ends in themselves.

In the same year as Young's influential but problematical book, Carlos Baker's first of four editions of *Hemingway: The Writer as Artist* appeared. Its very title indicated a focus less on Hemingway the historical figure than on what and how he wrote. Although Young did not seem aware of the problem, his approach in *Ernest Hemingway* entailed risk for those without solid grounding in psychology or psychiatry. No wonder Hemingway reluctantly, after Young's pleadings, gave the professor permission to quote from his fiction. Freud and Jung were in the

air, and indeed their writings were to some extent derivative of literature ancient and modern. One kind of fiction built on another, and such
books have continued to be published through the 1990s. In an age and
in a country of rampant individualism, perhaps such emphasis should
not be surprising. Yet in the tradition solidly begun by Baker, not Hemingway but Hemingway's writing should provide the center around
which critical satellites revolve, and Gajdusek's criticism in this tradition always orients on true north.

During my service as Hemingway Society president, I recall with
sardonic amusement the telephone inquiry of a somewhat overly
assertive man who asked if he would be eligible to join the Society. He
wanted to be perfectly honest and clear that he was interested solely in
Hemingway the man and had *no* interest in his writing. I wondered
about the source of such a passionate certitude and attraction, but it was
his dime, and I said only that yes, he was eligible, since the charter the
Society had inherited by way of Mary Hemingway's will specified that it
existed to promote the study of Hemingway and his work.

A generation ago, in "Ernest Hemingway and His Interpreters of
the 1960s" (in a special Hemingway issue of *Rendezvous*, 5.2, Winter
1970), Richard Etulain wrote, in tacit agreement with at least that one
Hemingway Society member, that the publications relevant to Hemingway and his work since 1952 revealed that "Hemingway's fascinatingly
active life" and not his writing was "of chief interest to most readers."
Poor readers.

Thus I find Robert Gajdusek's essays about Hemingway's writing so
rich and refreshing. Gajdusek seems uninterested in the historical person but deeply and broadly committed to discovering the art, the craft,
the genius of Hemingway the writer, and he does so with considerable
art of his own. Just as reading the entire oeuvre of a poet or fiction writer
clarifies individual works that are perhaps puzzling or incompletely
understood, so the papers collected here reinforce each other, creating a
whole greater than the sum of all its parts.

I cannot help but think that reading this collection will be a post-
graduate education for even seasoned Hemingway devotees. I had been
reading Gajdusek's interpretations piecemeal for several years and was
beginning to see and admire how he reads. Here in this book's wonderful
range and variety we can discover connections between and among
Hemingway's writings and similarly between and among Gajdusek's
readings. The latter weave together and make *Hemingway in His Own
Country* one of the best books to help us understand Hemingway's writ-

ing, from the earliest *The Torrents of Spring* to the posthumous *The Garden of Eden*. For instance, the long-held received critical judgment of *The Torrents of Spring* was that it was merely a hastily written farce whose purpose was to break Hemingway's contract with the publisher Boni and Liveright (which it did). Furthermore, in satirizing Sherwood Anderson's *Dark Laughter* it supposedly revealed Hemingway as an ingrate. Gajdusek's brilliant reading of *The Torrents of Spring*—"Hemingway's Application for Membership in the Club"—simply subsumes the conventional wisdom and leaps beyond it to discover dimensions in Hemingway's book that transform it from a vaudeville posy to a stunning garden of ideas and art—always art. Gajdusek's reading of *The Torrents of Spring* is a marvelous tour de force. One can never again pass off that early book as a satirical jeu d'esprit or contract breaker. It was a breaker, all right, but a breaking out from his apprenticeship and a breaking into "membership in the club" of his fellow modernist authors.

Gajdusek's several essays on *A Farewell to Arms* constitute a monograph in themselves. "Hemingway and Joyce" is the most ambitious of his comparative studies, which include another essay linking Hemingway to Joyce, an essay linking Hemingway to Fitzgerald's *Tender Is the Night*, and, transcending literature, an essay linking *For Whom the Bell Tolls* to Velásquez's great painting *Las Meninas*. Such rich readings go on throughout the collection. For example, "A Brief Safari into the Religious Terrain of *Green Hills of Africa*," which studies another neglected Hemingway book, is another tour de force that convinces because of its detail. "Artists in Their Art" is inspired, original. I'm awed by its comparison of *For Whom the Bell Tolls* to a painting and its insights into fundamental aesthetic truths. The essay on a "mere" short story, "An Alpine Idyll," is remarkably broad in the context not only of Hemingway's work but also of world literature. It is a fine, deep reading that cautions us in taking received opinion for an adequate critical response. In "The Cost of Sin in the Garden," Gajdusek adds scholarship to his keenly critical/aesthetic approach. This may be the very best essay to date on *The Garden of Eden*. "On the Definition of a Definitive Text" is brief but important because of textual problems in Hemingway books (especially the posthumously published ones). It introduces complex issues of textual accuracy and authorial intent too little understood and explored in Hemingway studies. "Gender and Role Reversal in Fitzgerald and Hemingway" makes fine comparisons of Fitzgerald's and Hemingway's "metaphoric transformations" in gender and other roles—without twisting the narratives into unrecognizable jargon.

One finds hope for the possibilities and importance of literary studies in contemplating these and the many other rich topics and varied presentations in Gajdusek's book. His is a brave, generous, and carefully attentive sequence of readings and studies. Gajdusek makes an original contribution to Hemingway studies in particular and to the analysis of fiction in general. He is a superbly sensitive reader whose papers and publications on Hemingway in the last fifteen years have earned him some claim to be Hemingway's leading contemporary critic. I welcome you to the remarkable feast he has spread before us.

Robert W. Lewis

Prologue
Set Piece

When Hemingway first came to Europe as an ambulance driver in World War I, the first task that was set before him was the gathering of the dead bodies, the pieces of bodies, that remained after the explosion of a munitions factory outside Milan. I like to think that the writer, the artist, was initially created on those fields as he went about assembling the fragments, putting together the parts of those who had been violently torn asunder. I see him there, the young boy, searching, stooping among the brambles and thistles, among the detritus and debris of wire, smashed tiles, broken masonry, and pieces of reduced machinery in the littered but green meadows. There had been a furious rending and the ending of life, and his search was a species of memory, sorting and groping amid the ruins for whatever remained, apprehensible only in fragments, of the now inapprehensible God. There had been an order, complete, whole, precise, and marvelous, and a cataclysmic eruption of violence; and as the boy knelt to put together, to establish order again, to bring discrete parts back into a relation to a lost whole and to reestablish the lost image of man, he perhaps came upon the unspoken name of his future vocation.

To the Reader

I believe that anyone who intelligently pursues Hemingway—whether in specific works, in his philosophy, in his biography, or actually in the landscapes he so enlivened with his perceptive presence—will find unexpected reward. Wherever he brought himself—as writer and artist, as sensually alert, involved participant in foreign lands and cultures, as passionate *bon vivant* with declared and discovered appetites for vivid experience—he was ever fully alive and involved in mankind. Because of journalism's distorted sensationalist image of the man, which aggrandized him in the imagination of his readers, the greatest surprises when exchanging myth for familiarity are in the discovery of his lifetime fascination for knowledge, his high and extraordinary intelligence, his omnivorous reading, and his unexpected shyness and solitudes.

He brings us himself always, whether as confidant and friend and intellectual equal with James Joyce, Ezra Pound, Bernard Berenson, Gertrude Stein, John Dos Passos, F. Scott Fitzgerald, Pablo Picasso, and a vast array of other great men and women of our time, or as the compassionate and committed companion of the unexalted GIs and soldiers, the cabmen and jockeys, the waiters and simple fishermen. Throughout his life he was a true democrat: though readily consorting with aristocrats and very rich, he was very often with the very poor, a compassionate sharer of the adversities, tragedies, and wonders of innumerable lives.

The geography of his wanderings he saw with a painter's eye—he often wished to be a painter, and he always stressed the necessity for keenness of sight. Equally a man with sensitive and acute receptivity to all sensations, he deplored in his culture the undeveloped art of listening. When we come to inhabit the hotels he stopped at, the houses he lived in, the towns and cities he brought to our consciousness by his avidity for life, they almost seem—as do Pamplona and Paris, Key West and Ketchum, Venice and the Michigan North Woods—to be invested with his presence. This is largely due to the heightened delight and intensity he brought to his living.

I have followed other writers where they have lived, getting to know whom they befriended and where and how they went, and usually such "tracking" is a pedestrian game. The average artist is an average man and living amidst interesting if rather average enthusiasms. This is decidedly not the case with Hemingway, whose mind went everywhere and who seemed to read and devour anything that came his way—a way selected by passions and awarenesses certainly uncommon.

Therefore, I hope to here bring you the excitement of my attempts to discover the mind, aesthetics, and style of this unusually hidden man. No one has been more exposed to cameras and reporters and few were more victims of celebrity; and, despite all that press coverage, no one of our century's artists, I am finally assured, has been less authentically seen and understood. He is a great, great artist—probably our best and most studied craftsman—but we as a culture still often read him as though he had but offered us portraits and accounts of hunting and fishing, of wars and travel in diverse countries, and of careless sequential loves. The truth is, we have to look to Whitman and Melville for comparable force, to James and Emerson for comparable sensitivity to manners and nature, to Wyeth and Audubon and Eakins for equal sight, and to Stendhal and Tolstoy for a similar understanding of war and society. I offer these essays as indices to his authentic mastery of his métier.

This collection of essays is a gathering of insights and recognitions and discoveries that came into being as waystations on my journey toward a new understanding of Hemingway based on a closer look at the paradigms and patterns that structure his work.

These are not just textual studies. This is not a book *about* Hemingway; nor is it a history or biography studying the creation of his remarkable writing. Rather, it is twenty-six separately focused essays that examine such topics as (1) the influences upon him ("Hemingway and Joyce: A Study in Debt and Payment," and "Dubliners in Michigan: Joyce's Presence in Hemingway's *In Our Time*"); (2) a remarkable passage or section in an individual work ("Pilar's Tale: The Myth and the Message"); (3) a presiding theme organizing a specific work ("A Brief

Safari into the Religious Terrain of *Green Hills of Africa*" and "The Cost of Sin in the Garden: A Study of an Amended Theme in *The Garden of Eden*"; (4) a metaphor sustained throughout his work ("Bridges: Their Creation and Destruction in the Works of Ernest Hemingway," "The Suspended Woman in the Work of Ernest Hemingway" and "Sacrifice and Redemption: The Meaning of Boy/Son and Man/Father Dialectic in the Work of Ernest Hemingway"); or (5) Hemingway himself as man and/or writer ("Harder on Himself Than Most: A Study of Hemingway's Self-Evaluation and Self-Projection in His Work" and "Hemingway's Late-Life Relationship with Birds").

The danger of such a gathering of fugitive insights gained through a pursuit of understanding over a long period of time has been a certain occasional redundancy. The process of unlocking the secrets of a style has been one of discovering and enunciating a succession of insights and delivering them to a succession of audiences never precisely the same. This has meant some inescapable repetitions as perceptions gained from one work have subsequently been applied to others. The experience of returning again and again to certain fundamental principles or modes of research may be for the reader occasionally similar to that of reading several novels by a mystery writer that feature the same detective, who brings with him or her a perhaps familiar apparatus and manner, of inquiry, though applying them to a new and intriguing case. The chapters can be read independently, whatever reinforcement they may give to one another.

The essays are not unified by a chronology or a developmental thesis, and they are deliberately arranged not chronologically but to a certain extent arbitrarily so that readers may feel a certain freedom of movement through a variety of texts—perhaps something like what they felt when they first came upon and read Hemingway's works or what a wanderer in the stacks of a fine library might feel upon inadvertently finding unexpected riches there. Each essay is a unique pursuit of a special problem, and I think each opens new doors. It is my hope that this process of discovery may be for the reader a series of excitements and recognitions, carrying something like the delight and fascination I found during my own scholarly journey. Welcome, fellow adventurer, once again into the remarkable landscape laid open for our travels by this very great artist indeed. In this terrain, his own country, you may be led to new and fresh ways to read him.

Introduction

Society is often unqualified for judgment on genius, for, ranging beyond the familiar, genius eludes quick and too-familiar intellectual embrace. Additionally, seeing and knowing and living with genius that may walk common roads may not qualify one for judgment—"mostpeople" (as e. e. cummings has it), are distracted by the human and troublingly awkward apparatus with which spirit functions to get through this world. I love Dylan Thomas's remark, "How *could* that man be a great devotional poet—I saw him fall downstairs yesterday in his suspenders."[1] When we are dealing with Van Gogh or Picasso or Beethoven or Hemingway or Pound, or any other of those special temperaments capable of journeying where none have gone, out beyond the usual perimeters, there must be special sight or special insight that also transcends nomenclature and recognition. Remember how Hemingway always insisted that every new work of art must go beyond where others have been. The acts of special grace that make Hemingway Hemingway and not just another aspirant for fame are there to be seen, but usually, even inevitably, they reveal themselves as ambiguities and incomprehensibilities, as discrepancies and bizarre dislocations that need to be adjusted to inadequate terminologies.

It is informing that, despite a continuing series of biographies, the mystery of Hemingway the man seems radically unexplored. Most such studies are intent upon making him accessibly familiar or on judging him by moral or ethical standards implicit in the critic's perceptions. The facts and data found seem to insufficiently register upon sensibilities eager to see him in their own image.

To give one broad example, the Hemingway of Paris in the twenties has not yet been sufficiently understood; no one has satisfactorily explained or defined the mystery of Hemingway's early effect and success, his genius when young. How does a Midwestern boy out of a suburban high school, whose image in his yearbook reads like a typical American success story, whose associations and activities tend to suggest his immersion in and emergence from the upper middle class American dream, become the very great artist and craftsman that he so surely almost instantly became and was? There is no biography that adequately accounts for his very special genius. There were surely thousands of literary aspirants in that Paris of the twenties, each intent in her or his own way on glory, and it was only Hemingway who in a matter of months had become not the acquaintance but the familiar and friend and companion of James Joyce, Allen Tate, Ezra Pound, Gertrude Stein, Archibald MacLeish, John Dos Passos, F. Scott Fitzgerald, and Ford Madox Ford—great writers all (and in a few cases geniuses in their own right), who never suffered fools gladly. The list is too long to name. The point should be made that in all the annals of the emerging literary lights of Paris, one finds *no* other figure who is so consistently described as extraordinary. Hemingway had an extraordinary magical effect upon the artists and writers of Paris of that time. Its unusual power and swiftness need to be noted. While Hemingway was still a young man in his early twenties, and before he had written his first novel, Ezra Pound told Ford Madox Ford, "He's the finest prose stylist in the world. . . . He's disciplined, too" (Rood 197), and Ford, called the dean of English letters at that time, acknowledged, "I did not read more than six words of his before I decided to publish everything he sent me" (Rood 197). John Peale Bishop, on meeting Hemingway in 1922, described this twenty-three-year-old as having "the most complete literary integrity it has ever been my lot to encounter" (Rood 197). Allen Tate spoke of him in those early Paris years as "one of the most intelligent men I know and one of the best-read" (Wickes 169). Samuel Putnam, who met him at that time, said of him, "No successful writer was ever less pretentious or more cordial toward others engaged in or associated with the craft" (132). One of Fitzgerald's first gestures on meeting Hemingway was to write to Charles Scribner to pronounce that Hemingway was "the real thing" (Rood 171–72). The list seems endless. These were comments by the leaders of humanistic thought in that time, not about someone who had long been similarly acclaimed, but about a very young man who had just recently come to Paris from the middle-class American heartland. Nowhere has criticism adequately faced up to that extraordinary take-over of twentieth-century letters by an unknown interloper.

Although what Denis Brian later wrote may be true, that "probably of no other living man has so much tripe been penned or spoken" (61), in the Paris of the twenties there was one sure and amazing thing: the sustained and almost unqualified acclaim of a talent like none other. The words that are repeated in a score of accounts are "complex" and "complicated." Mary Hemingway, years later, would still call him "the most decent and complex man she had known" (Brian 3). Malcolm Cowley pronounced him "a very complicated man" (Brian 51). To Tommy Shevlin later, "he was a complex, very difficult man" (Brian 98). To Harry Sylvester, "he was a complicated guy" (Brian 105). His attraction and charisma then were legendary and scarcely to be believed. Hadley was able to say of him, "He was the kind of man to whom men, women, children and dogs were attracted" and that he was "one of the most sensitive people I have ever heard of" (Brian 53, 52). Malcolm Cowley described him as "one of the most truly charming people I've ever met. He could charm a brass doorknob off the door" and later said, "By 1929 almost everyone in Montparnasse was talking about him. The charisma began to sprout like wings out of his shoulders" (Brian 51). Gilbert Seldes's wife urged her husband, "Forgive him everything—he writes like an angel" (Brian 61). These messianic dimensions expand: he is described as taking up all the air in a room, of filling a doorway, of having "larger than human proportions" ("Indestructible" 20). This is the stuff of myth. Nathan Asch's portrait is merely exemplary—note the awe and reverence:

> It was an event when this towering figure passed the sidewalk tables at the Dome, as arms waved in greeting and friends ran out to urge him to sit down with them. The occasions were charming little scenes, as if spontaneous, although repeated. In view of the whole terrace, Hemingway would be striding [past] and he wouldn't quite recognize whoever greeted him. Then, suddenly his beautiful smile appeared that made those watching him also smile. And with a will and an eagerness he put out his hands and warmly greeted his acquaintances, who, overcome by this reception, simply glowed and returned with him to the table as if with an overwhelming prize. (Brian 54)

C. J. Guest acclaimed "something magnetic about him" and Robert Cowley later said the only other man he had ever met who matched Hemingway's "magnetic personality" was John F. Kennedy (Brian 243, 197). George Saviers attributed the spells he cast to "more zest for life than most people" (Brian 243). Now, accounts like that are, first, everywhere from those who saw him and knew him, and, second, radically unlike those surrounding his contemporaries. Is there another young writer of that time and place for whom the record of "sensitivity"— whether in conversation, acts, or behavior or in his prose—is more full, or another writer of that time and place of whom the words "humility" and "generosity" were more used by those who had indeed so experienced him as to know him? Where is the writer whose literary and personal conscience was more active? He held himself ultimately responsible. It was Adrienne Monnier, owner and manager of the great French Les Amis des Livres bookstore, who admonished his contemporaries in the cafes, saying that he perhaps alone would be the one remembered, because, as she put it, "he cares for his métier" (Bryher 213). No one but Hemingway then could have defined what is moral as being "what you feel good after" (*Death in the Afternoon* 4)[2]—the sort of inner attention and honesty that such a definition demands is extraordinary. (My own essay "Harder on Himself Than Most," in which I document numerous instances of his sense of personal accountability and his rigor in matters of exacting conscience, is included in this volume.) The point of all this quotation is that Hemingway was and is exceptional, in ways that criticism has allowed to be muted. It has not yet enough questioned a "hail fellow well met" image or a public guy image, and it has permitted such to obscure the reality of an artist incomparably dedicated, a craftsman intent upon certain linguistic strategies beyond any conceived, an essentially poetic, shy, and unique man whose fundamental decency and princeliness of manner are yet not part of the public legend. It took one of his enemies, Zelda, to note his "beautiful manners."[3] It took James Joyce to tell us that there was much more behind Hemingway's form than people knew. That is still, of course, the case.

    It was not the failure of his craft that denied him the careful readers he sought but rather the increasing narrow, provincial, adoption of so-called liberalized ways of thinking that led many to deny to Hemingway what Europe permitted Joyce, what even was readily granted Eliot. During the thirties, a sudden demand for socialist and egalitarian assumptions created an atmosphere in which Hemingway was viewed with disfavor. Further, his quick rise to fame provoked a rather nasty reaction of envy and malice, even the formation of a cabal that sought to repress him, to force him down among the many ordinary others about him, refusing to him the sense of the meaning of his special language and extraordinary style, and demeaning and refusing to define or extend the specialness that the twenties of Paris had been exultant to recognize. It has been par for the course since then to snipe at Hemingway, to pretend that the special province of his imagination was devoured by his enthusiasms, to discuss "his decline" from the 1930s on. All that is nonsense, but it has become publicly paraded nonsense.

No, criticism does not know and has not explained this Hemingway. He is immediately submerged in his public persona, and just about every account studies his friendships with and resemblances to other artists, so that the nature of his unique and undefined large effect and talent is obscured. It is this same insistence that he should somehow conform to a general ethos that keeps his very special craftsmanship from being fully explored. Criticism cites his special effects—richly lyrical passages of prose and amazing subtleties—while leaving the many complex strategies of the corpus of his work only sketchily explored. The average American goes on thinking of him as an inspired nature or travel or adventure writer, a cross between a naturalist and a writer of popular fiction. However, anyone who reads closely the available letters knows that Hemingway knew he was writing, not for a buying readership—"Who cares for fame overnight!" (Breit 62)—but for posterity, and that he did so knowing full well that he was an artist challenging Homer, Maupassant, Flaubert, Tolstoi, the ancient Greeks, and Shakespeare, as well as his more inspired contemporaries.

He always "went for broke"—to do, as he repeatedly said, in each work what had never been done before. He remains essentially unknown when the authentic aesthetic base of his readability and his work remains unexplored—as it still does. Despite our cultural nods to his genius, Hemingway criticism has not adequately defined, cited, or proclaimed the real formal and structural achievements of not only his art but his life—the fashioning of living objects or acts in time destined for immortality by virtue of the way they were built or crafted, and not because of what they described or said. This is why he is *il miglior fabbro*,[4] the greater craftsman, who built the works that he sails on the seas of time to endure the conditions and requirements of their destination, the eternal isles.

Hemingway's *Paris Review* interview with George Plimpton ends with what I must assume is his most important point: "You make something through your invention that is not a representation but a whole new thing truer than anything true and alive, and you make it alive, and if you make it well enough, you give it immortality. That is why you write and for no other reason that you know of. But what about all the reasons that no one knows?" (Plimpton 129).

Now, that highlighted and stern final declaration must give his critics pause. The writer is then almost a god or priest—as Joyce would have it—who brings life out of matter and puts it into matter by the certainty of his craft, who resurrects out of the world a living new form imbued with life. Seeing Hemingway's emphasis on this, how is it possible for criticism to have listened so desultorily to his pronouncements? "I always try to do the thing by three-cushion shots rather than by words or direct statement" (*Selected Letters* 301). "Always," he said.

Having given his readers hints about the "fifth dimension"[5] of his prose in *Green Hills*, and the calculus of his method in *Across the River*,[6] he warned:

> It is very bad for a writer to talk about how he writes. He writes to be read by the eye and no explanations or dissertations should be necessary. You can be sure that there is much more there than will be read at any first reading and having made this it is not the writer's province to explain it or to run guided tours through the more difficult country of his work. (Plimpton 120)

He knew how much he shared with Joyce, and he defended their craft and trade secrets: "Joyce was a very great writer and he would only explain what he was doing to jerks. Other writers that he respected were supposed to be able to know what he was doing by reading him" (Plimpton 117). He has challenged us, head on:

> Well, I thought, Now I have them so they do not understand them. There can be no doubt about that. . . . And as long as they do not understand them . . . you are ahead of them. O sure, I thought, I'm so far ahead of them now that I can't afford to eat regularly. It would not be bad if they caught up a little. (*A Moveable Feast* 75)

What can be a more frontal challenge, which he knew that we would fail? For if in *Green Hills* there is lament for the distance between criticism and himself—"None of us great shots is appreciated. Wait till we're gone!" (81)—in *Across the River* he directly appeals not to his readership and critics then but again to posterity[7] for understanding. In the mid-1930s, he knew "that from the lice who crawl on literature" (*Green Hills* 109) he could expect no knowing praise.

This Hemingway, the artist contesting with every word the existing history and body of existing art and of existing things, remains essentially uncelebrated. The major texts are, as works of art, still considerably unknown.

NOTES

1. The source for this remark cannot be obtained.

2. This important definition was first ventured by Hemingway in his first novel, *The Sun Also Rises*, when, in chapter 14, he has Jake Barnes reflect, "That was morality: things that made you disgusted afterward, No, that must be immorality" (149).

3. The source for this remark cannot be obtained.

4. T. S. Eliot used this phrase in dedicating *The Waste Land* to Ezra Pound.

5. "There is a fourth and fifth dimension that can be gotten" (*Green Hills* 27).

6. "In writing I have moved through arithmetic, through plane geometry and algebra, and now I am in calculus" (Breit 62).

7. "He was addressing no one, except, perhaps, posterity" (*Across the River* 168).

WORKS CITED

Breit, Harvey. "Talking with Mr. Hemingway." *Conversations with Hemingway.* Ed. Matthew J. Bruccoli. Jackson: UP of Mississippi, 1986. Originally published in *New York Times Book Review,* 17 September 1950: 14.

Brian, Denis. *The True Gen: An Intimate Portrait of Hemingway by Those Who Knew Him.* New York: Grove Press, 1988.

Bryher [Winnifred Ellerman]. *The Heart to Artemis: A Writer's Memoirs.* New York: Harcourt Brace and World, 1962.

Hemingway, Ernest. *Across the River and into the Trees.* New York: Scribners, 1950.

———. *Death in the Afternoon.* 1932. New York: Scribners, 1957.

———. *Ernest Hemingway: Selected Letters, 1917–1961.* Ed. Carlos Baker. New York: Scribners, 1981.

———. *Green Hills of Africa.* New York: Scribners, 1935.

———. *A Moveable Feast.* New York: Scribners, 1964.

———. *The Sun Also Rises.* 1926. New York: Scribners, 1964.

Hemingway, Mary. "Introduction: The Enigma." *The True Gen: An Intimate Portrait of Hemingway by Those Who Knew Him*. By Denis Brian. New York: Grove Press, 1988.

"Indestructible." *Conversations with Hemingway*. Ed. Matthew J. Bruccoli. Jackson: UP of Mississippi, 1986. Originally published in *New Yorker*, 4 January 1947: 20.

Plimpton, George. "The Art of Fiction." *Conversations with Hemingway*. Ed. Matthew J. Bruccoli. Jackson: UP of Mississippi, 1986. Originally published in *Paris Review* 5 (Spring 1958): 60–89.

Putnam, Samuel. *Paris Was Our Mistress*. New York: Viking Press, 1947.

Rood, Karen Lane, ed. *Dictionary of Literary Biography*. Vol. 4. *American Writers in Paris, 1920–1939*. Detroit, MI: Gale Research Co., 1980.

Wickes, George. *Americans in Paris*. Garden City, NJ: Doubleday, 1969.

1

Hemingway and Joyce

A *Study in Debt and Payment*

This may be wrong and I would be glad to have anyone disprove the theory as what we want is knowledge, not the pride of proving something to be true.

—Ernest Hemingway, "Out in the Stream: A Cuban Letter," *Esquire*, August 1934

Ernest Hemingway is one of the few modern writers who have been able to appropriate with any degree of success the essence of James Joyce's style and vision. That this has not been adequately acknowledged is the result of a dominant and now almost traditional idea of the nature of Joyce's technique and of Hemingway's, which locks them into seemingly irreconcilable stylistic camps. Carlos Baker's analysis in *Hemingway: The Writer as Artist* has also unduly influenced many scholars to believe that Hemingway eschewed Joyce's method. This is unfortunate, for Baker largely meant to distinguish between Hemingway's method and the "mythologizing" of Joyce in *Ulysses*, and it was not his intention to come to terms with the style of *Dubliners* or other aspects of Joyce's style. According to Baker, "If he had wished to follow the mythological method of Eliot's *Waste Land* or Joyce's *Ulysses*, Hemingway could obviously have done so. But his own aesthetic opinions carried him away from the literary kind of myth-adaptation and over into that deeper area of psychological symbol-building" (88). But it is precisely this other area of "psychological symbol-building" that was most important for Hemingway, and it was such psychic architectonic that he did learn primarily from Joyce, and it is in that area that he most resembles this master.

It is usual when seeking influences on Hemingway to look to Sherwood Anderson, to Gertrude Stein, to Ezra Pound, to Henry James, to Gustave Flaubert, to Ivan Turgenev, to Paul Cézanne, and even to Johann Sebastian Bach and the King James version of the Bible but to fail to consider Joyce carefully, Joyce whom Hemingway well knew personally, Joyce who uniquely worked with Hemingway on his manuscripts, Joyce whom Hemingway uniquely reverenced and extolled without any sustained qualification throughout his lifetime. He is one of the few writers whose name turns up in Hemingway's work repeatedly with an aura of sanctity surrounding it. It was, significantly, Hemingway who was responsible for the introduction of Joyce's *Ulysses* into the United States, and the story told in Sylvia Beach's *Shakespeare and Co.* of how Hemingway masterminded the clandestine border-running operation that brought the copies of those banned books over from Canada bespeaks a dedication more than common.

In *Hemingway: The Writer as Artist*, Carlos Baker describes Hemingway's disciplined study of Joyce's prose and his companionship with that master. He states that with regard to writers the "greatest of them all, in Hemingway's opinion, was James Joyce" (28) and that Hemingway "would keep up his friendship with Joyce as long as their paths would cross" (28). Yet despite all this, he concludes, remarkably, that Hemingway "felt no call to imitate any of his contemporaries" (29). This same amazing and disturbing refusal to allow for Joyce's influence can be found in George Wickes's *Americans in Paris*. Wickes writes that Hemingway always revered Joyce as the great writer of his time and that he promptly ordered several copies of *Ulysses*, yet he hastily adds that "[Hemingway's] acquaintance with Joyce was purely social; he may have been an occasional drinking companion, but never a disciple" (161). One does not need much knowledge of the Hemingway of those early Paris years to recognize that his dedication was not to society but to art: he went to the greatest artists and craftsmen for what they could teach him, insight into craft, and he subsequently studied their techniques, tricks, and masteries to compete with them.

Critics again and again acknowledge that Hemingway respected Joyce above all other artists of his time but immediately follow this acknowledgment with an earnest attempt to suggest that of course Hemingway took little or nothing from him. One exception to this tendency, an important one, is Frank O'Connor—also an artist, a major short story writer, and a studious and dedicated craftsman. He writes in his essay "A Clean Well-Lighted Place":

Ernest Hemingway must have been one of the first of Joyce's disciples. Certainly, so far as I can ascertain, he was the only writer of his time to study what Joyce was attempting to do in the prose of *Dubliners* and *A Portrait of the Artist as a Young Man* and work out a method of applying it. It took me years to identify Joyce's technique and describe it with any care, and by that time I realized that it was useless for any purpose of my own. So far as I know, no critic had anticipated me, but Hemingway had not only anticipated me; he had already gone into business with it on his own account, and a handsome little business he made of it. (85)

O'Connor goes on to declare, correctly, that "Joyce was the most important single influence on Hemingway" (85). The other major critical insight into the Hemingway-Joyce connection is that of James Schroeter, who writes in the *Southern Review* in 1974 that *Green Hills of Africa* "has to be read, more or less, in the way we read Joyce" (95). He also points out that

to Hemingway, Ford Madox Ford, Gertrude Stein, Ernest Evans, Scott Fitzgerald, Ezra Pound, Evan Shipman, the people Hemingway portrayed in *A Moveable Feast*, the literary people one met at Sylvia Beach's bookshop or at Lipp's or Montmartre, Joyce was the one who had been there first, who knew absolutely the literary landscape, who could see what constituted a working subject. He was the explorer, tracker, and guide who taught them what it was all about; not as the literary critic does by saying what is right or wrong after someone has already done it, but by doing it—the only kind of knowledge and teaching Hemingway ultimately respected. (102)

There is the oft-repeated story that when James Joyce used to go out drinking with Hemingway and "a fight would start" and "he couldn't even see the man," he would leap behind Hemingway, seeking shelter, and cry out, "Deal with him, Hemingway; deal with him!"[1] If that is the role Joyce chose for Hemingway in life, perhaps that is also the role Hemingway carefully, aesthetically chose for himself—defender of James Joyce and his sight, his vision. There is a hint of this in a letter

from Hemingway to Bernard Berenson in 1952, where Hemingway says
of Joyce:

> He was the best companion and finest friend I ever had. I remember
> one time he was feeling fairly gloomy and he asked me if I didn't
> think his books were too suburban. He said that was what got him
> down sometimes. Mrs. Joyce said, "Ah, Jim could do with a spot of
> that lion hunting." And Joyce said, "the thing we must face is I
> couldn't see the lion." Mrs. Joyce said, "Hemingway'd describe him
> to you Jim and afterwards you could go up and touch him and smell
> of him. That's all you'd need." (Hemingway, *Selected Letters* 789)

Hemingway seems instantly to have understood the basis of Joyce's
excellence. He told George Plimpton in a *Paris Review* interview that
"Joyce was a very great writer and he would only explain what he was
doing to jerks. Other writers that he respected were supposed to be able
to know what he was doing by reading him" (Plimpton 26). When
Plimpton asked if Hemingway found himself influenced by what he was
reading at the time, Hemingway answered, "Not since Joyce was writing
Ulysses. He was not a direct influence. But in those days when the words
we knew were barred from us, and we had to fight for a single word, the
influence of his work was what changed everything and made it possible
for us to break away from restrictions" (26). We should not be put off by
Hemingway's disclaimer of direct influence, for, as he stated, Joyce
expected other writers to know what he was doing by reading him, and
knowing what Joyce was doing would be equivalent to studying his
technique and craft. The assumption is that Hemingway knew precisely
what Joyce was doing, for in this same interview Hemingway goes on to
observe that

> It is very bad for a writer to talk about how he writes. He writes to
> be read by the eye and no explanations or dissertations should be
> necessary. You can be sure that there is much more there than will
> be read at any first reading and having made this it is not the
> writer's province to explain it or to run guided tours through the
> more difficult country of his work. (Plimpton 29–30)

Morley Callaghan quotes Hemingway as having said, "James Joyce
is the greatest writer in the world" (28), and he documents that Hemingway took proofs of his work to Joyce for criticism and discussions.[2]

In 1932, Hemingway wrote that "any poet born in this century or in the last ten years of the preceding century who can honestly say that he has not been influenced by or learned greatly from the work of Ezra Pound deserves to be pitied rather than rebuked" (qtd. in Baker, *Ernest Hemingway* 236). He went on to add, "It is as if a prose writer born in that time should not have learned from or been influenced by James Joyce" (236)—obviously including himself among those influenced. Solita Solano described Hemingway as watching Joyce during their dinner together at Michaud's in Paris in 1934 in "a stupor of silent worship" (qtd. in Baker, *Ernest Hemingway* 258). But in a letter written some years afterwards to Arnold Gingrich, Hemingway qualified this relation: "I don't worship Joyce. I like him very much as a friend and think *no one* can write better technically. I learned much from him" (Hemingway, *Selected Letters* 384; italics mine). Elsewhere, in a letter Hemingway remarked, to Bernard Berenson, "You always had a good time with Joyce because he was never conceited with his equals" (814–15). He told Charles Scribner, "I haven't known a writer who was a good guy since Jim Joyce died" (678). And he wrote to Arthur Mizener: "Jim Joyce was the only alive writer that I ever respected. He had his problems but he could write better than anyone I knew. Ezra was nice and kind and friendly and a beautiful poet and critic. G. Stein was nice until she had the menopause. But who I respected was Mr. Joyce and not from reading his clippings" (696). These anecdotes of Hemingway's admiration are unique—there was *no* other writer for whom Hemingway expressed such profound appreciation.

Joyce was also Hemingway's intimate. The tales of their drinking suggest greater trust and intimacy than is usually assumed: Carlos Baker records the night Hemingway came out of a café with Joyce over his shoulder, "like a half-empty sack," and how on the rue Galilee "he carried the great man upstairs," kicking in Joyce's door to open it (*Ernest Hemingway* 236). There is also A. E. Hotchner's account of Hemingway returning with Joyce to meet Nora's breezy "Well, here comes James Joyce the author, drunk again with Ernest Hemingway" (58). Hemingway confided to Hotchner how Joyce would create an uproar and suddenly depart, expecting him to "handle the characters in his wake" (58). This last phrase, where Joyce's "wake" can be additionally read as *Finnegans Wake*, seems designed by Hotchner (or Hemingway) to suggest that Hemingway was he to whom the master's mantle was to pass.

Hemingway said many times that his own work contains more than meets the eye. Joyce, who must have well understood what he was up to, wrote, "There is much more behind Hemingway's form than people know" (qtd. in Ellman 708).[3] In *Green Hills of Africa*, Hemingway referred to a "fifth dimension" that can be gotten into prose (27), and he spoke to an interviewer about the "calculus" of his method that the critics of *Across the River* could not fathom (Breit 14). In *A Moveable Feast*, he reminisced about his early short story experiments in prose:

> Well, I thought, now I have them so they do not understand them. There cannot be much doubt about that. . . . And as long as they do not understand them . . . you are ahead of them. O sure, I thought, I'm so far ahead of them now that I can't afford to eat regularly. It would not be bad if they caught up a little. (75)

Hemingway's debt to Joyce is more carefully revealed in *Green Hills of Africa*. John O'Hara has wisely called the work a poignant book. It is, for what shows through behind *Green Hills* is exasperation and weariness, a contempt for the critics who have missed him, who have failed to understand him, thereby making his effort, although aimed at posterity and immortality, less and less truly appreciated or known. When Hemingway writes in *Green Hills*, "None of us great shots is appreciated. Wait till we're gone" (81), it sounds like petulance, but it is pain. All through that work, as author and narrator, he goes on making 'great shots' that perhaps only a Joyce could adequately honor, and having the trophy taken away—P. O. M. gets credit for killing the lion that has Hemingway's bullets in him—while the real "kudu" (or kudos, glory) that he seeks eludes him. Only painful exasperation driven to grief could have created the plot of *Green Hills*:

> For we have been there in the books and out of the books—and where we go, if we are any good, there you can go as we have been. A country, finally, erodes, and the dust blows away, the people all die and none of them were of any importance permanently, except those who practiced the arts, and these now wish to cease their work because it is too lonely, too hard to do, and is not fashionable. People do not want to do it any more because they will be out of fashion and the lice who crawl on literature will not praise them. Also, it is very hard to do. (109)

Here his disdain is sharp; his loneliness in the midst of incomprehension is terrifying. Joyce expresses this same loneliness and exasperation in *Finnegans Wake*, where he berates the critics and deplores the mis-readings of *Ulysses*, speaking of "Missed Understandings" (175) and lamenting "a hundred cares, and a tithe of troubles and is there one who understands me?" (127).

Although, in *Green Hills*, Hemingway acknowledges many literary debts explicitly or implicitly, he singles out Joyce for special attention. Speaking of Joyce as "a small man . . . who wore his eyes out,"[4] he quotes the line from Edgar Quinet that Joyce kept quoting the last night they were together: "fraiche et rose comme au jour de la bataille." The line, which in context refers to the ever-recurring freshness of the eternal natural forms of wildflowers, recognizes immortality through cyclical return (the basis, by the way, of Hemingway's title *The Sun Also Rises*) and implicitly refers to the return of forms that, perhaps original with Joyce, now hold new life in Hemingway's own art. Hemingway contin-ues: "I didn't have it right I knew. And when you saw him he would take up a conversation interrupted three years before. It was nice to see a great writer in our time" (71). Given that "in our time" is the title, origi-nally published in lowercase, of Hemingway's own book of short stories, Hemingway is here declaring that Joyce is alive and can be seen in Hemingway's work. (Hemingway pointedly puns in the same way in *Across the River* when he writes, "It was simply a splendid portrait painted as they sometimes are in our time" [267].) By his emphasis on recurrence, on the reestablishing of what was alive before, he resurrects Joyce through himself, and it is significant that Hemingway's eyes that "saw" and "see" him are offered to replace those of the man "who wore his . . . out."

Later in *Green Hills*, Hemingway tells Pop about his last night in Paris, when "Joyce and his wife came to dinner and we had a pheasant and a quarter of *chevreuil* with the saddle and Joyce and I got drunk because we were off for Africa the next day" (195). Hemingway, a mas-ter of the meticulously used pronoun, here places *we* in "we were off for Africa" so that it ambiguously means not only Pauline and Hemingway but also, and more emphatically, Joyce and himself. It is Joyce who hunts with Hemingway in this African book, as is evident from the mode of hunting carried on. Hemingway writes: "I was watching, freez-ing myself deliberately inside, stopping the excitement as you close a valve, going into that impersonal state from which you shoot" (76). Remembering Joyce's dictum of the creative writer who creates like a god, aloof, indifferent, paring his fingernails, and noting that Heming-way in *Green Hills* uses hunting as the metaphor for writing, one sees the resemblance clearly. But more importantly, as Schroeter has argued, Hemingway has established an important "link between Pop and James Joyce," and the "parts of *The Green Hills* [sic] which concern Pop in an important way also allude to Joyce" (100), so that Hemingway does indeed hunt with Joyce. It is Hemingway's way of responding to Nora's concern—"Ah, Jim could do with a spot of that lion hunting"—and of giving Joyce a singularly great gift.

After Hemingway has told Pop the story of dinner with Joyce, he and Pop have the following exchange:

> "That's a hell of a literary anecdote," Pop said. "Who's Joyce?"
> "Wonderful guy," I said. "Wrote *Ulysses*."
> "Homer wrote Ulysses," Pop said.
> "Who wrote *Aeschylus?*"
> "Homer," said Pop. "Don't try to trap me." (195–96)

The signal of meaning is loud: *Ulysses* is italicized when mentioned by Hemingway but not when referred to by Pop. Hemingway's sentence emphasizes the art, the work of a writer, but Pop's response shows how a writer creates art out of life, how a man "written" by another man becomes a work. Then Hemingway italicizes *Aeschylus* and by so doing makes the artist inseparable from art. Homer is now declared the creator of Aeschylus, so Aeschylus here becomes not what he himself creates but what has since been created out of what Homer created: he is an extension of the works of Homer, Homer the man who wore his eyes out. Thus, Joyce's *Ulysses* was born of Homer, who received his work from Ulysses the hero, and—implicitly—Hemingway is created by Joyce.

What is fascinating about all of this is not that Hemingway has affirmed his debt but that he has found it necessary to do so almost covertly, in code, in hidden fragments that are strategically placed. This in itself should suggest the need for a closer look at the work of both men to discern the nature of the debt for which the payment was so assiduously made.

Jackson Benson has written that one kind of criticism surrounding *The Old Man and the Sea* has produced a superstructure of such technical complexity as to suggest that the work can rival, word for word, the intricacies of James Joyce's *Ulysses* (*Hemingway* 169). He goes on to note that "Hemingway appears in that work to be carefully mapping out a cosmos, with each element, heavenly body, and animal species in its place, precisely balanced, counter balanced, and diagramed in regard to its influences on the human archetype that stands at the center" (171). Such precision of plan and formal structure may indeed work against the total artistic success of the work, as Benson notes, but the point is that it *seems* to be there. Similar structure is there in most of the Hemingway works: it is equally rigorous in *A Farewell to Arms*, in *Green Hills of Africa*, in *To Have and Have Not*, and in *Across the River and into the Trees*. Failure to see this is, in Hemingway's terms, due to a persistent attempt to read with an arithmetically trained mind a structure put together by calculus. Benson points out the extraordinary inequity of a situation in which critics continue to read Joyce with exquisite care and refuse the same service to Hemingway ("An Overview" 302).

Hemingway's prose is often as dense as Joyce's, but in another way, and his technique has appropriated much from Joyce. Since Hemingway is an artist, every word in the novels resonates structurally; since he is a student of Joyce, these structures tend to be mythic and multileveled. His texts offer far more than naturalistic surfaces—that is their greatness. His prose in *Green Hills*, *To Have and Have Not*, *For Whom the Bell Tolls*, and *Across the River* is only superficially unlike the prose of Joyce—dense, a composite of layered meanings, religious and mythic patterns and rituals, puns, allusions, and overtones. Most images in the novels are functioning multidimensionally and radiantly rather than linearly. Hemingway himself has warned us, "I always try to do the thing by three-cushion shots rather than by words or direct statement" (qtd. in Kenner 93). The magic of Hemingway's craft was to fashion a naturalistic surface that expertly concealed the dynamics of his structure. The clarity, purity, and freshness of that almost classical prose are his greatest achievement; still, the greatness is not in its simplicity but in its almost immeasurable complexity within apparent simplicity. Such a style says a lot about temperament and underscores a point made repetitively by those who knew Hemingway best in his early years: the wide discrepancy between his macho public image and his actual vulnerability and defensiveness, between his intricate subtlety of mind—which crafted a multileveled and intricate prose—and the public misconception of his writing as simple and naturalistic, a style that could by a Wyndham Lewis be misconstrued as that of a "dumb ox" (Donaldson, *By Force of Will* xii). Hemingway's language became his externalized sensibility, and he built into it all the subtlety and strategy for survival and intricacy of double and triple meaning that he needed to keep himself from sacrificing integrity to pose and from sacrificing internal precision to external form. Joyce was exactly the master that Hemingway needed, one who could show him a controlled, highly suggestive language loaded with multiple levels of meaning. Wallace Stevens wrote of Hemingway, "Most people don't think of Hemingway as a poet, but obviously he is a poet, and I should say, offhand, the most significant of living poets, so far as the subject of EXTRAORDINARY ACTUALITY is concerned" (qtd. in Gerogiannis xxiii–xxiv).

Close textual reading is nonetheless one of the least developed aspects of Hemingway criticism. Michael Reynolds, in his book *Hemingway's Reading: 1910–1940*, has urged acknowledgment that the influence of Hemingway's diverse and deep reading "will not be found on the fiction's surface" (26). He has correctly charged that critics, "blinded by scandals and feuds, by memoirs and hearsay . . . have not looked beneath the surface, have not pursued the difficult questions. . . . We must resume the practice of the trade for which we were trained" (28). Hemingway can be redeemed from his legend, that persona that he probably fashioned partly in scorn for those who would not (not could not) read him, only through intense textual study. Lack of attention to the very real details of the published text not only keeps thousands of wonderful jokes and puns and Joycean word games from being read but, more importantly, keeps the real man from being known. There must be extraordinary weariness in the writer who breaks the frame of his fiction in *For Whom the Bell Tolls* by having Robert Jordan give up trying to explain to Fernando just why he has called the guerrillas' cave "la cueva de los huevos perdidos" and merely says, "Take a book to tell you" (199). The point is that it *would* take a book, a work almost as long as *For Whom the Bell Tolls* itself, to spell out in detail the elaborate mythosexual implications of the comment and its preceding incident, in which Pilar fails to guard adequately Jordan's two sacks of dynamiting equipment, with the result that her husband, Pablo, from whom she has seized authority, is able to slit the sacks open and steal and throw away the exploder devices that they contain. Here we have metaphors of eggs, a cave, a domineering father/destroying mother figure, and a surrogate father who destroys his son's equipment—and this is but one structure among many that are carefully, exquisitely fashioned in the work.

Study of Hemingway's letters shows that his scorn for criticism, and specifically his contempt for its failure to "read" him, rose in a crescendo from 1925 to the mid-1930s. Two remarkable letters written in 1935 and 1936 reveal Hemingway as goaded to suicidal paranoia and despair by what he felt were the unperceptiveness and the malice of the critical establishment.[5] The flaws of his play *The Fifth Column*, written at this time, can be attributed in part to that disgust.

In *The Fifth Column*, Hemingway steps out of the frame of the drama to stand on a stage before an audience and blatantly announce his symbols, to reveal his armature of art. The play is painful reading: its ostensible subject is a hero who is publicly mistaken for a playboy, and that in itself says much about Hemingway's need to be respected, whatever his pose, for the technique that still had to remain covert—but its underlying drama is about a writer almost at his wits' end, unable to comprehend critical incomprehension. In his protagonist, he speaks of himself and his style and the critics who would put him out of business. Similarly, in *The Old Man and the Sea*, he describes himself in Santiago as the older great fisherman who knows best how to keep his lines straight and go deeper with them than others and whose achievements (great fish) will be stripped from him by the critics (sharks). In *The Fifth Column*, Philip Rawlings, who is a dedicated "stylist" in his métier as saboteur and operator behind the lines, is taken even by those closest to him for an often drunken whoring playboy. Trying to vindicate himself from such charges, and aware that there are those who are out to destroy him, he strips away some of his disguise and coolness—and Hemingway himself does the same. To say that liquor has been used in his works, as in Joyce's, with religious and ritualistic meaning, he has Dorothy remark to Philip, "He's so full of life and good spirits" (5) and has Preston rejoin, "The spirits are getting awfully bad at Chicote's" (5). To reveal that, like Joyce and Lawrence, he uses the verb *come* with its sexual, religious, and normal meaning, he has Dorothy ask Petra to ask Philip to "come in here." Petra is intermediary: "She says come." And Philip muses, "What a word. What a word" (32). This is not drama; it is drama caught in its poetics. In the play, Hemingway insists that the world know that *The Sun Also Rises* was just the first of his large works playing with an Apollonian-Dionysian structural opposition, and he highlights this opposition for his audience by having Philip come upon the scene with a Moorish tart and an electrician, the dark bitch goddess and Apollo. Lest the point be missed, he has Preston remark that the electrician does not seem awfully *bright* and Dorothy demand that the Moorish tart, Anita, be *muzzled*. This bestial bitch with a feared and potentially devouring sexual mouth (she is introduced as "the comrade that bit Vernon Rodgers") is opposed to the not-so-bright electrician, a pitiful representative of the Apollonian. In keeping with the electrician's dimness, there is a general failure "to concentrate on electricity" (7). The

Apollonian word is opposed to Dionysian sex—the prostitutes must have the signs read for them, and Anita says, "All time *talk*. . . . What we do here?" When she asks Philip if he is "with" her or not and he says he has to answer "in the negative," she rejoins, "What you mean take picture? You think me spy?" (13). The play on *negative* seems a feeble joke, but it is rather an almost pathetic attempt on Hemingway's part to reveal to his readers—out of exasperation—his judgment of this conceptually (light- and word-) oriented man, whose denial of dark sexuality and the woman is a betrayal in that it involves taking refuge from life by seeking detachment and attempting, like a photographer, to immortalize the living moment in a fixed frame. The camera that for Anita is hidden behind Philip's *negative* is a revelation of a metaphor that Hemingway in his other works would never deign to reveal. When the electrician finally announces, *"Camaradas, no hay luz!"* and does so "in a loud and almost prophetic voice, suddenly standing up and opening his arms wide" (17), he is not the first of Hemingway's dramatic parodies of Christ. In the very first pages of *Green Hills*, Garrick theatrically stands up, spreads his arms wide, and announces, "It is finished," (17), and at the end of *A Farewell to Arms* the waiter pronounces the same *consummatum est* as Catherine, by dying in childbirth, suffers the martyrdom of her sainted namesake on the classic iconic wheel of biological necessity. Hemingway the hunter has supreme contempt for the dramatic *consummatum est* that begins *Green Hills* and for the "theatrical" Garrick who declares it, partly because Garrick's assumption of the sacrificial son role supports dramatic pose at the expense of life and truth and partakes of the same cynicism that urged Hemingway the author to write drama in *The Fifth Column*—the cynicism that in both works he is striving to overcome and eradicate in himself. In *Green Hills* Hemingway the hunter makes a moral journey in which he overcomes and rises above his own competitive meanness and moral narrowness; and the title of *The Fifth Column* tells us of the enemy within that must be destroyed, the cynical betrayer inside the citadel of self that Philip Rawlings learns at last to cast out. Hemingway was well aware of his tendency toward self-dramatization (which was eventually to create the "Papa" persona and its destructive envelopment of his truly sensitive and shy nature), and at this time he well knew the dangers of his ambivalence, which had been, in part, encouraged by his use of a covert system and style.

What we recognize in *Green Hills* and *The Fifth Column*, therefore—given their tone of exasperation and their focus on revelation—is Hemingway's loneliness within his continued alienation. If his art had been consciously or unconsciously forged to effect a reconciliation with humanity, to affirm a common bond that his genius as artist had called in question, it had surely failed in this end. These two works seem to have come into being to restore him to his imperceptive audiences by removing the difficulties that stood in the way—the special pride, the extraordinary idealism, the querulous and demanding persona of the protagonist who is in specific ways much like Hemingway. But that pride was based on accomplishment, which in turn was based on an intricate covert (and therefore alienating) technique, partly learned from Joyce and deserving recognition.

In a way Hemingway was at this time like a spy who has been "out" too long. He was suffering from his own and others' confusion of his "cover" with his identity, but he was too proud and dutiful to destroy that cover; meanwhile, the very people he served continued to offer him no authentic recognition or gratitude. Applauded and celebrated for his false identity, he could only be forced toward cynical awareness of the terrible gap between himself and his real audience, which, he correctly perceived, would have to be "posterity."[6]

Given the depth of Hemingway's fascination for and association with Joyce, to what extent was he influenced? Hemingway was an original and creative genius who fashioned his own inimitable style. He learned from other artists but was never slavishly dependent, and he borrowed only what he could assimilate and refashion in terms of his own vision. Influences of Joyce or anyone else were always less the appropriation of another's method than the enlargement of his own technique as insights gained from others were passed through the alembic of his own highly alert sensibility. He never resorted to copying, borrowing, or mimicry, yet he never discounted the need for models, for masters and teachers. The malice of Gertrude Stein and Sherwood Anderson to the contrary,[7] he was a superlative student; his "passionately interested, rather than interesting eyes" (Stein 212) were those of an astute observer who had learned when young how to see and to hear and overhear. He was well aware that some writers "were born only to help another writer to write one sentence" (*Green Hills* 21), and although he was to write that "education consists in finding sources obscure enough to imitate so that they will be perfectly safe,"[8] it is well established in his letters that he sought out for competition and emulation only the truly great.

Hemingway's debt to Joyce was complex. Joyce gave Hemingway insight into and a means of dealing with psychic contents through externalized signs and a recognition of the inseparability of individual dilemma from cultural or mythic history. He gave Hemingway a manner of dealing with myth that Hemingway made over in his own style, which built mythic structure invisibly beneath naturalistic surfaces. Joyce also gave Hemingway specific techniques, devices, and metaphors—a whole literary arsenal.

As Helen Georgi has noted, James Joyce's dramatic form "bequeaths material . . . and lets the reader perform the action" ("Unity" 6). This technique of suggesting the missing part, of writing in the white space, is exemplified in *Portrait of the Artist* by the young Stephen Dedalus, who learns to force his thought into the caesuras and spaces in the sermons and into the intervals in the footsteps of his teachers, and in *Dubliners* by the boy narrator of "The Sisters," who must supply thoughts to fill the silences in Old Cotter's speeches. It must have been one source of Hemingway's theory of "the iceberg" (expounded in *Death in the Afternoon*), which posits that the written work of art is only the negligible part of the total form, the tip that shows and indicates the far greater mass concealed in the depths. It is a way of creating the evidence of things unseen, the work of art as surrogate for the unseen godhead structured in the imagination of an experiencing believer.

In terms of Joycean structure, Carlos Baker (*Hemingway* 218) and Philip Young (198–99), among others, have pointed out that the Marie Morgan soliloquy that ends *To Have and Have Not* is a probable imitation of Molly Bloom's soliloquy that ends *Ulysses*. Baker additionally notes that a scene in the unpublished large novel *The Garden of Eden* that ends with Barbara Sheldon's interior monologue is probably also indebted to Molly's soliloquy. He has observed Odyssean parallelism in *The Sun Also Rises* and has suggested that the last half of chapter 2 of *The Torrents of Spring* is indebted to *Dubliners*. Young (198) suggests that the war veterans' brawl in *To Have and Have Not* has its source in the Cyclops episode of *Ulysses*. Both Malcolm Cowley (66) and Nicholas Joost (112–13) comment that Hemingway's early writings are true epiphanies in the Joycean sense, and Joost goes on to observe that in "The Undefeated" the epiphanies of Joyce gleam above the metaphors of Imagism. He affirms that "They All Made Peace—What Is Peace?" and "The Snows of Kilimanjaro" owe much to Joyce's stream-of-consciousness prose (59). Sheldon Grebstein acknowledges that Hemingway "doubtlessly profited from Joyce's examples in the writing of interior monologue and the use of the limited-omniscient narrator" (2–3).

Joyce's story of the Jew among Gentiles in *Ulysses* probably influenced Hemingway's choice of Cohn as the similarly isolated and persecuted Jew in *The Sun Also Rises*. Also, Joyce's conceptualization and use of the scapegoat undoubtedly in some part determined Hemingway's elaborate scapegoat characterization of Robert Cohn and his allusions to Cohn as the biblical Esau and Moses and to Jake Barnes as the biblical Jacob. And Hemingway's use of a Christian iconography of the suffering redeemer to portray these and subsequent sacrificial protagonists—Robert Jordan, Harry Morgan, Colonel Cantwell, Santiago—resembles Joyce's use of this iconography in his portrayal of the Jewish Bloom. The adopted scapegoat motif determines the frequent use of the word *kid* in all Hemingway's works as a carrier of the scapegoat idea. "Don't kid me" often becomes, in Hemingway, the rejection of the scapegoat role. The dualism that for Joyce underlay the Western male psyche—a dualism that he explored in such pairs as the twins Shem and Shaun—became in Hemingway the inner dualism of his always flawed protagonists who struggle to be made whole in a ritualized individuation process. Such paired characters in Joyce's stories as Little Chandler and Ignatius Gallagher, Corley and Lenehan, and acolytes and priests prepare the way for Hemingway's "code heroes" (Young's term for protagonists whose behavior seems determined by a code of values that they share with others of their acquaintance) and their acolytes: Hemingway and Pop, Jake and Romero, Scripps and Yogi. Jake Barnes's attempt to cast off his alter ego companion Robert Cohn—the Robert Cohn whose coat he wears and whose bed he sleeps in and who holds his seat for him on the bus to Burguete—and to replace him with Romero is based on and equivalent to Stephen Dedalus's abandonment of Buck Mulligan in the Martello tower and his search for and discovery of an alternative surrogate male principle. The young Hemingway was undoubtedly drawn to Joyce in part because Joyce, in his portrayals of the flawed father, Simon Dedalus, and the denied mother (who evokes in Stephen "the agenbite of inwit"),[9] dealt with an intimate psychological family situation much like Hemingway's own.

However, it was not these devices but rather the larger, more insistent controlling structure of Joyce's art—from the early *Dubliners* to the late *Finnegans Wake*—that became a model for the art of Ernest Hemingway. Joyce well understood the distance he had to bridge between ascetic Stephen and sensual Molly, and he perceived this in terms of a psychic dialectic between dualism and organic unity, between patriarchal vertically structured dichotomies and the whirlpool of the Great

Mother. He recognized that the real battle was between language and matter, between the uncreated or inarticulate and the articulate, between the world and the word, between holistic merging and the ascetic denial of such synthesis, between spiritual-materialistic, masculine-feminine war (in *Portrait of the Artist*, "Foetus" [89], carved as a word on a desktop, inspires revulsion in the young Stephen) and feminine-masculine crossover ("Heavenly God," exclaims Stephen "in profane joy" [17] after his eyes have met the eyes of the wading girl).

Joyce's philosophy can be summed up in that moment when Stephen sees the wading girl with the sign of seaweed "upon her flesh" (171), for in that instant he fuses the patriarchal absolute godhead with the feminine, tidal, moon-driven, mortal cyclical forces, and he acclaims both the spirit *and* the natural physical world. It can be equally summed up in Stephen's abandonment of his male companions in the Martello tower, his subsequent search for a surrogate father, and at last his communion with Bloom while urinating in the garden at night, under the circling moon and stars and under the lamp lit window that denotes the unseen but acknowledged presence of Molly, whose unpunctuated flow of thought and metaphoric identity are those of a cyclical force. Hemingway throughout his life created similar symbols of cyclical forces. When Frederic Henry in *A Farewell to Arms* leaves his own Martello tower of male camaraderie to journey across Italy in pursuit of a father surrogate—Rinaldi, the priest, Valentini, Count Greffi—and ends up supporting Catherine in childbirth as she is being martyred like her namesake on a Catherine wheel, but one of feminine biological cycles, and then seems to become part of that process as he walks away in the rain, the pattern is remarkably Joycean. For Hemingway, the cyclical forces that Molly Bloom implicitly represents and that perpetual principle of flow that is first the river Liffey and subsequently Anna Livia Plurabelle become initially the cyclical encirclings of Circean Brett and later the cyclical feminine principle so carefully embodied in Marie Morgan, in Pilar, in Renata, and most completely in the Gulf Stream. In *To Have and Have Not*, the Gulf Stream is the medium in which Harry Morgan fishes and navigates, and it is to its moon-driven tides that he releases himself as he lies dying. Such Hemingway heroes as Robert Jordan of *For Whom the Bell Tolls* and Thomas Hudson of *Islands in the Stream* do not accidentally bear the names of rivers, as the texts make clear, and Jordan himself mentions that rolling river's origin in the Holy Land (438). When Jordan tells himself, shortly before his sacrificial death and before he gets himself "turned over" and placed in firing position (467), "Roll, Jordan, Roll" (438), when Frederic Henry in *A Farewell to Arms* commands, "We'll roll" (202) shortly before he flees to Switzerland, where Catherine doesn't mind "there not being rolls . . . I don't mind it at all" (278), when P.O.M. in *Green Hills* declares, "All we see or hear is revolutions. I'm sick of them" (192) after an earlier elaborate illustration, in the description of the death circles of a wounded and self-devouring hyena, of what "the horrid circle" (38) ultimately means, and when Colonel Cantwell in *Across the River* advises his driver, "We probably ought to roll now" and "Let's roll" (30) shortly before his heart "roll[s] over" (83) for Renata, they all acknowledge the cycles to which they must become at last reconciled.

William York Tindall, in *James Joyce: His Way of Interpreting the Modern World*, explores the basic cyclical pattern that Joyce chose to support his worldview. He writes that "to replace Christianity Joyce needed a system in which man could occupy the center" (65) and that "cyclical recurrence became Joyce's substitute for metaphysics" (65). The Catholic Joyce who grew up in worldly Dublin badly needed a way of reconciling spiritual and carnal modes and therefore probably gladly found a solution in such church fathers as Nicholas of Cusa, whose central tenet was the coincidence of contraries, the claim that "existence is a circle which begins and ends in God" (qtd. in Tindall 84). From Giordano Bruno of Nola he learned that "reality is circular and decay . . . is the beginning of generation" (qtd. in Tindall 84). It is not surprising, therefore, that the major journeys of *Ulysses* are to the cemetery and the maternity hospital and that in *Portrait of an Artist* the rhymes chosen by Stephen for his poem are *tomb* and *womb*. In *Portrait*, Temple finds "the most profound sentence ever written" in a zoology book: "Reproduction is the beginning of death" (231). Hemingway, who begins *In Our Time* with similar fusions of birth and death in "On the Quai at Smyrna" and "Indian Camp," underscores the philosophical importance of what he means to accomplish in *A Farewell to Arms* when he begins the novel by presenting soldiers who march toward death in battle as if toward childbirth (looking, with their gear stowed under their capes, "as though they were six months gone with child" [4]), and by ending the novel with a woman going toward a childbirth that will be her own death. It is interesting that the protagonist sees the dead Catherine as "a statue" (332); in doing so he wrests an absolute form from the flow of living experience in the way an artist does. Similarly, chapter 1 of *Green Hills* offers us Hemingway fetally crouched in a hole of ashes and dust (birth and death) in a time of dying light, and the novel ends as he answers

P.O.M.'s lament about how Pop is dying in her memory—"In a little while I won't be able to remember him at all. Already I can't see him"— by promising her a work of art that will grant Pop life in immortality, the book we have just read: "I'll write you a piece some time and put him in" (295). These fusions of birth and death place immortality against time as aesthetic creativity and immortality emerge from temporal biological cycles.

Although Plato, Shelley, Yeats, Jung, and Spengler taught Joyce more about cyclical recurrence than Giambattista Vico did, most scholars agree that Joyce probably found Vico's tricycular structures most readily assimilable to his trinitarian Catholic background. By taking the absolutes of dogma and doctrine, of the absolute godhead, and placing them, as Vico did, in a recurring pattern that imposed cyclical return on fixed, static postulates and positions, Joyce discovered a way to maintain a trinitarian spiritual center in a cyclically recurrent life pattern, a tricycle. As Tindall comments, "By retaining the language and machinery of the divine . . . Joyce gave divine weight to human pattern" (77). Finnegan goes through the cycle of death and resurrection, as does his son Shaun. Life is sacramentalized by the fusion of the divine pattern with the secular cycle. "God the Father in *Ulysses* is a metaphor for Bloom" (Tindall 76).[10] Vico, who finds eternity in time, offers Joyce the possibility of God being a shout in the street. Such synthesis allows Joyce the "eternal" flux of Anna Livia. Hemingway, who sought to sacramentalize life, filling it with rite, sacrament, and ritual, and who made the human being the measure of divine possibility, using the iconography of Christ to portray such men as Santiago, Jordan, and Cantwell, was able to arrive at the descriptions of the "eternal" Gulf Stream in *Green Hills* (149) and the "permanent rain" in *A Farewell to Arms* (4) and repeated fusions of birth and death and love and war without Vico, because he had Joyce.

Modern Joyce critics like Michael Zimmerman and Helen Georgi ("Myth in Ulysses") have convincingly shown that *Ulysses* places the masculine trinity of Father (Bloom), Son (Stephen), and Holy Ghost (Macintosh) in relation to the cyclical feminine principle (Molly). This achievement Hemingway well understood, and its influence is shown early in *The Sun Also Rises*. Bill elevates wine and recites a blessing, thereby establishing sacramental rites of communion for himself and Jake, in chapter 12, the most textually dense and Joycean chapter of the novel, but before he does so, this exchange takes place:

"You don't work. One group claims women support you. Another group claims you're impotent."

"No," I said. "I just had an accident."

"Never mention that," Bill said. "That's the sort of thing that can't be spoken of. That's what you ought to work up into a mystery. Like Henry's bicycle."

"It wasn't a bicycle," I said. "He was riding horseback."

"I heard it was a tricycle."

"Well," I said, "a plane is sort of like a tricycle. The joystick works the same way."

"But you don't pedal it."

"No," I said, "I guess you don't pedal it."

"Let's lay off that," Bill said.

"All right. I was just standing up for the tricycle."

"I think he's a good writer, too," Bill said. (115–16)

The point about the joystick of an airplane is that it is at once a sensual tool and a device facilitating elevation or descent. It has to do with flight, escape from earth, and transcendence, yet appearing as it does in a discussion that has focused on both Henry James's supposed impotence (see Crawford and Morton 106–9) and Jake's dephallused state, it has a strong sexual connotation. Additionally, in many planes the joystick is at once a stick *and* a wheel (masculine and feminine). Historically, the joystick was originally the Joyce stick, taking its name from its inventor, a man named Joyce[11]—a fact that Hemingway undoubtedly knew. Therefore, Hemingway's joystick is his Joyce stick— or Joyce trick?—a way of reconciling masculine and feminine possibilities in one image even as it allows one to mediate between or reconcile air and earth, abstract masculine and physical feminine realms.[12] Elsewhere in the same chapter, Bill's joking remarks about the marriage of irony and pity, about how caffeine can put "a man on her horse and a woman in his grave" (165), and about the role of lesbians and homosexual men in the American Civil War make clear that Hemingway's concern here is psychic split (Civil War) and integrative synthesis of masculine and feminine. At the meal in the wilderness that Bill and Jake share, Bill's claim to "reverse the order [of food items] . . . First the chicken, then the egg" (121) as he alternately raises the drumstick and the egg (the phallic baton or the cyclical source of cycles), questions whether the masculine or the feminine shall take precedence.

When Bill says, "Let us kneel and say: Don't eat that, Lady—that's Mencken" (122), the "Men" of Mencken is meant to be stressed just as readily as the "Man" of Bishop Manning whom Bill mentions almost immediately thereafter. The contrast between Bill, who has been with Mencken at Holy Cross and with Bishop Manning at Loyola, and Jake, who "went to Notre Dame with Wayne B. Wheeler" (123), suggests that Jake can combine the immaculate and spiritual feminine (broken away from the reproductive wheel, as is Jake) with the cyclical masculine, whereas Bill can connect only the masculine with the spirit.[13]

Given the density of structures and techniques used in chapter 12, it is not overreading to see Bill's preface to his prayer in the wilderness, "Let us rejoice" (122), as "Let us re-Joyce," another tribute to rites of worship learned from another James. Hemingway, who so delighted in giving his characters two first names (e.g., Frederic Henry), must have enjoyed putting the explicit "Henry" of Henry James—the initial conversation about "Henry's bicycle" was covertly a discussion of the legend of sexual impotence in James—together with the implicit "James" of Joyce to perfect the double attribution signaled in *too*: "I think he's a good writer, too" (116).[14]

Throughout the passage, Hemingway is additionally playing, as Joyce did, with metaphors of trinity and cycles, sky and earth, spirit and flesh, antitheses that must be reconciled at last in an emblem of peculiarly Joycean synthesis, the tricycle. Joyce stood up for the tricycle, and so did Hemingway throughout his career.

Metaphoric interaction between cyclical nature and fixed abstractions determines the form of *In Our Time*, where eternal values, related to the spirit, are carefully structured by Hemingway to be integrated with, or seen in relation to, the seasons of the earth. The boy's sense of immortality in "Indian Camp" is placed against his experience of cycles, which necessarily and by definition include both the birth and the death that he witnesses. At the end he gains a sense that he will never die, as the lesson of the concentric rings widening in the water is recapitulated for him in the enduring cycles of life that enclose him. In "Chapter III," to cross the garden wall is to fall down into the garden and to so discover death. This fall, placing death against life, as it did for Adam in another garden, establishes the cycle of life by fulfilling it with death. The man who struggles to get over the wall to the other side discovers there not the absolute Eden but the penalties for Adam's transgression,[15] the very cycles in which he dies. "The End of Something" bestows death upon a love that Marjorie had romantically considered unending; the point is that apparently eternal fun has become in time not "fun anymore" (*In Our Time* 110). A companion story, "The Three-Day Blow," bestows the hope of a renewal or *cyclical* resurrection of lost love upon a boy who had believed himself a victim of eternal loss. In "Soldier's Home," the central story of the fifteen, Krebs rejects both the breast of the mother (when he denies loving her and feels nauseated by her reminiscence about holding him next to her heart when he was a baby) and the suggestion that he is "in His Kingdom" (*In Our Time* 98). Refusing both the cycles of life and the life-transcending spirit, he is somewhere between. "Mr. and Mrs. Elliot" try desperately to have a baby (create cycles), while Nick in "Cross-Country Snow" tries to forget he has fathered one, and the man in bed with his wife in "Cat in the Rain" dominates the situation, which might lead to his becoming a father, with the abstract, fixed words that he reads, and denies his wife the cyclical fulfillment that she seeks. Mr. Elliot's alternative to child begetting is to write "a great deal of poetry during the night" (*In Our Time* 114), whereas Nick's is to ski—intent upon the high, clear, cold conditions of season-arresting heights, Nick knows that life is not worthwhile "if you can't" (*In Our Time* 147). Poetry practiced by night and skiing practiced at heights seem the transcendent alternatives to the cycles of pregnancy. In "A Very Short Story," Luz's betrayal of her lover, despite her protestations of "absolutely" and "always" (*In Our Time* 85), provokes his contemptuous gesture of having self-destructive sex—he contracts gonorrhea—in the back of a cab with a salesgirl who works in a department store in the Loop. Here, the circles of the wheels and the Loop (and the idea of multiple repetitive sales and exchanges) evoke cyclical repetitions (based on reversals) that undermine assurances of eternal fidelity and fixed devotion. It is Hemingway's irony that in the story "The Revolutionist" the protagonist wraps up reproductions of pictures—fixed (squared) images of the (immortal) virgin—in a copy of *Avanti*, a revolutionary (cyclical) daily, and that this takes place in September, the ninth or birth month. The story, and the book, end with the patriarch, the king, a prisoner of the revolutionists in the garden.

The title *The Sun Also Rises* records the implication of the fixed Apollonian sun in planetary cycles—it *also* rises—and hundreds of poetic metaphors throughout this work celebrate the immersion or implication of the fixed in the cyclical. We are told that Jake's "taxi rounded the statue of the inventor of the semaphore" (41), that Jake saw Marshal Ney's *sword* gesturing . . . among the green new horse chestnut leaves" (29), and that Brett and he drove "straight down, turning around" the Lion de Belfort (27) statue. In all these instances, Hemingway's conjunctions of opposites—like Santiago's lions (mythically associated with the sun and the Apollonian principle) playing in his dream beside the sea (a metaphor more drastically extended in *Across the River* in one richly allusive expression, "Phoebus the Phoenician" [213])—record reconciliations that, in plot, become Cantwell's, Jordan's, and Morgan's knowing acceptance of death. The three fixed statues immortalize exemplars of the very dualism that establishes abstract dialectics—semaphore communication, war, and the lion that evokes a solar principle and linear rays of light—but these are in each case encircled by cycles, as Robert Cohn, who sees Brett as "absolutely fine and straight" (38), will be encircled by the wreaths and coils of that Circean woman.

In *The Sun Also Rises*, Jake walks by the toy boxers, whose combat is a result of the invisible thread connecting them to the apparently disassociated girl, just before he sees a roller rolling the word *Cinzano*[16] in "damp letters" (35–36) on the sidewalk. Hemingway shows in such an image that masculine dualities or antitheses (boxers) may have a feminine source (a girl)—as they do later in the novel when Cohn fights with Jake, Mike, and Romero because Brett has played the men against each other—and that the Word (and the spirits that it means) descends to accept the turning earth as a result of being cycled: "damp letters," or the immersion of the Word in the waters of cyclical life, says it all. It was general critical failure to acknowledge such poetry—the shots that the great hunter was making—that bred his justified contempt. The epigraph from Ecclesiastes has, after all, been chosen by him to announce the constant cycle of the eternally turning earth, and often throughout the work, whether one circles the square or squares a circle is vitally significant. It is when the moon dominates and the rivers are high that Jake falls under the spell of Brett, goddess of cycles, and agrees to place in her hands the solar hero, Romero. But earlier in that same chapter he signals his devotion when, under the arcades, he circles the main square, and the chapter begins as the sea, itself a metaphor of eternal cycles, gains victory over the heights: "fog had come over the mountains from the sea" (170), cutting off their tops.[17] When the rain makes the flags hang wet from their poles and drives "everyone under the arcades," the metaphors speak of the victory of flow over fixity, arches over squares, and feminine cycles over patriarchal power. Similarly, in part 1 of *To Have and Have Not,* after three revolutionists are killed by those who come "across the square" at them (7), Harry Morgan, who at this point does not believe in words or ideals and will take no risks for any other person's belief, slips out "behind" and "in back" to go "clean around" the outside of "the square" (8).

Hemingway's first novel, written when he was most under Joyce's spell, was one that brought together the scapegoat Jew and the lady of cycles. It is important to recognize that this is Joyce's structure in *Ulysses*. Idealist Cohn, in Hemingway's novel, is suffering throughout, like Bloom in Joyce's novel, for feminine infidelity, here that of cyclical Brett, who (like Molly) has warned that she can never stop anything or finish what she starts. She is identified with decadence in its root sense, rot and ashes, and she is opposed by those who occasionally attempt to arrest the wheeling world with words, style, grace, or rituals of transcendence, or with symbols of arrested cyclical process such as hard-boiled eggs or stuffed dogs, and, at the end of the story, the raised baton that brings traffic (the wheels) to a halt. The complication of the novel is created by Cohn, who would idolatrously declare the goddess of cycles "absolutely fine and straight" (38).

In *A Farewell to Arms*, Frederic Henry and his men flee in a retreat where lines that separated and kept Austrians and Italians distinct from one another have not been held, where the front line has dissolved in an attack in the rain. Finding it impossible to keep things "clear" to the clearing station or to hold a "line" or to get orders "straight," Frederic retreats, first checking the differential of his car. But differences are lost as his anarchist soldiers look forward to sleeping in the king's bed "with the queen" (192). Finally, as a result of "blind" roads and soft earth,[18] they are trapped in mud where the car wheels spin and dig deeper and deeper until the car rests "on its differential" (203). Unable to get a "straight pull" (205), they are victims of the cycling wheels. As a result, a man dies. Retreating finally on foot, Frederic nearly dies because in the chaos of retreat nothing exists any longer to distinguish him from the enemy. Breakthrough is the source of loss of distinctions as Austrians become mixed with Italians on the other side of the broken line, and this is complicated by Americans like Frederic who have crossed over to be in Italian uniform.

Book 1 ends in chapter 12 with Frederic lying in the stretcher slings on a hospital train. Sick and vomiting, picked up, carried, cleaned, and fed by others, paying "a penny" for an orange he sucks on, he has become the "baby" that Rinaldi insistently calls him. As the chapter shows, he is childish emotionally as well as in his desire to accommodate and please others. The result of his denial of his own identity is his inability to hold a conversational line. He rushes to agree with whatever the major and Rinaldi say and quickly loses all distinction or ability to distinguish either himself from another or the masculine from the feminine: Rome becomes "the mother and father of nations" (76), and Romulus is described as "suckling the Tiber" (75). Hemingway's point is that maturity requires identity and that identity is something fixed. Without it, Western dialectics is impossible and there is only regression toward the womb. Earlier, on furlough, where "the room whirled" (13), Frederic was "unknowing" and "uncaring," unable to make distinctions and finally unable to tell about "the difference between the night and the day" (13). This is very much the way Pamplona becomes in *The Sun Also Rises* as Brett presides as goddess of cycles over the Fiesta; distinctions are lost until the trophy that stood for grace under pressure, the ear of the bull, is indistinguishable from ashes, and a man dies "all for fun" (197). In that novel Jake sullied himself by bringing Spanish Romero across the invisible boundaries defined by Montoya to "mix" with the foreigners. Such imagery shows how associations accumulate around the concepts of line and circle in Hemingway's vocabulary: rain, blindness, softness, cowardice, defeat, descent, dissolution, and loss of distinctions through mixing and mingling are associated with cycles. There are similar associations in the other novels. That which is straight, clear, distinct, and individualized strives for whatever control it can exercise against such revolutions.

The title of *A Moveable Feast* forces together unvarying solar calendar logic and that of the turning moon. *Islands in the Stream* and *Green* (or fertile) *Hills* (not valleys below) poetically speak of reconciled or yoked antitheses, as do *To Have and Have Not* and *Winner Take Nothing*. The point is that all of Hemingway's work is structured to arrive at a moment when the temporal cycles and that which seems to transcend them, eternity, become one. That is what those fallen pine needles mean that begin and end the cyclical novel *For Whom the Bell Tolls*: they are the *nondeciduous evergreens* that nevertheless fall.

In "Big Two-Hearted River," Nick Adams lies on his back in the shade of the giant pine trees above him, looking up at the sky beyond the branches. His back and head rest upon a circular floor of fallen pine needles. He closes his eyes, then opens them again, then shuts them and falls asleep. Before falling asleep, he observes the bare space that the trees once covered with shadow before they grew tall, a bare space now light in the sun. The pines are evergreens, trees that seem to transcend deciduous cycles with the absoluteness of an unchanging condition.

They bring evergreenness to the colorful alternations of seasonal cyclical forests—yet, as Hemingway carefully notes, they too are caught in cycle. He carefully studies the brown (dead) and fallen needles supporting the (living) resting head; the alternation of light and darkness, sight and blindness, sky and earth, consciousness and unconsciousness that are reconciled and supported by the joined antitheses of the fallen pine needles; the linear measure of time in the now-tall tree trunk that rises high above the earth, though resting upon it, and in so doing restores the sun where there had been darkness; and the cyclical measure of time in the generations of fallen needles—the "fall" implicit in the cycle. It is because the fine poetry of his young observation eluded his readers that he was able to return to it to base the circular structure of *For Whom the Bell Tolls* again upon it: the last sentence of that novel (as in *Finnegans Wake*) returns us to the first—in my end is my beginning, the lesson of eternal cycles and of the book. In the first sentence, Robert Jordan is seen lying "on the pine needled floor of the forest" (1), and in the last sentence he hears his two-chambered heart beating "against the pine needle floor of the forest" (471). This reexperiencing of the fallen pine needles can occur only after he has gotten himself "turned over" (467) and as he is "completely integrated now" (471). Ready for death in life, he looks "up at the sky" and touches the "pine needles where he lay" (471).[19] Reconciling spirit with its cycles, the sky and the earth, he rests on his elbows to evenly brace his body (effectively split by his injury into a nonresponsive left and responsive right side) and looks through his gun sight, which has the (male) oblong of the foresight secured in the (female) notch of the rear sight, to target the "enemy" he is about to kill. In doing so, he moves toward the moment of ultimate reconciliation with his victim, which will occur in "the sunlit place where the first trees of the pine forest join the green slope of the meadows" (471), where the evergreens meet the eternally turning leaves of grass.

For Pilar, the woman who dominates in the cave and "cows" (effeminizes) male authority, the forest of pines is a forest of "boredom" (97), and she is "tired of the mountains" where there are "only two directions" (97). The mountains are equally boring to Agustín, the man whose mouth makes everything "unprintable," the enemy of word. But Pilar is not Maria. Nor is she like Renata of *Across the River*, who dreams of traveling through the American West with Colonel Cantwell, taking "turns driving" (264) so that they can see where the Wagon Box Fight was fought (a wagon box is a wheeled or circling square) and see trees when they wake up, both pine and aspen, and how aspens "turn" yellow (265).

Maria in *For Whom the Bell Tolls* is also called Rabbit so that she may represent both the Queen of Heaven[20] and the reproductive cycle. Renata, in *Across the River*, is by her name the very principle of cyclical rebirth, rising like Venus (and Venice) from the sea, and is also actually called "Queen of Heaven." When, in *Across the River*, Hemingway writes, " 'It was easy,' said Giotto as he drew the perfect circle" (54), he has announced the artistry that consummately achieves a reconciliation of opposites: a real ideal, a living abstraction. Structurally, Hemingway's plots are determined by this need. *A Farewell to Arms* cannot end until Catherine has become "a statue" (332) after suffering on the iconic wheel of her namesake's martyrdom her death in childbirth that life's seasons have brought her to, and as Frederic Henry walks off in the eternal rain. The rain is announced in the first chapter as the "permanent rain" (4), change held within changelessness.[21] (Similarly, in Joyce's "The Dead," Michael Furey, not on Calvary but under Gretta's window, accepts his own death in the rain—"he died for me," says Gretta [*Dubliners* 200]—and God and man become one.) It is impossible for Santiago in *The Old Man and the Sea* to gain a victory over his great fish, which is carefully described as an icon of the perfected patriarchal trinity; it must go back into the maw of process, the gullet of the sharks and the belly of the eternally turning sea. What has been successfully extricated from the depths in great mythic and psychic victory must at last be returned there.

In *The Old Man and the Sea*, the sun is described as "rising for the third time . . . when the fish started to circle" (86). Such interlocked cycles establish the conditions of the battle with nature to which Santiago brings his faith: "I'm not good for many more turns," he says, but immediately amends this by telling himself, "You're good forever" (92). As the marlin swims in its third "circle," its pectorals "spread wide," Santiago notes the three-foot sucking fish that swim "around him." Such situations bring the trinity, the cross, and the cycle into inescapable interplay. As a result, there can really be no resolution in this work without the simultaneous victory/defeat of the old man. It is a statement of psychological necessity that his dream is of the solar lions that play beside the eternally rhythmic moon-driven sea, so what Santiago redeems from the deep and raises above it must be given again to it. This is to say that the sharks *must* attack *and* devour what he has raised. The religious imagery of the work makes the fisherman a Christ who suffers a crucifixion as he struggles to raise the spirit out of the deeps (the undifferentiated unconscious); the fish is an emblem of Christ himself and the spiritual redemptive principle. Hemingway makes it impossible for us to separate the man struggling for victory over the fish and that which is raised. The fish is described many times in many ways to make its iconic identification with Christ inescapable: diving with the sacrificed tuna crosswise in its mouth, it becomes both the cross itself and that which dies because of it; with its pectoral fins spread wide, with an eye like that of "a saint in a procession," (96), and finally as it hangs in the air above Santiago's head, it establishes compelling correspondences. Yet if it does suggest the sacrificed, raised and resurrected Christ, it also suggests spiritual presence and the good father principle from which it cannot be separated, just as in the Trinity, three are one, so that no one of the persons can be regarded as separable from the others. Therefore, when we see Santiago lash the fish beside his boat, after he has struggled against it, though honoring it, and has finally mastered it, and when we see him wish to take from it the "spear" or spike that projects from its upper jaw so that he may then be given the weapon to do battle with the shark enemies of the fish, which are simultaneously Santiago's own enemies, we are informed by Freudian and mythic parallels that we have witnessed the struggle between son and father, their consubstantiality, and the desired transfer of the phallic power of the father to the surviving son, who must go on to do battle, reinforced by the gifts and powers of the overthrown father. That the fish is a dying-son figure embodied in the image of the good Father and the Holy Ghost merely externalizes the fictional or mythic meanings that must be fused to the reality of Santiago, who is at once the son figure who struggles against the father, the good father figure (as he relates to Manolin), and the perpetual spiritual presence in the mind/heart of Manolin that prompts him to serve and honor something larger than himself or "the others." Finally, Santiago is inseparable from the medium in which he works, the subject with which he struggles: "Is he [the fish] bringing me in or am I bringing him in?" Santiago asks. This is another level of meaning for Hemingway in the novel, the aesthetic, and who brings in whom is the question.

But the story of raising or rescuing the symbol of spirit from the deep—in itself a parable of how the primitive unaided human being separates out what we might define as "soul" from the undifferentiated unconscious—would be a nineteenth-century heroic battle. And Hemingway is, in contrast, a modern, the first of our real moderns after

Joyce, because he knows that the true story ends in the undoing of the hero; the true heroic battle in our time must be lost (*Winner Take Nothing*). Elevated spirit must be returned to and seized back by the ravenous maw of process, by the sea and its toothed gullets of perpetual hunger, and the Father principle must die and be given to the maternal process of the sea, just as Bloom must at nightfall return to Molly. Spirit must be stripped by the biological mouth that is not accidentally the feared vagina dentata of the collective unconscious and of the profound depths that Santiago has been probing with his lines and rods in order to gain his identity and craft. To raise the fish from the deep is a crucifixion/resurrection, and Santiago must concomitantly redeem/resurrect the dead part of himself, the unconscious paralyzed and betraying hand, that it may live again. As the fish comes "alive with all his death in him" (94), the dead part of Santiago begins to live. It would reduce the story to simplistic Christian parable to say that the redemption of the fish permits the concomitant redemption of its worshipper, for throughout, Santiago's battle has been a primitive battle between a human being and elemental natural forces, of the kind described in all Hemingway's works. The metaphors point far more readily to the necessity for psychic integration through reconciliation of opposites—holistic integration. The two-stage battle tells us that the battle with the fish or spirit must be followed by—yoked to—the battle with nature and its process, with the sharks; whatever transcends life must be wedded through death to the cycle. Santiago must acknowledge the greatness of the fish (the spirit) and equally acknowledge and accept the forces that take the fish from him (the cycle). To do so he must integrate love and hate, and his good side must come to accept his betraying bad side.

Another major Joycean metaphor that Hemingway found most fundamental to his work is psychic and religious crossover.[22] Joyce shows us how the dichotomized Western sensibility is Easternized into an organic individuated self through masculine/feminine, intellectual/sexual, noumenal/phenomenal crossover. That is the point of Gabriel Conroy's necessary journey in "The Dead," even as it is the point of Stephen's journey in *Ulysses* from the male camaraderie of the Martello tower to his communion in the garden with Bloom beneath the lamp-lit window behind which Molly pours forth her cyclic, unpunctuated soliloquy; it is equally the strategy behind the interaction of Shem and Shaun in *Finnegans Wake* that is set against the eternal flow of Anna Livia. Joyce studies men and women of the Western world in their dichotomized sensibility and their reluctance to cross over to the other feared and different side. "Heavenly God" shouted in "profane joy" is a religious victory, but for a new religion.

Could not Hemingway have explored such dualism without Joyce? Of course—dichotomized Westerners' crossover pursuit of human transcendence achieved through a possession of eternity in time is certainly the one great theme of art. But Joyce emphasized a tricycular victory. Tindall says of Joyce's work that "the basic tricycle . . . is completed by . . . the rhythmic alternation of opposites" (65) and that "the maternal triangle reconciles the warring twins" (81). Hemingway's need for this trinitarian cyclical pattern emerging from dualism probably led him toward a consistent structural use of Christian trinitarian iconography, so that his protagonists—Santiago, Cantwell, and Robert Jordan—bear the wounds or undergo the agony. But Joyce showed him an iconography and strategies of crossover—of bridge building and destroying—as these relate to cyclical immortality, and Hemingway, discovering that he needed these, immediately seized them.

In *The Sun Also Rises*, Jake's missing phallus[23] is the device that allows Hemingway to study the difficulty of crossover to the other side, here the realm of the feminine, when a bridge, here the bridge of sexual intercourse, is lacking. *A Farewell to Arms* is practically a handbook on the dangers of crossover, of two becoming one—militarily, after breakthrough; politically, as anarchy overthrows discrete identity; conversationally, as desire to agree creates absurdity and childish regression; and, of course, in love and sex, where it can cause madness and death. In *To Have and Have Not*, Harry's persistent question is whether it is a good night to cross, and the island and the mainland (Cuba and the United States) are related by crossover. Jordan in Spain must cross over behind the lines to function and, when he is wounded, must get himself "turned over" (467), or rolled into firing position, at last. Renata in Venice makes Cantwell's heart "turn over" (83). Cantwell breaks the ice to lure the birds of the air down to the waters, thereby bringing these small living things to their deaths. He himself cannot die until he and the boatman, who are essentially enemies, come to terms; the man in the bow must enter into rites of communion/atonement with the man in the stern. At the end of the novel, when he for the first time gives up control and gets into the back seat of the car, he has learned at last how to cross over and to accept death. Santiago's betraying and crippled side must, like Cantwell's, be brought to cooperate with his good side, and Nick's burned-over, ravaged interior landscape must be related to and resuscitated by its living external counterpart. Hemingway's hunters, who must place the masculine front wedge of the foresight of their gun in the feminine notch of the rear sight in order to integrate themselves, as killers, with those they kill, and his fishermen, who must learn how delicate the relations are between the cycling reel and the straight line (or the butt of the rod and the socket) that allow them to be connected above with the unknown forces of the deep below, are engaged in psychic bridging that is extraordinarily Joycean. Crossover is the fundamental rite and ritual that permits individuated wholeness through an acceptance of life that is also an acceptance of death. Whether Hemingway was dealing with such authentic mysteries as "getting cockeyed . . . on wine" (*Sun Also Rises* 122), a phrase that connects the Apollonian associations of the cock and the eye with the Dionysian associations of the wine, or dealing with women's masculine names (Edna, Jo, Georgette, Frances, Brett) or androgynous names (Gracie Allen, Sylvia Sydney, Marie Morgan, Babe Ruth, Ginger Rogers, Helene Bradley, Helen Gordon, Freda Richards, Dorothy Hollis), which suggest attempts to bridge masculine and feminine, or with the lost patronymics of most of his characters,[24] which point to the disrupted connection with an absent father principle, he was studying bridges, broken or functional. Structurally, the therapeutic crossover means the inextricability of birth and death and creates novels of love and war.

Hemingway's studies of crossover naturally take him into realms of sexual ambiguity and sexual crossover—into a study of Brett as one of the "chaps," or of extreme transvestite inversions in *The Garden of Eden*. They also lead him to study the effects of "absolutely perfect" (*In Our Time* 43) barricades that block passage across integrative bridges, whether in the coward in battle who wants to live forever, in the homosexual, or in the dephallused Jake. In the chapter following Catherine's announcement of her pregnancy at nine o'clock in the ninth month,[25] it is Frederic who, in his bout of nausea from jaundice, metaphorically assumes the morning sickness, as if attempting to take on the dilemma of her pregnancy; and before the chapter ends, Miss Van Campen, who suspects him of malingering to avoid returning to the front, will, in taking away his "sack" of empty bottles, attempt to strip him of womb attributes (145). The old lady's bags that fall on Mike and injure his nose in *The Sun Also Rises* (78) are a sexual joke—one among scores in Hemingway—and the two "mail pouches" (106) that must be swung aboard the bus look forward to Bill and Jake's masculine communion rites at Burguete (their eating, drinking wine, and bonding while engaging in a parodic rite of a mass) and also to "la cueva de los huevos perdidos" (199) in *For Whom the Bell Tolls*, where Jordan's two sacks of dyna-miting equipment are in a sense rendered impotent when, after he fool-ishly leaves them in the cave (which is associated with the mother principle), Pablo, as corrupt, jealous "father," steals the exploder devices from them. When Cantwell takes the green emeralds that Renata has inherited through the matriarchal line and puts them in his pocket, then wonders what it must be like to have that in your pocket every day of your life—addressing "no one, except, perhaps posterity" (168)— he has effectively crossed over to femininity by assuming feminine fertility. Similarly, when Renata tells him the bad news that she has her period and Cantwell kisses her hard so that he tastes the blood from his bruised lip in his own mouth, he is assuming menstruation so that he can empathetically actualize the reality on the other side of masculinity. Watching her put on her lipstick, make a new mouth, he knows the spec-tatorial isolation of Apollo, who observes the changing cycles of the moon. This Hemingway protagonist, who takes unto himself feminine fertility, feminine pregnancy, and feminine menstruation, is hardly the macho womanizer/hunter of journalistic and biographical mythology.

Another technique Hemingway learned from Joyce was the use of rituals, sacraments, and rites, often in perverse inversions and rever-sals.[26] Hemingway's works are filled with deliberately banalized, secular-ized rites of communion, sacrifice, atonement, expiation, purgation, and exorcism. From his earliest work he plays with Christmas and Easter iconography of divine birth and crucifixion, and he structures the ritual of the mass to his own ends. "The Three-Day Blow," which begins with an apple retrieved after "the fall," (*In Our Time* 45), talks of cyclical resurrections after a supposed absolute death, and Frederic Henry, who returns to Catherine on the third day, returns as the resurrected spirit of her dead lover. Later, snow that comes three days before Christmas forces divine resurrection and birth, or absolutes and cycles, together. After three days of rain, Frederic and Catherine descend to the lake, rather than ascending to the skies. Robert Jordan lives a lifetime in seventy-two hours; Colonel Cantwell's story takes him from Friday to Sunday; Hemingway in *Green Hills* has three days left in which to get his kudu; and Santiago kills the giant fish on the morning of the third day on its predictable ninth circle.

Even more elaborate Joycean rituals surround Frederic Henry's first major crossover to the other side as he is wounded and experiences both death and resurrection, or rebirth, in the aptly numbered ninth, or birth, chapter. The first chapter of this novel has shown us the soldiers who look as if they are "six months gone with child" (4) as they march toward death, and the ninth chapter, from the first paragraph's description of the drive down the cornstalk-covered tunnel to the caves in the mud bank, symbolically recounts a journey to the womb and a subsequent Caesarean birth process during which Frederic, who has suffered an almost fatal wound, must be extricated from the dugout hole in which he lies and be cut loose and cleansed.[27] The hole in which he lies after having undergone a wounding that is an apparent death (from which he is returned to life) is originally reached after a journey down a cornstalk-covered tunnel to the cave where he is fed, wounded, and found. He is extricated from that "cave" and carried back to the operating table, where a surgeon does the "severing." It is then asked whose son he is, and the chapter ends as he is in a sense baptized by blood that drips on him from the soldier in the slings above him. All of this happens after a meal in the dugout, described in ways that reveal it to be a rite of communion (in an inverted black mass[28]) where Frederic Henry officiates as the false, spoiled priest. (Given how priests and doctors—those who minister to the spirit and to the flesh—are importantly paired and opposed in the novel, it is but balance that Frederic sees himself as a phony doctor when he stands ineffectually at Catherine's bedside at the end of the book.) Such covertly described rituals are the essence of Joyce's technique. Frederic's crossover to Switzerland, a crucifixion without death and a descent from the cross,[29] follows a chapter in which Frederic twice crosses over to what can be seen as "the other side." First, he and the barman go out to the island, and he fishes while the barman rows but then reverses roles with the barman on the return journey. Second, that evening he plays billiards with Count Greffi, speaking English for the first fifty points in a hundred, then reversing to speak Italian for the last fifty. These crossovers that precede the lake crossing portray the new integration that Hemingway's Frederic seeks.

Similar crossovers are everywhere in Hemingway's work. In *Across the River*, Hemingway presents Colonel Cantwell's ritual expiation/ atonement for the offense of his men—their shouting "Evviva d'Annunzio" (51) at a service for the dead where silence was commanded, an act that asserted resurrection/life against death. He carefully moves toward the colonel's communion/atonement with his boatman at the end so that the novel can be resolved and his hero completely integrated before his death. Finally, when Cantwell, who usually sits in the front seat of the car to stay in charge, moves to the back seat, he integrates front *and* back, as he has studiously integrated consciousness and unconsciousness, the dualistic mode of war with the integrative mode of love, so that he can truly at last arrive at "the grace of a happy death" (240). The action of the novel binds together the good and the bad hand, the good and the bad man (the rough and the gentle), "really" and "truly," art and life, and love and war.

Throughout *Green Hills*, the narrative operates smoothly and simultaneously on at least five fully defined and structured metaphoric levels.[30] To look only at the religious level, *Green Hills* begins with a magnificent Kafkaesque parable of modern man: curled fetuslike, with "knees high, [head] low" (5), in a "hollow half full of ashes and dust" (5), Hemingway watches the dying of the light without hope or faith. Against this dwindling light, Garrick stands up: "It is finished," he says, as he spreads "his arms wide" (3). Denying this theatrical Christ,[31] Hemingway observes, "I had never liked him and I liked him less now" (3). Garrick's *consummatum est* is pronounced on the first page of a book that ends beside the Sea of Galilee as Karl decides not to walk on it— "It's been done already" (294)—and as Hemingway wonders why the water birds (those that reconcile air and water) were never mentioned in the Bible: "I decided that those people were not naturalists" (294). The book is written in a time when, in the United States, "Fishermen all turned carpenters. Reverse of the Bible" (191). The novel is able to end, therefore, only after Hemingway has achieved his own glory by getting his "miracle" (232) kudu, the marvelous beast with "unbelievable" (231) spiraling horns, that he must touch "to try to believe" (231), and after Hemingway's desperate attempt to force the others' faith in the absent principle of the great lost sable bull against a climate of growing unbelief: "He was not there. He had disappeared. He had vanished. Perhaps he had never existed. Who could say he was a real bull" (264). Hemingway knows "you could not hunt them [the animals] against that unbelief" (264). Karl, the Christlike "kid" who "took real punishment in the hills"—"he did not believe in the flats" (137) in the sense of being able to find there the game that he was looking for—is no help. Toward the end, the Roman shows Hemingway the way—"I liked the Roman very much and had a high regard for him" (276)—and the journey through the thicket of thorns, as they stumble and fall several times under the great weight of the marvelous "widespread" (231) "miracle" beasts' heads upon their shoulders, echoes the Calvary/crucifixion imagery elsewhere in the book. Eating beside the fire, watching meat on a stick overblown with ashes—Has there ever been a more wonderful or profane symbol of crucifixion without resurrection?—they perfect their trinitarian icons: kidneys between two pieces of liver on a stick, a trinity of the organs of repetitive purification. When Hemingway earlier shows off to Droopy after shooting a reedbuck by taking out the liver and placing the kidneys beside it, Droopy takes out the stomach, turns it inside out, places the liver and kidneys inside it, sews it together and places the whole as a bag on a pole. He then hangs the buck in a tree and lets Hemingway come into camp, "the tripe bag over my shoulder" (55). Such an icon of the encirclement of the trinity of purification by the emblem of assimilative process is a gift given to the white man by the natural savage. But the buck hung on the tree is only half of the redemptive iconography. Later in the novel, as Hemingway holds a cup of tea, he sees the "meat on the stick, not looking nearly as admirable and very overblown with ashes" (246), while the Roman stands "making an oration with gestures in the direction where the light was beginning to show" (246). This mass is celebrated just before the hunters find the "miracle" (249) of the elephant track, the size of which is described by the reconciling gesture of making a circle with one's arms and joining one's hands. This spiritual transformation of the beast has been prepared for since a rhino was early seen—as though walking upon water upon the hill (50).[32]

Hemingway has previously refused three tins of tea that M'Cola brought him. Morning usually begins with "bloody chai" (182), but when Hemingway here says "the hell with tea" (182), he is rejecting redemption through crucifixion or by way of the cross alone. Tea in Hemingway means the letter T—the visible sign, as it was in Joyce, of the cross itself, the tau cross. The rejection of the tea (T) echoes the rejection of Garrick that began the book. So it is that Harry in "Snows" cannot be taken up to his apotheosis on Kilimanjaro in the tri-cycling Puss Moth[33] that has descended for him until this same tea problem has been resolved. "What about the tea?" cries Harry. "I don't really care about it you know," answers his sky pilot (75).[34] The device is borrowed from Joyce's Bloom, who carries his "ha" along with him, the circle of human sweat having erased the "t" that Bloom and, at last, Stephen are willing to forego (Ulysses 56). As Helen Georgi writes, "Joyce consistently uses the letter T to symbolize the cross of suffering" ("Myth in Ulysses" 96).[35] It identifies "the scapegoat and sufferer" (97).

In To Have and Have Not, Mrs. Tracey, having come to the yacht basin to find her missing husband, is accidentally shoved into the water, where she loses her teeth. This black comedy explains itself when she cries out, upon being "raised from below," "Basards! Bishes!" and "Alber. Whersh Alber?" (252). Asked if she's "all right?" she screams back, "All rie? . . . All rie?" (253). Pointedly, what is missing is the "T," and that is what Mrs. Tracey lost in the waters, her teeth. To underline his fundamental meaning, to connect the lost T with the scapegoat sacrifice, Hemingway on the same page describes the bodies of the dead bandits as "the greatest sight the town had seen since the Isleño had been lynched . . . hung up to swing from a telephone pole" (253). The lynching of the Isleño recalls the crucifixion of the scapegoat in earlier times, and we know now who is missing in the waters and not hung up on high: Albert. Albert is described (with the same verbal play used to describe Harry) as "poor bloody Albert, Christ" (148); he stands up on the stern to exclaim, "Christ, they're robbing the bank, Christ, what can we do?" (152); he is hit by three bullets as he says, "don't" thrice; he slides "down on his knees" with "his head slipped sidewise" (153); and he is finally dropped into the sea after being taken "under the arms" by Roberto and by "the legs" (160) by Harry. The imagery of execution and descent from the cross that surrounds Albert identifies him as the false scapegoat god who is marked by Hemingway (and by Joyce) with the T of the tau cross.[36] Bringing Albert to the sea, where he turns over before disappearing, and bringing the Isleño to a death where he will "swing" on a pole (253) is equivalent to bringing the sun to the sea and a death by drowning in the image of "Phoebus the Phoenician." These are "T" in the sea or Joycean wetting-of-the-tea rituals that restore lost potencies. Mrs. Tracey's lost teeth are just one of the Joycean riddles Hemingway has posed for us about the missing T. The last book of *Islands in the Stream* that brings Thomas Hudson to his death focuses intently on Hemingway's tea rituals. One wonders when Hemingway began his Joycean games: "Chrise . . . Jesus Chrise," cries Nick happily in "Big Two-Hearted River" (188), having arrived where he wanted to go without having to go the bloody route.[37]

If the missing T in Hemingway's work has its origins in the missing T in the works of Joyce, I would posit that the missing K has a similar origin. The problem of why Frederic Henry's first name lacks the anticipated K at its end—a K that repeated generations of Hemingway scholars and students inadvertently replace—can be solved by attention to Joyce and numerology. Frederic's missing K is the important missing element of *A Farewell*, important in the way that Jake's missing phallus is to Hemingway's first novel. Frederic not only lacks a genuine patronymic and a father in *A Farewell* but also lacks the K.

Scholarship has shown Joyce's complex use of letters as he studied them in the Roman, Hebrew, Celtic, and Welsh alphabets. K is one of the major symbols of *Ulysses*. In that work's "Aeolus Episode" (chapter 7), the key to Bloom's pursuit throughout the novel (and indeed to the novel) is revealed to be the two crossed keys of "Alexander Keyes, tea, wine and spirit merchant" (119). For Joyce, K is the "Key" and also stands for Keyes and what he means: In that episode, in a subsection entitled "Kyrie Eleison!" it is clear that this K stands for Christ: "Kyrios! Shining word! . . . Kyrie! The radiance of the intellect" (132). Another subsection of the same chapter, "Memorable Battles Recalled," concludes with "—A perfect cretic! the professor said. Long, short and long" (126). The word *cretic* means the metrical foot of a long, a short, and a long syllable. As Joyce well knew, this signal in Morse code is the letter K, the eleventh letter of the alphabet. (Importantly for Joyce, eleven is also a number that brings one together with one [one plus one] to make two: it is the sign of the "both/and" of individuality amidst dualism or of synthesis in separation.) Most importantly, K as the eleventh letter suggests the eleventh station of the cross, the crucifixion. Joyce plays with the *leaven* in *eleven*, that which helps it rise. The number eleven becomes in *Ulysses* the divine penultimate, for it precedes twelve, the final number on the clock or in the cycle of time, which stands for the void, or the nada beyond. It is the moment in time before resurrection when birth and death become one, the uroboric moment when the snake eats its own tail. Hemingway perfectly understood and frequently used this moment. "On the Quai at Smyrna" begins Hemingway's first book with the moment of midnight, the twelfth hour, when the women scream. "I do not know why they screamed at that time" (*In Our Time* 87), his narrator innocently says, but I think we do, for the story, like "Indian Camp," which follows it, reveals what it is like to be in a time when birth and death are forced together, creating the midnight or "twelve" condition. There on the pier, an unspecified "they" "take . . . away finally" (87) the dead babies in the living mothers' arms so that, out of the seemingly unsurpassable moment that is the end of one cycle at the beginning of another but where life hangs onto death, the hope of new life may be resurrected. Life locked to death, like incest, rejects tomorrow. Time begins again as the position of arrest, when the big and little hands of the clock seemingly become one, is passed beyond. "On the Quai at Smyrna" was probably belatedly placed as the introduction to *In Our Time* because it states the conditions of "our time" against which the other stories must be read: the world is at the twelfth hour, the hour of nada, when the spirit is absent and we are without God the Father or hope of resurrection.

In the "Scylla and Charybdis" episode of *Ulysses* (chapter 9) Bloom finds "Keyes' design for keys," and Stephen, the godlike artist, argues "the son consubstantial with the father" (194) as he develops a history of Shakespeare. It is here that Stephen acknowledges Christos Krystos, the bearer of the K, the eleventh letter that he bore and on which he died at the eleventh station: "the heavenly man. Hiesos Kristos, magician of the beautiful. . . . I am the sacrificial butter" (183). Hemingway, in ridding Frederic of his K, does precisely what he later does in *To Have and Have Not*, in *Green Hills*, and in "The Snows of Kilimanjaro" when he rids his protagonists of tea, or T: he takes off their cross and denies them their otherwise necessary bloody crucifixion. This is one reason why Frederic is alive at *A Farewell's* end, for he refuses the role of sacrificial scapegoat victim and, as he is no redeemer, leaves his world without redemption: at the novel's end he walks off in the falling rain, leaving the world to the eternal cycles of birth and death. If Frederic deserts duty and Italy to avoid being a scapegoat and effectively takes off the cross—indeed, lacks the K that would have meant his death on the cross—Catherine is not similarly stripped of the means of her martyrdom, her wheel, the biological wheel of life that she bears and on which she dies. In *To Have and Have Not*, when Harry Morgan, wounded unto death, is described by Hemingway as one who "hung against the wheel" (173), a similar substitution has been found for the cross of martyrdom.

I am fully aware of the danger of suggesting such an extraordinary and arcane source for the missing "K" of "Frederic," which may seem to many an insignificant detail and one that may ultimately be explained by someone as due to a typesetter's error or a whim, but I feel that the reading is in the correct direction, suggesting as it does Hemingway's intricacy of involvement with apparent minutiae, an involvement that goes far beyond where the critic has usually permitted Hemingway to go. It seems to me extraordinary impertinence to assume that we, who study him because of his great achievement, should be the delimiters of his imagination.

It is important to recall an encounter between Morley Callaghan and Hemingway in Paris in 1929. According to Callaghan (107–8), Hemingway was carrying the proofs of *A Farewell to Arms*, and he specifically stated that he was taking them to Joyce for an arranged conference and that this was an appointment between intimate professionals who were going to be going over the proofs and discussing the craft of writing together. Such professional talk would be ruined by the intrusion of an outsider, Hemingway insisted, and Callaghan was politely debarred from that meeting. It is equally important to remember why the extraordinarily perceptive Adrienne Monnier predicted fame for Hemingway as early as the 1920s, singling him out from among the many others and claiming that "Hemingway will be the best known of you all" (qtd. in Bryher 213). Monnier based her insight, as she revealed to Bryher, on the fact that after a hard day's work and some equally hard drinking, Hemingway went to a printer's shop in the late evening to learn to set up type so as to know exactly how his manuscripts, to the last comma, would look on the printed page. "He cares for his craft," was Monnier's verdict. Such precision and care she well knew how to evaluate.

In *A Moveable Feast*, Hemingway tells of his early reading and the literary influences upon him, but it is in the chapter on Sylvia Beach and Shakespeare and Co. that he focuses on his desire to pay for the books he has borrowed. Notably, he has not paid for what he has taken. He says to Sylvia Beach, "I'll be back to pay." She answers, "You pay whenever it's convenient," and he replies, "When does Joyce come in?" (36). What is an apparent non sequitur is actually the point of the exchange. It will be convenient for Hemingway to pay his literary debt only when Joyce is there. Such explicit, if covert, acknowledgment of debt is a sign, as payment has always been in Hemingway, of integrity and honor.

Notes

1. Scott Donaldson is one who retells the tale in his book *By Force of Will: The Life and Art of Ernest Hemingway*.

2. Willard Potts also notes that Joyce "read [Hemingway's] manuscripts, something he apparently did for *no one* else" (n. 79; italics mine).

3. Further, in 1936, Joyce told Ole Vinding that Hemingway "writes well, he writes as he is, we like him. He is large and wonderful and robust like a buffalo, athletic, created to live the life he describes and that he could not describe without his physique, but such giants as he are bashful." He went on to say, cryptically, "Beneath the surface, Hemingway is more intensely 'Hemingway' than has been assumed" (Vinding 148).

4. Joyce's eyes caused him excruciating pain, and he was close to blindness during the years in Paris when Hemingway knew him best. Hemingway undoubtedly attached special meaning to such suffering, for he brought great sympathy and compassion to Joyce's problem, and his own mother's eyes also had given her great pain and limited her life. All of this should be considered in the context of Hemingway's own visual handicap and the awe with which he

regarded his father's abnormally keen sight, which he celebrated in "Fathers and Sons."

5. On December 17, 1935, Hemingway wrote to John Dos Passos: "If nobody can tell when a book is good, why the hell write them? If anybody would take on my dependents—aw well what the hell. You can be goddamned sure nobody would. I would like to take the tommy gun and open up at 21 or in the N. R. offices or any place you name and give shitdom a few martyrs and include myself" (*Selected Letters* 427). On September 26, 1936, he wrote to Archibald MacLeish: "Nobody that I know likes what I write anymore. Me, I like life very much. So much it will be a big disgust when have to shoot myself. Maybe pretty soon I guess" (*Selected Letters* 452–53).

6. In *Across the River*, Colonel Cantwell, reflecting on the meaning of one of the novel's most beautifully structured metaphors, the green emeralds, addresses "no one, except, perhaps, posterity" (168). Hemingway's "perhaps" here suggests his essential loneliness and isolation.

7. In *The Autobiography of Alice B. Toklas*, Gertrude Stein and Sherwood Anderson gossip maliciously about the pupil who "does it without understanding it" (216). My judgment is that Hemingway understood precisely what he took and what he discarded.

8. Ernest Hemingway, MS No. 489, Kennedy Library, Boston, qtd. in Reynolds (3).

9. This medieval phrase meaning "prick of conscience" is associated in Stephen's mind with a sense of guilt for having refused his dying mother's deathbed request; for him, it represents a denial of the mother.

10. Joyce has Stephen in *Ulysses* declare, "I am tired of my voice, the voice of Esau" (211), the voice that cannot gain the father's recognition. In Hemingway's *The Sun Also Rises*, the absence of the father and the fathering principle, as suggested by the absence of Jake's phallus, leaves Jake as the eternally unredeemed and errant son, Jacob, who needs his father's blessing before he can receive his patrimony. Hemingway may have named his hero Jacob to express his own hope of extracting from the blind father, Isaac (Joyce?), the blessing that he sought.

11. According to Smart, the joystick was "named after its inventor, Capt. Joyce" (66). I thank Professor Jim Hinkle of San Diego State University for this information.

12. It is Joyce in *Ulysses* who pointedly makes Molly's feminine cyclical world physical and Stephen's masculine world intellectual and abstract.

13. Hemingway had begun to play with such structures early: the fourth of the six sentences he wrote in 1922 and called "1922" studied "Notre Dame grey and dripping in the rain" (qtd. in Baker, *Ernest Hemingway* 90–91). It is no accident that *The Torrents of Spring* records Scripps's movement from his Mancelona wife to Mandy, by way of Diana (goddess of the moon and sister to Apollo), and that references to the Bookman, the Mentor, the Manchester Guardian,

Hart*man*, Sher*man*, and Francis Park*man* abound in the work. The complication of the novel is, after all, the dilemma of impotent (unmanned) Yogi and the frozen, arrested, cyclical season, and Hemingway studies the source of this impotence and stasis with metaphors of voyeurism and masturbation.

14. Critics who are not themselves creative writers frequently tend to be suspicious of such structures and fail to recognize the sheer joy and delight that artists take in playing with their medium. Art emerges from such play, and artists gain their mastery from it, even though, unfortunately, the medium is all too often treated with sobriety by the critic. Artists, to amend this error, often emphasize the reciprocal relations between labor and play. Yeats writes in "Among School Children" that

> Labour is blossoming or dancing where
> The body is not bruised to pleasure soul,
> Nor beauty born out of its own despair,
> Nor blear-eyed wisdom out of midnight oil
> (214)

He also writes in "Lapis Lazuli":

> They know that Hamlet and Lear are gay;
> Gaiety transfiguring all that dread . . .
> . . . their eyes,
> Their ancient, glittering eyes are gay.
> (292–93)

"Lapis Lazuli" perhaps explains the concluding paragraph of chapter 1 of *For Whom the Bell Tolls*. When Hemingway writes, "There were not any gay ones left," he is at once lamenting the loneliness of the true artist and explaining to the reader at the beginning of his "political" novel that art does not emerge from a political imagination: the stress is on "left" as opposed to "right."

15. The moral meaning of transgression rests upon the root meaning of the term, to pass over a limit or a boundary. Hemingway's vignette is almost an elucidation of these fascinating unstated relationships.

16. Hemingway uses the metaphor again in *A Farewell to Arms* where he has Frederic Henry, while in his hospital bed in Milan, lift a bottle of Cinzano "up" from the floor and place it "straight up" on his stomach. While it makes "rings" there and while he watches the progress of darkness as "swallows circled around" (87) overhead, the nurse brings in some *eggnog* with sherry in it. Each element is mythically active.

17. The point really is that one "could not see" the tops of the mountains. Sight, in Hemingway, is classically associated with the absolute Apollonian principle, and blindness and darkness are classically associated with the feminine maternal principle. It is no accident that Nick's father, in trying to educate him, urges him to "see," or that Nick's mother is first introduced as a woman

lying in a darkened room behind drawn blinds. That Hemingway's father, like the remembered father of "Fathers and Sons," had fabulous eyesight, and that his mother, like the mother of "The Doctor and the Doctor's Wife," guarded her eyes against brightness, undoubtedly helped to establish for Hemingway personally what is a classical Western metaphoric bias. Throughout Hemingway's work, humidity and dampness seem to assault and overwhelm the higher mental, spiritual, or visual faculties. His hunters must create stratagems to guard their glasses against mist as carefully as they must protect their guns against rust.

18. Softness in Hemingway is ominous. In "Cross-Country Snow," Nick is spilled and spun "over and over . . . like a shot rabbit" when he hits the "soft . . . hollow" (*In Our Time* 183). The imagery suggests what the story elaborates: man becomes a victim of the reproductive cycle, one of the threats associated with the soft hollows. The hollows bag—encircle, entrap, bring down, and effeminize—the deft skier of hard heights. Nick is reduced to the cyclically reproductive rabbit by his inability to remain on top of the hard crust in linear control. Similarly, in "The Short Happy Life of Francis Macomber," it is Macomber's softness that leads him to run "like a rabbit" (*Short Stories* 7). One might speculate that Hemingway's pursuit of danger was an attempt to forge armor—that out of dangerous encounters he acquired the hardness necessary for endurance and survival, even as, wounded, he might grow "stronger at the broken places." Given the metaphoric structure of "Cross-Country Snow," it is not far-fetched to see the story's title as studying the interaction of the "cross" (spirit) and "cunt/ry" (flesh) amid the cyclical-frozen, arrested-rain: "snow." Certainly, when Hemingway writes at the end of chapter 5 of *Green Hills*, one of the most covertly sexually allusive chapters he ever wrote, "we had seen a lot of country" (123), he is using *country* in this fashion.

19. Similarly, as Thomas Hudson lies dying at the end of *Islands in the Stream*, he acknowledges "the sky that he had always loved" (466) and the sea, "the great lagoon" upon which his ship rests.

20. Robert Jordan's prayer that Maria should "come" to him echoes against Joaquin's dying prayer to Mary. That Maria is Mary is made clear by Agustín's remark "That I should never have the Maria is nothing. I will go with the whores as always" (293) and by Jordan's ironic recognition of Pilar's "wanting to keep her hold on life. To keep it through Maria" (176). As Robert Jordan is later seen as "our ex-Lord himself" to whom Maria brings the sheepskin, she is asked, "Must you care for him as a suckling child?" (203). Jordan calls out her name separately, thrice, and then cries out, "Oh, Maria, Maria, Maria," placing the circular cycle of O (a Joycean trick) against the three-become-one name. He does this as he acknowledges "I must care well for thee" and as he distinguishes between woman and word: "And I love thee and I love thy name Maria" (263).

21. In *Across the River*, Cantwell remembers "when the rain fell always, or at least always when there were parades and speeches to the troops," (50) moving from the initial statement of an absolute toward an ironic and relative hyperbole.

22. This may have been because Hemingway himself experienced such a crossover at Fossalta, when he "died" and was reborn, or it may have been because the healing of a psychic wound that had caused almost unbearable schism demanded a therapeutic restoration of balance. Certainly the need after a psychic wounding to restore balance, whether of a checkbook (*The Sun Also Rises*) or of inner and outer reality ("Big Two-Hearted River"), seems a pattern in the works.

23. Hemingway insisted that Jake's wound was not castration and had not caused impotence. He told George Plimpton, "Whoever said Jake was 'emasculated precisely as is a steer'? Actually he had been wounded in quite a different way and his testicles were intact and not damaged. Thus he was capable of all normal feelings as a man but incapable of consummating them" (230). Arthur Waldhorn notes that "in an unpublished letter addressed to Philip Young, he indicated that his model was actually a young man whose penis had been shot away but whose testicles and spermatic cord remained intact" (238). This letter has since been published.

24. To name a few characters and references: Frederic Henry, Robert Jordan, Thomas Hudson, Freddy Wallace, Eddie Marshall, Harry Morgan, Edouardo Giovanni, Robert Preston, Albert Tracey, Tommy Bradley, Richard Gordon, Herman Fredericks, Benny Sampson, Frederick Harrison, and Franz Joseph. Frequently a seeming patronymic hides what is really a given name: Nick *Adams*, Willie *Adams*, Jackson *Phillips*, Nelson *Jacks*, Harold *Tompkins*, Roger *Johnson*, Wallace *Johnston*, Douglas *Johnson*, Jon *Jacobson*.

25. In *The Sun Also Rises*, it is nine o'clock when Jake, about to leave France and enter Spain, arrives in Bayonne. Book 3 begins, after the carefully studied death of the masculine principle at the end of book 2, with death-rebirth symbolism ("In the morning it was all over. The fiesta was finished. I awoke about nine o'clock" [227]) and the cycle begins again: in San Sebastian, Jake establishes rites of cleansing, purgation, and integration-renewal that begin with the balancing of his checkbook. (In Joyce, the two washerwomen by the River Liffey renew the cycle by washing dirty clothes.) But numerology is important everywhere in Hemingway, as it is in Joyce: the three-four pattern of *Across the River* and *To Have and Have Not*, the use of forty and its variants in *To Have and Have Not*, and the three in *The Old Man and the Sea* are representative.

It is at five o'clock that Frederic Henry descends to meet Count Greffi at the billiard table, and it is five o'clock when the bank is robbed in *To Have and Have Not* and Harry Morgan confronts the murderous revolutionaries. These two protagonists go to their encounters at the same hour that Jake Barnes goes in his "suit" to meet the sea at San Sebastian, *a las cinco de la tarde*, the hour of the bullfight. Description of the even and level yellow sand of the shore in the exact phrases used to describe the sand of the arena where Romero goes to meet his bull tells us clearly that Jake is at last able to emulate Romero and, like Stephen (the "hydrophobe" of *Ulysses*, who finally overcomes his fear of water as he pronounces "Vidi aquam!" in the Circe mass), cross over and engage the powers of darkness. (Earlier, beginning his masculine rites of integration-purification as he boards the bus for Burguete, he "spills" the wine as he is startled by a klaxon, or horn.) Such a detail tells us that he, like a young torero, is not yet able to hold the purity of line under the pressure of the horn. Colonel Cantwell, in *Across the River,* is irritated by seeing in the road ahead of him a "cyclist" who pedals his bicycle while reading a newspaper that he is holding with both hands: word disdains cycles. "Give that cyclist some horn" (13) is his advice to his driver, and the horn makes the cyclist move over and accept the other side.

The billiard table in *A Farewell to Arms* is the lighted arena in which the men with long lances control the triple cycle—there are three balls in billiards that are reconciled through rectilinear control in one shot. This three-in-one image is no less functional than the image from Hemingway's tale in *Green Hills,* told just as he prepares for his final encounter in the country on the other side of the virgin stream he fished where on one cast of one line he caught three fish.

26. The deliberate parodies of the mass in the Telemachus and Circe episodes of *Ulysses* are representative.

27. The symbolic Caesarean birth process of "The Doctor and the Doctor's Wife" should not be overlooked, for it establishes the technique of chapter 9 of *A Farewell to Arms.* The story is in part a mirror reversal of "Indian Camp," for here a father and son and another man bring their tools and equipment from the Indian world to help extricate the logs that are stuck in the sand of the lake shore, while in "Indian Camp," a similar male trio, but white, bring tools to dislodge the child still tied to the placental shore of the mother's amniotic sea and needing assistance to be born. In "The Doctor and the Doctor's Wife," the men loosen the log in the sand until it moves and is finally "rocked" and "rolled" free; then they wash it so they can see "who it belongs to" (27), and the doctor (father) is accused of not owning the logs that he has claimed as his own. The sexual taunt, "'Don't go off at half cock, Doc,' Dick said" (27)—who could ever believe that anyone could ever write such a line without joy and tongue-in-cheek?—and the image of the tobacco juice that is spat on the log and slides off, "thinning in the water," suggest ejaculation, adulteration, and a challenged paternity. "Indian Camp" introduces the same theme of questionable paternity for the Indian father, as Uncle George is the one to distribute cigars to the Indians.

28. Little details—"Macedonias," the "mess" of the road, and the "mess" tins with which the men prepare for the elevation of the cheese, which is raised by Frederic ("Lift it high, Tenente") and from which "a mass loosened" (53)—all prepare the reader to recognize the bestial communion that is taking place as, with "chins close over the basin, tipping their heads back" (54), the men partake of what Frederic administers.

29. During the lake crossing, Frederic holds onto the two outer edges of a widespread umbrella whose handle goes between his legs and is hooked over

his seat. The image of crucified Frederic must be visualized. As it goes inside out, Catherine finds the image funny but asks him not to "be cross" (273). Later, she and he observe nets "spread on racks" (277) and discuss the nail holes in Mantegna's Christs. She asks to see his wounded hands. Frederic reassures her, "There's no hole in my side" (284). As the chapter ends, they are "down on the pavement," and Catherine observes, "You've been up a long time" (285).

30. At least five levels are fully developed and intricately structured in the book. First is the realistic level: hunting in and exploring and describing Africa. Second is the religious level, here only sketchily defined. Third is the aesthetic level, treating the shots made and the techniques of hunting, tracking, and shooting as metaphors for an artist's approach to his trophy, or "kudu," and taxidermic immortality as an equivalent for the achieved book. Fourth is the psychosexual level, which studies masculinity and femininity; the search for manhood in the midst of jealousy, infidelity, and sexual threat; the sexual rivalries between Hemingway, Pop, and Karl for possession of the mother (P.O.M.); and the son figure's entanglement with the father and mother—Pop and P.O.M.—and his need to find and achieve his own sexual identity. Fifth is the psychic level, which carefully develops the stages in the individuation process and studies the almost ritualized movement from phase to phase as egocentric childishness yields at last to reconciliations and acknowledgments necessary to integrative wholeness; this movement is emblematized by the phrase "Let's pull ourselves together" (85). These may be the five dimensions that Hemingway declares a writer can get in his work (*Green Hills* 27). Another level, the sociological level, studies the way societies technologically and unimaginatively abuse and destroy the environment, but this seems less elaborately structured and recurrent than the preceding five levels. On this level, Hemingway portrays nature as manipulated, soiled, and destroyed by greed, capitalist exploitation, and neglect—some of the same moral deficiencies that in the novel Hemingway as narrator strives to overcome in himself.

31. Lest the reader be unsure of this identification, Hemingway has Garrick aptly throw his arms wide twice more in the novel. At one moment Hemingway points out Garrick to Pop. "Look what we have." "Christ," (186), says Pop, and turns away. Hemingway often uses this trick of post hoc ergo propter hoc labeling. In *To Have and Have Not*, as Harry lies sleeping after having made love to Marie, with "the stump of his arm out wide on the pillow" (114), Marie watches him "sleeping just like a baby" (115) and remarks to herself, "I better stay awake so as to call him. Christ, I could do that all night" (115). "To call him Christ" is the point, especially here where he has given her happiness with sex and told her of the loggerheads (turtles of the land and of the sea) who "do it" for "three days" (113). This tricycular fucking introduces Harry as the Christ who gives Marie her desire to "do it and never sleep. Never, never,

no never" (115), thereby creating the cyclical absolute of eternal sex. Marie last sees him as being "like a kid" (115)—a warning that he is about to become the scapegoat sacrifice.

If Garrick has been a disdained embodiment of Christ throughout *Green Hills*, M'Cola has been the contrasting principle of cycle. He wears pieces of rubber tires on his feet; he has a highly developed lower body and relatively undeveloped upper body; and he is a Mama worshipper who would elevate Mama on his shoulders for glory on a basis of intuition, mystery, and faith that despises the rationality and logic of the Western world. He is the "black China-man" who insists on water (life principle) with whiskey (spirit[s]) and who at last reconciles Hemingway with humanity and with his black brothers.

32. Hemingway places his seemingly profane Joycean sacraments throughout the novel. Early in *Green Hills*, Abdulah scratches his name "on the black skin of his leg" (the word become flesh) and "M'Cola looked at the word without a shadow of expression on his face" (4) (a denial of the received Word). A few pages later, however, "to crown [a] fantasy," they all come upon "three tall conical mounds" (10) of elephant dung in the road. Hemingway touches one. It must be touched to be believed—the evidence of things seen. Such substitute profane trinities are here not new in Hemingway: at the end of book 2 of *A Farewell to Arms*, Frederic Henry's baggage is a big rucksack and two musettes. He sees in the leather goods shop the carefully arranged pyramid of "rucksack in the center, the riding boots on one side and the ski boots on the other," with "highlights" shining on the oiled leather (147).

33. The name Puss Moth correctly puts together the cat of nine lives and the moth of resurrection. The cat itself eternally cycles, for as it reaches the end of its ninth life, in its apparent last cycle, it approaches death as birth—the end of a nine-cycle being the symbol of birth and beginning. This symbolic meaning undoubtedly explains in part why in his later years Hemingway had so very many cats at Finca Vigía in Cuba and helps explain book 2 of *Islands in the Stream*, which records Thomas Hudson's love for Boise, his cat. The moth is the metamorphic moth of resurrection. Helen Georgi (in "Riddles in *Ulysses*") describes the moth in Joyce's work as "the everflying moth, an image of the soul." Thus, in itself, the plane is the right vehicle for cyclical transcendence. This thrice-circling plane must avoid the warthog holes if it is to become airborne and so reach the square sunstruck top of Kilimanjaro high above the (cyclical) fetid jungles at its base, which are last seen in the story in darkness and corruption. In "The Short Happy Life of Francis Macomber," Macomber, crossing to the "far side" (*Short Stories* 27), must equally avoid warthog holes, and in *Green Hills*, as the hunters cross over to the "virgin pocket" (25) on the other side, they must first confront a huge warthog boar. For Hemingway, the mythic journey to "the other side" must dare the hazards of the guardian at the gate, the pig with tusks.

34. When Joyce writes in *Finnegans Wake* of how the mail-awaiting (male-awaiting) woman is hoping "for the ladder [letter] to turn up with a cupital tea [capital "T"] before her ephumeral comes off without any much father" (p. 369, lines 30–33), the complex of associations can readily be seen: T, tea, and the lost father principle. Such phrases as "Homeo Capite [cup of tea, capital "T"] Erectus" (p. 101, lines 12–13) and "Houseanna! Tea is the Highest! For auld lang Ayternitay!" (p. 406, line 28) reveal a consistent set of associations.

35. Hemingway's letter T is certainly not simply Joyce's letter carried over with all its Joycean implications intact. In *Green Hills*, Hemingway is hunting with and for Joyce to some extent, but he is always his own hunter; consequently, his T is his own and is used for his own purposes, however much it participates in Joyce's schemas.

Margaret Solomon, in her book *Eternal Geomater: The Sexual Universe of Finnegans Wake*, focuses upon Joyce's use of the letter T. She sees "three" and "tea" as "closely associated with the tripartite aspect of the letter 'T'" and as related to the "power historically represented by a father-god" (59) as Joyce uses it, but she places her emphasis on the sexual characteristics of T, its potency. For her, the "double references to the performance of the sexual trinity and the holy suffering of the divine man" certify the "profane relationship, symbolized by the T-cross" (62). I think she accurately traces back Joyce's use of "T" to the Tuncpage of *The Book of Kells*. It is the "T" that "Biddy Doran rescued . . . from the theological dungheap" (68). She well establishes the alliance of tea and the capital "T": "Joyce's tea-ology is based on a sexual trinity, an impudent parody of the Christian Father, Son, and Holy Spirit" (80).

36. Hemingway's scapegoat Christs are inevitably finally cycled. Even as Harry in *To Have and Have Not* will be "hung against the wheel" (173) and finally take "the roll" of the moondriven sea, so Albert turns over twice in the sea before sinking, whereas the gun goes "straight down" (161). This cycling of the scapegoat Christ owes much to Joyce's Molly and the fate of his Bloom, but it is interesting to note the equivalent strategies used by D. H. Lawrence in *The Man Who Died* for cycling his scapegoat Christ. The alert reader should also note that when Richard Gordon in *To Have and Have Not* is hit by the wide young man, "the lights . . . wheeled round" and he comes to with "ringing" head and the room "wheeling." He tries thrice to strike MacWalsey but is finally carried out "between" two men and put in an old "model T taxi" (219), his head lying back "at an odd angle" (219). MacWalsey, for whom he becomes the scapegoat sacrifice, is unlike M'Cola of *Green Hills*, whose name carries the apostrophe to stand for what is omitted and denied, the "Mac" (son of). M'Cola's opposition to Christlike Garrick and his elevation of "Mama" as a matter of faith are typical for one who refuses the logic of the son of the Father.

37. If this suggests precocious knowledge, it is intriguing to speculate how much Hemingway knew when, in his high school story "A Matter of Color," he described the boxing ring as "the squared circle" (Cappel 49).

WORKS CITED

Baker, Carlos. *Hemingway: The Writer as Artist*. Princeton, NJ: Princeton UP, 1989.

———. *Ernest Hemingway: A Life Story*. New York: Scribners, 1969.

Beach, Sylvia. *Shakespeare and Company*. New York: Harcourt Brace, 1959.

Benson, Jackson. *Hemingway: The Writer's Art of Self Defense*. Minneapolis: U of Minnesota P, 1969.

———. "An Overview of the Short Stories." *The Short Stories of Ernest Hemingway*. Ed. Jackson Benson. Durham, NC: Duke UP, 1975.

Breit, Harvey. "Talking with Mr. Hemingway." *New York Times Book Review*, 17 September 1950: 14.

Bryher. *The Heart to Artemis: A Writer's Memoirs*. New York: Harcourt Brace and World, 1962.

Callaghan, Morley. *That Summer in Paris*. New York: Coward-McCann, 1963.

Cappel, Constance, ed. *Hemingway in Michigan*. Waitsfield: Vermont Crossroads Press, 1977.

Cowley, Malcolm. *A Second Flowering*. New York: Viking Press, 1973.

Crawford, Frank D., and Bruce Morton. "Hemingway and Brooks: The Mystery of Henry's Bicycle." *Studies in American Fiction* 6 (1978): 106–9.

Donaldson, Scott. *By Force of Will: The Life and Art of Ernest Hemingway*. New York: Penguin Books, 1978.

Ellmann, Richard. *James Joyce*. New York: Oxford UP, 1959.

Georgi, Helen. "Myth in Ulysses: Quest for a Central Theme." M.A. thesis, San Francisco State University, 1970.

———. "Riddles in *Ulysses*: Squaring the Circle." Unpublished manuscript.

Gerogiannis, Nicholas. Introduction. *Ernest Hemingway: 88 Poems*. New York: Harcourt Brace Jovanovich, 1979.

Grebstein, Sheldon. *Hemingway's Craft*. Carbondale: Southern Illinois UP, 1973.

Hemingway, Ernest. *Across the River and into the Trees*. 1950. New York: Scribners, 1970.

———. *Ernest Hemingway: Selected Letters, 1917–1961*. Ed. Carlos Baker. New York: Scribners, 1981.

———. *A Farewell to Arms*. 1929. New York: Scribners, 1969.

———. *The Fifth Column*. 1938. New York: Bantam Books, 1970.

———. *For Whom the Bell Tolls*. 1940. New York: Scribners, 1968.

———. *Green Hills of Africa*. 1935. New York: Scribners, 1963.

———. *In Our Time*. 1925. New York: Scribners, 1958.

———. *Islands in the Stream*. New York: Scribners, 1970.

———. *A Moveable Feast*. New York: Scribners, 1964.

———. *The Old Man and the Sea*. New York: Scribners, 1952.

————. "The Short Happy Life of Francis Macomber." In *The Short Stories of Ernest Hemingway*. New York: Scribners, 1953.

————. "The Snows of Kilimanjaro." In *The Short Stories of Ernest Hemingway*. New York: Scribners, 1953.

————. *The Sun Also Rises*. 1926. New York: Scribners, 1964.

————. *To Have and Have Not*. 1937. New York: Scribners, 1965.

Hotchner, A. E. *Papa Hemingway: A Personal Memoir*. New York: Bantam Books, 1966.

Joost, Nicholas. *Ernest Hemingway and the Little Magazines: The Paris Years*. Barre, MA: Barre Publishers, 1968.

Joyce, James. *Dubliners*. New York: Viking Press, 1964.

————. *Finnegans Wake*. New York: Viking Press, 1958.

————. *A Portrait of the Artist as a Young Man*. New York: Viking Press, 1965.

————. *Ulysses*. New York: Modern Library, 1946.

Kenner, Hugh. "Writing by Numbers." *Harpers* Apr. 1981: 93.

O'Connor, Frank. "A Clean Well-Lighted Place." *The Short Stories of Ernest Hemingway: Critical Essays*. Ed. Jackson Benson. Durham, NC: Duke UP, 1975.

Plimpton, George. "The Art of Fiction." *Hemingway and His Critics: An International Anthology*. Ed. Carlos Baker. New York: Hill and Wang, 1962.

Potts, Willard, ed. *Portraits of the Artist in Exile*. Seattle: U of Washington P, 1979.

Reynolds, Michael S. *Hemingway's Reading: 1910–1940*. Princeton, NJ: Princeton UP, 1981.

Schroeter, James. "Hemingway via Joyce." *Southern Review* 10.1 (1974): 95–114.

Smart, Lawrence L. *The Hawks That Guided the Guns*. N.p., 1968.

Solomon, Margaret. *Eternal Geomater: The Sexual Universe of Finnegans Wake*. Carbondale: Southern Illinois UP, 1969.

Stein, Gertrude. *The Autobiography of Alice B. Toklas*. New York: Vintage Books, 1960.

Tindall, William York. *James Joyce: His Way of Interpreting the Modern World*. New York: Scribners, 1950.

Vinding, Ole. "James Joyce in Copenhagen." *Portraits of the Artist in Exile: Recollections of James Joyce by Europeans*. Ed. Willard Potts. Seattle: U of Washington P, 1979.

Waldhorn, Arthur. "The Sun Also Rises." *A Reader's Guide to Ernest Hemingway*. New York: Farrar, Straus and Giroux, 1972.

Wickes, George. *Americans in Paris*. Garden City, NJ: Doubleday, 1969.

Yeats, William Butler. *The Collected Poems of W. B. Yeats*. New York: Macmillan, 1935.

Young, Philip. *Ernest Hemingway: A Reconsideration*. Rev. ed. University Park: Pennsylvania State University Press, 1966.

Zimmerman, Michael. "Joyce's Personal Catholicism and the Meaning of the Man in the Macintosh." Paper delivered at the James Joyce Symposium, June 1982, University of New Mexico, Albuquerque.

2

A Brief Safari into the Religious Terrain of *Green Hills of Africa*

It should have been impossible for *Green Hills of Africa*, structured as it is, to have been read as simply a book about hunting or an autobiographical record of a hunting safari. Hemingway had carefully, in his foreword to the book, warned his readers that although none of the characters or incidents in the work would be imaginary, he was attempting to see if a controlled rendition of the forms underlying real experience could compete with "a work of the imagination" (vii). He had, in other words, carefully told the reader that his work, however historically based, was meant to be read *as though it* were a novel, a work of art.

Indeed, what are we to make of a book that begins and ends as this one does? It begins with Hemingway, in "a hollow half full of ashes and dust" and "dried leaves" (5), in a time of the dying of the light, awaiting the advent of the great kudu bull who has never come to him. Suddenly, his "theatrical" (2) tracker, Garrick, rises, spreads his arms wide, and pronounces the *consummatum est*, "It is finished" (2)—these are the first dialogue words in the book. The book ends on the Sea of Galilee, as several of the party watch spreading wakes made by grebes upon the water. Hemingway, wondering why the birds are not mentioned in the Bible, decides, "Those people were not naturalists," and Karl declares, "I'm not going to walk on it. It's been done already" (294). Even the casual reader cannot fail to note the Christ analogues that begin and end the novel or to note that Hemingway's rejection of Garrick in this image—"I had never liked him and I liked him less now" (3)—and his criticism of "those people" (294), who have seemingly ignored nature in the texts they left to establish their religion, confront the reader at the beginning and end of his work with a seeming rejection of biblical authority. The only remaining lines in the book at the end are P.O.M.'s lament that she cannot keep Pop alive in her mind, as he is receding beyond recall, and Hemingway's assurance that he will try to keep him alive for her: "I'll write you a piece some time and put him in" (295). The wonderful tour de force is that the promised piece is the very one that has just concluded with those very words and that Pop, the otherwise lost spiritual Father of the hunt, has been resurrected from oblivion by Hemingway and made to come and stay alive. Taxidermy tries to preserve the experience of the hunt in the mounted heads with which the hunters return, but Hemingway's art keeps all of their human experience intact and alive as it makes verbal absolutes out of otherwise passing moments, while behind the trophies of the hunter or the artist seems to lurk the absent principle of the lost vital bull or Father.

James Schroeter, in his article "Hemingway Via Joyce," and I, in my "Hemingway and Joyce: A Study in Debt and Payment," which is reprinted in this book, attempted to suggest the multileveled Joycean structure and technique of *Green Hills of Africa*. Indeed, we both imagined that *Green Hills* was Hemingway's epistle to Joyce in which he was trying out elaborate Joycean structures for Joyce's commendation and approval. Even as the son figure of this book again and again tries to demonstrate shots and techniques to please Pop, so Hemingway throughout the work is with great style making aesthetically incredible and unbelievable "shots" to please father Joyce. Joyce is elaborately present in this book, embedded in anecdote, reference, allusion, and technique. In a letter to Bernard Berenson in 1952, Hemingway said of Joyce:

> He was the best companion and finest friend I ever had. I remember one time he was feeling fairly gloomy and he asked me if I didn't think his books were too suburban. He said that was what got him down sometimes. Mrs. Joyce said, "Ah, Jim could do with a spot of that lion hunting." And Joyce said, "the thing we must face is I couldn't see the lion." Mrs. Joyce said, "Hemingway'd describe him to you Jim and afterwards you could go up and touch him and smell of him. That's all you'd need." (*Selected Letters* 789)

Hemingway therefore acts as the master writer's eyes, and the book is the gift he returns with to lay at Joyce's feet. In view of such shooting as Hemingway demonstrates throughout, there is genuine irony and lament in Hemingway's "None of us great shots is appreciated. Wait till we're gone" (*Green Hills* 81). My purpose here, however, is not to address Hemingway's Joycean patterning but rather to examine a particular manifestation of Hemingway's Joycean technique in the religious structures of his work.

The novel is written to make the kudu bull seem the focus of Hemingway's quest. But *kudo* means glory as reward, and *Green Hills* is a book, on one level, about Hemingway the writer's pursuit of the recognition of the craft that he brings to his kind of hunting—a recognition equivalent to the taxidermically mounted heads that testify to the hunting prowess used to acquire them. Hemingway the writer needs the fame and the renown that he knows he deserves for his prose, in which he has made the incredible "shots" that arrest the flow of life in the stasis of art. In the book, Hemingway describes the hunt for kudu as an ardent pursuit that involves tracking by an intricate and laborious technique and that is driven by an almost desperate yearning for success and recognition. This pursuit seems to be analogous to the writer's pursuit of *kudos* for his aesthetic prowess. The book is certainly an elaborate guidebook to a writer's craft in which shots well made and strategies of the hunt are thinly veiled metaphors for the technique of the literary artist in pursuit of his subject and fame.

Another of the several levels on which the book is structured, however, is that of a religious pursuit: an attempt to establish a connection to the idea of glory itself and also to the presiding and invisible "bull" or Father ("Pop") spirit behind the hunt. Implicit is the question of how one does this in a time that all can recognize as a time of dying light, with the famine country ahead and the locusts, the rains, and the floods coming. The distance between the death without resurrection that begins the book and the successful literary resurrection that is demonstrated as it ends is the distance that the read book has come, and we, as readers, are hard pressed *not* to see a religious pattern controlling the book. This elaborate and sustained religious patterning is intricately worked.

Malinowski and other anthropologists, notably scholars of the Lascaux and Altamira caves, have traced the sacred, magical, and religious impulses behind the hunt. Hunting as rite or ritual, as propitiation of gods, has been well studied, and Hemingway's fascination for the hunt always had its mystical components. He was attracted to cultures where primitive rhythms were readily still available, whether in the prizefight, bullfight, or cockfight, and where food and drink—game, fish, or wine or spirits—could be pursued to their sources in nature. That such cultures are still vitally mythically/religiously connected to blood rituals as devices of bonding with the divine may help explain aspects of such works as *Death in the Afternoon, Green Hills of Africa, The Old Man and the Sea,* and *True at First Light* and may also help focus on Hemingway's sense of a direct relation between virtue in the hunter and the spirit alive in the noble beast or the great fish. One need but recognize the psycho-spiritual rewards gained at Burguete (in *The Sun Also Rises)* or at Big Two-Hearted River, or those gained by Santiago on the Gulf Stream, by Romero in the corrida, or by Francis Macomber in the bush, to recognize that the alert pursuit/confrontation of the animal can be for Hemingway regenerative. Stewart Edward White, in *Lions in the Path*—a book, published in 1926,[1] to which Hemingway might well have had or sought access, given the evidence, in Michael Reynolds' biography *The Young Hemingway,* of Hemingway's extraordinary admiration for White and the influence of White's work on him[2]—similarly describes the way the African lion hunter in his quest so bonds himself to the landscape by virtue of his alertness and projection of himself outward "into [his] surroundings" (143) as to enter into a mystico-religious harmony: "One's consciousness, wandering thus far afield, blends with and becomes part of one's surroundings" (143). In such mystical joining, the Hemingway scholar will recognize Nick at Big Two-Hearted River as well as Hemingway himself at last in *Green Hills*. This religious component of the hunt is present throughout *Green Hills*, but to express the magical properties in landscape and in beasts and primarily to take the reader beyond to larger questions of faith and the spiritual dilemma of our time, Hemingway creates an elaborate net fashioned of Christian iconography.

In *Green Hills*, lest Garrick, the "theatrical" one, be seen as only inadvertently related to Christ by virtue of his opening parodic cruciform *consummatum est*, Hemingway maintains the identification throughout the book. Later, Garrick throws his arms wide again, looks up to the sky, and bares his teeth in anger (178); another time, he throws his arms wide to indicate the horns of the great bull they must pursue— who turns out to be a cow (188); and another time, he preens and postures before Hemingway, and when Hemingway calls Pop's attention to Garrick with "Look what we have," Pop responds, "Christ" (186).

Garrick's opening words in the book are not the first or the last time Hemingway has carefully used or will use the *consummatum est,* and they are not the first time he has parodically presented the crucified god. In *A Farewell to Arms*, while Catherine in labor is being crucified at the end on her Catherine wheel of life/death and childbearing that she cannot escape, in a scene that looks like "a drawing of the Inquisition" (347), Frederic goes to eat in a cafe nearby, where the waiter lets him know that he is exiled from life's feast: "It is finished" (351). In *The Fifth Column*, the ineffectual and incompetent electrician, who cannot bring light to the darkness, pronounces, *"Camaradas, no hay luz!"* while Hemingway describes him as speaking "in a loud and almost prophetic voice, suddenly standing up and opening his arms wide" (27). It is important to note the imagery shared by these examples of the biblical trope: in *A Farewell to Arms*, there will be no son (and therefore no father), and in *Green Hills*, the womb hollow in which the hunters are held is for them a hollow of death, not birth. In this later work, Hemingway carefully describes the hunters as waiting against a time of dying of light, crouched in a "hollow" of ashes and dust with their "knees high, heads low" (5), in what is patently a fetal posture in a lifeless womb of death, not birth. As these metaphorically fetal dead arise, the book begins with a birth that is also a resurrection. All three of these Christ metaphors deny the advent of light, and all three occur during or in anticipation of rains. Apparently, neither the *Fifth Column's* electrician nor the seeming Light of the World who is Garrick can function in a situation where light is disappearing from the world about him.

Against the sense of failure that begins *Green Hills*, another tracker, Abdullah, "the educated one" (4)—Abdullah means "Slave of God" in Arabic—seems to try to bring what support he can: when he scratches his name on the black skin of his leg, Hemingway watches without admiration, and M'Cola, his other tracker/hunter, looks "at *the word* without a shadow of expression" (4; italics mine). Although Abdullah seems to have made the word become flesh, the word, so received, elicits no response. It is no help. The darkness has finally unrelievedly fallen, taking them from the much-sought great bull kudu that they believe in but cannot capture.

Technology, replacing theology in our time, has broken man's bond with nature. Hemingway's hunt is ruined initially because of the clanking truck that frightens away what they wait for. Kandisky, its owner, Germanic Western man, more interested in the life of the mind than of the body, out of relation with the technology he uses (for the truck hates him and he it, and it has the noise of death within it) has "spooked" the hunt. This opening scene, which presents the failed pursuit of the bull kudu, is matched at the end with the great final scene of the failed pursuit of the bull sable. There, too, Hemingway reflects on the technological source of man's failure in nature: "The earth gets tired of being exploited. A country wears out quickly unless man puts back in it all his residue and that of all his beasts. When he quits using beasts and uses machines, the earth defeats him quickly. The machine can't reproduce, nor does it fertilize the soil, and it eats what he cannot raise" (284). This last hunt is not spoiled by the machine— indeed, Hemingway has been able to hunt in one of the few unspoiled virgin pockets of nature left—but he knows the diminishing terms in which the hunt is carried on. He recognizes that modern human beings have broken the cycle of nature and that in that broken cycle they are quickly defeated.

As Hemingway at the book's beginning momentarily retreats, he considers the problem: he knows that the biblical situation now does not apply. One cannot lift up one's eyes unto the hills from whence cometh the help of the Father, for, as he carefully says, now the *cows* are "in the hills" and he *"doesn't believe"* (14; italics mine) the bulls are also there with them. This lack of belief or faith in part determines the hunt that follows, and the book ends with the great and partially unsuccessful hunt to find the elusive and invisible bull in the hills. The loss of this absent bull or patriarchal principle is the central subject of Hemingway's first book, *In Our Time*. The Western dilemma in the midst of this loss is what *Green Hills*, in its historical and religious dimensions, is partly about—what to do when confronted by the absence, ineffectuality, or inaccessibility of the Great Father principle and the consequent need for the son to assume that responsible role. The son's inadequacy to this responsibility can be read at its most simple as what can be done by Hemingway without Joyce or, in a more complex way, as how the son can prove himself—how Hemingway, as character, can solve the problem of his immature, competitive, petty, and vain temperament, or how the *virtu* and knowledge of the father (Father) can be passed on to the son. On the religious level, as Hemingway studies it, the story has much to do with a reconstitution of the Son-Father figure within the Christian trinity.[3] To attempt to reorder modern humanity's psychic pantheon in the interest of restoring and reviving the lost religio-mythical bond with nature is a grand intention indeed. Hemingway was, in this work that is so oriented toward Joyce, seldom unaware of Stephen Dedalus's seemingly arrogant hope "to forge in the smithy of my soul the uncreated conscience" of the race (253).

During the hunt itself, Hemingway, the acolyte as hunter, takes en route what reassurances he can: coming on three conical mounds of elephant dung in the road before him, he reaches out to touch them. Doubting, in need of faith, he lays down the coordinates of his naturalist's faith in the world before him—which becomes, in the hunt, pursuit of the "marvel" of the horns (231), the "miracle" of the kudu (203, 232), and "the ever miracle of elephant tracks" (249)—to find sensory verification through such accepted signs of things not seen. Hemingway's focus on the profane trinity left behind by the elephant is but one example of literally scores of such ironically inverted Christian emblems that Hemingway presses into service throughout his work.[4] Though Karl says he won't walk on water at the book's end, early, as the wind blows the grass in "*waves*," and the trees of the forest grow so closely that "it looked as though you could *walk on* their tops," Hemingway sees a rhino "moving with a quick *water*bug-like motion across the hill" (49–50; italics mine). The elephant dung trinity, the water-walking rhino, and the "miracle" horns and feet of kudu and elephant, as well as the kudu that must be touched to be believed and the bull sable that Hemingway feels he could "stay with forever," are meant in the book to be natural equivalents for supernatural myths.

That the book is structured initially as a pursuit of kudu/*kudo* (glory)—one that finally leads Hemingway into a desperate attempt to restore lost faith or the belief of others in the vanished or absent bull principle that has disappeared into the hills—should suggest one of the main lines of religious development of the piece. On this final hunt, which is at once the hunt to gain glory—the kudu/*kudo*—and also to create belief in the vanished bull, "the Roman" leads them and shows them the way. He is there before them, and his role in the final success is central. The reader must remember that the Roman Catholic Pauline is the P.O.M. of this piece, and it is explicitly for her (as the last paragraph of the book makes clear) as well as for the apostate Joyce that the book is written.

The text is dense with intricate religious reference and allusion. Here, however, let us mainly consider the last part, part 4, which, concluded, brings the hunting party finally to the Sea of Galilee, where Hemingway, having learned how religious belief and faith rest upon the pursuit of the natural creature and not the supernatural god, judges the biblical fathers "not naturalists" (294). Hemingway himself, before the book ends, is absolved of his own corruption—his pettiness, his meanness, his materialism; indeed, the book has been throughout a concomitant study of the amendment/reconstruction of the morality of Hemingway the hunter. As he finally accepts the three kudu heads, all grouped together, he accepts the three-in-one emblem of the vanished spirits they represent, who have finally all become one, *and* the integrated, sharing, not competing, natures of the hunters for the game: Karl, himself, and Pop, the spirit behind the hunt. Finally looking at the three-in-one group of heads, he thinks, "I had accepted the big one now" (293). That his spiritual journey has been directed toward this consummation the text makes clear, for as Hemingway describes to Pop what he hopes to find in the new "virgin" country where he *does* gain his final moral and spiritual victories, he recounts a past trip to "a river no one had ever fished," where with the first cast of his rod he was "fast to three fish" that he landed (210). As he affirms his tale of a three-in-one victory by saying "I swear to God," Pop twice pronounces, "God save us" (210–11).

There are two major parts, chapters 12 and 13, to the concluding fourth book of the novel, which is appropriately called "Pursuit as Happiness." The first of these records the pursuit and attainment of the long-sought kudu, which Hemingway gains, significantly, by *not* following Garrick's advice and by disassociating himself from Garrick. The last chapter records failure to capture the great invisible bull principle that has seemingly vanished into the hills. That chapter does not end, however, until Hemingway has demonstrated that waning belief in the evidence of things not seen is instantly restored through an imaginative reliance upon memory. Having gotten his kudus and tried to take what pictures he can against the dying light, he finally admits that what essentially matters is that his *faith* in what he has experienced is internal and absolute: every animal he has ever shot he remembers "exactly as he was at every moment" (235). Later this memory will keep the father (Pop) alive, as it enables him to construct the work of art—which substitutes for religion, as Joyce would insist it should, in keeping faith at once in absent presence and in life.

As chapter 12 begins book 4, the hunters enter the deer park–like country. It is the loveliest that Hemingway has ever seen—so lovely that he cannot believe they have come upon it; to him, it is like the country of a dream, a "virgin country" (218), an unhunted "pocket" in Africa. There, immediately confronted by a back-erect, "*un*curling"-tusked, bright-eyed warthog boar, unafraid of them, they make "a curve to the right and left the warthog" (218). Not only have they at once encountered a seeming guardian at the gate, a fearless male, happy within this feminine Edenic land, but the sentence that describes their evasion of him reveals within it the reconciliation of opposites that they will discover in this virgin nature—"a curve to the *right and* left."[5] The hunting party then quickly comes upon a Masai village, where they are surrounded by handsome, smooth-moving men who all seem to be of the same age and who are all "the tallest, best built, handsomest people I had ever seen" (219). That Hemingway has entered a land the most beautiful he has ever seen—like a dream—and there found a people the most beautiful he has ever seen should alert the reader to the imaginary/mythic dimensions of this final hunt. The Masai men give Hemingway the gift of a rabbit they have run to earth, and this rabbit goes, via M'Cola—the Mama-worshiping tracker to whom "all religions were a joke" (38) and whose sandals are "cut from old motor-car tires"(47)—back to the Masai, who then release it to the earth to run free, emblematizing a healthy life-affirming cyclical bond with the earth that this highly prolific reproductive rabbit confirms.[6]

As the hunting party leaves the idyllic country behind, they cross to the other side of a thorn-brush fenced cornfield enclosure and there meet Africans like none Hemingway has ever seen: intelligent, large-eyed, high-cheekboned, poised, and dignified men who have classic features and Grecian noses and who wear a sort of Roman toga. Again, the writer emphasizes the surreal nature of this adventure/hunt. The classical "Roman" elder that Hemingway meets here will be the one to finally lead him to the fulfillment he seeks.[7]

From the beginning of the book, the emphasis has been upon hunting that focuses ever more importantly upon the frustrating inability of Hemingway to get his kudu and achieve his glory and reward. He has, as a last resort, finally come alone, with his guides and trackers, and here, after having passed through virgin country where the male principle is handsome, heroic, and unafraid, he puts himself in the hands of the "Roman." He asks this Roman elder, "Where do we go?" (225), and he follows where the Roman leads. This Roman now spreads his arms, as Garrick frequently ineffectually did, to *correctly* show the largeness of the kudu bull's horns while he pours out a torrent of words.[8]

The Roman goes on ahead, spots the bull kudu first, and pulls Hemingway bodily to the earth before revealing the animal to him. In pursuit of this first bull, after it is wounded by Hemingway, the Roman has his toga around his neck and runs naked, crashing through the brush.[9] He pulls Hemingway down a second time as he sees the second bull kudu and similarly reveals it to Hemingway. Such gestures emphasize not only the Roman's extraordinarily important and controlling role in

Hemingway's victory but also the bond with the earth that he establishes that aids in the visionary quest. Both bulls are killed in this hunt. The characteristics of this animal that has been pursued throughout the book are special. He is "a huge beautiful kudu bull . . . his horns in great dark spirals" (231); he is described as "wide-spread and unbelievable," with "great, curling, sweeping horns," and Hemingway touches him "to try to believe it" (231; italics mine). The reader is reminded of the opening pages of the book, when Garrick—who now can be seen in retrospect as, ironically, a Christian icon of faithlessness—was "wide-spread and unbelievable" as he denied the advent of the great bull and pronounced the end of the light and the hunt. In contrast, the kudu itself, though dead, still verifies faith.

Where, in chapter 1, Hemingway turned away in disdain from the "theatrical" one's human words and *consummatum est* and toward the trinitarian icon of elephant dung that he reached out to touch, here he finds faith in the beast itself, "wide-spread and unbelievable," the verification of all his own belief and the destruction of all his doubting, as he reaches out to touch it. What is consummately revealed to Hemingway in the spiraling horns before him is the evidence, finally given, of what has been unseen: the presence of the glorious marvelous beast who embodies the psychic synthesis Hemingway seeks. In the hunt that has taken Hemingway across and into the "other" *rolling* virgin side, and also in the beast himself, whose masculine sky-ascending vertical horns nevertheless cyclically spiral magnificently upwards, he finds the icons and acts of reconciliation. (Notice how *rolling* and *virgin* reconcile biological and immaculate conception, or human and divine birth principles, as do Maria and Rabbit, whom Hemingway makes one in *For Whom the Bell Tolls*.) Here, in the beast itself, Hemingway has come upon the natural supernatural, a "cyclical absolute"[10] upon which he has imposed, in this fantastic country, a basic mythology. Hemingway touches the first kudu bull and puts his belief in the "wide-spread unbelievable" beast that he calls the "miracle," the "bull of bulls" (232). This Great Father principle, however, as Hemingway looks upon him, has "not a mark on him and he smelled sweet and lovely like the breath of cattle and the odor of thyme after rain" (231). This beast of both power and loveliness, beauty and strength, gathering in himself the scent of thyme (time) and the eternal cycles of rain and cattle, whose horns pronounce both the heroic male principle and the cyclical feminine, is reconciled by the imagery to the seasonal life cycles. The unbelievable has been made and proven to be real and believable, and belief is established: back at camp, Kamau will kneel before the heads, his eyes shining, as he ecstatically feels the ears and croons.[11]

The celebration rites for the realized kudu are *kudos* indeed; Hemingway's thumb is taken by the Roman and subsequently by the Wanderobo and pulled with great intensity in their fists while they look him "in the eyes fiercely" (232). This is a rite that Hemingway reciprocates: "me pulling his thumb too" (232). The thumb/fist-pulling ritual is a scarcely masked male-female integrative rite. Eyes meet fiercely above as the thumb meets its hollow below, with Hemingway being at once both hollow thumb holder/receiver and the thumb that is so held and pulled.

Throughout his work, Hemingway profanely inverts Christian symbolism and ritual so that he may better study the common man as Christ, the simple activity as sacramental, the banal as participant in the sacred. In *A Farewell to Arms*, mess becomes mass, a lake crossing becomes a crucifixion, and a vulgar meal crudely eaten before Frederic and his men are wounded becomes a communion mass; in "A Clean, Well-Lighted Place," the litany is profanely parodied; in "The Light of the World," a prizefighter is inextricably identified with Christ, as elsewhere are common men in their seemingly incidental activities: Robert Jordan, Santiago, Cantwell, and Harry Morgan.

In *Green Hills*, as Hemingway, the old man, and M'Cola take the heads, *heavy on their shoulders*, back to the camp, all three fall under the weight of the *widespread* heads, the old man *falling* again as he goes through *the thorns*—all this in mock parody of Calvary and the stations of the cross. At the fire, Hemingway's things are *spread on sticks* to dry, and as Hemingway rests with *his back against a tree*, he takes *whiskey*, which acts to "*straighten*" (238) him, the diction and imagery delineating a carefully structured crucifixion. The hunters put aside the special canned provisions—three tins of *Christmas* special mincemeat, *three* tins of *salmon*, *three* of mixed fruit, and a tin of *Special Christmas* Plum Pudding—and instead eat *meat on a stick*. Putting aside food to celebrate divine birth, they choose instead food to celebrate divine death and resurrection. *Spreading* his raincoat, Hemingway *stretches* his legs while *leaning back against the wooden* wall, and before him the old man is "roasting *meat on a stick*" (239; italics mine). Hemingway could hardly have been more deliberate in his delineation of the profane crucifixion imagery that underwrites that feast: spreading and stretching, which reenact Christ nailed to the cross, or flesh placed on the wood, take place multiply as Hemingway's back is placed "*against the wood*" (229;

italics mine), and meat on a stick is prepared as the sacrifice for the celebratory communion feast that each has prepared for himself. In these actions, in primitive hunting rites before the fire, the hunters honor both humans' and animals' interdependent cycles of renewal in nature through death and resurrection. Hemingway drinks the beer (which he elevates) to chase down the liver while he wonders where the kidneys are—both are the organs of purification—and then distributes the beer. The old man is "crouched by his meat sticks holding the bottle lovingly" (241). (Freudians will recognize the loving synthesis in stick and bottle.) The emphasis in this celebratory communion, as it has been in the Calvary/stations of the cross imagery of the journey in the darkness through the thorns, is on *each* man's solitary yet participatory reenactment of the passion, just as each man, as an altered Christ surrogate, finally has his own meat on a stick that he confronts with the spirits "lovingly," though he is still celebrating with the others.

As Hemingway before the fire tries to win his new followers' belief in his almost magical powers, he *spreads* out six cartridges. Giving them the names of the animals of the field that he has slain, like God in Genesis, he *names* the cartridges lion, lion, rhino, buffalo, kudu, kudu, and pronounces "*God's truth*" (242; italics mine) to get the natives to accept his evidence of things not seen. Then, as the natives work on the skins to be sure they will not spoil, Hemingway puts a piece of kidney between two pieces of liver on a stick. This trinity of organs of purification pierced on the stick is what Hemingway here chooses as an apparent spiritual alternative to the flesh, for he accepts it just as he is denied his sexual wish for the sister of the girl-like boy who is with them.

The chapter ends as he makes M'Cola "*suffer*" as he promises to lead him into extreme danger on the morrow "*in those hills*" (244; italics mine). Twice he "kids" M'Cola, who tries to tell him that Pop would not wish this. To create the "kid," or scapegoat, who begins to "suffer" as he anticipates his possible death in the hills is another structural device, akin to meat on a stick overblown with ashes, whereby Hemingway speaks of sacrificial death with or without resurrection. *Kid* is used with its scapegoat overtone, as it is throughout Hemingway's writings from *The Sun Also Rises* on. It is of interest that M'Cola tries to suggest that the absent Father (Pop) would himself not wish the scapegoat death of his servant in the hills. The next and last chapter begins with Hemingway, tea in hand, observing the meat on a stick "very overblown with ashes" (246) while "the Roman was standing making an oration with gestures in the direction where the light was beginning to show" (246).

(I have suggested in "Hemingway and Joyce: A Study in Debt and Payment" how Hemingway often plays with tea and tea drinking as a reference to the tau cross and the crucifixion of a scapegoat Christ.) This mass, being celebrated by the Roman before the "spread and neatly salted" skins (while tea drinking and dead meat on a stick are pointed out), should not go unnoted.

One problem in *Green Hills* is how to understand Hemingway's acceptance of the Trinity, so emphatically structured at the end of the book, if indeed, in his detestation of Garrick, he has seemed to deny the crucified scapegoat Christ. There is ample evidence throughout Hemingway's work that he was never able to accept what seemed to him the scapegoat role of the son figure in the Trinity, that he considered asking or using another to die for one's own sins to be at once cowardly and—as it related to the suffering Jew Robert Cohn—abominable. Whether masochistically invited by the sufferer or sadistically offered by the perpetrators, it undoubtedly seemed to Hemingway unacceptable. That is partly why Santiago, Colonel Cantwell, Harry Morgan, and Robert Jordan are *not* redeemed by Christ but rather iconographically take *his* identity upon themselves. It also helps explain why Harry and Albert in *To Have and Have Not* both carry such identification. The answer to the problem of how Hemingway can reject the sacrificed son but accept the Trinity is, I think, given in the kudu hunt, which ends with *each* of the three men finally equally sharing and participating in the Calvary—the stations of the cross, the crucifixion, and the agony. Redemption through a trinitarian base of belief seems possible only if *each* is part of the Trinity and participates in the death/resurrection rituals that underwrite it. Karl, Hemingway, and Pop, who is the presiding spirit overseeing the hunt, lurk behind the trinity of heads finally amassed, the three-in-one that Hemingway finally accepts; but just a chapter earlier, Hemingway, M'Cola (the Mama worshipper), and "the old man" construct the active trinitarian base in the kudu hunt and together emblematize a male-centered masculine and feminine bond that participates with the loving spirit of the old man to complete the reconstituted icon. The thumb-jerking ritual expresses the male-female integrative rituals that Hemingway tried to fuse with his Christian emblems. D. H. Lawrence and Joyce, among others who influenced Hemingway, frequently fused pagan and Christian emblems in similar fashion. This participation mystique, in which *each* is obligated to participate with and suffer with the others, allows Hemingway to build a trinity on the basis of his own painfully gathered trophies (the flesh) *and also* on the basis of the words (the spirit) that at last resurrect for P.O.M.—and for us!—the absent Father, believed in and recovered by virtue of them.

It must be recognized that the crossover to another "rolling" and "virgin" side, where male-female psychic syntheses are attempted, occurs coevally in *Green Hills* with Hemingway's attempted mastery and elimination of his competitive sense. But this mastery of the male-centered competitive psyche, caught in either/or dialectics where one part wars with the other, occurs in *each* of the major novels. That is why it is wrong to designate Jordan and Cantwell as types, for they are not—they are in amendment and in transition. When Cantwell reconciles himself with the boatman in the stern, when he cries out, "The shooting's over" (294) and gets in the back seat of his car to die, he is emphatically not the Richard Cantwell of the early chapters. Jordan, Pablo, Harry Morgan, Cantwell, and the Hemingway of *Green Hills* have all come to acknowledge the feminine part of their psyches before their novel's end. When Catherine dies like her namesake on the martyring biological wheel; when Harry Morgan hangs on the wheel and accepts the "roll" of the moon-driven sea, able at last to say "a man alone ain't got no bloody fucking chance" (*To Have and Have Not* 225); when Robert Jordan, having accepted not Maria, but Maria/Rabbit, and gotten himself turned over at last, lies on the fallen, thus cyclical, though ever-green needles; when Cantwell lets the matrilinearly inherited green emeralds be placed in *his* pocket and lets Renata resurrect from unfeelingness the insensate side of himself; when Santiago brings back to life and cooperation the paralyzed side of himself; and when Hemingway of *Green Hills*, like Francis Macomber, explores at last the rolling "other" side to acknowledge and come to terms with it—we are watching complex religious iconography in action.

In *Green Hills*, the pattern of Christian iconography is meticulously drawn. As Hemingway falls and is mocked; as the old man bearing the weight of the great sacrificed beast on his shoulders falls, and, bleeding, resumes the climb but falls again going through the thorns; as these communicants at the celebratory feast after the killing of the great male beast (whose unbelievable widespread horns mean attainment of glory) set aside the Christmas meats and then elevate the beer; as they drink and watch the meat on sticks before the fire while Hemingway's back rests against the wood—as, in other words, they participate in rites of communion, sacrificial death, and resurrection and undergo in almost mock parody the agony of stations of the cross and the processes of purification-redemption—new strategies for religious belief are set beside the old.

In the penultimate chapter, a religious structure has underwritten the hunt. It seems to insist that brotherhood and a bonding with the earth and its cyclical processes—like Joyce's whirling Molly at the end of *Ulysses*—supports and restores man's faith. The next and final chapter, which begins with the performance of a pagan mass as the light is beginning to show, will study the ebbing and failure of belief as the basis of patriarchal faith, the great bull principle, vanishes and leaves finally no valid trace to support dying belief that he ever existed. What can be done if the patriarchal or bull or Father (Pop) principle is lost, has vanished and cannot be seen, seems to be the question. Hemingway's answer, given in the Holy Land, seems to be Joyce's; that the artist, as priest of the eternal imagination, will resurrect him imaginatively and so reaffirm through the Word the validity of his power.

Notes

1. I owe the insight into Stewart Edward White's fascinating book *Lions in the Path* to Professor Robert O. Stephens, who called it to my attention.

2. Reynolds describes the young Hemingway as "raised . . . on the adventure stories of . . . Stewart Edward White" (24) and says that Hemingway named White one of "his three favorite authors" (39). He cites Hemingway's "The Last Good Country" and "Judgment of Manitou" as stories based on White's settings and fictional modes. More significantly, he shows that Africa "caught and held [Hemingway's] imagination forever" (230) and that Hemingway read White's five African books, devouring maps and details. It is highly unlikely that Hemingway, constantly alert to whatever was being published in 1926, would have overlooked White's new book, *Lions in the Path*.

3. This need, which restructures a psychic religious pantheon, may indeed have much to do with Hemingway's creation of himself as Papa while he was still a young man. It may be important to remember that in *For Whom the Bell Tolls*, Robert Jordan's insight at the train station into his father's vulnerability and sentimentality is described as having basically deprived him of his youth.

4. The dazzling virtuosity of Hemingway's imagery, frequently shocking in its inversions, has yet to be adequately acknowledged. *For Whom the Bell Tolls*, for example, describes Robert Jordan beginning to find walking difficult as he thinks of Maria. This is in a passage where the imagery's implication, "evidence of things not seen," is central. I suggest that to make a hard-on a vehicle for religious belief is brilliant.

5. This is a structural device that Hemingway also uses in *To Have and Have Not:* "He turned to the right as he left the dock" (146). He plays with a variation of it in "The Snows of Kilimanjaro," as he describes antelopes with "quick dropping heads and switching tails" (*Short Stories* 58).

6. These "good" people, whose disinterested friendliness and instant and complete acceptance wins them nobility in Hemingway's eyes, are described as having the attitude that "makes brothers" (*Green Hills* 221). It is of interest that these handsome Masai, into whose country Hemingway has come for his climactic hunt, "no kill to eat. Masai kill man" (220). They are proud warriors, not hunters.

7. It is worth speculating that Hemingway also needs these Grecian/ Roman guides to get where he wishes to go—to suggest that he, like Joyce, had to go to classical models to find the way to his subject, even as Joyce went to Homer to get to his own *Ulysses*.

8. The horns and torrent together name the male and female principles that through him, and in the very beast they hunt, will be elaborately reconciled. Wet to the waist, Hemingway forces the hunt in the last hour of dying light. He changes to dry things, drinks whiskey and water, and, as he sees the Roman coming for him, cleans both foresight and rear aperture on his gun and drinks the remainder of his watered whiskey that rests on the ground. Close reading of Hemingway's style in this Joycean work should teach respect for such details: fore and rear, wet and dry, whiskey and water, and spirits and the earth are reconciled in ways that prepare Hemingway for the hunt, even as the joining of the liquid cascade of the Roman's words to his celebration of the widespread horns names the male/female syntheses being achieved.

9. Barbara Lounsberry sees this as a reversion to the primitive and a casting aside of classical restraint: "The reader is back to the time of aboriginal man" (24).

10. My essay "Hemingway and Joyce: A Study in Debt and Payment" (reprinted in this volume) rather elaborately explores the "cyclical absolute" as the icon that Hemingway pursues throughout his work, a figure he learned from Joyce that substitutes for a trinity based on a scapegoat sacrifice. It should be noted that the spiraling ascending horns of the kudu are not unlike Yeats's gyres, which, cycling while ascending, enable human beings to get beyond the eternal cycle, to escape the eternal round.

11. During the skinning out and the taking of the heads, Hemingway struggles between participation and detachment, wishing to keep memory intact and perfect as the basis of what he will truly keep of value. He knows that memory rests on involvement, for he states, "I had skinned-out or seen skinned-out every animal that I had ever shot." Yet he also knows that he remembers "every one exactly as he was at every moment, that one memory does not destroy another" (235–36). Two kinds of taxidermy are taking place: the movements and activities necessary to have the heads, which will be the

evidence and proof of what is and was, and the mind's strategies of holding and keeping what is and was. Memory becomes the imagination's means by which the artist bestows immortality on otherwise vanished spirits.

12. In *The Old Man and the Sea*, Santiago is similarly crucified throughout his ordeal: Hemingway, while describing Santiago's wounded hands and brow, and the feeling of a spear through his side, many times emphasizes how Santiago's back is forced against the wood.

Works Cited

Hemingway, Ernest. *Across the River and into the Trees*. New York: Scribners, 1950.

————. *Ernest Hemingway: Selected Letters, 1917–1961*. Ed. Carlos Baker. New York: Scribners, 1981.

————. *A Farewell to Arms*. 1929. New York: Scribners, 1957.

————. *The Fifth Column*. 1938. New York: Scribners, 1969.

————. *For Whom the Bell Tolls*. 1940. New York: Scribners, 1968.

————. *Green Hills of Africa*. 1935. New York: Scribners, 1963.

————. *The Old Man and the Sea*. New York: Scribners, 1952.

————. *Short Stories of Ernest Hemingway*. New York: Scribners, 1966.

————. *The Sun Also Rises*. 1926. New York: Scribners, 1954.

————. *To Have and Have Not*. 1937. New York: Scribners, 1965.

Joyce, James. *A Portrait of the Artist as a Young Man*. New York: Viking Press, 1965.

Lounsberry, Barbara. "*Green Hills of Africa*: Hemingway's Celebration of Memory." *Hemingway Review* 2.2 (1983): 23–31.

Reynolds, Michael. *The Young Hemingway*. Oxford, UK: Basil Blackwell, 1986.

Schroeter, James. "Hemingway via Joyce." *Southern Review* 10.1 (1974): 95–114.

White, Stewart Edward. *Lions in the Path*. New York: Doubleday, Page, 1926.

The Ritualization
of Death and Rebirth

The Reconstruction of Frederic Henry

The ninth chapter of Ernest Hemingway's *A Farewell to Arms* is an important stage in the development of that richly structured work. In it, Hemingway establishes the symbolic and intellectual coordinates of his novel: he ventures into death to covertly explore in ritual and myth the significance of rebirth, and he studies both the process and the sexual, religious, and mythic necessities for effective psychic rebirth.

That this takes place in the ninth chapter is itself an important fact, for numerology is as structuring a device in this early work as it was to be in *To Have and Have Not, Across the River and into the Trees,* and *The Old Man and the Sea*. In this novel, Catherine announces the fact of her nine-month pregnancy at nine o'clock in September, the ninth month. Such use of nine as a generative symbol, suggesting the beginning of a new cycle, appears frequently in the novels. In *The Sun Also Rises,* for example, Jake, beginning a new cycle in his experience, arrives in Bayonne at nine; after the metaphoric death of the male principle at the end of book 2 where Jake, Cohn, and Romero are all defeated or injured in actual fights or in moral encounters or humiliations, the third and last book begins as he awakens at nine. In this work, Catherine's nickname, Cat, allies her with the mythical cat whose life proverbially ends on its ninth cycle, Catherine's own fate. But in the cat/nine metaphor, Hemingway has joined the opposites of birth and death. That which gives birth at the end of the ninth cycle is joined to that which ends at this same moment; the moment of death is made into a simultaneous moment of birth. Birth and death are forced together, as in the first chapter, when the soldiers who go toward their deaths with their gear bulkily stowed under their capes are described as looking like women heavy with child, and as in the last chapter, when Catherine dies in childbirth. When Hemingway gives his character both the name of Catherine, the saint who underwent her martyrdom on the wheel, and the nickname of Cat, he joins cat and saint in one person and outlines much of the intellectual action of the novel. Later, in *For Whom the Bell Tolls*, he similarly gives a character both the name Maria and the nickname Rabbit to bind together eternal reproductive natural cycles and the virgin of immaculate conception. Hemingway's ubiquitous cats—whether the 57 that Norberto Fuentes recorded Hemingway as keeping at the Finca Vigía outside Havana (79) or the one who represents fertility amidst sterility in "Cat in the Rain," or Boise, the one who tries to reconcile Thomas Hudson to life after the death of his trinity of sons in *Islands in the Stream*—continually express the healing synthesis of opposites.[1]

In chapter 9 of *A Farewell to Arms*, where Frederic experiences death-in-life and undergoes death and cyclical resurrection, opposites are joined, even as they are when love is thrust into the midst of war. These oppositions, studied in dialectical opposition as well as in synthesis, prepare the reader for the antagonisms and loves of lovers and the battles and capitulations of warriors. *A Farewell to Arms* exists to force love and war together. This is partly because Hemingway was both warrior and lover. His ironic recognition, however, is that each may become its opposite: Love, which tends to bond lovers together creatively, and war, which tends to oppose warriors destructively, are the archetypal sources of birth and death, but they may invert, so that love begets death (as it does for Catherine and Frederic) and war creates birth (as it seems to in the imagery of the "pregnant" soldiers and in Frederic's multiple violent rebirths that the novel studies).

Frederic's mythic journey, in which he travels by night to the other side, is wounded, and returns bearing the special knowledge of that other kingdom, has the classical features of all such journeys: the ninth chapter is, as completely as "Indian Camp," a traumatic exposure of the culture hero to the mysteries, by way of a birth/death journey to the underworld, and his subsequent return with wisdom. But Hemingway has carefully prepared for this crossover and its religious, mythic, and psychic meanings in the immediately preceding eighth chapter, when, in describing Frederic Henry's reconnoitering visit to what will be the scene of his life/death encounter, he has him recognize in the external world the necessary syntheses and reconciliations that he must, in the ninth chapter, at risk of death, psychically experience. In the eighth chapter, in elaborate landscape description that is filled with religious overtones, he has Frederic Henry ascend into the hills while the dust is rising under the wheels—an image that is in itself a sharp, controlled metaphor (taken from *The Sun Also Rises* and the first chapter of *this* novel) speaking of death and resurrection caught in cyclical recurrence.

On his physical journey, Frederic climbs hills to confront distant peaks in the snow and then descends to valleys to study the waters, farms, and produce there: he encounters both the sterility of the heights and the fecundity of the low places. He takes his four cars up into the hills, always conscious of the three he can see and not see. It is equally a journey where he must weave back and forth between the two sides of the river, between the heights and the lowlands, actively stitching them together in his movements as he observes imaginatively from his vantage point above the turning wheels. He thinks, as he drives, of the two facing but separated armies, and he considers the water in flow as well as its pebbly bed. In sun and then in shadow, he looks forward and back, to the north and to the south, and above and below. He is alert to the lines and curves of the river and, in the valley, to the *straight* line of the railroad bridge as well as the *arched* stone bridges. He considers the *lines* of trees that lead his sight to the flowing river and later lets the trees lead his sight to the *line* of the river. The road goes back and forth—there are straight ways and rounded turns—and, climbing and descending, he considers the high white loveliness of the mountains and, below, the low green darkness. On the journey, he is responsive to road line, river line, tree line, crest line, snowline, and battlelines between armies, as well as to both sides of the river, the road, and the bridges and to the sides taken by armies in the larger picture of war. But this is a journey to the front and its divided landscape that Frederic, being a soldier constrained by the requirements of war, must undergo; and the whole chapter is based on the necessity to separate or divide Catherine and Frederic Henry in their love—the two lovers who have attempted in their love to become one indivisible whole.

Before Frederic goes toward the front, Catherine, who is staying behind, gives him a Saint Anthony in a capsule to wear. Later, on the journey, an interval separates his spilling the saint into his hand and then spilling him back into the capsule: in that interval, he watches his driver take a similar Saint Anthony from under his tunic with his right hand while his left holds the wheel. To emphasize the split/synthesis of spirit and flesh (hand on the saint or hand on the wheel), Hemingway writes, "His right hand left the wheel."[2] In *To Have and Have Not*, he will similarly play with words: "He turned to the right as he left the dock" (146). Play of this sort is a sure index to the density of the intellectual structure being built. But this play with the encapsulated saint is the paradigm of the spirit's separation from and return to the flesh that Hemingway studies in the ninth chapter when Frederic feels his soul slide out of his body and then slide (spill?) back again. All the landscape dynamics of the eighth chapter are preliminary to the event they are meant to focus upon: the death and resurrection, life/death experience of the wounded hero that he undergoes in the next chapter.

In the ninth chapter, Hemingway develops a consistent imagery of birth that runs alongside incidents and imagery of death. Carefully, he sets the stage for a Caesarean birth that is no less difficult than the one in "Indian Camp," though this one is metaphorical. His first sentence reads: "The road was crowded and there were screens of cornstalk and straw matting on both sides and matting over the top so that it was like the entrance at a circus or a native village." Few have noted how inappropriate an imagery of circuses and aboriginal simplicity is to the frontlines of battle. It is, however, necessary to Hemingway, who is establishing at the very beginning of his ninth chapter an imagery of cycles of nativity and of return to primitive sources. *Native* speaks of natal. The cornstalk screens additionally speak of Demeter/Ceres and Persephone, of birth and death and cyclical renewal, of seasonal fruition and the birth of crops, and of the death and reaping of the harvest. Hemingway lets us see that this entrance to the place of experiencing wounding and death is patently a return to the womb itself. As Frederic and the ambulance crews drive slowly down the straw matting–covered tunnel to emerge in a bare cleared space sunken below the level of the riverbank, they confront holes in the earth that are filled with infantry. These men in the holes will variously emerge to live and die. Some will die in the holes—a foreshadowing of Catherine's child's death in the womb later in the novel; others will need assistance to be lifted from the holes and brought to life. The uterine journey inward down the covered tunnel of life and death (made of materials that speak both of death and of life and the cycles of life and death) has literary precursors of which Hemingway could scarcely have been unaware. Perhaps only as we re-read Melville's story "Tartarus of Maids" do we discover that we are being taken, *not* on a tour of a paper mill, but rather on an expedition through the biology, the reproductive organs, of a woman and that these indeed are the Tartarus of maids. In Hemingway's biological journey, the holes in the earth where the doctors function are described as the ovens of this setting, which was a brickyard. The sense of the oven as a hot source out of which emerge fully formed and created "bricks" is part of the total structure, and Hemingway twice emphasizes a distinction between the straw matting of the tunnel and the life-endorsed "obstetric" ovens from which may emerge men restored to life. In the main "oven," Frederic notes the instruments shining in the light and the basins. This is the oven to which he must be brought after he is wounded and before he is finally delivered to the world. But before rebirth, he must first undergo wounding and death. In the wounding, he knows he is "dead," and then he feels himself "slide back." The shock of this moment is carefully described as a "blastfurnace door . . . swung open." Hemingway so describes it to suggest the trauma of a man being destroyed or that of an infant being expelled from the womb, and he describes it in terms that carefully and distinctly relate it to the "oven" from which he will later emerge, fully restored to life. When Frederic goes on to exclaim that it is a mistake "to think you just died," the bewildering "just" is a real clue to one major insight of the novel: birth as death, death as birth. This journey into death and back again into life is the replication in miniature of the mythic heroic journey to the other side that the true hero must make—the rebirth-return as important as the death journey in the archetype of heroic adventure.[3]

Much of the birth imagery of the chapter is associated with the feminine reproductive system of the mother, which is associated with death, darkness, and disorder. But *this* imagery is associated with a sustained parallel imagery of the father/obstetrician role in "delivery," which is associated with light, control, and spiritual resurrection/redemption. The two strands of imagery together produce an imagery of a doubly endorsed rebirth/restoration, one part of which is physical, the other spiritual: however, it is the spiritual resurrection that seems to save Frederic from encirclement in the womb, the fate his son will suffer.

The birth/rebirth imagery takes the reader on an internal journey to the womb itself where primitive feeding occurs. It is a world of oppositions, a place where there are conversational interchanges but no resolution and where passion and reason are mixed. Life in that dugout hole is a sitting on the earth or a crouching in darkness. As a small lighter is lit and passed around by these men—whose backs are most frequently described as being, in the telling Hemingway phrase, "against the wall"—

one of the soldiers says, "Why didn't we see?" Frederic, saying, "I'll go and *see* now," prepares to go back to the lighted world of the doctors that he has left; when he goes out, it is to "look" and to "see." The point is made that his men can either stay where they are *or* "look around" but that sight is not a function of the cave.[4]

In this almost sightless sunken hole, the men are nurtured and prepared for either life or death. Passini dies there, and from there three others emerge naturally under their own power. Frederic has to be forceably lifted out and brought to the doctors in the light, who subsequently "cut" him free and act to set him forward on his journey into the world. Hemingway uses the word *severing* to describe the doctor's action; then "The flesh was cut," and this child/man of questionable paternity is carried toward the waiting world, undergoing a baptism of blood as he goes.

Hemingway carefully lets us see the intricate relationship between father and son in this victory over death and process. It is described as a spiritual victory of paternal expertise and definition over darkness and chaos in a maternal realm where dirt rains down and where multiple inversions and dissolutions are proposed. The major who is responsible for the food Frederic receives and the medical attention he is given, and who has great expectations for Frederic, is one of a group of three doctors whom Frederic Henry knows. To emphasize his alliance with the paternal doctor ideal, later established in Valentini, the major is given the same rank and upturned mustaches as Valentini and bears wound stripes to tell of his own successful encounters with death. With this trinity of doctors, Frederic first shares spirits in this lighted place surrounded by darkness. When he later returns to this same lighted arena to get food for his men, he finds the major sitting on a box and then sees, as the major again offers him spirits, the instruments "shining in the light" and the basin and stoppered bottles.[5] Frederic is given food for his men—pasta asciutta and cheese, significantly retrieved from a dark hole in the back and out of sight—and he receives it in a basin. This separation of the cheese/pasta from the alcohol/light—a careful separation exercised in that lighted oven/hole in the earth—speaks of the demarcations and sunderings overseen by the father figures. Later, after Frederic is wounded and after he has officiated via that basin with cheese and wine at a black mass communion that he offers as perverted priest to his men, the religious significance that Hemingway has been developing about the trinity of doctors with their implements, whose operation to save/restore the body vaguely suggests a mass to sustain the spirit as well, is established.

After Frederic is wounded, he is unable to move, so he must be lifted out: "Some one took hold of me under the arms and somebody else lifted my legs." Before he is lifted, he notes that a trinity of persons has survived: the explosion that almost meant his death has effectively removed from him the contaminating fourth, Passini: "That left three." As he is carried to the oven where three doctors await, he is twice dropped. The imagery of his wounding is that of death/resurrection, and that of his lifting is the classical imagery of Christ's descent from the cross. The subsequent falls on the journey to the oven suggest the stages of the cross on Calvary. That this imagery seems reversed should not trouble a critic who has studied similarly frequent ironic inversions of religious ritual in *The Sun Also Rises, Green Hills of Africa,* and "A Clean, Well-Lighted Place." Such inversion is central to Hemingway's statement: Frederic is, after all, coming back to life through a sort of rebirth and not being brought to heaven through death.[6]

The spiritual/obstetric part of the process of spiritual/physical rebirth takes place at the main oven, formerly dominated by the three spirit-giving doctors. Here the question of paternity is the important first question raised. First, Frederic is called the legitimate son of President Wilson; then he is described as "the only son of the American Ambassador." At this frontline aid station, he now confronts a new trinity of totally admirable paternal role models. Later, the reader will see Frederic in Milan confronting three inadequate nurses (mother figures), then three rear-echelon impotent ineffective false doctors (surrogate fathers)—all before Valentini arrives to look after him. Now, at the ovens, the first man of three who take charge of Frederic is the tall British driver who has arrived there with three ambulances. He is active, effective, concerned, and spirited. He steps carefully among the wounded, speaks perfect Italian, bypasses procedure and protocol by seizing control of events, and establishes Frederic's fictional paternity to give him special status and attention, as he also anticipates Frederic's subsequent needs. The next man is a little Italian major who oversees the operating room, readily speaks French, shows resilience as he accommodates to the driver's rearranged priorities, and shows active control as he continues to operate on others while accepting Frederic. A third officer takes Frederic on his operating table. As he dictates and talks while investigating, probing, injecting, and cutting Frederic, he demonstrates the easy reconciliation of humanity and expertise, efficiency and humor, objective curiosity and concern, speed and accuracy, that mark the humanity of the Hemingway hero: his hands move "fast," his bandages are "taut and sure." He offers brandy (spirits) to Frederic and has a cross marked on both Frederic's legs. Frederic offers him three exclamations, saying once, "Christ, yes!" and, twice, "Good Christ!"

It is part of Hemingway's sustained iconography that as Frederic emerges from under the care/concern of these three "fathers," he comes out to have the sergeant-adjutant kneel down "beside me where I lay." The phrasing of this iconic image bears a religious overload, and the chapter ends as he is baptized by the stream of blood that falls upon him from the man who dies above him in the slings.

Throughout the novel, the struggle between the priest and Rinaldi and the other officers over who is to be mocked or to have authority at the mess establishes the alternatives of mess and mass, an ambiguity that suggests the alternative meanings of these feasts—life as biological process or life as spiritual sacramentalized event. What Frederic first brings to his men to share in communion together are *Macedonias*— but he brings them to men who prophesy that the road will be a "mess" and who prefer to eat, and it is to honor their request that Frederic gets "mess" tins and food. They have effectively converted the mass to mess.[7] However, as Frederic prepares the food for his men in the dugout, he carefully separates the dust and dirt from the cheese while Gavuzzi at his side hands him the basin. He then elevates the cheese and macaroni. Hemingway writes:

> I . . . lifted. A *mass* loosened.
> "Lift it high, Tenente."
> I lifted it to arm's length and the strands cleared. I lowered it into the mouth, sucked and snapped in the ends. [italics mine]

He describes the taking of the food: "They were all eating, holding their chins close over the basin, tipping their heads back." This profane communion mass, where Frederic officiates as the profane priest, seems to be a challenging fusion of mass and mess that is answered immediately by three celestial comments from the skies. The communion is of cheese and wine, and although Frederic and his men eat four times, he drinks wine three. As he takes this profane communion the second time, "something landed" and "shook the earth." As the men return to their eating, a second explosion "shakes the earth," but then, just as Frederic eats the cheese and drinks the wine once more, the "blastfurnace door" swings open and the third explosion strikes, the one that is his "death"/ wounding. There are actually four pagan communions answered by three blows from heaven. The last of these almost fatally wounds Frederic and does fatally wound Passini. It is significant that of the four men, Passini is the unbeliever-anarchist who would break down the definitions that Frederic tries to uphold—the man who refuses to cross over into and attack, or intellectually venture into, the side of his enemy and who instead wants to bring Frederic over to *his* "side," to "convert" him. Dying, Passini, true to character to the end, cries out to both "purest lovely Mary" and "Mama mama mia"—avatars of both spiritual and biological birth. He refuses to accept the patriarchal terms of battle, duty, and orders that he doesn't comprehend, and he refuses to go out across the frontline to meet what may be death on the other side. He is identified with anarchism, sexual prowess, and being "always with the girls." He says, "I do not believe," and then "I don't believe," and at one point exclaims that "even the peasants know better than to believe in a war." The argument between Frederic and the unbelieving Passini is basically between dualism and synthesis. The upholding of legal and military forms or the anarchistic abolition of them is the issue. Passini, whose argument endorses the "both/and" ambiguities of the mothering cave, dies in that womb enclosure, crying out, in his last words, "Mama mia." Frederic, in contrast, is separated from the cave and borne away from it to the fathers and by them cut loose and carried clear. His cry is neither "Mama" nor "Mary," but rather "Oh God . . . get me out of here." It is the doctors in the light who "cut" him free and act to set him forward on his journey into the world.[8]

The religious imagery has a double function: to sacramentalize Frederic Henry's relations with the world—this explains the perverse inverted mass at which he officiates as priest, as well as the redemptive spiritual iconography associated with the three-in-one father image—and to establish his unique role as the sacrificed and resurrected god/child returned to the world. That Frederic is last seen in the chapter being raised to the "top" by wheels is part of a pattern that is clearly present throughout Hemingway's work and that expresses Hemingway's unique religious belief. His Christ/Savior imagery, so lavishly overlaid on Santiago, Cantwell, Robert Jordan, Harry Morgan, and Steve Ketchel, to name a few of his protagonists, always shows these redeemed redeemers as resurrected to an eternal return. They come to terms with and, as part of their redemption, *necessarily* accept the cycles of life, the wheels upon which they discover the still point. They do *not* disappear into isolating and abstract heavens. The novel ends as Frederic, having seen Catherine in death as a fixed "statue," at last walks away "in the rain" that Catherine has feared. The rain is the icon of those cycles that include death (and also the birth that causes her death) and so deny the changeless state she desires and, for a short while, seems to have attained. Colonel Cantwell, possessor of the unchanging portrait of Renata, accepts the back seat of his automobile as the place of his death, so that he dies while riding on wheels; Robert Jordan, who has found his eternal Now in orgasmic love, whose ecstasy moves the earth, who has discovered a lifetime in 72 hours, in his last gestures acknowledges and accepts the fallen pine needles beneath him that speak of the cycles of the unchanging evergreen; Harry Morgan, after sacrificially hanging on "the wheel," accepts the "roll" of the eternal cyclic moon-driven sea that he has resisted throughout his life; and Santiago lies with his Christlike wounded hands outspread on the bed of sleep from which he will arise in the morning. As emphatically as D. H. Lawrence, who in *The Man Who Died* mated his Christ with a Priestess of Isis so that she might become pregnant by him, Hemingway rewrites received orthodox belief to refuse his nature gods an escape into the skies: bound to the wheel, like the sun that must forever "also rise," they endorse spirit bound to life, where eternity can be found in time and can "always" be rediscovered.

It is important to note the many details of "Indian Camp" that resurface in chapter 9 of *A Farewell to Arms*. The protagonists in both undergo a crossover night journey to a wounding in a primitive, dark place where a Caesarean birth is finally accomplished only by virtue of the sight, light, tools, and technique of a father figure with his basin beside him. This father figure brings out of darkness into light a child whose paternity is covertly questioned. In "Indian Camp," the host that is elevated is the newborn child itself, who is released from the darkness of the womb and brought out into life; in *A Farewell*, the host is the cheese that the men eat together, but its elevation and the communion that follows set in motion a similar "birth" out of womblike darkness. In "Indian Camp," Nick himself is the surrogate newborn (or reborn) given to life at the end of the story. There, he goes forward into a new day with a sense of immortality, achieved partly through his father's command and partly through the reconciliations he himself has made between two discrete realms—reconciliations emblematized by his endorsement of the cyclical rings that spread about him and envelop him. Frederic Henry makes comparable affirmations, having visited both sides of existence and debated and observed their differences. In "Indian Camp," a second father figure dies in a bunk above. We might ask just whose blood falls at the end of this chapter upon Frederic, given that the man who dies about him in the slings is unseen and anonymous. I would like to know if that detail was added to the novel or written after Hemingway's own father's suicide.

With the above, my essay on chapter 9 of *A Farewell to Arms* ends. However, I would like to add a brief coda to illustrate, through one example, elements of Hemingway's modernist style in another chapter of that work. Readers accustomed to reading Hemingway as a naturalist or as a writer who employs a simple style and direct prose need to break down passages of *A Farewell to Arms* to discover its often very elaborate structures. In chapter 16, Catherine, who has chosen to prepare Frederic for his operation in Milan, administers the pre-operative enema to him, which she does so deftly and circumspectly that the action goes almost unrecognized. All we see of it is her "There, darling. Now you are all clean inside and outside." However, the themes both of the enema and the operation, which go inside to bring things out, and of the war and Catherine and Frederic's love, which have been carefully developed in their metaphors of crossover (like Frederic's wounding and operation), are elaborately prepared for and underscored in the first paragraph of chapter 16. In that paragraph, real elements in the scene in Milan in the hospital are shown with extraordinary precision—not only the lovers in the central foreground but the world that they inhabit about them. Hemingway's style is one that uses the unaltered elements of reality to tremendous symbolic, thematic, and intellectual advantage:

> That night a bat flew into the room through the open door that led onto the balcony and through which we watched the night over the roofs of the town. It was dark in our room except for the small light of the night over the town and the bat was not frightened but hunted in the room as though he had been outside. We lay and watched him and I do not think he saw us because we lay so still. After he went out we saw a searchlight come on and watched the beam move across the sky and then go off and it was dark again. A breeze came in the night and we heard the men of the anti-aircraft gun on the next roof talking. It was cool and they were putting on their capes. I worried in the night about some one coming up but Catherine said they were all asleep. Once in the night we went to sleep and when I woke she was not there but I heard her coming along the hall and the door opened and she came back to the bed

and said it was all right she had been downstairs and they were all asleep. She had been outside Miss Van Campen's door and heard her breathing in her sleep. She brought crackers and we ate them and drank some vermouth. We were very hungry but she said that would all have to be gotten out of me in the morning. I went to sleep again in the morning when it was light and when I was awake I found that she was gone again. She came in looking fresh and lovely and sat on the bed and the sun rose while I had the thermometer in my mouth and we smelled the dew on the roofs and then the coffee of the men at the gun on the next roof.

The details that Hemingway introduces here begin to fill out the background reality that surrounds the lovers and becomes part of the sense of the Milan interlude of the novel. If images might be considered tonal and heard as music, we would be hearing a short fugue, whose counterpoint Hemingway probably learned in the year he was kept out of school to study Bach. It is, however, a fugue whose basic action is this: Something outside comes inside through the connection between the outside and the inside that those inside use to observe the outside. The light inside is created by the light outside, and the creature now inside acts inside as though it is outside. After it goes outside, those inside see a light outside and feel inside a breeze from outside that comes inside, and they also hear inside men outside talking. Frederic, inside, worries about somone outside coming inside. He wakes to find that Catherine, who was inside, has gone outside, but he, inside, hears her outside coming back inside to him. She tells him she had been outside and there had heard people inside; but she has returned with things to eat and drink, things outside to still the hunger inside, but she knows that whatever Frederic takes inside will have to be taken outside once more. She again goes outside only to come back inside to put a thermometer inside his mouth, something outside put inside to tell those outside what is happening inside, and the passage ends as they, inside, take inside themselves the intense fragrances of the morning that come to them from outside. Now, all this is something of an indulgence—starting from "There, darling. Now you are all clean inside and outside"—but it does illustrate the extraordinary lengths to which style has gone to establish its bonding of opposites. Hemingway has composed a fugue in the form of a brief philosophical treatise on the relations between man and nature, a short version of "Big Two-Hearted River," that intricately studies the vital and necessary interaction between man and his world. It is patently an elaborate study of crossover, densely structured, and, most importantly, it is a supremely dense example of the way Hemingway insists upon forcing antitheses into extremely intense bonding. The outside is made to be part of, is annealed to, is forced hard against, the inside in every detail of the passage, and this introduces a chapter where medicine is trying to get the inside outside (via the enema) to support an operation to go inside Frederic's leg to get what is inside, the shrapnel fragments, out. Yet, one would be hard put to say that any element in that scene, the coffee of the men on the next roof, for example, existed more because it was "there" (or because Hemingway wanted to convey the keen sense of the fragrance of coffee against the smell of dew on an early crisp morning) than because he simply needed an illustration of something essential and incorporeal that might cross over a barrier to be experienced by someone on the other side of that barrier, and he needed it to be a balancing element in an established rhythm that he did not wish to break. He could have used visual or olfactory sensation, and he may have chosen scent to balance the visual and auditory crossovers he had already studied. In being an introduction to the "enema" chapter, one that has to do with physical cleansing through rites of purification accomplished through crossover, this passage is about the lovers who are trying to inhabit, or dissolve, the barriers or boundaries between them. So what about the mise-en-scène which includes bats and coffee and thermometers and anti-aircraft batteries? They are patently notes in a progression that is musically organized for rhythmic and intellectual purposes. Details here, as throughout the novel, demand to be participants in the sort of fusion of opposites which is ardently struggling toward the dissolution of boundaries, which the breakthrough at Caporetto and the pregnancy seem to symbolically and tragically epitomize.

Notes

1. The imagery of chapter 38 portrays Frederic's rowing across Lago Maggiore to Switzerland as a crucifixion/death/rebirth. When the journey has at last been successfully made to Brissago, Frederic exclaims, "I couldn't be any happier," and immediately "A fat gray cat with tail that lifted like a plume crossed the floor to our table and curved against my leg to purr each time she rubbed. I reached down and stroked her" (279). This cat who both crosses and

curves, whose terminal tail lifts like a plume, reconciles death and life and welcomes Frederic and Catherine to their momentary idyll in Switzerland.

2. Throughout this chapter I quote briefly from chapter 9. I do not, however, include for these quotes page references to a specific edition, since the text I quote from is at once so readily and variously available and so very circumscribed.

3. A series of watery deaths and rebirths is structured for Frederic throughout the novel, and after each he is seemingly offered the alternative of one or the other of two surrogate "fathers." After his wounding, he is offered the services of either Rinaldi, who calls him "Baby," or the priest, who is truly a padre. When he emerges from the Tagliamento and crawls ashore after his escape from execution, the imagery suggests his similarity to a newborn child, and he is soon under the aegis of two father surrogates, the barman and Count Greffi. After his night crossing of Lago Maggiore, where he is portrayed by imagery of a Christ crucified, he emerges from the lake and steps ashore to come under the alternative care/concern of the two quarreling customs officials, who insist on opposing alternatives for the direction his life will take.

4. It is interesting that the "lighter," which is described as shaped like "a Fiat radiator," does not give light (although it is associated with radiation), only fire for the linear cigarettes. The men in the holes hand "around" the lighter and twist their cigarettes to keep the tobacco from spilling. Such circulating of the light and cycling of the line should not be missed.

5. The square, sunstruck top of Kilimanjaro is just one of many descriptions in Hemingway to suggest that the box (square), light, and spirits found in this passage are all related to the Father principle.

6. Students of film may remember Elia Kazan's brilliant reversal of the order of execution, death, the Pietà, and stations of the cross imagery in his *On the Waterfront*, created by a similar need to reverse redemptive imagery and ritual.

7. Frederic's men prophesy, "They'll shell the ____ out of us" and warn that the road will be "a mess." Through such remarks, Hemingway focuses on the virtue/ heroism of "holding fast" as opposed to the moral and physical self-soiling of spilling or not being able to hold fast. He lets the reader see that these men, whose coordinates are mouth and anus, have chosen flesh over spirit: "soul" and "mass" are the antitheses of "shit" and "mess."

8. This opposition between Passini and Frederic, suggesting their alternative devotions, involves significant inversion: physical Passini uses words (abstractions) to destroy faith and spirit, whereas mental Frederic uses food to restore faith.

Works Cited

Fuentes, Norberto. *Hemingway in Cuba*. Trans. Consuelo E. Corwin. Secaucus, NJ: Lyle Stuart, 1984.

Hemingway, Ernest. *A Farewell to Arms*. 1926. New York: Scribners, 1969.
———. "Indian Camp." *In Our Time*. 1925. New York: Scribners, 1958.
———. *To Have and Have Not*. 1937. New York: Scribners, 1965.
Lawrence, D. H. *The Escaped Cock, St. Mawr, and The Man Who Died*. New York: Vintage, 1953.
Melville, Herman. "The Paradise of Bachelors and the Tartarus of Maids." *Stories, Poems, and Letters by the Author of Moby Dick: Herman Melville*. Ed. R. W. B. Lewis. New York: Dell, 1962.

The Suspended Woman
in the Work of
Ernest Hemingway

It may prove valuable to glance at a group of metaphors that Hemingway has used with some consistency throughout his work. For want of a ready name, let them be called metaphors of "feminine arrest."

In a wonderful but neglected short story, "An Alpine Idyll,"[1] Hemingway carefully prepares the reader throughout for his deftly created metaphor, one that appears to be at once grotesque and perverse. The wife of Olz, the seemingly crude peasant from the high mountains, has died in the winter, and since she cannot be buried in the iron-hard, ice-covered ground until the spring, when he will be able to take her body down to softer ground and sanctified burial in the churchyard in the valley, Olz places her body in the woodshed, where, for lack of space, it is propped up against the wood. During winter nights, when he goes out to the shed to get wood, he finds no place convenient to hang his lantern, so, in apparent callousness, he hangs it from the lower jaw of his wife's mouth. The deformation that this gradually creates over time and the very act itself are used to shock and awe those in the story who finally learn of it, and the story's readers share their shock. Part of Hemingway's focus is carefully kept on the dead woman in a state of frozen suspension, removed from processes of decay and immune to rot. That she, so used, becomes a source of light for the man is a necessary part of the metaphor.

Catherine, in *A Farewell to Arms*, dies on the biological wheel[2] that she cannot escape, as it is part of the biological "trap"[3] that Frederic considers their lot, and not even his metaphoric assumption of morning sickness the morning after her announcement of her pregnancy can take that cross, the wheel on which she is to be martyred,[4] from her. The idyllic days spent in the frozen heights above Montreux are at last ended when three days of rain[5] confirm the thaw and break in the weather. As Frederic and she descend to the waters of Lac Leman, it is the beginning of an unarrestable progress toward a birth/death due to love (death in childbirth) that recalls the suggestion of a birth/death due to war in the first chapter of the novel, when the soldiers going toward deaths in battle are described as seeming big with child. Life—which was apparently suspended or arrested at the chilly heights of the Swiss Alps where the couple lived and celebrated Christmas, or divine birth based on immaculate conception—is seemingly set once more in motion by the thaw, and Catherine, in descending from the heights, moves toward her inevitable death within a biological birth process. Her wheel is, however, halted at last when, after her death, Frederic last sees her as a statue, an image that seemingly opposes the image of the rains of cyclical process that enclose the narrator in the novel's last words. It is almost as if Frederic's image of Catherine takes her from the biological wheel and arrests her in an aesthetic immortality, frozen into an "object" like Olz's wife. We might posit that Catherine, as the "statue within the mind," has been a similar bearer of light against darkness/death for Frederic/Hemingway and has demanded her own story, the work of art that is the novel we have read—the novel that Frederic was by guilt impelled to write. Joseph Flora has well argued that in "An Alpine Idyll" Nick, as auditor of the story of the frozen suspended wife, is learning how to gather his materials for his own creative work. (209)

These two plots suggest that heights remote enough to arrest decay or process, rot and decay, and thawing,[6] as these are related to the suspended state in which a woman might be held, are an intricate metaphor that relates to the creative process itself and the role of the woman as muse within the imagination. This suggestion leaves room for the speculation that the fear and avoidance of "consequences"—that is, attempts to avoid pregnancy and outwit the natural creative birth process—appear with great frequency throughout the Hemingway canon and are related to sacrifices made to the creative process. Early in Hemingway's work, the imagination of the creative artist seems duped into believing that it needs either the woman set apart (as possible muse) or a free space unprejudiced by complicating bonds with the earth. I say "duped" because Hemingway as a mature artist mocks these attitudes, knowing that the risk of death and "consequences" is what defines the bravery of the true *torero* or artist, even as it defines for him whether a man is a man. However, in the early work "The End of Something," Hemingway studies how the fear of going with Marjorie—which is spelled out as the fear of "consequences," or pregnancy, in the following story, "The Three-Day Blow"—is answered by the artificial, largely verbal, and adolescent abstract male world of Nick and Bill. This latter story focuses distinctly on Nick and Bill's distancing themselves from the sources of their language and imagery as they relate to life through literature and the abstract tales and legends of others while they drink the father's spirits. These stories of the puerile fears of youth set up a pattern that stories like "Cross-Country Snow," "Cat in the Rain," "Hills Like White Elephants," and even "Soldier's Home" extend to more seemingly mature protagonists—stories where fertility-avoiding males try to maintain absolute controls, either by imposing artificial or sterilizing situations or states of suspension on their women or by attempting to distance themselves in states of abstraction from the fear of consequences. Hemingway carefully studies the vapidity of such boy-men and the attendant dilemmas of their women. The insulated, storm-protected house of "The Three-Day Blow," where the boys drink the father's spirits by the fire while shutting out nature and the wet and shutting themselves away from Marjorie, is a compelling paradigm of the antisepsis of the life-fearing male.

The wife of "Cat in the Rain" is held in a state of expatriate suspension by her careless husband, detached from friends, associates, and things familiar or known, and initially out of contact with the rain, the cycles of life, potential pregnancy, and her own nature or growth. This suspension is carefully judged in the story as a result of the husband's domination of the bed—he reverses himself in the bed, and, solitarily reading, places his feet where their heads might be—and his advice that she choose a similar strategy of insulated life avoidance through the abstract word. The wife's willingness to expose herself to getting wet as she descends for the sake of the cat is a sign of her desire to break out of the aridity and sterility and also the abstractness of her suspended state. In "Hills Like White Elephants," the conversation between the girl and the young man again carefully focuses upon their detachment from familiar life and on their insulation and expatriate isolation. They are suspended in a foreign medium where sights, ideas, spirits, and "letting in the air" are abstract devices and where abortion, or frustration of the cycle of life, is the male obsession. Mr. and Mrs. Elliot, in the story of that name, are also expatriates suspended in such an environment; as they desperately try to beget a child, Mr. Elliot alternatively strives to beget his poems. The detached husband in "Cross-Country Snow" considers his own state of suspension in skiing while contemplating the necessary process to which he must return as he descends to those lower valleys that will mean normal life patterns and acceptance of his wife's pregnancy. In each case, the male who yearns for detachment or arrest of the natural cycles of decay—as Harry does in "The Snows of Kilimanjaro"—is one who in life avoidance gives himself to high artificial or abstract verbal or literary alternatives. The woman, who by virtue of his detachment is frequently a victim of suspension or of arrested natural process, is thwarted or thwarting in her desire for or state of pregnancy or is the figure who reminds him of the biological love/death that life means. Life as art and life as process are the alternatives. Colonel Cantwell, in *Across the River and into the Trees*, carefully considers the living/dying girl who is Renata against and in contradistinction to the "unmaneuverable" image of herself in the painted portrait that she gives him. The alternative Renatas are (1) an abstract immortality established on a reality-denying fictional base and (2) the warm, if compromised, girl.

Images of arrested life, seemingly frozen in time within an immortality that dispenses with the cycles of time, are everywhere in Hemingway's works and are usually seen in opposition to the eternally turning wheels of process—rot—and time. The image of the dead Catherine as an implicitly stone statue in *A Farewell to Arms* is carefully placed against the birth process that cannot separate itself from death and the falling rain, just as, at the beginnings of "The End of Something" and "Big Two-Hearted River," the white stones of the foundations of the earlier lost worlds of the mill and Seney are placed against second growth, the renewing green, and the eternally renewing life of nature. Brett, in *The Sun Also Rises*, a story of expatriate suspension, is a woman who can't seem to stop anything. She is the goddess-icon at the center of the whirling dance, and she is shown in relation to Jake, the would-be writer who tries to stop the room from wheeling by fixing his eyes upon the word, in a novel where the momentary arrest of the cycle— the policeman's raised baton that brings the taxi wheels to a halt— is the final image. Brett's exclamatory marker is "Rot!" and she leaves a trail of ashes behind her; this suggests that as Hemingway studies the pull of the woman toward Circean cycles, he creates the dephallicizing of Jake as a poetic device to enable him to avoid consequences and cycles and to achieve the immortality of stasis. The novel is really a handbook of devices and rituals to enable a state of arrest for the male, to be achieved through rituals of synthesis, whether the rituals of camaraderie through fishing at Burguete, where time seems temporarily suspended; or the rituals of the *torero*, who knows how to cross over—as Jake cannot—into the territory of the "other" without loss to the self; or Jake's ordering and cleansing rituals of San Sebastian. These rituals are equivalent psychic achievements to the art of the artist.

The lost or denied mother is frequently in Hemingway's works a statement of male denial or replacement of the maternal creative principle. The substitution of Bill for Marjorie in "The End of Something" and "The Three-Day Blow" removes Nick from the perils of her potential and feared pregnancy, and Catherine's fatal pregnancy in *A Farewell to Arms* leaves Frederic to his world of men. *Torrents of Spring* offers Diana's anecdote of how she lost her mother. It is an elaborate paradigm of the operation of the creative process, and in its account of how a French general assumed her "lost" mother's place in her bed, Hemingway explores how a man can fictively and at risk take over the reproductive/creative role of the mother. The cost, of course, is the forever lost mother, but, as Hemingway observes, "The general . . . always seemed to us like a pretty brave man" (107). In "The Doctor and the Doctor's Wife," another lost mother, screened off behind drawn blinds, is denied and rejected by both son and huband. The same denial is implicit in the direction finally taken by Krebs, in the interest of truth, in "Soldier's Home." It is not without profound meaning that in such early works as "On the Quai at Smyrna," "Indian Camp," "Chapter II" of *In Our Time*, and the ending of *A Farewell to Arms*, those who attend upon the biological birth process react with a vivid sense of horror and trauma. The distance between biological birth and immaculate conception seems to be the distance between nature and spirit, between time and immortality; and the son or potential father figure, who seeks immortality as a replacement for his implication in the biological birth process, is the creative artist who, in abstract media, himself becomes begetter/creator.

All kingdoms where time seems stopped are finally exemplified in the remote heights of Kilimanjaro, where the leopard lies undecaying—heights imaginatively sought by Harry, the dying unfulfilled artist. We should remember, however, that it was in the early *Torrents of Spring*—whose very title speaks of the emergence from the suspension stasis of winter, as the thaws of spring create a release to life for a would-be writer, Scripps, who is learning his trade—that Hemingway first elabo-rately studied the relations between biological and aesthetic creativities and impotence. In *A Farewell to Arms*, Catherine was too quick to see the frozen heights of Switzerland, remote from the war and "conse-quences," as a place where time was similarly stopped and there were "no rolls"; and for a while, before the thaws of spring when the cycles reasserted themselves, the place was that for her. With the resumption of seasonal cycles, however, a descent to the waters is necessary. There are obviously no cyclical decay processes on the square top of Kiliman-jaro that "The Snows of Kilimanjaro" describes. We are in a world like that described in Keats's *Ode on a Grecian Urn*, where the figures on the urn are eternally in a state of immortal arrest: "forever wilt thou love and she be fair."

In *The Forest Lovers*, whose plot situation Nick reflects upon in "The Three-Day Blow," a sword placed on edge between the sleeping lovers keeps them apart, but, as Nick tells Bill, if it falls over flat, you can "roll right over it." (*In Our Time* 50). In *The Sun Also Rises*, the road to hell is "paved with unbought stuffed dogs" (73) because neither a stuffed dog nor a taxidermically mounted trophy nor a hard-boiled egg—all of which place life in states of suspension—will permit the rolls that the life process demands.[7] Artificial or mythic ways to circum-vent natural biological process, like immaculate conception, order much of Hemingway's work. It is, significantly, a Christmas story that is told in "God Rest You Merry, Gentlemen," in which a boy who seeks a life-transcending purity and yearns for a state of suspension within what are to him the demeaning cycles seems to emulate Jake Barnes as he fatally dephalluses himself.

This extended elaboration should make the patterning of *The Gar-den of Eden* more visible. In the original Eden, the penalty for transgres-sion, or the eating of the forbidden fruit, was removal from the Edenic state of suspension; it meant expulsion into that world of decay and process where Adam and Eve were gifted with biological birth and death and Eve was to bring forth her progeny in pain. David's story, which he finally is able to write, attempts to tell of a state of innocence before his own fall and his subsequent losses, and it seemingly can be told only by means of David's detachment from life, during which he perfects his craft. That detachment suspends Catherine and keeps her in a state of expatriate malaise where trying new cities and hotels and beaches and drinks, like trying on new hats, seems an artificial series of excitements that have no contact with reality around her. David and Catherine have few friends, and the only person introduced intimately in their life is a "pick up," Marita, chosen for experimentation. Catherine, like her namesake in A Farewell to Arms, is the uneasy victim of the need for a biological creativity whose frustration is her undoing. She is the wife of "Cat in the Rain" driven toward an ultimate craziness by her suspension from any significant activity or identity. Unable to abstractly create—she can neither write nor paint—yet jealous of the dedication and success her husband has found in his art, she chooses to impose unnatural patterns upon real living flesh and to become, like God, a creator in the real.

The original holograph manuscript in the Kennedy Library makes abundantly clear that Hemingway's first conception of the novel focuses upon Catherine's rage at her thwarted motherhood, which, according to her, is David's doing, since her sterility is the result of his having contracted gonorrhea or syphilis when young. This holograph version views the source of the couple's dilemma as their biological infertility. Marita, when she enters into relationship with David, quickly presents herself as the fertile alternative to his sterile relationship with Catherine, and her lovemaking with David is fully focused on the begetting of a child.

The motivations in the holograph help us to understand underlying patterns in the novel as published. The pregnancy/fertility that Hemingway has explored thematically in many other works, as early as the stories of In Our Time, and that is part of a ubiquitous tendency to place process, childbearing, decay, and death in dialectical balance or struggle with abstracting heights, whether of art/word or expatriate disengagement, is stripped from the published version of The Garden of Eden, but it is still the unexpressed alternative to the state of suspension and arrest in which Catherine finds herself. The story that David needs to tell and has never told, the story on which he focuses his creativity, has to do with his complicity in the destruction of the great white elephant that he really loved. In "Hills Like White Elephants," the white elephant, an unwanted gift, is, metaphorically, the unwanted child whose abortion is the unstated subject of conversation. If we imagine for a moment that the elephant might remain somewhat similarly coded in The Garden of Eden, then David's tale is, on one level, the tale of the way he participates in a "father's" killing of an unwanted child. It seems an almost mimetic act when Catherine then styles her destruction of David's manuscript the killing of a child.

Throughout the holograph version, David's abstract creativity as artist is opposed to Catherine's sterility as childbearer, or aesthetic creativity is balanced against biological fecundity, and maternity is seen as compromising or competing with the male artist's art. Thus, Catherine accurately labels David's writing as a practice of solitary vice in a wastebasket filled with clippings. Such onanism, or spilling of seed upon the ground, rather than with potency into her womb, is the source of her growing rage; his art, in her image of it, is a waste, and it supports, as she sees it, a vanity. In *For Whom the Bell Tolls*, Robert Jordan, seemingly sexually denied Maria for the night, momentarily allows himself abstract and imaginative fulfillment after having rejected Maria's offer to help satisfy him. As he does so, he thinks about Onan, who spilled his seed on the ground. Asking himself, "Whatever happened to Onan?" (342) he concludes that we never heard any more about him, and the unstated conclusion is that there is no immortality to be had by that route. Before the chapter ends, Jordan has affirmed his ethical position that he will not accept self-satisfaction without the satisfaction of his partner and that only through mutually fulfilling sex is any true and lasting immortality to be had. In *The Garden of Eden*, the opposing poles, as Catherine initially sees them, are either feminine biological fulfillment or a feminine state of suspended arrest from process as a result of the male's dedication to his art. When David finally detaches himself from Catherine and begins to write, he creates a hunger; he satisfies it as he eats not only his own eggs but Catherine's eggs as well. That they have been getting cold is his justification. In the detached and high abstract state in which creativity takes place, however much Catherine and David may be creatures of the Riviera, giving themselves to the sun and the waters, *her* eggs have been getting cold.

The suspended woman in Hemingway's work, then, is not unlike the leopard on Kilimanjaro. She is in an unnatural place, in a condition of suspension from natural process, and her dilemma is integrally related to the artist's desire to find fulfillment on the square sunstruck top of the Mountain of God. Yes, it does seem as if Hemingway's artists sought a woman who would be willing to accept for their sake the unique conditions that their art might impose upon them. The wife in "Cat in the Rain" and the girl in "Hills Like White Elephants" are exemplary. It also seems that, unlike many, Hemingway was fully aware of the costs of such an art and that he labored throughout his lifetime to come to terms with the dilemma created by that cost; that he strove to find aesthetic means to declare his guilt and a way in which the woman might be spared that price. That the men in "Cross-Country Snow," "Hills Like White Elephants," and "Cat in the Rain" are mocked is patent. In "On the Quai at

Smyrna," the story that Hemingway later added to be the real introduction to *In Our Time*, the mothers with dead babies at their breasts are
the paradigm for the suspended and arrested women who follow in the
stories. The male attempt to take those dead babies away is the attempt
to outwit such suspension—which is a result of male dialectics since, in
the story's logic, it is the men who orchestrate war—and to return
process to its normal cycles.

The Garden of Eden, I would imagine, is an unfinished novel, as
Keats's "Hyperion" is an unfinished poem, because it could not be completed. Nothing in the holograph version of *The Garden of Eden* war-
rants the promising ending of the published version, or even an
aesthetically satisfying conclusion to David's dilemma, for the extraordinary search for alternatives to the cost of the creative process has
not been successful—even though Marita is offered, at least in the published version, as a satisfactory solution. Hemingway knew, and his story
shows that he knew, that there is no good place for the woman who is
the cost of an artist's art. "Get a Seeing-Eyed Dog" is a superlative
example of a story in which the creative artist well sees the penalty that
his art exacts, for he carefully evaluates his wife's suspension in a state of
sterility and dependency on him. In Keats's "Eve of St. Agnes," the
lovers abandon the frozen castle, fleeing from that suspended state into
the southern storms, where they are forever lost to us. They have
exchanged their images as statues in art—Catherine's final state in *A
Farewell to Arms*—for love and life, and they are finally devoured and
obscured by time, as most things outside of art are. They cannot accept
dying into life upon the urn, as the Catherine of *The Garden of Eden*
cannot; and Hemingway—who, I affirm, never could accept the role of
the martyred scapegoat victim, whether that victim is a Christ absolving us of our sins or the wife in "Cat in the Rain"—repeatedly exposes
the victimization. Catherine, in *A Farewell to Arms*, may have become
a statue to Frederic, but the fact that she has drives Hemingway as artist
into his confessional self-laceration. He repeatedly excoriates himself
for the fate of suspension that he, as a seemingly life-careless, abstract-
oriented male, has brought upon his consort, and I think it is important
to note that the husbands in "Cat in the Rain," "Out of Season," and
"Cross-Country Snow" were modeled on Hemingway himself. A story
like "After the Storm" becomes unbearably poignant as the suspended
woman, clearly seen floating behind glass, somehow seems to be both
the treasure that the protagonist so desperately needs to recover and also
the sacrifice permitting the accessibility of that treasure. As he batters

at the round porthole with his useless pole, the sexual and mythic dimensions of the painful quest suggest themselves.

Given that a self-reflexive concern for the creative process of the work being written permeates the Hemingway canon, one can see dephallused Jake as the suspended man aware of the cost of his detachment. However, his attempt to master the cycles of the seemingly un-arrestable wheel, to stop the room from wheeling, is somewhat similar to Frederic's attempt, in A *Farewell to Arms*, to master the destructive cycles by which Catherine will finally be slain by taking her to the heights of Switzerland and by viewing her as a statue after her death. The suspension of the woman becomes in such a case ambiguously charged with meaning: it may be a knowing illustration of the way the woman becomes a sacrifice to art, and yet it may be the only way the au-thor can mythically attempt to protect her from the destructive aspects of the cycles of her life that lead to inevitable death. Either way, the suspension exists within a work of art, and the message—whether "In my rhyme you live" or "Life is the cost of art"—is an artist's sensitive perception.

NOTES

1. See my "'An Alpine Idyll': The Sun-Struck Mountain Vision and the Necessary Valley Journey" in this volume.

2. Catherine in A *Farewell to Arms* and later Catherine in *The Garden of Eden* are carefully named after the saint whose icon is the wheel on which she was martyred. Both novels study the biological wheel of pregnancy that is the dilemma for both women, one of whom attempts to find absolutes—"always," "forever," words or immortalities—to replace death, time, and the biological trap, and the other of whom attempts to take over the role of the male.

3. In A *Farewell to Arms*, after Catherine tells Frederic that she is preg-nant, he remarks, "You always feel trapped biologically" (133). Toward the end of the novel, as Frederic foresees Catherine's death in childbirth, he thinks to himself, "This was the end of the trap" (303).

4. Crucifixion on the wheel rather than the cross is a frequent Hemingway inversion: we see it in A *Farewell to Arms* in Catherine's death at the end of her nine-month cycle, in a scene like "a drawing of the Inquisition" (308), and in *To Have and Have Not*, in Harry's dying, while he "hung against the wheel" (173).

5. Hemingway delights in forcing birth against death in "On the Quai at Smyrna," "Indian Camp," and A *Farewell to Arms*, so he frequently mentions three days—the interval between Christ's death and his Easter resurrection—

in the context of Christmas. In *A Farewell to Arms*, snow comes "three days before Christmas," but later, after three days of rain, which should in the re-ligious symbolism be answered by spiritual transcendence of death in resur-rection, Catherine and Frederic descend instead to biological process and biological death. The suggestion seems to be that nature outwits God—that the cycles of natural process, for Hemingway, take precedence over spiritual powers. That is essentially the meaning of *A Farewell to Arms*: its ironies every-where announce the ineffectuality of the word, prayer, or God as they try to go against "life."

6. A master's thesis by Susan Ormandy Simons, "A Grand Illusion: The Motif of Mountains and Snow in Hemingway's Fiction," skillfully explores the relations between freezing, thawing, and flow in Hemingway's work.

7. "Let's roll," commands Colonel Cantwell to his driver, Jackson, in *Across the River and Into the Trees* (30); "We'll roll," commands Frederic Henry to his ambulance drivers in *A Farewell to Arms* (193). In both instances the actual directions being taken are toward the beloved and also toward possible death.

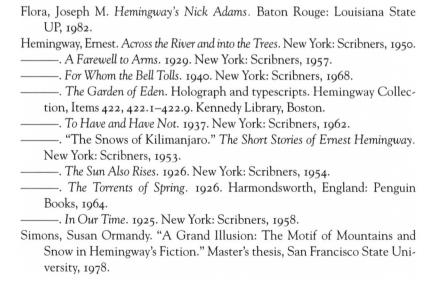

Works Cited

Flora, Joseph M. *Hemingway's Nick Adams*. Baton Rouge: Louisiana State UP, 1982.

Hemingway, Ernest. *Across the River and into the Trees*. New York: Scribners, 1950.

———. *A Farewell to Arms*. 1929. New York: Scribners, 1957.

———. *For Whom the Bell Tolls*. 1940. New York: Scribners, 1968.

———. *The Garden of Eden*. Holograph and typescripts. Hemingway Collec-tion, Items 422, 422.1–422.9. Kennedy Library, Boston.

———. *To Have and Have Not*. 1937. New York: Scribners, 1962.

———. "The Snows of Kilimanjaro." *The Short Stories of Ernest Hemingway*. New York: Scribners, 1953.

———. *The Sun Also Rises*. 1926. New York: Scribners, 1954.

———. *The Torrents of Spring*. 1926. Harmondsworth, England: Penguin Books, 1964.

———. *In Our Time*. 1925. New York: Scribners, 1958.

Simons, Susan Ormandy. "A Grand Illusion: The Motif of Mountains and Snow in Hemingway's Fiction." Master's thesis, San Francisco State Uni-versity, 1978.

5

Artists in Their Art

Hemingway and Velásquez—
The Shared Worlds of
For Whom the Bell Tolls *and* Las Meninas

In the Prado in Madrid one may see, as many of you may have by now seen, a truly remarkable painting by Velásquez entitled *Las Meninas* (*The Maids of Honor*).[1] It shows the Spanish Infanta Margarita and her maids-in-waiting dressed in the ceremonial dress of the royal court. It also includes, however, the artist himself, who is engaged in the very act of painting within a painting, perhaps painting the very painting we observe. In a mirror on the far wall, we additionally see the faces of the proud parents, Philip IV and his wife, who, while seemingly real subjects being painted by the artist in the painting, are also onlookers almost unseen by us at the scene we witness, a scene in which the Infanta is centrally placed and apparently dressed to pose for her portrait. The king and queen are revealed only by their mirrored reflection; they are related to us, the modern spectators, by being, like voyeurs and not participants in the scene we see, outside that scene in history in approximately the same relationship that we are—we seem to stand on the plane where they must have stood—and are only, as it were, accidentally included within it. This painting, regarded as one of the world's most profound and complex works of art, has inspired many artists to emulate its patterns or to study its composition. It has led them into making their own creative statements. Although there is no mention of *Las Meninas* in *For Whom the Bell Tolls*, Hemingway was surely well aware of it, and I will try to show that Hemingway almost appears to be playing with its technique throughout his novel.[2]

There are several overlapping and complex levels of awareness within the scene. There is that of the Infanta, who is looking beyond her time and toward us where we must meet her eyes, and there is that of her maids-in-waiting, who are scattered about the scene but held there by the central reason for their existence—the child. There is that of her parents, who observe their daughter together with her friends, and who also observe the artist who paints them and for them and is at their service. They may additionally perceive the illusion of themselves briefly caught in the virtual imagery of a reflecting mirror on a far back wall within the painting. And there is the vision of the artist, who can include in his regard all that he chooses to include—who can alter or distort history at will, transgressing the boundaries of reality by intro-ducing imagination and fancy in his treatment of it. Staring as he is ap-parently toward his patrons, who are in part there to judge his service and talent, he is also looking directly toward us, for Velásquez has made us assume approximately the place where these real subjects stand. We are thus the other spectators at the scene through whom he undoubtedly acknowledges the posterity for whom he additionally works, con-cerned as he is for the immortality of his subject and his art. There is another figure, outside the room on its far side on the stairs beyond it, seemingly hesitating momentarily before retreating backward and disappearing into the history from which he briefly emerged. The re-flecting interfaces of these several points of view make the canvas an exceptionally thrilling one that connects us to the artist and to his milieu, to his situation and the time he is disappearing into, even as he labors to find a way to transcend them. By the painting we are related to its time, the time and court within which Velásquez painted, where we study his interpretation of himself as well as his environment. We are related also to our own anticipated time, from which we peer into that world of anterior event, trying to interpret images as diverse as those distorted and manipulated within the very painting we contemplate. In the inverted virtual images in the mirror we see images within the painting that, intriguingly, the artist *within* the work does *not* see but that are painted and seen by the artist *outside* the work. The artist *within* the work might see us; the artist outside it looks away from us and engages us, as Perseus did Medusa, only by reflection.[3]

I belabor details of Velásquez's painting so that I may better address Hemingway's *For Whom the Bell Tolls*, a work of similar strategy and complexity that presents many of the same overlapping frames of appre-hension within it and a work whose artist and hero, Hemingway and

Robert Jordan, have taken a stance that is very much that of Velásquez in *Las Meninas*. I am less concerned with the enclosing frames within the novel than I am with the artist's—Hemingway's—portrait of himself that he has, like Velásquez, placed in the center of *his* canvas. But these similar frames are there, and I will treat them first.

Robert Jordan is not of the milieu he comes to serve. He is an outsider, somewhat like a court painter, who has taken service inside the special world where he brings his unique talents. These are talents, as we learn, not only for destruction but for creation. He labors throughout a religiously significant three days to find ways, like an artist, of moving the "now" of dying life to the "always" that the lovers finally do achieve through caring love. One of the major questions of the novel, Jordan's concern, is how to achieve eternity and immortality in time—how to expand time and, partly by the powers of love and imagination, master life through ecstasy so that time, though finite, becomes infinite. The "now" and the "always" become one in Jordan's and Maria's passion, and Hemingway suggests that Jordan has managed in three days to live a lifetime. Velásquez as artist similarly challenges time and, on his canvas, unlike the film of a cinematographer, makes it come to a position of seemingly eternal arrest.

Jordan and Hemingway are also concerned, however, with saving Maria from death, and at the end she is sent on by the pen of Hemingway and the planning of Jordan over the hill toward life and also toward posterity. Her salvation, Hemingway pointedly affirms, is also that of her artist/creator, for by surviving while Jordan remains behind to die in his duty and craft, she carries with her all that can ever remain of *him*. The last pages of the novel reiterate strongly that he lives in her, that there is no death as long as she, made constant by her fidelity to his memory (that they have fashioned together through love), carries what they have created beyond and into the future, where we, the contemporary readers, have it to evaluate, to judge, and to experience again. However, she cannot save herself unaided; she is carried forward toward the safety that keeps her alive for us by the cherishing attention of her metaphorical adoptive "parents," Pablo and Pilar. Balanced between the two, held there, she is carried over the hill and to that safety that has been identified with immortality. In his painting, Velásquez expresses the concern of the parents for their daughter, whom they are giving to immortality as their patronage yields her to art. It is an obvious parallel. Their cherishing assures the Infanta later life beyond her aesthetic existence in Velásquez's painting.

The crude outlines of the Spanish court seem also almost parodically drawn in the revolutionary imagery of an antiaristocratic guerrilla band. Pablo and Pilar are the controlling rulers in the primitive "court" of the cave where the interloping artist/dynamiter comes to grant immortality to them and their "daughter." Spain is the milieu. The Loyalists are those who have given the craftsman/artist Jordan a service to perform for them, a performance that, if successful, will help to perpetuate their order. Pablo and Pilar are the ruling parents who provide Jordan with the dual subject, themselves and Maria, who is to be *his* means to immortality as he brings her back to life through the intricately integrated arts of love and bridge destroying. In the foreground is the band of guerrillas that surrounds and guards Maria, who is identified throughout the novel as a parodic, profane manifestation of a raped/virgin Mary; their attention, though scattered, is often fixed upon her. In the background, characters like Agustín, Anselmo, and Fernando briefly "hesitate on the stairs" if you will—that is, they briefly note, observe, and judge the Jordan/Maria relationship before they themselves disappear into history, except as they are momentarily captured by the sensibility/craft/memory of Jordan/Hemingway.

I have made too much of a partially arbitrary resemblance, and an expanded metaphor has become a conceit. What matters most are *not* these overlapping congruent frames but rather the figure of the artist in the center of his own canvas, involved and disengaged at once, confronting in one moment the world he is immersed within and is paid to paint and the world beyond it where the spectators and audience wait to appreciate: the man caught in time and the man concerned with its transcendence, aware of death and eternity.

In Velásquez's canvas the girl-Infanta is centrally placed and lit for us and seen therefore to have been a central focus of concern of the artist, while actually the canvas that holds her in her own time reveals that her only accidentally seen parents may be the real, if concealed, subject of her artist's craft. It has been suggested by some critics that *For Whom the Bell Tolls* was the novel where Hemingway at last came to terms with his own parents, given as projected surrogates in powerful Pilar, who cows her mate, and cowardly Pablo (who in turn echo *Jordan's* own parents, a bully of a mother and her cowardly, suicidal consort that she intimidated), and that this double reflection has its real source in Dr. and Mrs. Hemingway. It has also been suggested that Hemingway's avoidance of explicit profanity, within his elaborate strategy of euphemisms, was one way of making a belated gesture of conciliation toward his morally fastidious parents. Such concern for the mirror-revealed parents who look on at the morally guarded world of the Infanta, and are therefore related to the audience, ourselves, suggests that the artist's real subject is, as it is in Velásquez's *Las Meninas*, not the one indicated in the title. The true subject is the dialogue going on between the artist and the audience that observes—and, out of that audience, some observers, the royal parents, who specifically receive the artist's authentic attention—and it is through the reflective strategies of his art that the artist is able to come to terms with them.[4] Certainly Jordan's final reconciliation with Pablo, the cowardly surrogate father, occurs almost simultaneously with Jordan's forgiving-understanding of his real father and, I would affirm, Hemingway's acceptance/forgiveness of *his*.

Like Velásquez, Hemingway paints himself, the artist at work painting the very canvas we witness, in the center of his art. There is enormous daring and effrontery[5] in this exchange near the end of a 470-page novel:

> [Pilar says violently, raging] "What passes with that Ingles? What is he obscenitying off under that bridge. . . . Is he building a bridge or blowing one?" [*Anselmo responds*] "Patience, woman. . . . He is terminating his work." [*Pilar*] "But what in the name of the great whore does he take so much time about?"
>
> [*Anselmo*] "*Es muy conciuenzudo!* . . . It is a scientific labor."
> (444)

When Pilar shouts obscenities suggesting that Jordan's work under the bridge can be regarded as masturbation, Anselmo replies, "Calm yourself, woman. . . . He is doing an enormous work. He is finishing it now" (444). The person completing the enormous work is not only Jordan but Hemingway, and the woman's view of the writer's creative endeavor as masturbation is recapitulated in the holograph version of *The Garden of Eden*, where Catherine describes David's writing as a spilling of seed into a wastebasket.

There were not many artists of Hemingway's time who had either the daring or the need to paint themselves at their easel in the midst of and painting the very work that the reader was reading. And Hemingway does it consistently: this self-reflexive technique determines the shape of *Green Hills of Africa* as well as that of *Death in the Afternoon*, *Torrents of Spring*, *The Fifth Column*, *The Old Man and the Sea*, and *A*

Moveable Feast. Hemingway does it in part by making the moral and practical disciplines of a protagonist concomitantly the strategies of the artist. In *For Whom the Bell Tolls*, war becomes a mode of art as the artist creator, purifying himself of subjective, personal concerns in his dedication to and immersion in his subject, annihilates himself so that something else, something lasting, can exist: "Once you got rid of your own self, the always ridding of self that you had to do in war. Where there could be no self. Where yourself is only to be lost" (447). In opposition to Jordan's movement towards self-sacrifice and redemption, which is also the writer's self-transcendence as he replaces self with character and situation (in Joyce's description, holding himself "aloof, indifferent, detached, like a God paring his fingernails"), the novel shows Pilar, the enemy of absolutes, ridiculing the arrogance of the artist: "Thou and thy perfection" (448). She does this as Jordan/Hemingway focuses upon the intricacy of the formal problems he faces in the completion of his great work. The author's delight in his solution of stylistic/narrative problems is one of the delights of reading *For Whom the Bell Tolls*. His sense of what he has solved and of the prize he thereby deserves is very real.[6]

As Jordan nears his death at the conclusion of the novel, he thinks, "I hate to leave it, is all. I hate to leave it very much and I hope I have done some good in it. I have tried to with what talent I *had. Have, you mean. All right, have*" (467); and then he reflects, "I wish there were some way to pass on what I've learned, though. Christ, I was learning fast there at the end" (467). It is terribly exciting to witness simultaneously the approaching death of Jordan, the character painted, and Hemingway's exultation at his own aesthetic lessons learned, which have become his triumph, *his* way toward life everlasting. Of course, that is what is happening whenever we watch an artist at work, as he translates life-feeling into its death-suspension state of abstraction in art, but it is rare that the artist consciously paints the process or finds an imagery for the revelation of both events. All of this prepares us for the major achievement at the very end of the book as Hemingway/Jordan sends Maria—and us, the readers!—on over the hill toward our own safety. As we exult in our catharsis, we note that it has been purchased at the cost of the victims. As we the readers are freed, we should be aware of all that has ceased to be. Jordan and Hemingway recede, retire, and speak further from the great silence and darkness into which they now both have gone, while life and feeling are loud within us. "If thou goest then I go with thee. It is in that way that I go too. . . . Thou will go now for us both. . . . I am thee also now. . . . You are me now" and "Thou art all there will be of me" (463–64). Crying out against relentless time, Jordan/Hemingway achieves the victory of the artist who lives on through and in the reader/spectator whom he inhabits.[7] The tour de force of simultaneous aesthetic, pragmatic, and religious levels of victory is obvious as he concludes, "I am with thee" (465). Hemingway has affirmed that the artist lives only in the experience of his reader and that the end of a work of art is its translation into the sensibility/memory of the one who has possessed it.

Throughout the novel Hemingway has, in the character of Jordan, expressed the problems and dilemmas of the artist who, while thinking and speaking as his life-involved hero, is debating his own aesthetic strategies. "I don't know whether anyone has ever done it before. But there will always be people who will do it from now on, given a similar jam. If we do it and if they hear about it. If they hear about it, yes. If they don't just wonder how it was we did it" (370–71). His concern is very real that the readers, the recipients of his work, should penetrate its façade—not just wonder about it but study it to learn exactly how it was done and thereby to learn truly what it has to pass on, what its real accomplishment was. He knows that what he has to hand on are a set of forms and formulas, the formal solutions that are an artist's ultimate gift to the community of artists.

The identity of reader and Maria that I have shown is early established as the intensely mentally active Jordan/Hemingway does not wake the sleeping Maria, but instead goes on planning, plotting, and arranging his materials while she remains unconscious of his work. This is, as Jordan says, the "ring" he gives her, the artist's gift to his audience; *unconsciousness* of the details of construction in the midst of aesthetic experience. Hemingway plays with the alternative identities of his hero who is at once character, Jordan, and Hemingway, artist. The ambiguity creates genuine problems in structure. "Afterwards," Jordan thinks, "I'm going to write a true book. I'll bet, he said. I'll bet that would be easy" (163). Much later he reflects, "All right. He would write a book when he got through with this. But only about the things he knew, truly, and about what he knew. But I will have to be a much better writer than I am now to handle them, he thought" (248). The reader of such a passage is witnessing the artist at work, trying to create readiness, capacity, and compassion for the act of identification-understanding that is art. Early, Hemingway/Jordan knows, sees, and understands too little to be in mastery of either his situation or his materials. This is not a critic's observation. It is Hemingway's, the artist's, recognition. Only later, as he warms to his work, does he attain that command over situation and materials and find a control of them that leads him to exult at the end of the novel in his powers and his achievement, in the speed with which he has finally worked and the perfection of his execution. During the body of the novel, he again and again girds himself for the task:

> No, himself said. You have no right to forget anything. You have no right to shut your eyes to any of it nor any right to forget any of it nor to soften it nor to change it. Shut up, he told himself. You're getting awfully pompous. Nor ever to deceive yourself about it, himself went on. All right, he told himself. Thanks for all the good advice. (304)

This schizophrenic inner dialogue between the involved and the detached, between the character and the author, between the self immersed in and inextricable from the world and the transcendent overseeing spirit, between the passionate and the cold reflective mind, is the product of the artist on the canvas, the painter painted standing in the room he paints.

Jordan confronts the catchphrases that possess his mind, to which he, as character and actor, has given absolute assent. They are revolutionary patriotic clichés, and he knows the need to be beyond such immersion, to be disciplined by the detachment of one uninvolved with this war. The problem of being at once immersed in his medium and detached from it, of needing to transcend it while still being caught in it, is the dilemma of God in the flesh, of the author/painter in his medium/time. It is the problem of the Hemingway in Jordan. Hemingway early confronts this problem as he prepares Jordan, caught in history and *his* story, in which he must die, to become Hemingway, the transcendent, detached, godlike manipulator/overseer and comprehender of that material:

> But he noticed, and listened to, and remembered everything. He was serving in a war and he gave absolute loyalty and as complete performance as he could give while he was serving. But nobody owned his mind nor his faculties for seeing and hearing, and if he were going to form judgments he would form them afterwards. And there would be plenty of material to draw them from. There was plenty already. There was a little too much sometimes. (136)

Hemingway has spelled out this difficulty, this remarkable problem of the author's identification with his creations—God's with his creatures—as he has studied Jordan's dilemma of separation from and concomitant immersion in the world in which he works. Jordan thinks toward the end, "There's no *one* thing that's true. It's all true. The way the planes are beautiful whether they are ours or theirs. The hell they are, he thought" (467).[8] Transcendence and immersion, disengagement and detachment of the transcendent imagination, character embodied in situation: these alternatives are the author's distance from yet immersion in his protagonist, the painter apart from his subject yet joined to it in the act of painting.

Jordan has recognized that his political feelings have religious analogues like one's first communion—but when he elaborates upon them, he finds that politics are inseparable from *aesthetic* response:

> It was authentic as the feeling you had when you heard Bach or stood in Chartres Cathedral or the Cathedral at Leon and saw the light coming through the great windows; or when you saw Mantegna and Greco and Breughel in the Prado. It gave you a part in something that you could believe in wholly and completely and in which you felt an absolute brotherhood with the others who were engaged in it. (235)

Reaching for an understanding of his political involvement, Jordan comes upon the brotherhood of artists who share similar aesthetic problems. His split is genuinely between his aesthetic and political-social dedications. This problem is elaborated as Pilar finishes her description of the massacre in Pablo's town.

> Pilar had made him see it in that town. If that woman could only write. He would try to write it and if he had luck and could remember it perhaps he could get it down as she told it. God, how she could tell a story. She's better than Quevedo, he thought. He never told the death of any Don Faustino as well as she told it. I wish I could write well enough to write that story, he thought. What we did. Not what the others did to us. He knew enough about that. He knew plenty about that behind the lines. But you had to have known the people before. You had to know what they had been in the village. (134–35)

Here, as author in the midst of his work, whose virtues he attributes to the skill of his character's art, he discusses the basis of the literary technique that has created the very experience we have just had, but it is a basis that we are led to assume neither Hemingway nor Jordan had. It is perverse: the doubled thinker, who yearns to write the book we are reading, denigrates his own abilities; at the same time, by disassociating himself from them and bestowing them on Pilar, he declares himself superior to Quevedo. It is, again, a magnificent tour de force of transcendence of subject in the midst of subject: it is Velásquez standing in the center of *Las Meninas*.

This technique of the artist painted in his art has always been Hemingway's. It accounts in part for the unfortunate tendency to read Hemingway into all of his creations. In Hemingway's work, the artist is most frequently inseparable from his subject. Even as Santiago cannot at last extricate himself or keep himself separate from the material he deals with—he asks about the fish, "Is he bringing me in or am I bringing him in?" (99)—so the death-dealing *torero* must be exposed to death, for the medium is the message, and the artist his art.

I am sure that Hemingway enjoyed the deviousness of *Las Meninas*, the exciting and exhilarating sense of being caught in destructive life and simultaneously aiming at an immortality that both he and Velásquez gained by placing themselves in the center of the arena of their canvas. Both men were addressing a posterity that might know how to evaluate the suspended brush in the artist's hand[9] and his inextricability from the world he best served by calling its categories in question and breaking its frames.

Notes

1. *Las Meninas* was completed in 1656, when the Infanta Margarita was about five years old and when Velásquez was fifty-seven. All but one of the figures in the painting were immediately recognizable as specific members of the court of Philip IV.

2. There is indeed precedent for his so doing, and since his novel was published, the painting has increasingly become the subject or basis of other art. Gustave Courbet's painting *The Painter's Studio* (1855) was recognized by his contemporaries as playing off parallels with *Las Meninas*. Much more recently Pablo Picasso made the first of his forty-five studies based on *Las Meninas* (that are now in the Picasso Museum in Barcelona) on August 17, 1957. Salvador

Dali and the Chilean painter Juan Downey have similarly based paintings on the Velásquez work—the latter using a copy of *Las Meninas* as the central theme of an installation and performance event at his New York exhibition in March 1975. It seems apparent that Jean-Luc Godard drew on Velásquez and this work of his for his film *Pierrot le Fou* (1965). Antonio Buero-Vallejo's short story "The Only Man" (1933) and his controversial play *Las Meninas: A Fantasia in Two Parts* (1960) both indicate the fecundity of Velásquez's conception for the artist.

    3. Interpretations of the painting vary widely. The major interpreters see it as a painting of the Infanta Margarita or of the royal family in its courtly setting. Indeed, even after being admitted to the Prado, the painting was variously referred to for many years as a portrait of the family, and its name *Las Meninas*, referring as it does to the maids-in-waiting who seem largely incidental to the whole canvas, was either only occasionally used or ignored by critics or official catalogues. Jose Lopez-Rey, who himself uses the title *The Royal Family*, indicates that the title *Las Meninas* was not entered in the Prado catalogue until 1735. One historian, Carl Justi, describes it as a portrait of the Infanta Margarita at the center of a familial scene in the life of the palace; but he goes on to hypothesize, leaning to some extent on legend, that it is a realistic depiction of a casual event, an instant in time, where the artist, at the suggestion of the king, capitalized upon what the king happened to see as *he* posed with his queen for *their* portrait in the studio—obviously, everything we see is from the standpoint of the king. Justi also says, "It is the picture of the production of a picture" (315), the latter being the portrait for which the royal couple was posing when the king noted the aesthetic possibilities in the scene that he, as sitter, looked upon. Bartolome Mestre Fioi speculates that the image in the mirror is that of the full-length portrait Velásquez is painting in *Las Meninas*. Critics like Enrique La Fuente (30), George Kubler and Martin Soria (268), and Hugo Kehrer conjecture that Velásquez is painting in the picture what the viewer sees and is perhaps even using an unseen mirror behind the king and queen to see what he paints. The author of one study regards the princess as at the center of an allegorical theme that emanates from her. Madelyn Kahr, in a chapter vital for the criticism of this Velásquez painting, "Interpreting *Las Meninas*," writes that the subject of the picture "stated most succinctly, is *The Art* of painting" (171). Luca Giordano, who was a court painter in the 1690s, called it the *Theology of Painting*.

    4. Madelyn Kahr sees the "intermingling of the reality within the picture and the reality outside, this essentially Baroque breaking of the bounds of the picture space," as "the magic of the mirror" (179). The room in the Prado where *Las Meninas* was solitarily hung included a mirror, apparently to add yet another dimension to the problem of reality/art.

    5. The two major paintings that can be distinguished on the wall in *Las Meninas*, both based on oil sketches by Rubens, are *Minerva Punishing Arachne*

and *Apollo's Victory over Marsyas*. It is noteworthy that both represent a divine chastisement for mortal artistic vanity or human creative acts that arrogantly choose to compete with the gods. Charles de Tolnay reads the paintings as symbolizing "the victory of divine art over human craftsmanship" (36).

6. The king conferred on Velásquez the title of Knight of the Order of Santiago on November 27, 1659; yet in *Las Meninas*, painted in 1656, the cross of the Order of Santiago is plainly visible on Velásquez's breast. Antonio Palomino, in book 3 of his *Museo Pictorico* (1724), says this "was painted after his death at the order of His Majesty, and some say His Majesty [Philip IV] painted it, for when Velásquez painted the picture he had not yet been granted this honor by the king" (Kahr 132). Students of Hemingway may well imagine the importance of this order and this title for Hemingway, who had named the protagonist of *The Old Man and the Sea* (for which he himself gained the Nobel Prize) after Santiago—the most important saint, I would hazard to suggest, in Hemingway's pantheon. Santiago is the terminus, the objective, of the great pilgrimage route across Europe.

7. Charles de Tolnay states that the self-portrait in *Las Meninas* shows the artist "in a state of dreamy rapture" (36) because showing him actually putting brush to canvas would be less dignified, as manual labor, than "the subjective spiritual process of creation [that] demonstrates the supremacy of spirit over matter" (37). Hemingway's elaborate use of Christian iconography throughout his novel, his creation of a cast of characters having correspondences with a Christian pantheon, and the pattern of the sacrificed-and-to-be-resurrected son that he uses at the end of the novel, as well as Jordan's admonition to Maria at the end, all argue for an intricately constructed message of the supremacy of spirit over matter.

8. Madelyn Kahr writes, "As for Velásquez specifically, he looked upon everything from water jugs to princesses with the same clear-eyed objectivity" (175). This fidelity to "truth" and refusal to be subordinate to subjectivity or bias, one of the major aims that Robert Jordan/Hemingway struggles to achieve in *For Whom the Bell Tolls*, should explain why Hemingway may well have taken the main idea for his major work from Velásquez.

9. The suspended brush in the artist's hand emphasizes, as Kubler and Soria suggest, the artist in the act of "considering an idea" (268), thereby emphasizing painting as an act of the mind. Madelyn Kahr sees the arrested moment as implying that Velásquez "did not flinch from the fact that in the end, after thinking, the painter must act" (167). The Hemingway scholar will note that the three days of special life that Robert Jordan is granted—during which he is living apart from the act of writing about his experience that he plans for in the future—is for him, as writer and expatriate, a suspended "moment" in time, and that the bridge blower, Jordan no less than Hemingway, was one to insist upon the integration of thinking and doing, reflection and action.

Works Cited

de Tolnay, Charles. "Velásquez *Las Hilanderas* and *Las Meninas*." *Gazette des Beaux-Arts,* 1949, 35ff.

Fioi, Bartolome Mestre. "El espejo referential en la pintura de Velásquez." *Revista Traza y Baza* 2 (1973): 16ff.

Hemingway, Ernest. *For Whom the Bell Tolls.* 1940. New York: Scribners, 1968.

———. *The Garden of Eden.* Holograph and typescripts. Hemingway Collection, Items 422, 422.1–422.9. Kennedy Library, Boston.

Justi, Carl. *Diego Velásquez and His Times.* Vol. 2. London, 1889.

Kahr, Madelyn. *Velásquez: The Art of Painting.* New York: Harper and Row, 1976.

Kehrer, Hugo. *Die Meninas des Velásquez.* Munich: Bruckmann, 1966.

Kubler, George, and Martin Soria. *Architecture in Spain and Portugal and the American Dominions 1500 to 1800.* Harmondsworth, England: Penguin Books, 1959.

La Fuente, Enrique. *Velásquez: Complete Edition.* London: 1943.

Lopez-Rey, Jose. *Velásquez: A Catalogue Raisonné of His Oeuvre.* London, 1963.

6

"An Alpine Idyll"

The Sunstruck Mountain Vision and the Necessary Valley Journey

"An Alpine Idyll" is a neglected Hemingway short story.[1] In 1975, when Jackson Benson edited his seminal work, *The Short Stories of Ernest Hemingway: Critical Essays*, its comprehensive bibliography listed only *one* essay on the story and less than a dozen commentators who had briefly made remarks on it in essays focused on major critical works. When such critical lack of attention is measured against the forty-three (often extensive) entries listed for "Big Two-Hearted River" or the sixty-three for "The Snows of Kilimanjaro," a just sense of the story's obscurity emerges. As of this writing, there are fewer than a half-dozen critical essays on the story in print.

Were "An Alpine Idyll" truly an inept or a merely shocking failure, as it has been judged, there would be no need for this essay or the few others that are now beginning to call for the story's rescue. It is, in fact, an astonishingly intricate, well-told tale that exemplifies the best in Hemingway—it is Hemingway all the way, pure and classic in form. It has undoubtedly been overlooked because, more successfully than other tales, it has demonstrated the iceberg technique at its most exemplary: the visible tip has, by a most startling exposure, kept the vast bulk hidden and unsuspected. Carlos Baker, speaking of Hemingway's short stories in *Hemingway: The Writer as Artist*, said of them, "They are so readable as straight narratives that one is prepared to accept them at face value—to admire the sharp lines and clean curves of the eighth of the iceberg above the surface, and to ignore the real causes of the dignity or worth

113

of the movement" (119). The problem is that when the eighth of the iceberg that is visible shocks or repels, there may be scant desire left to discover the "real causes" below the surface. It is partly for this reason that some of the best and most subtle Hemingway critics have been among those who have summarily dismissed "An Alpine Idyll."

Attention should be paid to this kind of dismissal, for the fact that the story has led even astute and sensitive readers to remand it to relative obscurity is itself fascinating.[2] There are many who have judged "An Alpine Idyll" not worth the reader's time. One leading Hemingway critic ascribes to it "a detectable streak of morbidity" and asks, "How else can one explain 'An Alpine Idyll,' a relatively pointless tale?" (Donaldson 284). Another major critic describes it as "very close to what was called several years ago the sick joke" and relegates "the masculine bravado here" to "the level of goldfish-eating" (Benson, *Writer's Art* 54–55). To Richard Hovey it is a "grotesquerie" (9), and Arthur Waldhorn joins others in judging it "a grotesque tale" (37). Many of the most extensive studies on Hemingway have utterly ignored it, and it exists in major commentary largely in remarks of dismissal. Yet when Klaus Mann reacted to "An Alpine Idyll" and "A Simple Enquiry" in the *Neue Schweizer Rundschau* in 1931, he said, "They are masterworks . . . extracts from life in which each word is loaded with destiny. The essence is bitter, but wonderfully strong" (qtd. in Kvam 5). Hemingway's style, to Mann, was "nothing other than a miracle" (qtd. in Kvam 6). Carlos Baker, recognizing Hemingway's metaphoric structure, suggested that one should read the story "with as much awareness, and as closely, as one would read a good modern poem" (*Hemingway* 121), and surely he is right. It is Joseph Flora who has seen this most fully, recognizing that "An Alpine Idyll" is a story "about perceiving stories," and that, within the confines of the story, only one who, like Hemingway himself, is sensitive to what is being said can interpret it, for "the narrator knows better than to accept conventional interpretation" (208). If Flora is right, and I think he is—his work on "An Alpine Idyll" is very perceptive—Hemingway readers must bring new poetic attentiveness to this familiar tale and a healthy skepticism toward existing critical responses.

Among those who have lingered to study aspects of the tale, there has been an almost fastidious revulsion from its central image. The story was initially turned down by Scribner's magazine for being "too terrible." Robert Bridges believed it would be "too hard a blow for the magazine" (qtd. in Baker, *Ernest Hemingway* 171), and Baker himself, despite his interest in the tale, speaks of the peasant's "inhuman lack of feeling for his wife" and indicates his belief that the tale itself grew out of a taste "for the macabre" (*Ernest Hemingway* 168). Richard Hovey speaks of the story's anaesthetization and dehumanization of love "through habit and routine" (9). Bernard Oldsey speaks of "the peasant brutality and coarseness" of the tale (68). Charles Fenton calls it "a brutal short story" (167). Kenneth Lynn calls it "a particularly brutal and guilt-drenched story" (*Hemingway* 341) and refers to its character Olz as "a bestial Austrian peasant" with "an oafish name" (342). Raymond S. Nelson describes Olz's "stolid imbecility" as "only a few cuts above Neanderthal man" (30). Such comments on what is read as the callousness of the peasant and his act, or on what is taken to be an immature desire to shock on Hemingway's part, accordingly account in part for the scant attention paid. As Joseph Flora said, "The story seemed to many too anecdotal, merely a study in the bizarre" (198).

Yet Carlos Baker is among those who have seen more in "An Alpine Idyll." He readily recognizes that it is only "apparently" a "simple tale" and that it is Chekhov-like. His deeper appreciation comes from his peripheral recognition of the iceberg: "The story is not 'about' the peasant" (*Hemingway* 119, 120). The story's aspirations or literary pretensions seem to have been perceived most by those who read it fresh in the 1920s. The editors at Scribner's magazine recognized that it was "like certain stories by Chekhov and Gorky" (Baker, *Ernest Hemingway* 171). Ezra Pound, early in 1927, responding to this story that Hemingway had sent to him for inclusion in *Exile* after it had been turned down by Scribner's, commented, "This is a good story (Idyll) but a leetle litterary and Tennysonian. I wish you wd. keep your eye on the objek more, and be less Licherary" (qtd. in Tavernier-Courbin 183). How later Hemingway critics, who were censuring the story's brutality and coarseness, accommodated themselves to Pound's sense of its Tennysonian echoes is unknown, but Pound's comment reveals his ready recognition of the story's ambitions. Kenneth Lynn felt that Pound's criticism of "An Alpine Idyll," where he charged Hemingway with "following too closely in the wake of H. J. [Henry James]," was suggesting that Hemingway "carried his jamesian facility for talk too far and allowed his characters to indulge in more of it than was wise" (*Hemingway* 328). Still, such recognitions of the story's aesthetic aspirations have been few, and even among those who have studied the story with some care, comments that dismiss it without really having come to terms with it are much more typical. Edward Hattam, who is listed in Jackson Benson's bibliography for the story (Benson, *Short Stories* 333) as having written the single existing article on the story as of 1966 ("Hemingway's 'An Alpine Idyll'"), treats the story of the peasant as a "tall-tale" told by the villagers to make fools of outsiders, and Fraser Sutherland finds the irony of the story "laid on so thick as to be slab-like" (42).

Undoubtedly the bizarreness of the story's subject is partly responsible for this fate, but the passivity of its narrator and his friend, who seem in the story to be there merely as witnesses to the tale about another, who is only peripherally seen and not understood by anyone in the story, is also responsible for critical oversight. This is ironic, for, in a way, the story is Hemingway's art carried to its perfection: its epiphany remains unstated, its meaning remains implicit, its point of view remains ambiguous, but all are carefully, elaborately established.

To describe the structure and significant imagery of the story, it will be necessary to retell it in part, stressing and citing details. The story seems another "Cross-Country Snow," but here Nick and, this time, his friend John have descended from the high Silvretta country, where they have been skiing for a month.[3] Unlike the other story, which ends with the protagonists still up in the mountains, lamenting what they see as their necessary descent and only looking forward to further skiing at some time in the future, Nick and John have on this occasion been "up" too long and are suffering from the effects of too much sun. In the high country they have not been able to get away from the sun, and it has finally spoiled the snow, creating "spring skiing," where the snow is good only in the early morning and again in the evening. This sun, in which they cannot rest, has made them tired of skiing. John, aware they have stayed too long, declares, "You oughtn't to do anything too long," and Nick agrees, "No. We were up there too long." To this, John, seemingly unnecessarily continues, "Too damn long. . . . It's no good doing a thing too long" (345). Their repetitions, like their ski runs, have become almost unconscious and drain the vitality from statement as from experience: their style of expression begins to establish the meaning of the piece. They are, therefore, finally, unlike Nick and George of "Cross-Country Snow," glad to be down in the valley and glad that there are other things in life besides skiing. Nick admits that the high mountain spring seemed to him "unnatural" when measured against "this May morning in the valley." The "too much sun" up above has ruined things (344).

As the two companions come down into the valley, they pass a churchyard where a priest, departing from a burial service in the yard, bows to them but does not speak, a fact that John makes much of: "A priest never speaks to you. . . . They never answer" (343). In the church-yard a sexton and a peasant are completing the burial of the peasant's wife, the peasant finally "spreading the earth evenly on her grave," like "a man spreading manure in a garden" (343). Later, drinking with the innkeeper and the sexton in the taproom of the inn, the boys learn that the peasant's wife died "last December" and has only now, in May, been brought down to the soft earth of the valley for burial. It has only been possible to bring the body down from on high for burial since the snow has melted and gone. There is no mystery about the wife's death—she died of heart trouble that everyone knew she had—but there is a mys-tery about the radical deformation of her features, and the sexton tells of the priest's demand that Olz, the peasant, reveal the cause. It is Olz's confession, however slight, that is at the heart of Hemingway's story; all other details of Nick and John's skiing and their drinking together in the inn are secondary to their reaction to this tale.

Olz says that after properly reporting his wife's death to the au-thorities, he first placed her body in his woodshed across the top of the big wood but that when he started to use this wood, he had to move her and so placed her "up against the wall" (348).[4] Her mouth was open, and when he came into the shed and had no place to hang the lantern, he "hung the lantern from it." The reader is the one, along with Nick and John, to imagine the gradual effect of this often-repeated process. The grotesque deformation of the woman's mouth is a result of her husband's need for light, which she, finally rigid and no longer supple, supports. Despite this "use" of his wife, Olz affirms that he "loved her fine" (348). The innkeeper, who has elicited the story from the sexton, thrice declares such peasants to be "beasts" and tells Nick and John thrice that they "wouldn't believe" the story he is about to reveal to them. Heming-way's story ends with John first interrupting the tale with "How about eating?" and then again interrupting its conclusion with "Say . . . how about eating?" and Nick responding "All right" (349).

Some of the readers of this seemingly perverse little tale have seen the point of it all as another stage in the gradual hardening of the boys to life's painful ironies and tragedies: "in our time," they affirm, one is gradually inured to the bizarre and horrible and gets on with the busi-ness of life in spite of it. Young has argued that "Nick is hardening a lit-tle. . . . A shell is growing over the wound to protect it a little" (60), and Bhim Dahiya seconds Young on this (43–44). Surely, John is shown throughout to be far less sensitive than Nick: he is largely concerned with sleeping and eating, and he falls asleep with his head on his arms soon after they enter the inn, while Nick is apparently sensitively and meticulously noting the details of the room, the table, the people in the room, and the world beyond the room that can be seen through the window.[5] John does not awaken when the sexton and the peasant enter the room to drink, when the girl takes or brings orders, or when the innkeeper comes to their table, but only when the girl brings the menu: "The girl brought the menu. John woke up" (346). He has not bothered to learn much of the language of the country, and he tunes out the tale being told: "I can't understand it, anyway. . . . It goes too fast for me" (347).

In radical contrast, the narrator carefully notes the peasant's final *conscious* disregard of the sexton, with whom he earlier drank a traditional drink—for which he insists on paying, "*Alles,*" before leaving for another inn, the Löwen[6]—and Nick carefully studies the peasant's disregard of others and everything in the room. The peasant is described as ignoring the innkeeper and not seeming to see the waitress, though she stands beside him. Twice he is described as looking out the window. His attention and his respect seem pointedly to be located elsewhere. That they are placed beyond the room itself, in the landscape beyond the window where Nick's attention also has come to rest, suggests a genuine bond between the peasant and Nick that goes unexamined and unstated. Hemingway has, on the other hand, with precision, and in sharp contrast to the peasant's apparent unconsciousness, placed on display John's real unconsciousness.

In "An Alpine Idyll," we are asked to solve the riddle of the psychological source of the peasant's behavior with his wife's body and also his detachment in the inn, as well as the reason for the innkeeper's excess. In every case, we are being taught by the writer that what seems is not what is. The black-bearded, high-booted, primitive peasant, who lives alone, far from others, "on the other side," and who is throughout much of the year apparently totally cut off from contact with the world below, obviously has his own proud and emphatic code of values. Hemingway, who is careful about the meaning of such things, makes him the only one in the room to drink pure spirits; he orders schnapps while the others consume beer and wine. Intriguingly, the peasant is the only one associated with both love—"I loved her fine"—and war—"He wore his old army clothes." Nick has earlier noted how "evenly" Olz spread the earth upon his wife's grave. (Although Nick has returned to the valley to find "many letters" awaiting him, at no moment is the reader given any sense of the source of these; his human relations, except with John, remain a mystery.) The peasant is also the only one native to the area; he is carefully defined as belonging both to the mountains and to the valley: "He lives on the other side of the Paznaun," we are told, "but he belongs to this parish." Seemingly coarse and crudely dressed, yet with patches on his elbows to suggest the care that he takes or that was taken with his person, he is nonetheless denounced as a "beast" by the innkeeper and condescended to by the sexton.

The judgment of Olz is the point on which everything turns.[7] Certainly this point is the one that radically divides the critics. Most of them, as described, read him, as do the sexton and innkeeper, as bestial and crude. Even Carlos Baker, whose reading is often sensitive, tries in every way to make excuses for him. Baker urges the reader to recognize that Olz "has lived too long in an unnatural situation" and that "his sense of human dignity and decency has temporarily atrophied" (*Hemingway* 120). It must be a need to absolve this man somehow of the terribleness of his deed that leads Baker to announce, "When he gets down into the valley, where it is spring and people are living naturally and wholesomely, he sees how far he has strayed from the natural and wholesome, and he is deeply ashamed of himself" (120). There is certainly little natural and wholesome about either sexton or innkeeper, and there is no way to substantiate this deep shame that Baker infers. To support it, Baker regards Olz's exposure to the priest and sexton as a "coming to judgment" and describes the "unspoken shame of the peasant, who could not get away from the open staring eye of the 'natural' people who in a sense brought him to judgment." I find small justification for this reading—just where do we see this sense of shame?—except perhaps in the critic's wish to exonerate or cleanse the peasant of what is judged to be his terrible guilt.

In contrast to Baker, Myra Armistead urges in her essay on the tale that the reader note how "the *valley people* [italics mine] have been telling and hearing [such] tales too long and have been insensitive to the feeling of their fellow men" (255–58). She perceptively points out the prejudice and lack of courtesy in the innkeeper, and she suggests that the attack on the peasant has its own covert motivations. John Atkins, also on the minority side, perceptively remarks, "There is a simplicity about the story and a dignity about the peasant which appeals . . . to me. . . . It did not occur to the peasant that he was outraging his wife's body putting it to such obvious use" (224). He refers to the peasant's love as "the crude, unsensational kind of love which exists among people who live hard, inarticulate lives" (224). This reading is given support by Hemingway's first wife, Hadley R. Mowrer, who wrote in a letter of February 11, 1965, that "the rough mountain peasants of these Alpine regions would joke about the frozen corpses awaiting springtime burial"(qtd. in Hattam 261–65).

J. Bakker argues that "love has nothing to do with conventional morality, and this is probably the 'point' of the story" (35–37). He portrays the peasant as one bewildered by the priest's morality, since, by his own set of values, he had not wronged his wife. Charles Fenton presupposes Hemingway's "revulsion at the peasant's callous treatment of his wife's corpse" (167–68), but Joseph DeFalco writes that "the peasant's unawareness of having done something unnatural indicates his own absolute coming to terms with death. . . . The point is, he has accepted her death. Those who criticize him cannot accept naturally the knowledge of death; in fact for them outward form has all the importance in any situation" (216). Joseph Flora also tries to put reaction straight: "Humor and disgust are not . . . the only possible responses to the story Nick has heard" (207). Flora acknowledges that "there have been moments in 'An Alpine Idyll' when Olz has appeared to invite more sympathy than curiosity. . . . Who is to say how another man might deal with grief?" (207).

Hemingway's portraits of the innkeeper, the sexton, John, and the priest are as carefully drawn as those of Chaucer's pilgrims, and they are meant to invite our moral judgment. The innkeeper is quickly revealed to be a rather noisy and intrusive busybody who almost sneeringly takes delight in eliciting and spreading about the story of the tragedy. But the reader is expected to note additionally that the innkeeper insists on labeling the others as unbelievers before the tale; that he quickly, loosely generalizes—"All these peasants are beasts"—and that he bridles when corrected in his inaccuracies:

> "She died last November."
> "December," said the sexton.
> "That makes nothing. She died last December then. . . ." (347)

Economically, Hemingway has revealed something important about the imprecisions of the innkeeper and his edginess when contradicted, while he has also introduced a hovering sense of the language in which they speak: the awkward "that makes nothing" readily suggests the probable *"Mach's nichts"* or *"Das macht nichts"* of the actual exchange.

When Nick asks what there is to eat, the innkeeper replies, in what the reader should begin to see is his characteristic failure to relate reality and the mind's creations, "Anything you want. The girl will bring the eating-card" (346).[8] The waitress, when she arrives, is shown to be almost too easily affable and also intrusive. The sexton, who is the only one in the room actually by role associated with the church, and who yet is familiarly addressed by his name, Franz, labels what the reader comes more and more to see as the pathetic encounter between Olz and the priest only as "very funny." When asked by Nick what he will drink, the sexton refuses, saying "Nothing," while shaking his finger; but when pressed—"Another quarter litre?"—he immediately yields: "All right" (347). Apparently neither his words nor his gestures mean much, and the turnabout is meant to seem appropriate for a man who has just drunk Olz's wine and is now about to share it with his enemy.

Early in the story John noted that Nick's spoken greeting to the priest in the churchyard was answered only by a bow: "It's funny a priest never speaks to you" (343). The silent response of the priest is meant to be heard against the garrulity and intrusive affability in the inn. These details that Hemingway delicately places with these slightest of touches establish that the curious group in the inn, who laugh at the tragedy, who gain status by what they know of the tale, and who gossip almost jeeringly over the sinister details, have no insight whatsoever into the peasant's psychology or values, as they also have none of his pride. John, on the other hand, who ignores the language he does not understand while remaining focused steadily on sleeping or eating, could far more readily be styled the "beast" of the piece. Only the priest—the man of God in this valley village who apparently has the official role of dealing with the problem of the events that have taken place high above in the unmelting snows—is kept apart and by that separation is made to seem of another order. Against the intrusive and eager desire to relay gossip on the part of the innkeeper and sexton, his initial reluctance to communicate with Nick and John comes to seem to define his integrity. As befitting a man of God, a keeper of the secrets of the confessional, his silences, like Olz's silences and like those cold and removed heights from which Olz has come, speak of detachment from the world. If this detachment seems alienating and cold, it only reinforces Olz's own seeming distance from normal human sentiment.

The mouth of the woman (Olz's wife) is a finely focused metaphor, relating as it does to the process of eating as well as to the spoken, but notably not written, word. Throughout the story the spoken word is often found as gossip, as a calumnious means of inaccurately judging others. The two silent people of the story are the priest and Olz, neither of whom is related to food. The most gross and bestial of those pictured is John, who ends the story as he keeps urging Nick to accept food. The metaphors of the story tell that, pointedly, death suspends natural process. The mouth of the wife that dealt with words and food is at last stilled. This momentary arrest of process by death would normally be followed by decay and rot.[9] However, here it becomes unnatural suspension. In the story it really is nature itself, the seasonal return of spring, that urges the resumption of the cycles of life and death and the necessity of burying the dead so that out of death may come birth again: it is on an early spring morning that the boys watch the peasant spreading the earth over his wife's buried body like "a man spreading manure in the garden." There is a primal necessity for the end products of the eating process and for life itself to become at last the fertilizers of life. In the very end of the cycle, the cycle is affirmed; death leads toward birth.

There seems to be a double meaning in the use to which the wife's mouth is put and what seems the almost deliberate deformation of that mouth by her husband, who, although he "loved her fine," goes about his solitary business apparently unconscious of the effect upon her that his needs cause. The mouth of the wife is altered from an emblem of process into a seemingly dependable source of light, and it is by this means that Olz can carry out his lonely tasks. The transformation suggests a victory over process, albeit one achieved through censurable detachment. But it is just as much a victory of absolutism and immortality over mortality as the frozen wife, at a great height, has become at last a source of light in what seems a victory of the spirit over the flesh. The real irony of "An Alpine Idyll" is that the seemingly callous and bestial Olz metaphorically participates in what seems a transcendent mastery of process. His repetitive movement of light rather than food to the mouth of his fixed wife metaphorically reads as a spiritualization of the physical. The dead woman, as undecaying, unchanging bearer of the light, has become in the poetics of the piece almost an icon of spiritual absolutism, of escape, however temporary, from the eternal wheel of existence. The reader should note how often such "spiritualizations" historically end in suspended death: eighteenth-century gardeners, reaching toward the "ideal" in the geometric patterns toward which they disciplined their plants, learned to replace aberrant life with fixed, colored gravel.

The delayed burial and Olz's retention and suspension of the dead woman, whom he keeps out of the processes of rot and decay at a great height, interrupt natural expectation and create an unnatural situation. But Olz unnaturally lives in an unnatural situation: he lives remote from mankind and without those connections and relations that might humanize his life. In that world of his, the unmelting snow is basically responsible for his isolation from others and life below. Hemingway has carefully established that there is complicity between nature and humanity, between the seasons and heights and snows and human beings' alienation and estrangement from humanity, for he has added to the priest's avoidances and silences and Olz's detachment and abandonment of the inn the setting of Austria that is also an actor in the drama. For a man to remain for long, as Olz does, at that height, where the snows are unmelting, is to exist in a bizarre state, and that elevation, keeping him "too long" away from those seasonal alterations and changes associated with natural process, seems a cause of monstrosity. If Olz lives in this unnatural world, the boys have been in it themselves "too long" and have equally suffered for their habitation of it. In "Cross-Country Snow," Hemingway let his readers recognize the unnaturalness of his protagonists' reluctance to give up their skiing: Nick's statement that life "isn't worth while if you can't [ski]" (*In Our Time* 147) has an absurd ring when considered in the light of the deferred responsibilities of fatherhood and life that await him below. Similarly, there is an absurd discrepancy sensed between Olz's "I loved her fine" and the actual use to which the body of the beloved wife was put.

In art, concrete detail serves thematic ends, and story is often parable. Olz has gone so far beyond his once well-loved wife that she merely at last serves to support his observation of other reality. Nick is meant to be led to reflection by the tale of Olz, as are we. Olz *seems* a common peasant who feels nothing as he uses his wife's inert body to hold his light, and that light seemingly serves no noble or abstract end, used as it is only so that the brute man may keep himself warm. The terrible image of the deformed mouth is patently placed to shock, and the shock of horror is meant to be there, in part to tell us how quickly we forget, distort, and get beyond the source of our recognitions—how rapidly we put behind us the means to our transcendence. To take this to another level, we might reflect on how quickly experience becomes word, which in turn becomes experience of the word and then neglect. Certainly Olz's silences and avoidances should not be taken for lack of feeling or guilt, nor should the image of the mouth merely elicit contempt and scorn for

Olz. The loquacious ones in this story seem particularly unqualified to pronounce on feelings, and the wife's deformed mouth, if rather horrifying, is also poignant. Implicit in the peasant's act and in the deformed image is, even more than the transcendence of process, a victory akin to an artist's victory over matter; and also significantly implicit in it is the cost of that victory: a seeming loss of humanity and the desecration of the bond with the feminine. Olz is neither artist nor intellectual, but he may well paint a moral and teach a lesson to Nick—who has perhaps remained too long away from those who await him—or to any artist who may never have known fear of an artist's abstraction and the cost of it. "An Alpine Idyll" is fundamentally a story about the creative process and its human cost. The woman's deformed mouth as its central image is brilliant and unerringly right.

The artist's godlike creative function makes him or her precisely the one to sacrifice nature to personal ends: the greater such idealism and the more rarefied such vision, the more fantasy and imagination play fast and loose with nature and the greater the deformations that nature suffers. The artist is always the one who, in often serene detachment and necessary transcendence of materials, can, like Whistler, paint a picture of his mother as merely "An Arrangement in Grey and Black" and can, like Hawthorne's and Poe's artists, scientists, and imaginative adventurers, translate living flesh to a tone, a pigment, an area of color, a balance on a canvas, or a formal compositional problem. Hawthorne's Aylmer (of "The Birthmark") and Ethan Brand, and Poe's narrator of "Ligeia" and artist of "The Oval Portrait," all sacrifice their women, however loved, to their absolutist fantasies of art or of high, cold, abstract perfection. In the work of Edgar Allan Poe, a host of Ligeias and women on rue Morgues are the cost of their or their narrators' broken ties with the real world and their unworldly desire to transcend the cycles of earthly process. Master of horror, Poe is also the writer who most fully explores the murderous cost of the imaginative creator's inhuman, creative vanity. Nathaniel Hawthorne's "Man in the Steeple" well knew that although he could gain a better and more accurate detached view of the world from his height, he *had* to descend finally and rejoin mankind in the streets below. Hemingway, who studied the problem, never doubted that the descent to the valley was the necessary balance for the mountain journey.

If I have argued for recognition of the aesthetic paradigm in the peasant's act, both Joseph Flora, in his pioneering study, and Ann Putnam, in her recent representation of Flora's arguments, argue forcefully for reading Nick in "An Alpine Idyll" as the writer and artist who, in detachment from and objective assessment of what he sees, is creating the materials out of which his stories will come. Joseph Flora contends that "An Alpine Idyll" is "an example of the artist's temperament—really the artist at work"—that it essentially is "the story of the coming into being of a story" (203, 204). He admits that "by extension, the story asks how people can treat those they love in the frightful ways they sometimes do," and he acknowledges that "it is a major theme of the short stories," but, finally, he knows that the question we are left with at the end is "what to do with a story" (209–11). This is Nick's problem, and he has been observing it carefully, considering the framing, placing, structuring, and disposition of the elements of the tale that he is being given in every nuance and gesture that he has skeptically yet precisely observed.

Hemingway was not extolling those who manage to escape natural process any more than he was extolling the somewhat cowardly and selfish Nick and George of "Cross-Country Snow" or the vapid men of "Cat in the Rain" and "Hills Like White Elephants" for having thwarted the natural desires of their consorts. Hemingway always knew how necessary it was for his creator protagonists to flee the high places apart, the tops of Kilimanjaros, where imaginative life, briefly separated from processes of rot and decay, or the disciplining and informing limitations of reality, might court its separatist dreams. He also knew that this way lay death and that too long and sustained a flight into rarefied ether—or simple expatriate rootlessness, as with Catherine and David on the Riviera in *The Garden of Eden*—could be unnatural and deadly. Eternity had to be bound to *now,* just as expatriate rootlessness finally needed authentic and native roots. Hemingway knew this as readily as Keats, who knew that he had to "wreathe a flowery band" to bind him to the earth as he set out on his own celestial journey in "Endymion." Only in death could Harry of "The Snows of Kilimanjaro" reach and remain at the sunstruck top of the Mountain of God in an extended and unbroken fantasy that would be the mountain's immortal equivalent.

There is a way in which "An Alpine Idyll" seems to be one of Hemingway's most poignant and most psychologically necessary statements, a work that at this point in his life he had to write. The deformed mouth of the woman arrested in natural process signals at once a violation she did not feel, being in her death beyond suffering, and a monstrosity in the husband who kept her there at that unnatural height, supporting his own needs and functions. That one emblem, the deformed mouth, speaks in "An Alpine Idyll" of the human and natural cost of an unnaturally prolonged victory over the cycles of nature. Bizarre and terrible as it is as an image, it affirms fully and directly, if metaphorically, Hemingway's aesthetic recognition of the human cost of his art. It is important, in an understanding of Olz and of Hemingway and of the artist behind the tale, to emphasize that Olz manipulates dead matter, that he deals with human but insentient materials, that his needs bring him to use human and emotionally bound materials, the mouth of his dead and beloved wife, toward abstract ends, those of illumination, and that such use implies distortion of them. Olz, however crude, stands in for the artist at work. Not as fastidious a statement as Henry James's "Maude Evelyn," but similar to it, Hemingway's story allows his readers to fall into the banalities of the sexton and the innkeeper as it seemingly endorses their harsh judgments of Olz. Like "Cat in the Rain," however, "An Alpine Idyll" leads us to and through a series of revealing questions that could well apply to either story: Does the writer share the husband's callousness? Is the writer insensitive to the wife's plight? Could an insensitive man create such a structure? Is not one of the most interesting aspects the extent to which the story invites the pillorying of the character who seems biographically an extension of the author? In these stories, as in all his work, Hemingway is harder on himself and more rigorously moral than the vast majority of his readers. Such stories come out of the artist's careful, meticulous consideration of the relations between life and art and also out of guilt for his art's effect upon his life.

As the story is read back onto Hemingway, with that unavoidable and intrusive biographical interest so often unfortunately brought to his works, the critic wants to acknowledge the events surrounding its composition in the first days of May 1926. Immediately and inescapably, the story seems a *mea culpa* for all the unnatural distortions of natural life that Hemingway's writer's life brought to Hadley, and this is the way Kenneth Lynn would prefer to read the story. He writes, "Out of this troubling confrontation [with Hadley over his infidelity with Pauline] Hemingway produced, around the first of May, a particularly brutal and guilt-drenched story called 'An Alpine Idyll,' in which he symbolically dramatized both his callous treatment of Hadley as nothing more than a convenience to him during their months together in wintry Schruns and the effective burial of their marriage in springtime France" (*Hemingway* 341–42). Lynn is so enamored of his biographically manipulated reading that he repeats it at length in an April 1988 interview in *Johns*

Hopkins Magazine (Lynn, "Interview"). However, Hemingway's emotional problems compounded with his aesthetic ones went far deeper than his guilt for infidelity or clandestine romance, as careful psychoanalytic readers can see in "Cat in the Rain," "Hills Like White Elephants," and "Out of Season." In the holograph version of *The Garden of Eden*, the artist's guilt, as he achieves abstract creativity at what seems to be the cost of his wife's biological sterility, is vividly shown. And if Harry in "The Snows of Kilimanjaro" at last leaves Helen below with his seemingly debrided, rotting, gangrened leg—that is all she sees of him dead—while he flies off in imaginative, deathlike fantasy to the sun-drenched top of the Mountain of God, the story as gesture seems a desperate acknowledgment of the lengths to which the artist may be driven to seize immortality in art out of otherwise wasted life. It is easy enough to speak of guilt for treatment of Pauline on safari, but that is not the whole of the story.

If the critic perhaps rightly refuses to be led from the work by biography, he or she nevertheless may see Nick—the boy become man become that older man who leaves his skiing at last to descend and pick up those many letters that await him in the valley inn—as a man who has better things to do than ski and who has learned through trying too long that to extend a brief flight into an extended and then unnaturally extended time in the sun can have a genuine human cost in the detachment and distance that the human emotions may take from normal patterns of behavior. This more mature Nick may be able to acknowledge that he can unknowingly have become to others, in his detachment, monstrous.

What makes the story classic Hemingway is the extent to which it recapitulates or phrases patterns and metaphors that are present throughout the Hemingway canon. Two young men without women, rootless in a country not their own, have been enjoying themselves in the camaraderie of shared delight in techniques practiced with care and precision somewhere beyond civilized society, in nature. This describes the young skiers of "Cross-Country Snow," the hunters of *Green Hills*, and the fishermen of *The Sun Also Rises* even as they epitomize the detachment, pride, and satisfaction gained in such mastery and disengagement. Also in the story is a woman who has been taken out of process—removed from the usual terms of decay and rot that accompany life and death—and who, in her rigidity and fixity within a medium of flow (water), held in a state of momentary suspension (snow), is inverted into being the basis and seeming source of light. Hemingway's works reveal this seemingly intricate pattern as recurring. At the end of *A Farewell to Arms*, Catherine, like her sainted namesake who died on the wheel, is seemingly also martyred on the biological wheel that she cannot escape. Turning toward her fulfillment within the seasons, she dies in time and in a falling rain that her wish for an immortality of being "always" in love cannot control. Martyred on the cyclical, reproductive wheel to which she is tied, she nevertheless is last seen by Frederic as a statue, a woman of marble who, in his imagination, we are led to observe, has become the light that has led him to tell the tale the reader has just read. In her achieved absoluteness, she remains in Frederic's mind to take him beyond the momentary, cyclical rain in which he walks away toward the abstract words he has finally fixed upon the novel's pages. Similarly, the peasant's wife remains in Nick's imagination, however John may impel him toward the absolving unreflectiveness of another momentary, cyclical meal. She also seems to remain in the mind of the peasant who has little to say to others and only looks out the window, like the Italian major in "In Another Country" whose wife has also died. With the melting of the snows of Les Avants above Montreux, the lovers in *A Farewell to Arms* are forced to descend from their unnatural sustained idyll to what will become again the turning, seasonal wheel of restored natural life in which Catherine will necessarily die, her abstract wishes for arrested time and immortal love destroyed by reality. Nick in "An Alpine Idyll" regards the high, alpine spring as "unnatural," and he and John descend from there to the fertile valley.

It is out of *arrested* cycles that the Hemingway hero again and again seizes his transcendent vision. Robert Jordan finds within a cycle of three days an eternity, and he realizes his "always" in the orgasmic "now" of love. Nick in "Indian Camp" takes from the fact of death in a place of birth a sense of immortality. Harry, in "The Snows of Kilimanjaro," realizes his imaginative visions and seizes his immortality only in a moment that is equivalent to his death. Such a moment can only be snatched from the jaws and claws of the hyenas and vultures, the predators who, in feasting on the dead, exemplify the eternally turning round of process in whose inescapable midst the dreamer contemplates the mountain. Stories like "Hills Like White Elephants" and "Cat in the Rain" have men who, in their detached existence or in dedication to abstract heights of imaginative speculation, try to take their women out of time by arresting their fecundity.

The holograph manuscript version of *The Garden of Eden* makes abundantly clear that Catherine's masculinization of herself and her sun worship are ways she tries to deal with David's inability to beget a child and that they are ways that take her off the potentially fecund, feminine, biological Catherine wheel. David as artist is a man so given to his high, abstract speculations practiced in his abstracted expatriate life that he has effectively arrested natural process for Catherine. Catherine recognizes her fixity, her removal from the wheel of life, as the cost of his art, but as she tries to find compensation and a means of imitating David, she gives herself to the sun too much, and, like Nick and John of this story, who also stay up in the cruel sun too long, she effectively sterilizes her life relations. Brett, in *The Sun Also Rises*, leaves behind her a trail of ashes and the incantatory refrain "Rot!" to remind the reader that this Circe indeed is the very wheel that Jake wants to get off or learn how to control.[10] Stopping the room from wheeling is part of that exercise for which his dephallused state has prepared him; it is also precisely what the peasant has managed to do as he has retained his frozen woman. Hemingway's title for his first novel names his mythic and desperate attempt to immerse the fixed, Apollonian sun in cycles that permit it the period of death and darkness that joins it with life. It is equivalent to the valley journey that must finally be added to the period of arrest at immortal heights.

"An Alpine Idyll" is an early exercise that carefully studies how the sun-given skiers must initially abandon the cycles of the valley world to explore an alternative world where indeed rot and process can be arrested, suspended, and momentarily escaped. But they stay there too long. John reminds Nick that, to him, nothing is good sustained too long, and this avoidance of continued states labels John's fear of absolutes and his fundamental carnality. The supposedly beastly peasant, who remains above and beyond the snows through most of the year and who translates what would normally be the rotting body of his dead wife into a repetitive source of light, by that act seems one who successfully masters the earth's eternal cycles. The reader's instinctive revulsion from the image of the cost of this success and Hemingway's placement of horror at the center of such disregard for process tell us what we need to know. The plot reveals not expiation but the restoration of order in nature. A day in spring, pointedly a day in May—the month that begins with a day dedicated to revolution and to celebration of eternally renewing spring—amends December's seeming eternity of death that is maintained in a state like life. It does so as the husband spreads the "new earth" upon his wife's grave as though he were "spreading manure in a garden"—as though he were bringing the products of natural process to nature to renew the reproductive cycle.

Throughout the story, with the slightest of touches, Hemingway has noted the need to balance abstract and physical worlds. As Nick sees the burial taking place on this beautiful spring day, he can "not imagine anyone being dead," but he immediately says to John, "Imagine being buried on a day like this." When John replies, "I wouldn't like it," Nick responds, "Well, . . . we don't have to *do* it" (343). The shift he insists on noting is from imagining to doing. Later, John confesses that "up in the hut I used to think about [beer] a lot," and Nick responds, "Well, we've got it now" (344–45). Such suggestions of the distance between abstraction and reality, the speculative and the physical worlds, help underwrite the basic theme of abstraction from natural process.

This theme is augmented by the innkeeper's revealed distance between himself and fact and is further augmented by Nick's minute observations through the window of the world beyond the inn. He sees the mill and the water wheel and the saw in the mill rising and falling, and he notes that the mill, like an inhuman process, seems to be operating with no one tending it. He also notes dust on the leaves and crows in the grass and sunlight passing through the empty glasses on the table inside the inn where he is sitting. This sight, which reconciles inside and outside, rising and falling, earth and sky, and which insists that we note how birds descend and how dust rises, prefigures the fundamental religious and psychic meaning of the tale, the need for fixity in flow, eternity in time, and the transcendent spirit in the realm of the rotting flesh. Urging food on Nick as the story ends, John is calling for the burial of the image of the frozen woman just as emphatically as spring called for the physical burial of the real but suspended woman. The valley journey, metaphorically suggesting as it does the acceptance of and immersion in the feminine, certainly seems in Hemingway's psyche to be the necessary therapeutic balance to the sunstruck mountain vision of his men.

NOTES

1. "An Alpine Idyll" was completed during the first days of May 1926. Already by the fifth of May Hemingway had dispatched it to Max Perkins for submission to *Scribner's* magazine for publication. When the story returned from them in June, rejected, Jeffrey Meyers tells us that Hemingway apparently sent it on to the Communist *New Masses*, which rejected it in turn in the fall of

1926. Undoubtedly, Hemingway then submitted it to Pound for inclusion in *Exile*, for we have Pound's letter of December 21, 1926, in which he discusses the too "licherary" story. Carlos Baker informs us that, at the publisher's request, on January 21, 1927, Hemingway sent his story on to Alfred Kreymborg, who took the story for his *American Caravan*, where it was first published. It was subsequently included by Hemingway in his *Men without Women*, published on October 14, 1927. Baker ascribes the source of the tale to Hemingway's conversations in Schruns with Fräulein Gläser, who, according to Baker, had a taste for the macabre and had often talked to Hemingway about death and suicide.

2. That such attention is now about to be paid was abundantly clear at the June 1988 Third International Hemingway Conference in Schruns, Austria, where the story was used as the centerpiece to focus the discussion of a heavily attended seminar on manuscripts and textual studies.

3. There is every reason why the unnamed narrator of the story should be regarded as being Nick, the somewhat older and more mature Nick of "Cross-Country Snow" and the other Nick Adams stories. Surely, it is not insignificant that he goes unnamed, and that fact should be stressed and interpreted, but there are many reasons why Hemingway meant the reader and critic to read into this narrator the history and sensibility of Nick Adams. Philip Young firmly declares of "An Alpine Idyll" and "The Killers" that "the I of these stories is Nick Adams," and of the former he says, "The story is utterly without a 'point' if not seen in the context of the other [Nick Adams] stories" (59). Young sees that the story's "focus . . . centers on the responses of the listeners. A change in their responses is the point" (60). His reading places the story in the corpus of Nick Adams stories and as a necessary and further stage in the development of Nick's awareness. Since Young judges that as its main function, for him it has no other "point" if not so seen. Joseph Flora seconds him, arguing, "On this point [Young] has been largely ignored, and that is unfortunate" (199). Noting the great number of correspondences with "Cross-Country Snow," Flora cites these as the best evidence for considering "An Alpine Idyll" a Nick story, and he finally asks, "Who is the narrator if not Nick?" albeit "an older, more Europeanized Nick" (199). Bernard Oldsey declares "An Alpine Idyll" to be "almost a continuation of 'Cross-Country Snow' or a slightly altered retelling (68). Flora astutely continues his argument to identify the narrator as Nick by suggesting that "'An Alpine Idyll' gains as a story . . . by keeping Nick unnamed, which is not to say that Hemingway did not mean for his reader to recognize Nick Adams, or to relate the events of the story to Nick's life. The pursuit of the artist's personality may be a part of the challenge for the reader" (211). Without joining in this argument now, I prefer to use Nick's name throughout interchangeably with the narrator of the tale.

4. The phrase "against the wall" is almost the incantatory refrain for the stories and vignettes of *In Our Time*, occurring insistently. It always carries with

it a sense of desperation and extremity, as it identifies a position of retreat beyond which one may not go, where the implied barrier radically separates two discrete worlds.

5. Those who look through the window, like Nick and the peasant, are obviously intent on what lies beyond, on the other side of possessed and given reality. The window suggests an invisible barrier between two discrete worlds and implies an abstract visual contact with what lies beyond. Others in the inn, who are intent only on wine or beer or sleep or one another, are suggested as materialistically held by their surroundings and as prisoners to them. It is important to note that Harry in "The Snows of Kilimanjaro" is, finally, similarly intent on what lies above and beyond him and is associated with immortality, while Helen and the hyena and vultures are all intent upon food and life and death and the realities before them.

6. That the peasant goes to the Löwen—"the lions"—seems important. The lion is a solar beast and as such is associated with the world of fixity and light from which the peasant has descended.

7. There is a genuine mystery about the peasant's detachment that a Hemingway critic needs to explore. Is the detachment due to a fundamental alienation or to his inwardly turned grief? To a constitutional unperceptiveness or to his almost implacable and unsocial temperament? Is it a result of his sense of estrangement from others, caused by his being from "the other side" and a genuine outsider in this community? He is not a man of these high valleys or one who intimately shares their customs or their garrulity and sociality—their ways are not his. Is this detachment perhaps a result of a focus of attention upon what are to him more important matters, the just-completed burial in the spring and his finally acknowledged severance from his wife who has companioned him, both living and dead, for so long? Olz has also come from a confrontation with the priest to a room where the judgments of those about him hover in this alien air. Has he absorbed something of the priest and sexton's earlier shocked reaction to his treatment of his wife's dead body, so that he now feels himself an outsider among judgmental strangers? Or is there a pride that separates him from these strangers and almost-sniggering "others," so that he studiously ignores and refuses to acknowledge their presence and quickly disengages himself from them to go drink where he need not suffer their presence? That he is willing to drink in the Löwen seems to suggest that it is only from the innkeeper's inn and set of people that he separates himself. Is there, then, special meaning in the remarks of sexton and innkeeper that come at the very end of the story? "'He didn't want to drink with me,' said the sexton. 'He didn't want to drink with me, after *he* knew about his wife,' said the innkeeper" (italics in original). Is the sexton's knowledge of Olz's treatment of his wife a factor in the peasant's alienation, or does it come from a disdain that has other sources? The sexton who sees the situation as "very funny with the priest" hardly seems to merit respect, but neither does the innkeeper, and for a dozen

reasons. And what about the innkeeper's qualification that it was only after "he" knew about "his" wife that the peasant refused to drink with the innkeeper? After who knew what? After he, the peasant, knew about his wife? But what was there additionally to know that he did not already know—that what he had done in perhaps innocence was wrong? Or is the innkeeper saying that the peasant chose not to drink with him after he, the sexton, knew about his, the peasant's wife—and knew what about his wife? Apparently the innkeeper is not in the room when the sexton comes into the inn with the peasant, but when they are there, the innkeeper goes over to the table and speaks in dialect to the sexton, who answers him while the peasant merely looks out of the window. It is immediately after the dialect speech, unre- counted, that the peasant stands and pays and leaves without drinking further, and seemingly pointedly refusing to even acknowledge the sexton with whom he entered to drink. I think we may infer that an insult was offered in the innkeeper's communication to the sexton, but the innkeeper seems to suggest that the refusal to remain was a result of "he" knowing "about his wife." We guess that the peasant must know that the sexton shares the priest's knowledge, but this suggests that what is known "about" the wife may be something the innkeeper has just transmitted to him. What is this "new" knowledge, whether new for sexton or peasant or both? Although little is known and everything remains ambiguous, a new and different suggestion begins to emerge of why the peasant may unconsciously have chosen to treat his wife as he did, and a second and metaphoric reason begins to be established for why her undecaying suspen- sion from rot is not only prescribed by weather but also a psychological and moral necessity for the peasant. His acts and her suspension are ways of artifi- cially maintaining her as an absolute and away from and out of "the world's" corruption. The author has told us little, but much has been suggested. In "Indian Camp," when we remember that it was Uncle George who distributed cigars, we have a renewed interest in "other" causes of the Indian father's sui- cide. So here we are similarly forced toward amplification of motivation and action.

   Hemingway often deliberately creates riddles that need solution, knowing that "the heart of the matter" in a story may be the way in which signs are read or misread, observed or overlooked, and that frequently the meaning of a story may be the figure in the carpet, seen or unseen. One of his most spectacular devices is his use of ambiguous pronoun reference: he not infrequently excites several thematic levels of meaning in a story through deliberate obfuscation of reference. He seems to legitimize several antecedents for a particular pronoun, and he shifts antecedents bewilderingly, allowing them to become multiple and contradictory. In this way, by bringing in simultaneous, alternative possibilities, he studies the complexity of the mind as well as the complexity of situation. Most frequently, he deliberately blurs motivational information so that the reader is left with something resembling life's riddles: Why does Nick in

"Indian Camp" feel he will never die? Why does the Indian father in that story kill himself? "Where did Uncle George go?" Part of the greatness of Hemingway's style is its disdain for mere information, its contempt for glib answers, and its abdication of exposition. He forged a style that allowed the reader participation in the implementation and discovery of meaning.

8. In Jack Clayton's film *The Pumpkin Eater* (script by Harold Pinter), there is a scene in which James Mason, in a café and about to order, suggests to Anne Bancroft that she can have "anything" she wants. He is summarily reproved by the waitress: "Anything on the menu."

9. Rot is one of Hemingway's major metaphors. It is Brett's favorite word, and as she moves through Paris and Pamplona, she leaves behind her a trail of ashes and rot. Her interjection "Rot!" frequently disciplines the vanity of arbitrary absolutes. Cohn, who would think of her idolatrously as "absolutely fine and straight" (*Sun Also Rises* 38), obviously knows little about her. "The Snows of Kilimanjaro" vividly opposes the rot of gangrene to the top of the Mountain of God where the leopard lies undecaying. The contrast between the fixed or the eternal and the rotting or decaying is a constant of Hemingway's work. "An Alpine Idyll" is another of many works based fundamentally on this opposition.

10. The reader should remember how important getting off the wheel is as a Hemingway metaphor. In *For Whom the Bell Tolls*, Robert Jordan's very life depends on being able to get off Pablo's "merry-go-round." In *The Sun Also Rises*, Jake spends much time learning ways to stop the room from wheeling, to get beyond the feeling that he is going through something he has been through before. Indeed, the metaphor is at the heart of the meaning of "An Alpine Idyll," as it is at the heart of *The Garden of Eden*. After all, Eden is that garden—unlike the one for which the peasant seems to be spreading his manure—where reproduction and the cycles of generation do not exist; it is the prelapsarian world.

Works Cited

Armistead, Myra. "Hemingway's 'An Alpine Idyll,'" *Studies in Short Fiction* 14 (Summer 1977): 255–58.

Atkins, John. *The Art of Ernest Hemingway*. London: Spring, 1964.

Baker, Carlos. *Ernest Hemingway: A Life Story*. New York: Scribners, 1969.

———. *Hemingway: The Writer as Artist*. Princeton, NJ: Princeton UP, 1972, 119.

Bakker, J. *Ernest Hemingway: The Artist as Man of Action* Assen, N.V.: Van Gorcum, 1972.

Benson, Jackson J. *The Writer's Art of Self-Defense*. Minneapolis: U of Minnesota P, 1969.

Benson, Jackson J., ed. *The Short Stories of Ernest Hemingway: Critical Essays.* Durham; Duke UP, 1975.

Dahiya, Bhim. *The Hero in Hemingway.* Atlantic Highlands, NJ: Humanities, 1982.

DeFalco, Joseph. *The Hero in Hemingway's Short Stories.* Pittsburgh: U of Pittsburgh Press, 1963.

Donaldson, Scott. *By Force of Will: The Life and Art of Ernest Hemingway.* New York: Penguin Books, 1978.

Fenton, Charles A. *The Apprenticeship of Ernest Hemingway: The Early Years.* New York: Viking Press, 1954.

Flora, Joseph M. *Hemingway's Nick Adams.* Baton Rouge: Louisiana State UP, 1982.

Hattam, Edward. "Hemingway's 'An Alpine Idyll.'" *Modern Fiction Studies* 12 (Summer 1966): 261–65.

Hemingway, Ernest. "An Alpine Idyll." *The Short Stories of Ernest Hemingway.* New York: Scribners, 1966.

———. *The Garden of Eden.* Holograph and typescripts. Hemingway Collection, Items 422, 422.1–422.9. Kennedy Library, Boston.

———. *In Our Time.* 1925. New York: Scribners, 1958.

———. *The Sun Also Rises.* 1926. New York: Scribners, 1964.

Hovey, Richard B. *Hemingway: The Inward Terrain.* Seattle: U of Washington Press, 1968.

Kvam, Wayne E. *Hemingway in Germany.* Athens: Ohio U Press, 1973.

Lynn, Kenneth S. *Hemingway.* New York: Simon and Schuster, 1987.

———. "Interview with Kenneth S. Lynn: Hemingway Heretic." *Johns Hopkins Magazine* 30.2 (April 1988): 22–29.

Nelson, Raymond S. *Hemingway: Expressionist Artist.* Ames: Iowa State UP, 1979.

Oldsey, Bernard. "The Snows of Ernest Hemingway." *Ernest Hemingway: A Collection of Criticism.* Ed. Arthur Waldhorn. New York: McGraw-Hill, 1973.

Putnam, Ann. "Dissemblings and Disclosures in Hemingway's 'An Alpine Idyll.'" *Hemingway Review* (Spring 1987): 27–33.

Sutherland, Fraser. *The Style of Innocence: A Study of Hemingway and Callaghan.* Toronto: Clark and Irwin, 1972.

Tavernier-Courbin, Jacqueline. "Ernest Hemingway and Ezra Pound." *Ernest Hemingway: The Writer in Context.* Ed. James Nagel. Madison: U of Wisconsin Press, 1984.

Waldhorn, Arthur. *A Reader's Guide to Ernest Hemingway.* New York: Farrar, Straus and Giroux, 1972.

Young, Philip. *Ernest Hemingway: A Reconsideration.* University Park: Pennsylvania State U Press, 1966.

Pilar's Tale

The Myth and the Message

Pilar's tale of the execution of the fascists in Pablo's town at the start of the revolution is one of the justly famed and celebrated passages of *For Whom the Bell Tolls*. It has drawn praise from numbers of critics, and some have not found the book equal to the achievement of her tale. Even critics on the far left, for whom the book was an indiscretion or an embarrassment, have praised Hemingway for the descriptive power of his prose in that section; and even Robert Jordan—to a degree a projection of Hemingway within his own work—is awed by the tale as told. Jordan, deeply moved by Pilar's description, thinks to himself:

> Pilar had made him see it in that town.
>
> If that woman could only write. He would try to write it and if he had luck and could remember it perhaps he could get it down as she told it. God, how she could tell a story. She's better than Quevedo, he thought. He never wrote the death of any Don Faustino as well as she told it. I wish I could write well enough to write that story, he thought. What we did. Not what the others did to us. He knew enough about that. He knew plenty about that behind the lines. But you had to have known the people before. You had to know what they had been in the village. (134–35)

Jordan's reflections on the narrative are interesting in and of themselves, for they well establish some of the fundamental aesthetic beliefs that were part of Hemingway's arsenal as a writer and that in part determined the composition of the tale. His commentary is intriguingly self-reflexive, for in it he stands in for the writer himself who is talking about writing the very passage he has written. Life and art come together in fascinating ways within his thoughts as he thinks of the tale that Pilar has "told" that needs to be at some future time written—that is, of course, the written story that we have already read. In this way, the future and the past are joined just as effectively as the tale has joined the fascists and the Republicans in deadly struggle. Indeed, Hemingway has even answered his political critics before they have begun to assail him: the need is not to know what *we* have suffered, which we already too well know and will therefore teach us little, but rather to know what we have done to *others*, which we may not sufficiently recognize. He here simultaneously explains, as fully as he needs to, the aesthetic basis of his vision, which, he anticipates, may be read as betrayal of the left. As Hemingway's protagonist Jordan argues for this self-transcendence and empathic projection into the "other," he not only defines Hemingway's own doctrine of composition, which demands in each of his major works that he cross over to the other side to explore,[1] but also substantiates his own position at the moment, for he, as a foreigner, has crossed over from his side of the lines to be in the territory of the "other."

He also defines the writer's job as making others see what they otherwise cannot see, and he suggests that a writer's craft depends upon the accuracy of his memory, the authority of his experience, and also a measure of luck. He even goes on to argue that if Pilar could tell that tale, it is a tale he could not, for to tell it so knowingly one would have to have had knowledge of those in the village that would depend upon a knowing "before," a prior exposure to and familiarity with *them*. But we know as we hear this that Hemingway has created "them," and whatever backgrounds and histories they may be inferred as having had, and that all that Pilar knows of them is just whatever Hemingway has created to be known of them. As he goes on to pit Pilar's tale telling against the writing of Quevedo, he demands that we acknowledge the told tale as superior to Quevedo's art. Therefore Quevedo, existing beyond any telling in the immortality of his writing, is one of the writers that Hemingway, in his writing of Pilar's tale, has taken on and has been sparring with. He, Hemingway, has outdone Quevedo.

When Jordan wishes that he might be able to write as well the tale that has just been told, and be the agent of getting Pilar's tale finally written, we must see that that is precisely the role Hemingway has himself already taken, and that Pilar's tale exists through and because of his writing/telling of it. Jordan's wishes are therefore singularly perverse, for the further we go in the novel, the more we see that Jordan's completion of his great work in the blowing of the bridge, and sending on those who survive the experience over the hill, into the future, carrying inside them the memory of his great achievement and his sacrifice to get it done, *and* the finishing or completion of the novel become in intricate ways ever more identical until the author and his creature fuse. What remains alive at the end is what Jordan and Hemingway have fashioned to remain alive within those who remember what they have passed through and from where they have come. Therefore Jordan's statement, of his insufficiency to this task now, exists to suggest a yet unfulfilled ideal and a journey yet to be made, but it exists against the amazing artistry he (and we) have just seen performed.

This looking back on Pilar's tale by Jordan is really a way for all Hemingway's readers to look back to what they have received by virtue of her telling and to reexamine it; placing Jordan's reflection here is but to follow Hemingway's directive for reconsideration of what has been received: reaction, prepared with hindsight, has become preface to what will now be examined.

Despite the great critical attention Pilar's tale has drawn, it has not yet been adequately judged the intellectual and psychological tour de force that it is, for in it Hemingway has written one of his most philo-sophical (and also Jungian) analyses of war. Pilar's tale is an intricately fashioned, deliberate, and highly particularized study of the psychic art of revolution, in which Hemingway analyzes just what is happening on the deeper mythic and psychic levels of being as a country engages in civil war, the war that he had described in *Green Hills of Africa* as the "best" kind of war for a writer (71). Here he acknowledges that he "had seen a revolution . . . and a revolution is much the best if you do not become too bigoted" (71). The reader of *For Whom the Bell Tolls* is being shown a revolution by someone who has seen one, and Hemingway, in the tale of the beginning of the movement and of the executions in Pablo's town, is revealing in an amazingly Jungian metaphoric structure the deeper psy-chic, mythic, and historical significances of just such a war.

The tale itself is rather beautifully framed against the mountain journey that the three—Maria, Pilar, and Robert Jordan—are taking in order to meet with El Sordo. It begins with Pilar's imposed sugges-tion that they rest and Robert Jordan's imperative sense that they should continue. Jordan, who wanted only to stop "at the top" (96), has been forced by Pilar to consider an alternative. He is in a hurry, but Pilar teaches him that "there is much time" (96). Indeed, by the time the bridge is blown, he has learned that one can live a lifetime in three days, and his typically Western zeal for attainment and completion has found moderation: he has learned how to have his cake and eat it too, that the journey need not be a sacrifice to its end, that love and war can coexist, as can time and timelessness.

As they rest by a cold mountain stream and bathe their feet, Pilar educates Jordan, and each detail, as she speaks in this setting that Hemingway intricately describes, is in fact a preparation for the tale of the executions she will soon tell. Hemingway tells us that it was "almost as though she were lecturing" (98). Pilar importantly insists that "the pine tree makes a forest of boredom" and that "a forest of pine trees is boredom" (97). Arguing for the character, beauty, and individuality of deciduous or cyclical forests, and against the absoluteness of pines, she singularly argues for the plains, declaring herself tired of the mountains, where "there are only two directions. Down and up" (97). This discussion should be significantly heard against the first sentence of the novel, where the reader is first given Robert Jordan lying flat on the pine-needled floor of the forest. It will be heard again against the last words of the book as Jordan's heart is described as "beating against the pine needle floor of the forest" (471). Both the beginning and the end, his beginning and end for us, and his end for himself, are phrased against fallen pine needles, and one important learning stage on Jordan's final journey is this point of arrest on the mountainside where Pilar's disdain for the pines is opposed to her love of deciduous cycles. Jordan at last at his end will have learned how to accept the absolute evergreen needles, which, whatever their absoluteness, are nevertheless implicated in cycles and have fallen to be the base upon which he lies and on which he will die. But at this point in his journey, Pilar goes on to point out to him the water wagtail, a "ball" of a bird, "no good for anything. Neither to sing nor to eat" (97), that can only bob and jerk up and down. She observes this as she unconsciously lights her cigarette from a flint and steel lighter and before she goes on to place beauty against ugliness— "Would you like to be ugly, beautiful one?" (she asks Maria)—and then acknowledges that she herself would have made "a good man" though she is "all woman" (97). Speaking of relations between the sexes as a sequential and repetitive male blinding and restoration of sight, controlled by the illusion of her beauty that a woman casts upon a man that will eventually be informed by the truth of ugliness, Pilar explains the cycles of male/female fascination: "then . . . another man sees you and thinks you are beautiful and it is all to do over" (98).

This rather long introduction to the telling of the tale of the killing of the fascists in Pablo's town is told as they have stopped halfway up the mountain and as they focus on the alternatives of deciduous or absolute evergreen trees, on mountains that compel ascent or descent, on the water wagtail that only goes up or down, and on the alternatives of ugliness or beauty as these relate to sight or blindness and desires for masculine or feminine identity. They talk as Pilar lights her cigarette with flint and steel. These many focused antitheses as they are skillfully linked and related by her to cycles are preparation for what follows. The tale that Pilar now tells, however specific and historically and topically detailed, studies fascist dialectical alternatives caught in revolution, or either/or dialectics caught in a cyclical process of renewal. Such a structure is pure myth. As given, it is so pure in its many elements that even small deviations from the mythic pattern are informative variations.

The structure that Hemingway establishes for the telling of the tale, the apparatus and technique he uses, is complex. As he essentially describes a psychic battle, he interprets his terms broadly and mythically: his major pattern associates the fascists with the Apollonian— and all that might be, by Nietzsche, Jung, or Neumann, associated with that[2]—and he largely places the cyclical, the "revolutionary," with the Dionysian. Most details in Pilar's tale that are identified with the old order are distinguished by their Apollonian attributes, and most that are identified with the Republican cause are given as Dionysian attributes. These polar oppositions become in a broader perspective and another vocabulary masculine and feminine, and the struggle between them emerges partly as a solar/lunar battle in which male powers accept feminine control and the solar world yields to the lunar.

The geography and architecture of the main square in Pablo's town determine the action. The square is one, like the square in Pamplona in The Sun Also Rises, largely surrounded by arcades, and this fact in this novel, as it did in Hemingway's first, compels a basic dialectic between the area where the sun might dominate the *square* and the area under the arcades where one might, in shade and shadow, *encircle* the square. In this town the arcade covers three sides of the square; the fourth side, where there is the edge of the cliff, is still, however, in shade and shadow, being under the trees that line that edge. In The Sun Also Rises, as Jake walks toward his introduction of Brett to Romero during which he will lie to Romero thrice, he twice encircles the square. It is in that novel that the reader also notes that the entire fiesta is placed in jeopardy as (cyclical) rain comes to dominate the square, rain that drives people under the arcades, and also as mist from the sea comes to cut off the tops of the mountains. Such changes in landscape or scene are changes in powers and principles. The reader should not forget that Margot Macomber (in "The Short Happy Life of Francis Macomber") begins to suffer badly from the sun as Francis, bonding with Wilson in masculine rites, begins to challenge her authority or that Brett's power is established over Jake (in *The Sun Also Rises*) preeminently when the night is dark and the moon and the river are high, and that it is in the dark lower wine cave that she is idolatrously enshrined as pagan goddess.

Crossing and circling the square are throughout Hemingway's work significant alternatives. Similarly, to accept the darkness or shadow beneath the romanesque arch of the arcade rather than submit to the terms of the sun in the square generally defines a retreat from Apollonian powers. Certainly, in Hemingway's aesthetics, as in any work of art, such basic oppositions are neither simplistic nor unvarying, yet they serve to define a struggle between opposing forces.

One of the major controlling submetaphors of the tale is that of the corrida, a ritual death dealing that usually takes place in a circular arena where *sol y sombra*, the dialectic of sun and shadow, oversees the action. However, *capeas* like the metaphoric one suggested in Pablo's town do often take place in Spain in enclosed squares where the entering streets are closed or sealed off by carts and doors. Hemingway is superbly alert to the way the ring in Pablo's town is fashioned from a square, or is a squared circle,[3] and his metaphors reflect it. If in his tale the ring and the square seem to have become one, this is also the case with *toro* and *torero*. The fascists readily seem to become, in the vocabulary of the life-and-death ritual of the bullfight, those who are to be slain, or representatives of the bull. This, however, is not simply the case in this tale, for Hemingway has deliberately complicated his symbolism by inverting its usual meaning—a frequent strategy in his work.[4] Throughout Pilar's tale the fascists are associated with those values that are usually associated with the *torero*, and it is the revolution itself that is rather given—in this scene especially—to be associated with the dark wildness and ferocity of the bull in its attempt to destroy the insulting and goading codified forms that have provoked it to its attack. Although the drunkard among the Republicans will cry out *"Qué salga el toro!* Let the bull out!" (109), in an attempt to establish those in the "box" of the Ayuntamiento as the bulls, Don Faustino, an amateur bullfighter, who emerges like a bull from the box, is described as the *torero* and is so taunted. "Don Faustino, *Matador, a sus ordenes*" (114), mocks one in the crowd; "Come, Don Faustino. Here is the biggest bull of all" (113), cries another; and another, after his death, declares, "He's seen the big bull now" (115). This deliberate confusion of *toro* and *torero* and killer and killed is a major device and part of Hemingway's intellectual and aesthetic strategy here and elsewhere in his work.

Hemingway has inverted ritual terminology for specific ends.[5] The deliberate ambiguity Hemingway has attached to the fascists and their killers can be well seen as Hemingway describes the two lines of men that connect the Ayuntamiento and the edge of the cliff where begins "the emptiness [the *nada*] beyond" (113). These lines conduct those who walk between them from linear prominence and authority high above to the chaotic darkness of death in the waters three hundred feet below, and the files of men are described as standing like those who "watch the ending of a bicycle road race with just room for the cyclists to pass between, or as men stood to allow the passage of a holy image in a procession" (104). The two similes are antithetical, the cyclists or the saints, and in being joined as one and the same, merge the two principles of the flesh and the spirit, the cycle and the cross, or cycles and absolutes, that Hemingway so frequently labors to fuse. Cyclists and/or saints, *toro* and/or *torero,* and square and/or circle suggest the ideal toward which the revolution unconsciously strives, a both/and existence that might replace the rigid dichotomizing either/or dialectic that the prologue called in question as it studied Pilar's ability to be a good man while being all woman or looked at the water wagtail, a bird of the air that is also a bird of the water that, bobbing up and down, is yet a "ball" of a bird (97). It is no accident that the last words of the novel are "the pine needle floor of the forest" (471), for simultaneously Jordan's heart and the pine trees themselves accept the cycles of the nondeciduous evergreen, the fallen and changing principle of unchangedness: human and vegetable life, both internal and external nature, man and landscape, rise from, attempt to transcend, and yet are caught in and ultimately acknowledge the terms of their engagement.

One of the keys to Hemingway's metaphoric structure in this novel is the fountain that dominates the center of the square, and it, at the very center of the action of the tale, is the archetype of that action. The sound of "the splashing of the water in the fountain" is one of the last details of the tale as told. The fountain is described as being apparently a statue of a lion from whose mouth protrudes a brass pipe through which water pours to fall into the bowl of the fountain below, "where the women bring the water jars to fill them" (105). In elaborate detail Hemingway describes the translation of the vivifying waters, whose source is identified as the linear masculine solar lion above, through a fall into the circular bowl beneath, where they are finally described as filling the feminine vessels. This translation is of the captive waters through the line to the circle, from the male solar principle to the cyclical feminine, and it is no accident that the action duplicates the flow of movement of the soon-to-be-"translated" victims between the lines above and down to the watery ravine beneath, just as it is no accident that the bowl should echo toward Pablo's wine bowl where he will search for his ideas or refer back toward the bowl from which Pilar seized her stirring-spoon baton of authority. What Hemingway is getting at is a theory of the restoration of absolutes through cycles, and of the masculine through the feminine, to create a both/and psychic base.[6] The Ayuntamiento on the square, across from the cliff edge and in which the fascists are imprisoned awaiting their execution, is described as a box, so emphasizing its association with the square. But landscape itself becomes the instrument of execution as those high above are cast out and down into the ravine far below. This overthrow of powers above, bringing them down, is the kind of therapeutic inversion that revolutions are meant to establish, to bring arrogant earth- and life-disdaining vanity down, to make that which is of the air, of the mind or the spirit—that which is too abstract or elevated—acknowledge and accept the waters below, as life is coevally forced to accept death. The ravine therefore becomes heavily coded as the place of darkness, descent, the waters, death, and fear—it is also patently, in a Freudian sense,[7] a feminine metaphor—and it is a clue to Hemingway's intricate structure in this novel that the action of revolution is the enforced synthesis of that which is above with that below, the sky with the waters. The blowing of the bridge, the major action at the center of this novel, in effect destroys the barrier between sky and water, air above and ravine below, and connects them, and this successful revolutionary act brings Pablo from the roadmender's hut below to join Pilar from above so that these two bracing and reconciled surrogate father and mother figures may disappear over the crest of the hill at last, Maria between them. This new integration and synthesis is a psychic trinity for the future. It is important to so explore these relations between the height and the ravine, and a few of the meanings implicit in the blowing of the bridge, for the major irony of this novel—which has to do with each

being part of the main, and no man being an island "intire of it selfe"—
is that its central metaphor is the blowing and destruction of a bridge
rather than the building of one. Metaphorically, it would be natural
to assume that Robert Jordan, as the American who has crossed over
to the other side to join others unlike himself so that he may be part
of their cause and share their lives, would be a bridge builder, not a
bridge destroyer. It is Pilar who understands this irony, and she is the
one to label his work in behalf of the common cause, as he goes on
laboring below the bridge to help destroy it, masturbatory solitary and
self-satisfying activity, perhaps practiced to *make* a bridge, not destroy
one. And, of course, what she says is true: Hemingway's art is at once
the building and destroying of a bridge.

Jordan once interrupts Pilar's tale to tell of the lynching of a Negro
he saw from the window of a house in Ohio when, at seven years of age,
he went there to be "the boy of a pair of boy and girl" for a wedding
(116). Maria remarks that she has never seen a Negro except in a *circus*.
A black man, related to cycles, raised in the air and given to fire during a
celebration of a synthesis, or wedding, is patently the exact metaphoric
antithesis to polarized men thrown headlong down a ravine to waters
beneath during a war. In Pablo's town Hemingway has, in almost pure
Jungian dialectical terms, illustrated the psychic meaning of revolution,
and in Ohio he has demonstrated the metaphoric meaning of patriarchal fascist control. It is exact that it should have been Jordan's mother
who pulled him away from the window, so destroying his spectatorial
Apollonian disassociation.

The killing of fascists in Pablo's town is specifically described as a
destructive activity that is coevally creative. It is a fertility ritual in
which fertility is assured through the separation of the chaff from the
wheat, through the threshing and harvesting rituals in which the act of
killing with sickle and scythe, or turning or tumbling with a wooden
pitchfork, is part of a death process out of which comes renewed life.
The threshing of the grain, the spilling of the blood that then waters
and fertilizes the otherwise barren earth, celebrates the relations
between death and birth. The killing of the old king is implicit and
underwrites the fertile reign of the new successor, as destruction is seen
to be implicated in creation—as the birth/death imagery and rituals of
A Farewell to Arms tried to show. To make this point explicit, Hemingway has one of Pablo's cohorts say, "We thresh fascists today . . . and out
of the chaff comes the freedom of this pueblo" (107). If, indeed, it is the
blood of the fascists that fertilizes the earth, they are nevertheless here

seen as the chaff, the part that is thrown away and that has been separated from the grain, and it is out of this that freedom comes.

As the other fascists are executed, their deaths are administered
largely by the hands of peasants, men who deal with the earth, and they
are killed in part by wooden instruments that relate to the crops and
seasonal harvests, to fertility and its cycles: flails, herdsmen's goads,
wooden pitchforks, and so forth. The sickles with which the priest is
pursued in their very name speak of the cycles, and by their shape they
mythically and precisely refer to the moon and to primitive pagan fertility rites. The priest's death therefore becomes a larger victory, specifically a lunar or maternal victory, of nature religions over Christianity.

If the killings are described as a threshing, a separation of chaff and
grain in a fertility ritual, in which all participate, they are also described
as a feast or an eating—again, that which sustains natural process. Pilar,
as the killings continue with less formality, feels she "has a bellyful," and
then has a nausea "as though I had swallowed bad sea food" (119). The
smell of vomit is prevalent throughout the square, and that night,
Pablo, eating, is described as "having his mouth full of young goat"
(127), suggesting the scapegoat sacrifice that has been served up to be
eaten. Hemingway throughout his work plays with the cyclical though
secondary meaning of *revolution* and *revolutionary*. His short story "The
Revolutionist" is a tour de force of such play, and in *Green Hills*, and *To
Have and Have Not*, he elaborately studies the deeper ways in which
revolutions are inevitably tied to cycles and generally create them,
restore them, implement them, and support them.[8] Now, at the beginning of Pilar's tale, as she begins with the story of the attack on the barracks, cyclical forces of the movement are pitted against rectilinear and
static oppositions.

The techniques and strategies of Pablo's attack and the modes
of execution reveal the mythos of the encounter. The Republicans
encircle their enemies in the barracks, cut their *lines and wires*, and, after
having destroyed the intact form of the building and so having brought
down much of the *roof*, execute the unwounded survivors by destroying
their *heads*. The exponents of the revolution throughout the tale will
either destroy or be unable to maintain linear controls. The destruction
or lowering of the head—or the roof—is the means toward overthrow
of their enemies, and the breaking or rupturing of intact forms their
need: "Open up! Open up!" (121, 122, 124) and "We're going in! We're
going in!" (121) are their cries. The four men executed at the barracks
are, predictably, all *tall* men who keep tight mouths, who discipline,

restrain, and control themselves, who speak, if they do, with *dry* voices, and who are described as *mother killers*. In their deaths, the patriarchal Apollonian is overthrown: the voice of one of the *civiles* is described as "grayer than a morning *without sunrise*" (101; italics mine), while the effect of Pablo's victory and destruction is to fill the air with dust that comes down over everyone as at a threshing. As the earth and passions rise, visual and mental clarity are part of the sacrifice. The officer commits suicide with his own gun, and this is then taken by Pablo and turned against the other *civiles* before it is given to Pilar, who then carries it with its muzzle encircled, its "long barrel stuck under the rope" (108) about her waist. This feminine appropriation and encirclement of the male phallic linear gun is a trope that finds several variations throughout the novel as it speaks of the shift of masculine powers into feminine hands. Pablo personally executes the *civiles* with shots to the head. His act subsequently is seen as having been egoistic, and thus, for the following executions, all are formed into lines between which the victims must pass, so that all may share in the administered blows and therefore in responsibility for the deaths that follow. In this way individuality yields to commonality and integration. The killings are throughout, as they were at the barracks, described as the execution of the male principle: as one revolutionist says, "Thanks be to Christ, there are no women," and Pilar asks, "Why should we kill their women?" (105)—suggesting that destruction is reserved for the masculine principle for male crimes.

Before the release of the first fascist from the box to the lines, water is swept in wide sweeping arcs to moisten the ground. Hemingway carefully also establishes that the land becomes truly the peasants' land when the fascists are "extinguished" (107), suggesting by the verb that the tale being told is one that recounts the struggle as additionally between light and darkness, fire and water. As though to emblematize the meaning of the deaths that follow, Hemingway has Pilar discard her tricorner hat taken from the *guardia civil* so that it can be "destroyed" (107). It is sailed far out into space to drop down into the ravine and river below. The destruction of the hat is an important metaphor for the assassination of masculine pride, vanity, identity, and power.[9] It establishes the paradigm for the deaths that follow it into the ravine, even as it establishes the values that the revolution discards.

The prototypical fascist death is that of Don Federico Gonzalez. Described as a "fascist of the first order" (109), he has been the owner of the mill and feed store, therefore proprietor/manager of the cycles and the cyclical processes of life. He is predictably tall, thin (vertical, linear), and balding (mental rather than virile), and he emerges unable to walk, "his eyes turned up to heaven . . . his hands reaching up as though they would grasp the sky" (109). This man who has "no legs to walk" (109), and "no command of his legs" (110), who seems to have no lower centers to relate to the earth but instead yearns toward the spirit and the sky, "never did open his mouth" (110). The iconography reveals a model of what is to be overthrown. The others who die are significant variations on this model—however different, they do not contradict or challenge the paradigm—like Don Ricardo, who, equally mental and earth disdaining, "trying to walk with his head up," nevertheless is overflowing at the mouth as he verbally vilifies the effeminized principle that destroys him: "I obscenity in the milk of your fathers" (111). He shrugs off the contamination of contact: "Don't touch me" (111).

The failed or spurious fascist ideal is represented in Don Faustino Rivero, who, despite his patriarchal credentials as the oldest son of his father, a landowner, and his tallness and sun-yellow hair, conceals behind his facade of masculine pride the coward who wanted to be an amateur bullfighter, "went much with gypsies," and was "a great annoyer of girls" (112). Though he "acts" brave, and looks handsome, scornful, and "superb," when he sees the "emptiness beyond" (113), the *nada*, he loses all his style and covers his eyes, "throwing himself down and clutching the ground and holding to the grass" (114). In this revelation of the failed or false fascist ideal, Hemingway reveals the coordinates of the patriarchate. Don Faustino's apostasy—as he compromises his belief with superstition, his male insularity with uxoriousness, his authentic pride with poses and assumed and not genuine feeling, and then overthrows sight, verticality, belief, pride, and form—expresses the overthrown patriarchal pattern.

Having given these examples of the authentic and spurious Apollonian ideal, Hemingway provides the portrait of Don Guillermo, a man killed largely by the drunkards who are no longer able to distinguish or comprehend what they kill. Don Guillermo is carefully described as of medium height, as nearsighted, and as a "fascist, too, from the religiousness of his wife which he accepted as his own due to his love for her" (117–18).[10] Moderate in height, in sight, in his masculinity, and in his faith, which he moderates because of love, he finally nearsightedly rushes towards death "blindly," believing he is rushing toward his wife who calls his name. His final blindness is an important self-dethronement of the Apollonian world, as it speaks of the substitution of the woman for sight. The anomaly of Don Guillermo speaks to the two worlds that are in delicate balance within him.

Inside the box, Pablo sits with his legs hanging down, rolling a cigarette, while Cuatro Dedos sits in the mayor's chair with his feet on the table. This inversion, where lower centers are emphasized or replace higher, is implicit in most revolutions; and the feet, legs, and cycling here speak of it. Outside the Ayuntamiento a drunkard lies on the one un-overturned table at the fascist club, his head hanging down and his mouth open. The unconscious prone man with inverted head and open mouth names what has, at this point in the revolution, replaced the vertical, keen-sighted, close-mouthed capitalist proprietors, and it is this state that has metaphorically been forced upon them. Overthrown, they have had their heads destroyed and brought low and into the dust and been projected down into the dark death in the ravine. In the background on the square the destroyed lines have now become a mob that chants, "Open up! Open up! Open up!" (121, 122).

Pilar witnesses the death of the priest. In order to see what is going on inside the "box," she has to stand on a chair to look over the heads of others, and with her face against the bars of the window, she holds on by them. A man climbs behind her on the chair and stands with his arms around her holding the wider bars. His breath on her neck smells like the smell of the mob, like vomit on paving stones, and as he shouts "Open up! Open up!" over her shoulder, it is "as though the mob were on my back as a devil is on your back in a dream" (122). Meanwhile the mob itself presses forward, and another man hurls himself again and again against the backs of the men before him. The image and the metaphor is an image of sodomitic rape being accomplished concomitantly with the overthrow of all order and the simultaneous death of the priest, or the spirit. Indeed, exactly as Pilar witnesses the fatal assault on the priest, the chair she stands on breaks, and she and the drunkard mounted on her back fall to roll on the pavement among the spilled wine, vomit, and the forest of legs of the mob, which is all that Pilar can now see.

Hemingway has written with keen irony a study of the almost instantaneous way a revolution, even as it is being established, creates the same competitive struggle for ascendancy and power based upon sight and visual control as existed in the capitalist world it tries to replace. As Pilar and the man on her back struggle for advantage, he pushes her head down and she hits him hard in the groin: the man tries to dethrone intimidating feminine mental supremacy, and the woman tries to castrate the man. This attempt to gain advantage over another in a competitive struggle for height and sight is pointedly at the cost of the one less advantaged. Hemingway has also suggested that erectness and verticality, sight and perception, are based on a relation to spirit, and that to deprive the body of the spirit is to bring it down to the underworld of legs and leavings, to roll in the dust.

Pablo's dismay at being deprived of his belief in the manliness and courage of the priest is answered by Pilar's wisdom: "I think he died well enough—Being deprived of all formality" (128). She is suggesting that to destroy the forms of life leaves it without the sacramental base through and by means of which human dignity can be maintained.

In the night after the killings, Pilar awakes and looks out at the square where the lines had been, which is now dominated by and filled with the moonlight. There she sees the moonlight on the trees, the darkness and the shadows, and hears "no sound but the splashing of the water in the fountain" (129). At the end of the executions, the once sun-drenched square is dissolved in darkness where amorphous and indistinguishable shapes and the sound of water falling seem to control the world. The solar (lion) principle has yielded to the lunar, the woman presides over the square, while Pablo, stuffed with goat, impotent after the day's deeds, lies unconscious, sleeping.

The mythic dynamics of Pilar's tale operate throughout the novel. One of the most poignant moments in this work is the exchange that, in a later chapter, takes place between Anselmo, Fernando, and Robert Jordan as they get ready to return to the guerrilla cave. "Back to the palace of Pablo," Jordan says to Anselmo. Anselmo alters his description, "*El Palacio del Miedo* . . . The Palace of Fear," and Jordan caps this retort with his own, "*La cueva de los huevos perdidos* . . . The cave of lost eggs." Fernando, in his usual unperceptiveness, asks, "What eggs?" and Jordan answers him, "A joke. . . . Just a joke. Not eggs, you know. The others." "But why are they lost?" Fernando asks, and Jordan replies, "I don't know. . . . Take a book to tell you. Ask Pilar" (199).

The exchange is one of the few places in a Hemingway novel where the frame is broken, and deliberately broken by a character who steps beyond his role to speak for the author and the author's controlling awareness. Another similar break in a novel's fictive frame takes place in *Across the River and into the Trees* and for approximately the same reasons. It is the moment when Richard Cantwell, having confronted a very similar recognition indeed, the significance of the green emeralds, which are the "eggs" of *that* novel, subsides to let the author intrude: "He was addressing no one, except, perhaps, posterity" (168). Here, too, the lament, the pain, if not the exasperation, shows—Hemingway is now beyond exasperation and he knows well that he cannot look for contemporary recognition of his deeper structures.

Both interpolations, in *Across the River* and *For Whom the Bell Tolls*, reveal an infinite weariness in the author, the weariness of an artist whose intricately crafted structures have created no public and scant critical awareness, who labors to establish deep patterns that meet no appreciative response, hardly a glance of recognition. When Jordan, in *For Whom*, says, "Take a book to tell you," he knows what his creator Hemingway well knows, that the intricate and detailed pattern that the writer has carefully laid down in the novel studies the rivalry for power within the primal cave, the eternal battle of the sexes for phallic power or authority, and the Oedipal son/father rivalries as they relate to that battle, at a level and in such depth that no explanation or speech or essay will reveal their mystery. Hemingway would need another book like the one being written to trace the many lines and ramifications he has placed in that remarkably complex story.

On the simplest of levels, the reference to the lost eggs is, of course, to lost testicular power or male potency in the struggle for power and authority that Jordan has witnessed within the cave, a battle that has culminated in Pablo's overthrow; he has been unmanned and cowed by Pilar, who, inverting her stirring spoon, has made the baton of her cyclical function the new emblem of power in the cave. On another level, the reference goes back to Jordan's two sacks of dynamiting equipment, which have early been carefully coded by Hemingway to develop their testicular/egg associations, and which Jordan has packed, we are told, "as carefully as he had packed his collection of wild bird eggs when he was a boy" (48). Those two male sacks were first studied by Hemingway in *The Sun Also Rises* when he described the driver of the stage that takes Bill and Jake up to Burguete as coming out "swinging two . . . mail [male] pouches" as they start off for their consummate male experience (106).[11] Now, again in Spain, these sacks are resurrected as the containers of Jordan's potency as a dynamiter, for in them are his exploding devices, his detonators, and his bundles of explosive charges, which can allow him to fulfill his mission and himself as a male.

As Jordan heads toward the mouth of the cave with a sack in each hand, Hemingway's earlier image from his first novel is revived. Jordan's "things" are now placed in the cave. Their being there can be recognized as the provocation to the scene that ensues, in which Pablo, a surrogate but cowardly father figure, will be overthrown. Jordan's "things," now in the cave after Pablo's authority there has been called in question and stripped from him, identify Jordan's new role with respect to Pilar and introduce new plot complications. Hemingway seems to be studying the situation that exists when a son figure takes his potency through the cave mouth and puts it in the care and under the supervision of the maternal figure at the hearth. Such metaphors are all heavily coded with the language of sexual power dynamics and rivalries. But these are only a few of the levels of the struggle that Hemingway studies. As Jordan said, for Hemingway, "Take a book to tell you."

What is important to recognize in Jordan's remark to Fernando is that he himself is only too well aware, superlatively aware, of the sexual dynamics of the power struggle that has been going on. He has been witness to much. He has seen the shift from patriarchal authority to matriarchal power and has recognized his own role in that as son-usurper. He has witnessed the subsequent humiliations of Pablo, who is now identified with a flaccidity, limpness, and inert inactivity that suggest his castration. The reader is, at this point in the narrative, not yet fully aware of Jordan's own history—one in which he effectively lost his own father, a cowardly man who was cowed, like Pablo, by Jordan's bully of a mother—and Jordan has not yet suffered the assault on his sacks. In that attack, Pablo, as he takes away Jordan's potency, slits the sacks in the cave, in an apparent attempt to effeminize that rival son and prevent the success of the action and task he hopes to perform. Hemingway has coevally let those readers who are aware of his self-reflexive mode in this novel see that Jordan's fulfillment of his task is simultaneously Hemingway's completion of his and that the "father's" interference with its success is their shared problem. Jordan's remark to Fernando occurs on page 199 in chapter 15 of the novel, yet it was exactly 100 pages earlier, on page 99 in chapter 10, that Pilar began to tell her remarkable tale of the execution of the fascists in Pablo's town. If we are to recognize another, still more profound level of meaning behind *"la cueva de los huevos perdidos,"* that tale must be carefully examined, remembered, and related to the larger patterns of mythic struggle that the novel exists to study.

NOTES

1. This pattern, which goes far toward explaining the psychic dynamics of Hemingway's art and its philosophical/psychological concerns, is visible in each of his major works: a necessary crossover from the known country into the

unknown, a binding together of two discrete and opposed worlds or modes. It may be projected as a necessary bonding of the conscious or unconscious parts of the psyche, of the masculine or the feminine aspects of the self, or of ordered realms of light with chaotic areas of darkness. I am convinced that the pattern is at once unconscious and conscious in Hemingway's work, being the compulsive need for integrated wholeness and mastery of an almost schizophrenic split (which is shared by most artists) and also his highly conscious recognition of the split that must be healed as the major dilemma of Western man in our time. Highly organized religious and mythic patterning in Hemingway's work suggests that he, like Joyce, sees the artist as the creator of the conscience of the race who forges in the smithy of his soul the sensibility for that possession. The major icon of the synthesis he proposes seems to be a cyclical absolute, which binds natural process to ideal structures (see my essay "Hemingway and Joyce: A Study in Debt and Payment" at the beginning of this volume). And the major metaphor of the needed crossover and fusion seems to be the bridge (see my essay "Bridges: Their Creation and Destruction in the Work of Ernest Hemingway" in this volume). In the details of the novels and stories, the problem may be seen in the imagery of the dephallused man and the highly sexually charged woman (*The Sun Also Rises*); the forcing of love and war together (*A Farewell to Arms* and *For Whom the Bell Tolls*); the unique relationship of the hardened old warrior and the young inexperienced Contessa (*Across the River*); or the mortal man dying of rot on the plain while dreaming of an immortality to be achieved on the high Mountain of God ("The Snows of Kilimanjaro"). It creates a dichotomized landscape where the author studies the interrelations between the haves and the have-nots, the winners and losers, and the split men—like Harry Morgan, Santiago, or Cantwell—who have had to come to terms with their betraying sides, or simply the undercover operators (Jordan or Philip Rawlings) or hunters (Francis Macomber or the Hemingway of *Green Hills*) or fishermen (Nick of "Big Two-Hearted River") who can only gain their victories by crossing into new and alien territory to explore and bind themselves to unexplored lands that are not understood, or to the psyches or internal dynamics of those "other" worlds. It demands the dynamics of *A Moveable Feast*, where the sacred and secular are joined in moments of fluid fixity, as well as the experimentation of a *Garden of Eden*, where the possibilities of androgynous male/female identity are studied. It was always Hemingway's way to empathically identify himself with and study his antagonist, so boxing and war and hunting/fishing and confrontations with death were his natural fascinations. To become a man, Macomber had to learn what was inside the lion or the buffalo, to know what it was feeling—just as Richard Cantwell had to imagine the virtues of his enemies. But that self-transcendence is anathema to revolutionary commitment and is seen as apostasy to "the cause." Caught as Jordan/Hemingway was between the aesthetic need to inhabit the "other" and the political need to ignore its justifications, Hemingway has Jordan observe, shortly before his own death, "There's no *one* thing that's true. It's all true. The way the planes are beautiful whether they are ours or theirs. The hell they are, he thought" (467). The quote is a beautiful example of the two sides, whose boundaries he needs to breach, warring within the artist/warrior.

2. The binary and polar oppositions that all three use to talk about psychic dialectics readily accept a terminology based in Apollonian/Dionysian, patriarchal/matriarchal, or solar/lunar, conscious/unconscious terms.

3. In one of Hemingway's high school short stories, "A Matter of Color," he describes the boxing ring as the "squared circle" (Cappel 49), giving any alert critic pause to consider the possible sophistication of this seventeen-year-old. Later in his work, the squared circle, or the absolute cycle, the mastery of time by eternity, becomes an important concern, demonstrated in this novel by Robert Jordan's triumph as he makes time stand still and makes of seventy-two hours a lifetime and of the "NOW" of orgasmic love an eternity.

4. When in *Green Hills of Africa* Hemingway relates meat on a stick to Christ on the cross, when in *A Farewell to Arms* he parodies the celebration of the mass in a scene of gross eating of pasta, and when in *Across the River* he parallels blood bruised to the lips by kissing with menstruation, he is forcing carnal and spiritual, and oral and genital, oppositions together. Such examples are frequent throughout his work.

5. We see this strikingly done in the "Hail nada full of nada" passage in "A Clean Well-Lighted Place," as well as in the profane black mass being celebrated by Frederic Henry in *A Farewell to Arms* just before his wounding and in several inverted religious ritual moments in *Green Hills*.

6. This may help as much as anything to explain the sexual dynamics of *The Garden of Eden*.

7. In chapter 5 of *Green Hills*, Hemingway develops the ravine, in a remarkably sexual chapter, as the cleft of the feminine into which the intrepid male adventures.

8. In *Green Hills*, P.O.M., finally exasperated, breaks out, "I don't want to just hear about revolutions. All we see or hear is revolutions. I'm sick of them" (192). But Hemingway is concerned with them, in how they go bad, and why they do so, though to get "on that wheel" can be as disastrous as being on Pablo's "merry-go-round." In *To Have and Have Not*, Harry Morgan turns away from revolutions when he asks what the "lady wrestler" Mrs. Laughton is drinking and, when told that it is "A Cuba Libre," says, "Then give me a straight whiskey" (134). The opposition is between revolution and straight spirits, or the circle and the line.

9. In Josef von Sternberg's film *The Blue Angel*, the taking away and, over time, the destruction of the professor's hat is similarly meticulously studied as the overthrow of patriarchal authority and the eradication of masculine power.

10. Richard Gordon, in *To Have and Have Not,* is portrayed as a man who sacrifices his wife to his vanities and his egocentric sense of self; in contra-distinction, Helen Gordon remembers her father, who "went to Mass because my mother wanted him to, and he did his Easter duty for her and for Our Lord, but mostly for her" (187). Men who sacrifice for their women, or women who do so for their men, like Maria's mother, are mostly throughout Hemingway's works contrasted with men and women insulated in their own sense of self, like the husband in "Cat in the Rain" or the young man of "Hills Like White Elephants."

11. This use of *mail* as *male* is found throughout Hemingway. One example: in *The Garden of Eden,* as Catherine begins to focus on the mail and to open the mail and David finally says farewell to the mailman, elaborate sexual joking is taking place.

WORKS CITED

Cappel, Constance, ed. *Hemingway in Michigan.* Waitsfield: Vermont Cross-roads Press, 1977.

Hemingway, Ernest. *For Whom the Bell Tolls.* 1940. New York: Scribners, 1968.

———. *Green Hills of Africa.* 1935. New York: Scribners, 1963.

———. *To Have and Have Not.* New York: Scribners, 1937.

8

The Torrents of Spring

Hemingway's Application
for Membership in the Club

In *That Summer in Paris: Memories of Tangled Friendships with Hemingway, Fitzgerald, and Some Others*, Morley Callaghan wonderfully tells of his immersion in the group of expatriate literati of Paris in 1929. I enjoy the book in part because that was the summer my parents and my brother and I were also wandering those streets, undoubtedly somewhere in the background of Callaghan's foreground portraits and reminiscences. I have always enjoyed beginning my "Expatriate Literature of Paris in the Twenties" course with the words "When I was in Paris in the twenties." Of course, I don't immediately mention that I was but four and the year 1929. Did I run into Hemingway then, or did he trip over me—or did Joyce, or Fitzgerald? I cite Callaghan here, however, because he tells of meeting Hemingway as he was on his way to see Joyce, taking the proofs of *A Farewell to Arms* to the master so that they could go over them together. It's revealing to hear Callaghan's description of that incident:

> We had got up and were walking slowly along the street. At the corner he said, "I'll leave you here. I'm late. I told Joyce I'd bring these proofs to him." And then he must have seen the envious look in my eyes. Suddenly he was boyishly apologetic. "I know you'd like to meet Joyce. I'd take you with me and have you meet him, Morley, but he's so shy with strangers. It's no good when you walk in on him.

He won't talk about writers and writing. This way it wouldn't be
any good. You understand, don't you?"

"Of course I do," I said. "I wouldn't dream of going with you.
You want to talk to him about your work." (108)

The anecdote, in addition to tellingly establishing Hemingway's
honest sensitivity and Callaghan's responsive understanding (however
excluded he might feel), tells us much more—that Hemingway and
Joyce were indeed intimates and fellow artists sharing the intricacies
and techniques of their work with one another. We have no reason to
doubt the anecdote, for Callaghan's memoir rings with a certain
unchallengable authenticity. It is another insight into the reasons that
Hemingway, alone among thousands of would-be expatriate writers,
almost immediately became the confidant and companion of Pound,
Ford, Joyce, Stein, Fitzgerald, and innumerable other great writers, and
by them was considered their equal—he had a delicacy of perception
allied with an exquisite dedication to his craft.

What we should not miss in that anecdote, however, is the carefulness with which Hemingway separates himself and Joyce in their focus
upon writing as a craft from Morley and his interest in being with Joyce.
Hemingway avoids suggesting that Morley is less an artist than they, but
the implication is that conversation between artists about their texts is
for them alone. We see that same sort of singling out of those who are
serieux and those who are not "in the know" in a comment Hemingway
made about *Torrents of Spring*: "I like it as well as anything I ever wrote
and so do Pound, Joyce, Wyndham Lewis, Allen Tate, Evan Shipman
and some others although plenty of citizens consider it worthless."[1] In
that sentence the condescension toward "citizens" is blatant as Hemingway establishes the fact that the book may indeed be an "in" book for
those for whom it is written, a book that artists will understand, though
not the average reader. That exclusionary comment is written by the
Hemingway who, on January 19, 1926—when he was twenty-six years
old and before he had yet published a novel—wrote to Horace Liveright to tell him that "everyone in your office, excepting, I believe,
Mrs. Kauffman, was opposed to *In Our Time*"—in that comment separating the many so-called editors and publishers' agents at Liveright
from the one or two who could know art when they saw it. He goes on
in that letter to say, "As you know I expect to go on writing for some
time. I know that publishers are not in business for their health but I

also know that I will pay my keep to, and eventually make a great deal of money for, any publisher" (*Selected Letters*, 191). *That*, written before the publication of his first novel? What incredible, almost incomprehensible prescience and arrogance! What self-knowledge and prophetic accuracy—at twenty-six years of age.

Hemingway's youthful bravado and certainty undoubtedly sprang from his knowledge that Pound, Ford Madox Ford, and others had already placed him among the masters of contemporary prose,[2] from his intimate association with Stein and Joyce, and from his recently established relationship with Fitzgerald[3] and other recognized men of letters who were among themselves in Paris at that time already acknowledging him as *il miglior fabbro*.[4] (For further discussion of these associations, see my book *Hemingway's Paris* and my essay "Hemingway and Joyce: A Study in Debt and Payment" at the beginning of this volume.) It was to that society of artists, those who knew and understood one another and who knew what they as artists were about and trying to do as artists—those "in the club"—that Hemingway appealed, leaving the verdict, as he always had, from his very first days as a writer, to posterity and to the true artists. He had said of Joyce that you were supposed to know what he was doing by reading him, suggesting that the medium itself, to one sensitive to prose, was the message, and he went on to say, "It is not the writer's province to explain it or to run guided tours through the more difficult country of his work" (qtd. in Plimpton 26). And here, it is my contention that *Torrents* was written as a prelude to *The Sun Also Rises*, actually written in an interrupted week as he was rewriting *Sun*, for those who he knew would know what he was talking about—for the other artists who would be his true audience.

The Torrents of Spring, however rich and dadaist and seemingly hysterical or gauche its humor, is metaphorically an elaborate parable of the workings of the creative imagination of the artist and an explanation and revelation of the delicate psychic poise of the creative writer—one that studies its hazards and pitfalls, its perils, its strategies, and its sacrifices. Thus, it is certainly in many ways a precursor to *Death in the Afternoon*, *Green Hills of Africa*, and *The Garden of Eden*, and it has strong affinities with stories like "Cat in the Rain," "Hills Like White Elephants," and "Cross-Country Snow," and the tragedies of works like *A Farewell to Arms*, where women as lovers, wives, or mothers are lost or sacrificed to, or used and manipulated by, the aesthetic strategies of their métier-intent men. No other work by Hemingway—with the possible exception of *A Moveable Feast*—is so literarily self-conscious, and, set in the real landscapes of Michigan and Paris, there saturated in the interrelations of artists.

Instantly, we see, however, that the comic style of the work dominates all: Hemingway's achievement here, as elsewhere in his writings, and as described by his own comparison of literary works to icebergs, most of whose substance lies beneath the surface, is to conceal the depths and profundities and serious business of his texts under material that often seems to indicate something utterly other. The *Torrents* text is filled with self-parody and self-mockery; pomposity, self-righteous absurdity and mad preening, insanity and inanity, cant and rant also mock the literary world and his own pretensions within it. Scripps and Yogi are like two sad clowns in a barrel, and within affectation and romantic posturing, the ideal and the real are tumbled, and the "business of literature" is excoriated and revealed. It's not just that it is a bravura performance, with a tone a generation ahead of his not-yet-modernist and postmodernist readers, but that this work, in its ability to mock pomposity and preciocity, to destroy self-justifying pretensions, reveals an extraordinary wisdom—one might feel it the wisdom of an old man of letters who has had deep intimacy with and has already lived through all the ironies and disillusionments the creative artist must endure and who in mad humor has found his mode.

Literary anecdote is one of the dominant techniques of the book, whether we are dealing with the many anecdotes, apocryphal or true, that Hemingway pours into his text from his everyday encounters with Dos Passos, Fitzgerald, Harold Stearns, Sinclair Lewis, or H. G. Wells; those that he brings in through Yogi's reflections on Anderson or Cather or Booth Tarkington; or Diana's or Mandy's older reminiscences about Wordsworth, Henry James, Ford Madox Ford, and Sir Edmund Gosse that Scripps appropriates for his own art. In this way Hemingway enunciates the process of art and shows how life and art interact and how the emerging writer is based on writers of the past and in his contemporaries. I need not enumerate who the authors are. They are not only named, quoted, and deliberately misquoted but alluded to and present behind innumerable images and situations throughout the work—Fielding in the epigraphs and Turgenev more than Anderson are the presiding figures over Hemingway's own book.

I like to think that Hemingway—who, as Stein said, "looks like a modern and . . . smells of the museums"(216)—was indeed consciously making his scholarly obeisance to the Muse, or call it "the literary establishment," knowing feelingly that he needed to open with a traditional formula that placed him in the company of the literary great. One of the mysteries of his genius is how he ever came to be as knowing and traditionally savvy as he was about what he was facing at that time (at the outset of his career as novelist) as he worked to create *The Sun Also Rises*. He knew that, however small his "in" audience, it would be an audience of those he had chosen to accompany him on the great adventure on which he was about to embark—and that was an elect audience because from the first he had placed himself among the elect. I ask a revealing question: How many general readers have any idea what is going on in chapter 12 of *The Sun Also Rises*? I am trying to emphasize not Hemingway's elitism—he was never an elitist—but the several levels of discourse he brilliantly concomitantly used. Certainly, if *Green Hills of Africa* is a private communication to James Joyce—and it is!— and *The Garden of Eden* a belated work delivered posthumously partly to F. Scott Fitzgerald, and *A Moveable Feast* an open letter to all artists explaining the artists and expatriates in the Paris of the twenties, *Torrents* is Hemingway's first work addressed to the intimate community of fellow artists he respected who were sharing with him his period, place, and time. It was of them, to them, and for them that he wrote. Even as the colonel in *Across the River and into the Trees* muses, "He was addressing no one, except, perhaps, posterity" (168), we can recognize that Hemingway did not necessarily expect contemporary appreciation. He took the full measure of his audience: his Robert Jordan in *For Whom the Bell Tolls* answers Fernando's query about why he calls the cave the "*cueva de los huevos perdidós*" with the comment "Take a book to tell you" (199). Hemingway's recognition of how far he had gone beyond his average audience sharply determined his wise assessment of just who that real audience was. He called it most frequently "posterity." The stress of this recognition—and the loneliness it forced upon him—is best illustrated in a moment in *A Moveable Feast* when he shows himself as a young man musing: "Well, I thought, now I have them so they do not understand them. There cannot be much doubt about that. . . . And as long as they do not understand it you are ahead of them. Oh sure, I thought, I'm so far ahead of them now that I can't afford to eat regularly. It would not be bad if they caught up a little" (75). But he did not compromise his texts then, as he later did with *The Fifth Column*, when the loneliness forced on him by an uncomprehending readership and literary establishment, augmented by his lack, in those Key West years, of the highly charged companionship of the literary great that was his in Paris in the twenties, led him to expose his devices.[5] In the Paris of the twenties, he knew that he did have that small coterie of artists—which is always any artist's real audience—with whom he shared his lonely endeavor. *Torrents* was addressed to them, and they were the ones, as he had said, who enjoyed, praised, and understood it.

In this small handbook for writers, written hilariously and with joy, rather than soberly and solemnly (he says in *Death in the Afternoon* that "a solemn writer is always a bloody owl" [192]), he sets up his symbolic landscape and characters. To recognize them for what they are, we need to be aware of Hemingway's determining arsenal of metaphors. The time is that between freezing and thawing; the chinook wind is beginning to blow, and the cycles of life and life itself, the subject matter of art, are seen against the stasis and frozen state that holds life in suspension, much as the landscape itself is held in a painter's landscape, or the nude beloved in her artist beloved's nude. Hemingway had considered the techniques of the *torero* in *his* art in the corrida as a means of speaking of the realm of aesthetics, and in *Green Hills* he had gone on to relate the shots of the hunters and their taxidermic "heads" to the literary process. The pump factory in *Torrents* is an important setting, a place where artificial means are created to enable connections to be made between that within and below and that above, where flow is induced to bring into the open what is otherwise unseen within. That is a pure metaphor of masturbation and of the often self-satisfying masturbatory art, writing, that it represents: how overt is Scripps's contempt for "an endless succession of days of dull piston-collaring" (48)? The pump factory is an exemplification of the process of art that additionally allows us to reflect on its sources and life-giving functions and its abrogation of these. Hemingway had already (in the written if yet unpublished *Sun*) deeply explored the meanings of the static work of art; his references to hard-boiled eggs and stuffed dogs in a conversation between Bill and Jake exemplify arrested processes of life, seen in facsimiles of life for which life itself is in problematic ways traded. (Scripps in *Torrents* is the perfect person to thaw the frozen bird and bring it out of form and back to life at his own breast.) Late in his career, in *The Garden of Eden*, Hemingway would be exploring the ways Rodin's fixed statues had instigated the transformative processes of creative David and perversely creative Catherine and their life strategies and the forms of their real and aesthetic scenarios.

Additionally, Hemingway knew, as well as Joyce, the intricacies of the alternative creative processes that supported and aborted one another: those of Joyce's Stephen Dedalus and those of Molly, of art and nature, of the aesthetic birth process and the biological birth process. It is not arbitrary that Hemingway's first story in *In Our Time*, "On the Quai at Smyrna," studies the interrelations of life and death, the meaning of life in death, and the artificial means necessary to break life out of stasis, to take the dead babies from the breasts of living mothers. Hemingway goes on in "Indian Camp" to study how to bring to the child unable to be born unique techniques and expertise to let it truly live. And in "The Doctor and the Doctor's Wife," "The End of Something," and "The Three-Day Blow," he keeps his focus on artificial and biological creative processes, on obstetrics and the Caesarean and the techniques and vanities of obstetricians, and he studies the sacrifices of life to language that are going on in birth-death situations. His focus is on real and metaphoric fathers and mothers and their children, on art and on life, and also on the sexual ambiguities forced upon all of those who enter the arena of writing, where seemingly passive men seem to parodically take upon themselves the role of abstractly reproductive women, bringing forth out of themselves the works of art—their paper babies[6] that might justify their disengagement and detachment and the abandonment and circumvention of their women.

The Torrents of Spring is a profound study of the dynamics within the psyche of the artist, who must be at once feminine and masculine, detached and committed, and it correctly rests on a parable of Yogi and Scripps, two men, one the active principle, the other the passive, alter egos of and implicated in one another. Where else in Hemingway than in the twelfth chapter of *Sun* (and in some passages in *The Garden of Eden*) is sexual ambiguity more openly studied than in *Torrents*? And as in dozens of Hemingway's works where a male bond exists, whether between Jake and Bill, Macomber and Wilson, or the protagonists of "Cross-Country Snow" or "An Alpine Idyll," the men's opposition to the cycles of life and their dependence on one another represent an inner split, an interior state, vaguely homoerotic, that must, for aesthetic and humanistic reasons, be challenged by active heterosexual alternatives. (Recognize that this challenge is precisely what active Brett poses to dephallused detached Jake.) This is the case as the naked squaw returns Yogi to life and Mandy returns Scripps to art. It is significant that, in the first paragraphs of the book, we see the confusion between Scripps and Yogi as Scripps momentarily forgets that it is not he but Yogi who had "his" adventure in Paris. The novel must end with Scripps inside the Beanery, a place where beans are translated into flatulent air;

here he is eternal listener to the abstract exemplifications of life offered to him by his woman, while in his imagination he is with Yogi and the squaw out in the wild outdoors, where Yogi nakedly follows his primitive squaw into the natural wilderness.

The Torrents of Spring, like chapter 12 of *The Sun Also Rises*, is a treatise on the necessary psychic poise of the artist amid the sexual inversions and ambiguities thrust upon him by his commitment to an abstract medium. It studies the elaborate strategies of disengagement and detachment that are necessary to the artist—like Scripps—who must endlessly remain dependent on and attached to, but not overwhelmed by, the cyclical feminine real world, the necessary anecdotal narrative sources in life of his art, which he must abstractly manipulate. Notice how these strategies of disengagement within engagement, of the overly verbal yet technically brillliant obstetrician father in "Indian Camp," are also but exemplifications of this special artist's situation. The necessary life relations of the woman, who as surrogate brings abstractly to her artist-lover the life information and contact and imaginative structures that he needs, is in part classically the meaning of the Muse, of Petrarch's Laura and Dante's Beatrice. (See Etienne Gilson's lovely book *Choir of Muses* for a fine scholarly expansion of this theme.)

In *The Torrents of Spring*, two central mysteries that are essential to a reading of this text are offered up to the reader within the major anecdotes of Diana, the elderly waitress, and Yogi. The first is the mystery of the lost mother; the second is the mysterious source of Yogi's impotence. In the first of these (107–08), Diana tells her tragic tale of how she lost her mother and subsequently became an expatriate wanderer.[7] Having come with her mother to Paris, the City of Light, she arises in the morning to find in her mother's bed in her adjoining room not her expected mother but a French general. The mystery of the mother's disappearance is solved for us: she, having become "violently ill . . . in the night," is judged by called-in doctors to be fatally ill with bubonic plague, and since Paris is on the eve of its Great Exposition, with millions expected, she is "made to disappear" by called-in authorities lest her death create panic and financial disaster—thus, her place in the created fiction is taken by the French general. Diana's pleas and attempts to tell the truth and find her mother are brushed aside, for the world has been conned, given a fiction to replace the lost mother—this in itself the most revealing of metaphors—and to suggest that the mother was only a fabrication or fantasy. At the end of the novel, Hemingway remarks that the French general, who took the mother's place in her bed, "always seemed to us like a pretty brave man" (107). The mother in this tale—of an event only able to happen where the father is absent (as he is notably absent in several contexts in *Torrents*)—is coded in the anecdote as a source of even fatal danger, and the assumption of her place and role as a great risk indeed. The man in this case who assumes these places himself in great danger and is instrumental in breaking the familial bond, finding an expatriate solution and, primarily, establishing a verbal fiction to replace the "truth," which resides with the lost mother. Note that all of these actions describe the role of the artist. What the tale tells is that any man who assumes the dangerous role of the mother—as does the artist, who takes unto himself her reproductive capacity and role in the abstract, that is, in "the tale,"—is a very brave man indeed. It is important to recognize that Hemingway is also showing in this anecdote how the truth—what Diana tries to affirm—really resides in what seems her fiction, while the official disseminated "truth" is the real lie.

Yogi's story of the source of his impotence (95–97) is more complex and fascinating, probably as germane to Hemingway and his art as a tale can be. Yogi says that one evening when he was a soldier on leave in Paris during the war, he was invited into a cab by a very beautiful lady indeed, who took him to a room in a mansion where what was to be for Yogi "the most beautiful thing that had ever happened" to him took place. Although the experience was to be but a "one-night stand"—the lovely lady had emphasized afterwards, before he was escorted out, that he would never see her again—he remained desperate to find her. Finally, in that despair, he let himself be led by a tourist guide to a mansion where he joined dozens of allied veterans and others in standing behind a wall looking through slits into another room. Into the room came a lovely lady with a young British officer, and as she took off her coat and hat and he his Sam Browne belt, Yogi recognized her to be the beautiful lady of his dreams. Since that moment, Yogi affirms, "I have never wanted a woman." This complex and simple source of his sustained impotence is a fascinating tale indeed. Before going into it, we need to be aware that it is based, like the wanderings of the multiply married Scripps, on "the lost woman"—a feminine ideal image in Yogi's mind that leads him in his search.

Initially, when Yogi was an unknowing participant in the event, living it in what was for him its unalloyed spontaneity, participating unconsciously in its fiction, it became in his mind and heart the most beautiful thing that had ever happened to him. Later, as he tells us, after he became an enlightened spectator to its reality, it was transformed

into the most ugly thing that had ever happened to him. Its ambivalence, its uroboric capacity for being at once two utterly antithetical
things, fiction and reality, is undoubtedly at the heart of its terrible
power over him. We as listener/readers should note that in this tale
unbroken fiction is the source of beauty and that truth is the source of
impotence and ugliness. The whole tale is on one level the ultimate
trope of the artistic creative act. The image of a man whose genuine
passions and excitements, his very life enthusiasms, are used in a fiction
as the base of entertainment for onlooking but essentially detached and
uninvolved others—ourselves, dear readers and listeners!—is the ultimate metaphor for the artist and his audience. His desire used as an
imagery in tropes of love and passion fulfills their voyeuristic needs,
while he, as a player in a game, remains ultimately unfulfilled; his
excitement in the moment of the structuring of the event is what he
will get of personal lasting fulfillment in the act. It is a consummate
metaphor for literary process, where the artist's desires used in his passionately informed forms are staged for the inert and abstract enthusiasms and passions of others, who pay so that they may be admitted as
voyeurs to the imaginative forms that the artist's real passions project
and can assume. The image of life reduced to art—become merely a
drama or play performed for an audience—is magnificently given in the
metaphor of the Apollonian eye applied to "the slit." This is a Freudian
trope, where the phallus that naturally should penetrate the slit is necessarily replaced by the eye of the passive, disengaged beholder. He who
should hold has become the discarded *beholder*; Apollo (or his sister
Diana) has displaced Eros. Metaphors such as these help enormously in
letting us understand the guilt and ambiguity that always accompany
Hemingway's confrontation of the role of art and artist. Like Poe's
"Oval Portrait" and Henry James's "Maude Evelyn," Hemingway's work
is, in parable, studying the dangers inherent in the creative process.

Yogi's tale tells us of a man being used by a woman in fictions that
she consciously supports and in artifice that she consciously sustains: he
is the one manipulated in the fiction. In *The Sun Also Rises*, we know that
Cohn is the fictionalist and Brett pragmatic in comparison, and that his
sentimental fictions that he casts over Brett, asking her in effect to be
"absolutely fine and straight"(38) and the beloved that she seemed
to be, echo against a Yogi who might indeed be imploring his beautiful
performing prostitute to convince him that what he took to be authentic ardor was truly such. Cohn can't believe that what was the most
beautiful thing was just a drama or a play, with him cast in a role to sup-

port Brett's image. Also, Agnes von Kurowsky undoubtedly must have seemed, to the utterly "snowed" and involved young Hemingway, to have been playing with him all along—writing to him on March 1, 1919, to say that he is "just a boy—a kid" and that she is "not," suggesting that she's in love with someone else and that all along she has been outside the myth of a "real love-affair" that he projected (Villard and Nagel 162–63). His need to believe that it was real, that they were ideal lovers and that she was his ideal love, was shredded when romance was reduced to reality, the fiction unmasked as such, and the ideal proven to be a whore. In *A Farewell to Arms*, the work in which Hemingway used many of the materials of his love affair with Agnes, Catherine can be seen as initially inveigling Frederic into a relationship where he is used in a fiction that she projects upon him, placing him in the role of her lost dead beloved—a "role" that he knowingly accepts. In *Torrents*, the metamorphosis of potency to impotence happens when Yogi, the subject of voyeuristic abuse, becomes the voyeur. The metaphor for the instant of that transformation is the Freudian trope of the artist's eye at the slit, his own active sexual life involvement replaced by voyeuristic abstract detachment. It is what happens when the authentic passion of the young artist finally is brought to see itself in its art, in its techniques and tricks, as having fictionalized, or profaned through abstraction, the real passion. But that is what an artist always does; he transforms real passion into its abstract forms, which he sells for others' voyeuristic delight, and he pays the price in seeing and knowing himself merely as the agent in a depersonalized interaction. The only way to absolution is to leave the room, the enclosed contaminating inner room where the masks and words have their play, and, like Yogi, to walk wordlessly, nakedly, out into raw nature, following his naked squaw, both of them stripped of all masks of costume or clothing or relations to others. It may be that the journey into nature as hunter or fisher, as searcher after replenishment and healing in its solitudes, as in "Big Two-Hearted River," was a necessity for a Hemingway who well understood the cost of art.

In terms of *Torrents* itself, it should take us but a moment to see that Diana's tales, her life anecdotes that are offered up to Scripps's passion for transformation into the tales and stategies of art for readers' voyeuristic delight, are but another projection of the beautiful woman's artful forms staged for the onlookers. And it should take us but a moment to see in how many ways *The Sun Also Rises*, being written at the time this metaphor is created, is a larger study of its meaning—after all, dephallused Jake looking for a solution to his sexual problem while fixated on the woman in his mind is surely Yogi trying desperately to be able to have the potent phallus he lacks, or to desire a woman, and we may need merely to look at the source of Yogi's problem to understand why the artist has written *The Sun Also Rises*. It all has to do with the artist's dilemma. Or, to go to the end of Hemingway's oeuvre, Catherine's conscious imposition in *The Garden of Eden* of her imaginative fictive erotic structures on David, and her forcing of David to use their authentic life as the conscious subject of his art, art for sale, has its echoes back in Yogi's dilemma.

Torrents is also a handbook of literary techniques and devices, and no remark in it is more pointed than its last words, "I will just say a simple farewell and God-speed, reader, and leave you to your own devices" (108). It lines out in detail the resources and strategies or "devices" of the creative artist. It focuses on the artist's necessary transcendence of origins and the sources acting within him toward deracination and expatriation. After all, the artist's real country, as Hemingway said, is the country of his heart. The reference to the Australian who takes on the identity of those he fought with and the story of Henry James becoming English and being awarded the Order of Merit on his deathbed are made to echo against Hemingway's own somewhat fictionalized version of his becoming Catholic and getting a military medal for valor for foreign service in Italy on his own metaphoric "deathbed." Diana's history and identity and her ability to embed her own foreign land in Scripps's imagination are part of this, as is his wife Lucy's having left him, so getting him away from home and on the road. (We are not wrong to see that Scripps, like Odysseus, is a man far from and dispossessed of his home, trying to find his way back.) The roots of *Torrents* are in the picaresque *Wander-erzählung*, man on the road, trying to find his home or substitutes for it. The deeper story of Wordsworth's own expatriate wanderings, hidden behind Hemingway's allusion to Wordsworth's "Lost Lucy" poems, highlights this pattern. Scripps's choices and actions sequentially present the stages that Joyce shows in *A Portrait of the Artist as a Young Man* and that he himself chose—and with Scripps on the road, his apprenticeship as an artist is studied. The symbolic journey that follows has analogues in Melville's parables "The Tartarus of Maids" and "The Paradise of Bachelors"—it belongs as a parody of the genre of Bunyan's journeys in *Pilgrim's Progress* and Dante's in *The Divine Comedy*.

To the telegrapher in Petoskey—who stands in for Hemingway's *Kansas City Star* apprenticeship—Scripps tries to tell his own story in journalistic telegraphese: "he would give the bare essentials." At McCarthy's barber shop, the narcissistic, vain, posing men let themselves be shaped to existing styles as they submit themselves to the barber's hands. Scripps will have none of this. Later, talking to Diana in Brown's Beanery, the place of a lot of hot air, Scripps, as a mental blowhard, confuses his flatulent excesses with his creative potential— "his head was clearing under the influence of the beans"—and he realizes that he is talking wildly and must pull himself together. He sees that Diana can be used for his creative ends—that he can use her story without her name—and he recognizes "what a fund of anecdote" is there, that "a chap could go far with a woman like that to help him" (55). Working in the pump factory, he takes Yogi's tales of experience and appropriates them to himself: "He would quiz Yogi. Get him to talk. Draw him out. Make him tell what he knew" (48) Yet the pump factory is patently a work place where he spends an apprenticeship in masturbatory creation. It is where he works with his hands, where the perfect pumps are selected from the misfits, the others discarded, and the best sent on to international competition. What he is learning from the two master pump makers, Borrow and Shaw,[8] as they "let the boys watch . . . their hands shaking a little between strokes" (46), are the arts of introverted masturbatory egocentric creation. And it is there that Scripps spends a year of dull piston collaring—the image explaining the introverted way in which material is drawn out of oneself. The considered feminine alternatives to such piston collaring are given ambiguously as "a poor wife ain't no better than no wife" and "any wife is a pretty good wife" (47). Married at last to Diana, Scripps functions for her as "all of America to me," and she helps him to transcend himself, as she is his access to tales, plots, and storylines as he imaginatively appropriates and capitalizes on *her* origins and experience. Meeting Mandy, he finds in her flood of talk an interminable stream of literary gossip moored in the more humanized base of talk and tale that he needs; and he discards with Diana the great fund of intellectual literary critical writing on which he turns his back—Mencken, the *Manchester Guardian*, Mercury; it was with these that she had hoped to hold him. As we last see him, he has achieved an apparent balance in his mind between Mandy's humanly based literary anecdotes and Yogi's nature-relating images. This is a new stage in an artist's literary sophistication.

The textual surface of *Torrents* is incredibly dense with the "in" jokes of artists. With the lost Lucy or Lousy (the daughter become mother), we are dealing with Wordsworth's strategy of Lucy for his

"Lost Lucy poems" and the suggested historical sacrifice of the woman (Annette Vallon) to the egocentric artist—Wordsworth being another artist, like Matthew Arnold (in his Marguerite poems), who has sacrificed the woman to his art. On the other hand, Scripps beneath Lucy's lighted window in the snow in Petoskey is a variant of Romeo (who will die for love) below Juliet's balcony, and equally of Michael Furey in the cold rain beneath Gretta's window in Joyce's "The Dead." Later, after we learn that the elderly waitress Diana is from the Lake District, "Wordsworth's country," she becomes to Scripps his mode of access to "England, the Lake Country, Scripps striding through the Lake Country with Wordsworth. A field of golden daffodils. The wind blowing at Windermere" (53)—in other words, the basis at once of his imaginative extrapolations and projections and of his nostalgia for home. The fact of her attachments and origins, even, as she tells her story—revealing the original cause of her being, like Scripps, a victim set upon the road and so at last an expatriate also—in part determines his choice of her, despite her being, at this point, an old waitress. (As Diana, her ties with Apollo are evident.) Whoever she classically is, we are essentially being asked questions about the role of the lost woman, the light beyond that is inside the devoted artist, whose loss (or sacrifice) forces him upon the road and into expatriate homelessness. It is a significant part of this single Wordsworth trope that Diana relates him to Wordsworth's home, Windermere[9] which was basically (Windemere) the name given by Hemingway's mother to his own lake home in his own Lake Country, from which, a few days after his majority birthday, she had ousted him, setting him on the road to his expatriate wanderings. It is vital that Diana should be the vehicle, in her life and her tale, her art, for the legend of the lost mother, and perhaps unavoidable that she herself should become the jettisoned woman—already a replacement for Scripps's earlier wife—when Mandy appears on the scene. Diana reminds Scripps that as an artist he is beginning to repeat himself—his tale of how his earlier wife left him is a "story" he has already told "so many times."

A major focus of the book is on the sexual ambiguities implicit and unavoidable in the artist's taken role. The lost (absent) father has placed upon Scripps his pseudo-impotent role: his massively pillared patriarchal home is forfeit to the fires of Sherman—she/he/her man—who asserts that if the father were there, "We could have it out as man to man" (31). *Torrents* hilariously spins variant surrogate fathers or alternatives to eternal boyhood: in the *Manchester Guardian*, in *Mancelona*, and *Mandy*, in the *Bookman*, in the *Mentor* and *Mencken*, in references to *Sherman* and Hart*man* and pull*mans*. We learn from Scripps that Scofield Thayer was "his best *man*" and that he himself is a "Harvard *man*." Diana's love declaration to Scripps is, "You are my *man* and more than my *man*," and she, "having a *man* now. A Man of her own," prepares what defense she can to hold him—"He was her *man* and she would hold him." Even the beautiful-ugly experience that un*mans* Yogi in Paris takes place in a "*mans*ion." Scripps, who has become the child at the mother's breast, who becomes the man guarding the bird at his own breast against the cold winds—the bird that is called "a *man*ly little fellow"—has his own masculinity called in question, as it may be for any artist who recognizes the psychic poise, costs, and transformations of art and the artist. The telegrapher may well take him for a "fairy" if he goes about with a bird at his breast, a bird suggestively allied with the imaginative lyrical principles of Puck and Ariel.

Yes, *Torrents* is an artist's letter to artists, and Hemingway was insisting that he be early acknowledged as a "member of the club." If it is a "contract breaker," enabling him to move from Liveright to Scribners, it is that tangentially and additionally—but certainly not primarily.

NOTES

1. Quoted from a letter by Hemingway. Exact source now unavailable.

2. While Hemingway was still a young man in his early twenties and before he had written his first novel, Ezra Pound told Ford, "He's the finest prose stylist in the world. . . . He's disciplined, too" (qtd. in Rood, vol. 4, 197), and Ford acknowledged, "I did not read more than six words of his before I decided to publish everything he sent me" (qtd. in Baker 123). John Peale Bishop, on meeting Hemingway in 1922, described him as having "the most complete literary integrity it has ever been my lot to encounter" (Wickes 162). Allen Tate spoke of him in those early Paris years as "one of the most intelligent men I know and one of the best-read" (qtd. in Wickes 169). Samuel Putnam, who met him at that time, said of him, "No successful writer was ever less pretentious or more cordial toward others engaged in or associated with the craft" (Putnam 132).

3. One of Fitzgerald's first gestures on meeting Hemingway was to write to Charles Scribner to pronounce that Hemingway "has a brilliant future" and "he's the real thing" (Fitzgerald 167).

4. "The better workman": this was T. S. Eliot's dedication to Pound in *The Waste Land*.

5. In the dialogue in *The Fifth Column*, Hemingway reveals in explicit statements and puns that the word *come* carries both its normal meaning and its

sexual ejaculative meaning—"What a word. What a word" (32)—and that *spirits* carries its obvious reference and also names alcoholic beverages (5). He punningly describes the electrician, who is there to restore the light, as not seeming "awfully bright" (7) and has him stand with his arms outstretched, like a Christ who brings no redemption, to pronounce, *"No hay luz"* (17). Speaking of muzzling (10) the bitch whore Anita, who has bitten a compatriot—during fellatio?—he allows both reality and metaphor to play openly and to so show his rhetorical hand. To "answer in the negative" is immediately punned photographically—"You see connection? Camera, take picture, negative?" (13). Only enormous weariness and exasperation (with a public unable to rise to his humor and punning) could have driven his prose to such ends.

6. Surely, Hemingway means his audience to feel the relation between Ibsen's Hedda Gabler and Catherine, the childless protagonist of *The Garden of Eden*, when she takes her revenge on David's manuscripts—in early holograph versions of the manuscript, being driven toward craziness partly because of her barrenness. Gaining her revenge on Eilert Lövborg's manuscripts, Ibsen's Hedda repeats, "I am burning your child" (353). Throughout *The Garden of Eden*, biological childbirth and literary creativity are at war, and this opposition is developed as the cause of the tragedy.

7. Ivan Bunin, "The Gentleman from San Francisco." I owe to Robert Lewis the observation that Hemingway may have been aware of Bunin's short story, which similarly deals with a tourist abroad whose sudden death in a hotel must be hidden and hushed up lest it injure tourism.

8. Is Hemingway alluding to George Borrow and George Bernard Shaw?

9. Windermere, Windmere. Wind is developed in many ways in *Torrents*, and in this essay I will not resolve such questions as the possible parallelism of the newspaper office ("Aeolus") chapter of Joyce's *Ulysses* and the reading and anecdote-reciting moments in Brown's Beanery. Wind is treated as agent of divine spirit and also of flatulent stink. *Mere* is "pond," but also "sea" in its root origins, and it also carries the French meaning of "mother." Afflatus and generation, even pregnancy in Greek mythology, are closely associated with wind, and a psychoanalytic reader will be well aware of the lost child and lost mother and childless and absent/lost father themes complexly scattered throughout *Torrents*. Nor will Windemere as the name of the Hemingway's northern Michigan cabin on Walloon Lake (pond) be lost on those who remember how Grace drove Ernest from that "home" in the summer when he undoubtedly raised the subject of her possibly lesbian companion. All this, playing against the gay jokes and the often-repeated theme throughout *Torrents* of indeterminate sexual identity, suggests the very large unconscious component in the work.

Works Cited

Baker, Carlos. *Ernest Hemingway: A Life Story*. New York: Scribners, 1969.

Callaghan, Morley. *That Summer in Paris: Memories of Tangled Friendships with Hemingway, Fitzgerald, and Some Others*. New York: Coward-McCann, 1963.

Gajdusek, Robert. *Hemingway's Paris*. New York: Scribners, 1978.

Fitzgerald, F. Scott. *The Letters of F. Scott Fitzgerald*. Ed. Andrew Turnbull. New York: Scribners, 1963.

Gilson, Etienne. *Choir of Muses*. New York: Sheed and Ward, 1953.

Hemingway, Ernest. *Across the River and into the Trees*. 1950. New York: Scribners, 1970.

———. *Death in the Afternoon*. 1932. New York: Scribners, 1957.

———. *Ernest Hemingway: Selected Letters, 1917–1961*. Ed. Carlos Baker. New York: Scribners, 1981.

———. *The Fifth Column*. 1938. New York: Bantam Books, 1969.

———. *For Whom the Bell Tolls*. 1940. New York: Scribners, 1940.

———. *The Garden of Eden*. Holograph and typescripts. Hemingway Collection, Items 422, 422.1–422.9. Kennedy Library, Boston.

———. *A Moveable Feast*. New York: Scribners, 1964.

———. *The Torrents of Spring*. 1926. New York: Scribners, 1972.

Ibsen, Henrik. *Hedda Gabler and Three Other Plays*. Garden City, N.Y.: Anchor Books, Doubleday, 1961.

Plimpton, George. "An Interview with Ernest Hemingway." *Hemingway and His Critics: An International Anthology*. Ed. Carlos Baker. New York: Hill and Wang, 1962.

Putnam, Samuel. *Paris Was Our Mistress*. New York: Viking Press, 1947.

Rood, Karen Lane, ed. *Dictionary of Literary Biography*: Vol. 4. *American Writers in Paris, 1920–1939*. Detroit: Gale Research Co., 1980.

Stein, Gertrude. *The Autobiography of Alice B. Toklas*. New York: Alfred A. Knopf, 1960.

Villard, Henry, and James Nagel. *Hemingway in Love and War: The Lost Diary of Agnes von Kurowsky, Her Letters, and Correspondence of Ernest Hemingway*. Boston: Northeastern UP, 1989.

Wickes, George. *Americans in Paris: 1903–1939*. New York: Doubleday, 1969.

9

The Cost of Sin in the Garden

A *Study of an Amended Theme in*
The Garden of Eden

On March 9, 1987, the *New Republic* featured on its cover a reproduction of the dust jacket of the Scribners version of Ernest Hemingway's posthumous novel *The Garden of Eden*. Across its face in great black block letters was stamped "THE GREAT HEMINGWAY HOAX"; beneath it, in large black type, was the subheading "Anatomy of a Literary Crime." Thus were readers introduced to Barbara Probst Solomon's controversial article "Where's Papa?" Such a challenging and provocative display, emblazoned with the loaded terms *hoax* and *crime*, was meant to be a cause célèbre; at the very least it was intended to create a literary furor. But there has been no furor, nor does it seem that there will be one. The issues that Solomon raised nonetheless continue to be important. Her chief complaint was that Scribners had "interfered imperiously with what Hemingway left us" (31), a charge based on her having studied the original Hemingway manuscript in the John F. Kennedy Library in Boston and having compared it with the published version of the novel, edited by Tom Jenks at Scribners. She concluded her article:

> *The Garden of Eden* was to have been nothing less than Ernest Hemingway's final summation on art and literature, on the nature of love and the body, on the possibilities of human life. But you won't find any of these strong conceptions in the book that Scribners has published in his name. . . . In almost no significant respect

172

is this book the author's. With all its disfigurements and omissions, its heightening of the trivial and its diminishment of the significant, its vulgarization of the great themes of Hemingway's final years, this volume is a travesty. (33)

The world is well aware of the major revisions of Thomas Wolfe's novels by Scribners editor Maxwell Perkins and generally has been grateful for them, feeling that, but for his wise emendations and excisions, what we have warmly received would never have seen the light of day. It is probable, given Carlos Baker's expressed doubts about *The Garden of Eden* (which he saw in manuscript), and the generally prevailing skepticism about the apparently badly mangled manuscript that remained at Hemingway's death, that, had it not been for what Solomon describes as Jenks's "interference" with the manuscript, we might not have seen *The Garden of Eden* at all. And yet, as she acknowledges, its reception was mixed, varying from fulsome praise to overt skepticism.

At the time of the book's release, many critics who had a genuine sense of the extent of editorial liberties taken were still deeply impressed by the published work. Allen Josephs wrote that "Mr. Jenks in some miraculous fashion has made this story hang together so that it sounds exactly right" (20). John Updike felt that Jenks "succeeded" in reducing "two shopping bags" of manuscript to a "trim, published text of sixty-five thousand words" over which "a chastening, almost mechanically rhythmic order has been imposed" (86), and he asserted that the story within the novel left us "with a better feeling about the author's humanity and essential sanity—complicated, as sanity must be—than anything else published since his death" (88). Anthony Burgess described the emerging book as "all pure Hemingway" with "the old magic" in it (93). Similarly, while E. L. Doctorow admitted that "this cannot have been the book Hemingway envisioned" (45), he nevertheless labeled the Catherine of the published novel as possibly "the most impressive of any woman character in Hemingway's work" (44).

On the matter of the editing of the manuscript, it is my judgment, based partly on several extended telephone conversations with Barbara Solomon and also on my careful reading of the holograph and typescripts of *The Garden of Eden* in the Kennedy Library,[1] that all of us would share Barbara Solomon's sense of loss were we to have access to those first penciled and typed drafts, for they include some of Hemingway's most fascinating ruminations on the creative process, on art, and on life and literature as they interact at the most profound of levels. Her rage at the Scribners "hoax" is a measure of her sense of deprivation. This sense is distinct for anyone who has even partially read the holograph of *The Garden of Eden*, for patently what is there, in those admittedly incomplete, unfinished, undeveloped notes, are ideas and conceptions that go far beyond where the novel itself, as published, seems to take us. What if, for example, we were to know that Catherine and David, in *The Garden*, get their idea for sexual inversion and role reversal experimentation from having together witnessed at the Hotel Biron, the Rodin museum in Paris, Rodin's experiments with sexual metamorphoses? We might immediately recognize (as we may not necessarily in Jenks's version) that art and life—which are interlocked throughout the novel in intricate ways that have much to do both with the antagonisms between aesthetic and biological creativity and with the play of imagination over the surfaces of a manuscript or of a living human body—are throughout all levels of the novel in a deadly and fundamental interplay. We would recognize that sexual play can be either biological or aesthetic and that the artist's study of passional problems in his art is one mode of addressing what another might be forced to consider in experimentation with love. These recognitions are fundamental to the novel that Hemingway writes.[2] Rodin in his art was fascinated by metamorphosis and sapphic subjects, as is this novel. The omission of the Rodin reference is thus of vital importance. Also omitted from the published novel are many discussions of art and artists, Catherine's descriptions of conversations with Picasso, and at least three major characters. It would stun most readers to know that in the Hemingway manuscripts for this novel—a novel that, in the published version, ends by predicting creativity and happiness—Hemingway's considered endings seem to include a violent death followed by a double suicide or a suicide and madness.

We must, in all fairness to Scribners and Jenks, and in all fairness to Hemingway, try, as we are able *without* the published holograph manuscript, to understand why the editing exists as it does, as well as, perhaps, to fathom why there has been no large-scale support among Hemingway scholars for Barbara Solomon's call to arms. The reason for hesitation in assigning responsibility for alterations is that the history of the manuscript is at the moment muddied. It is impossible to determine from a visit to the Kennedy Library if all variations and versions of the manuscript are known, just what the worksheets were from which Jenks worked, and whether a supposedly revised version from which the Scribners novel was largely edited had ever been received in Boston, even though both Charles Scribner, Jr., and Tom Jenks assured me that it had been mailed to the Hemingway collection at the Kennedy. Until all existing versions are specified and the publishing history is clarified, no one can truly know if an alteration was Hemingway's own revision of his work or an idea originating with his editors.

In his 1987 essay "Editing Hemingway: *The Garden of Eden*," Tom Jenks has indicated his unwillingness to "go public" with information the critics need, a position he also articulated in a letter to me of November 18, 1986:

> Then there is the truth that in editing the book I have really already said all of consequence that I have to say about it. The press comments at publication served a commercial purpose and once I got into it, my own vanity, and then were finally exhausting. I felt the responsibility to be responsive to those who had some legitimate reason to ask for a response, and I have tried to fulfill that obligation, and I have so far said no only once.
>
> And now I am not sure I could, even if I wanted, recreate for anyone the process through which I edited *The Garden of Eden*. The book, its author did pass through me in a powerful and intimate way. I asked myself most all of the questions that I think I can ever be asked about the material, asked them over and over again, from any number of points of view, and of course made some battlefield decisions. . . . I would enjoy a give and take with you . . . but. . . . All I know just now is that I cannot give more of my life to Ernest Hemingway, *The Garden of Eden*, or to anyone in that purpose. Moreover, you will find me somewhat perverse in saying I don't mind there being a little mystery. If there is any editorial magic in *The Garden of Eden*, it's on the page and I don't guess I'm really under any obligation to reveal it to anyone, though someday I might be moved to.

I have the report of Patrick Lufkin, a Hemingway scholar who is currently working with the *Garden of Eden* holographs, and who attended a talk given by Tom Jenks at Davis, California, on February 11, 1991, that Jenks there stated he had never worked with either the holograph or the Kennedy Library materials while he was editing the book. Jenks at that talk apparently repeated the story about Mary Hemingway delivering to Scribners a paper sack filled with materials, among which were the manuscripts that he subsequently edited. He described these materials as three typescripts of approximately 600, 800, and 1,200 pages, respectively. It is the large and unbridgeable discrepancy between what is at the Kennedy Library and what was published by Scribners that understandably fueled Barbara Solomon's charge of "travesty," and until we have a finely studied, fully documented explanation for all versions, and any possibly missing arrangements or versions, we must note differences without assigning either blame or responsibility.

Certainly the first question should be, "What do we have?" What do we know that we have in manuscript at the Kennedy Library, and to what extent are we in possession of the exact manuscripts out of which the Scribners version was fashioned?[3]

The second question should be, "Is the received text in the Scribners version accurate as we have it?" Certainly we know it is heavily edited, truncated, emended—but are we even sure that it is reasonably accurate in what it supposes to put before us? A comparison of only a few pages of the holograph and manuscript versions of the novel with the Scribners text yields at least four errors in transcription.

These are not editorial emendations but what seem to be simple basic errors on the part of a reader/copier at Scribners. In the published novel we find, "He treated evil like an old entrusted friend" (146). On the evidence of the holograph, this appears to be a misreading of what in Hemingway's hand is clearly "He treated evil like an old untrusted friend" (1, 3, bk. 3, ch. 25, 3). The difference is radical. Elsewhere in the novel as we have it, David is described as sitting "with a glass of whiskey and water in his hand and the rolled figs swept away" (139). The manuscript (1, 18, bk. 3, ch. 24, 2) has in Hemingway's hand the word the editors took to be *rolled* carefully rewritten in Hemingway's hand with the two t's unmistakably crossed, so that this very error should not be made: the difference between rolled figs and rotted figs is radical to one concerned with metaphor. Furthermore, the published novel reads, "Nor had he even worn the plaid corduroy jacket" (128), but the manuscript reads, "Nor had he ever worn" it (1, 17, bk. 3, ch. 23, 2 bis 1). These are mistakes found in only a very casual comparison of some paragraphs of the book and some paragraphs of the manuscript. Such alterations do not seem to be editorial decisions but rather simply careless reading and transcription. It should be a first imperative to cleanse the published text of such errors.

What literary scholars badly need is a university press scholarly edition of the Hemingway manuscripts of this fascinating book so that they may study the very act of composition/creation and see Hemingway's own several movements toward his final story and so that they may judge the editing job while not being deprived of much that appears in holograph but is excluded from the published novel. Such a volume would be the ideal solution.

There is genuine damage when a novel is this radically edited, certainly to the novel that is there somewhere among imagined hypothetical alternatives, and most certainly to the author, whose image is shaped by what is offered as from his hand. Hemingway has become the recipient of critical judgments that find his work's apparent intentions unfulfilled, its narrative justifications weakly supported, or its characters inadequately developed. Charles Corn, writing mainly appreciatively in the *San Francisco Chronicle*, suggests that *The Garden* is an "uneven, imperfect work" in which the author imposes "a conceit of bisexuality" that is often less than convincingly handled (10). Hemingway is also blamed for inadequate explanation: John Updike writes, "It is possibly a pity that Hemingway's own inhibitions, if not those of the changing postwar times, prevented him from telling us exactly what is going on here" (87). Updike notes that as Marita "turns increasingly sympathetic and heterosexual," after having "begun as a hardened, though attractively blushing, lesbian, she rather incredibly becomes a perfect man's woman" (87). He laments that the "plot solution the Scribners editors have used—perhaps the only one available to them in the uncontrolled manuscript"—is a "feeble one, compared with the dark soft power of the opening sections" (86). Such judgments, formed without knowledge of the extent to which the insufficiencies noted are absent in the holograph, nevertheless weigh against Hemingway.

In *Life*, Anthony Burgess, reaching in that magazine a far greater readership than most critics writing to more limited scholarly audiences, assures this readership (with amazing assurance for one who apparently has not seen the manuscript) that "Scribner's [sic] editors cut heavily, as they had to" and that the book "is all pure Hemingway, with no editorial intrusions or wanton excisions" and "is the work that Hemingway had in mind" (93). E. L. Doctorow, also without having seen the holograph, yet troubled that the original forty-eight chapters and 200,000 words have been compressed into one-third that space—a published novel of thirty chapters and 70,000 words—nevertheless argues that "Marita has not the weight to account for her willingness to move in on a marriage and lend herself to its disruption. She is colorless and largely unarticulated" (45). Of David he notes that the "deadness of the piece" is due to the way David's consummate self-assurance in everyday affairs "does not mesh" with his "incapability in dealing with the crisis in his relationship" (45) and that he is a man "hapless before temptation and unable to take action" (44). These criticisms are not of the editing, which he cannot judge, but of Hemingway and his novel, despite the fact that Marita's "weight" and lack of articulation, like David's ambiguity, may well, in a novel so heavily edited, be due to editorial excision and not authorial failure.

Robert B. Jones acknowledges that reviewers have "generally dismissed Catherine as two-dimensional" (4), and Frank Scafella affirms that it is only in the holograph version that "the origin and nature of Catherine's gamble for David's soul" is disclosed (22), and that in the novel as published we "experience little of Catherine's deep hostility" toward her husband's work (24). He goes on to argue that David's awareness of "the state of his own soul" and the "effect of Catherine's change on David" is to be seen in excised material in the holograph only and that only in the holograph, in certain "portions of dialogue and in David's extended meditations on his work" that are omitted in the published novel, can "the spiritual impact of the 'changeings'" (*sic*, 24) be seen.

All the suggestions that the editing undoes the Hemingway novel that is in the holographs come to a head in a version of Barbara Solomon's then-unpublished manuscript "Hemingway's Fiesta at the Prado," which she enclosed to me in a letter of October 6, 1986. In that work, she directly attacks Scribners's "minimizing and distorting Hemingway's intent . . . in the interests of making a modish, commercial yuppie quick read" (15). Her judgment is that nothing in the holograph "could conceivably lead to the . . . beachy happy ending" (8) and that the David that critics have found "askewly passive" (7) is a Scribners creation partly made as the "edit cuts out the way he talks and relates to other men about art" (6–7). Of Jenks she says, "He didn't understand why Hemingway was writing this book" (3), and the result is a "lack of conceptualization of what Hemingway was trying to do" (4).

Since much current criticism of *The Garden of Eden* focuses on the inadequacy of character motivation or definition, it becomes imperative to ask if that missing motivation and definition exist in the holograph. The ongoing debate suggests that a valuable exercise might be performed by placing side by side two versions of one theme, evident in both *The Garden of Eden* as published and in the holograph manuscript as it is to be found at the Kennedy Library. Without asking such vital questions as whose hand brought the theme as we originally see it in its first manifestations to its later altered state, questions that must at a later time be answered, we will be raising other radically important questions: Is the published revision true to Hemingway's hand as we have known it? Given the altered state of the theme, which, in the holograph version, is the explanation and determinant of action and character, is the theme still similarly functional in the novel? If not, are the new dynamics and causes sufficient unto *their* ends? These are not questions of whose was the hand that shaped, for which we can offer no firm answers here, but rather of the extent and logic of the reshaping, the aesthetic integrity of the published novel.

The theme to be studied here, in both holograph and published novel, is the theme of the child, the biological child absent for these lovers but always a possibility for them. In a work that focuses as does *The Garden of Eden* on David's literary creativity, as well as on Catherine's envy of that process from which she feels excluded, the woman's natural alternative of biological creativity is the omnipresent if often unstated alternative. Since the novel details Catherine's flight from her feminine identity and toward masculine or lesbian alternatives that confirm her childlessness, the possibility or impossibility of pregnancy—of natural physical fecundity as opposed to abstract creativity—becomes central. The theme of child begetting is crucial in both manuscript and novel, albeit amazingly altered in the published work.

Both the novel and the holograph focus on a conflict of creativities, of productive potentialities. The abstract creatures of David the writer's mind are everywhere placed in opposition to the potential if unborn children of Catherine's womb. She declares herself unable to write and unable to paint, and Hemingway looks hard at David's, the artist's, guilt for his biological neglect of his childless and so unfulfilled wife and also at her jealousy of *his* fulfillment in his chosen abstract métier. Life is thus transformed by David—undergoes metamorphosis—as it is remade into fiction in art; and Catherine, eager to find an aesthetic satisfaction similar to that of her husband, begins to manipulate life into unnatural fictive postures, in experimentation with hair and body odor and sexual styles and modes. Her consort becomes part of the material necessary for such artful metamorphosis: the active man is transformed by her desires into the passive feminine partner, as she, passive woman that she has been, becomes the aggressively active male—Catherine assumes the persona of Peter (her male self) as she commands David to become "Catherine."

In both the published and holograph version of Hemingway's manu-script, as Catherine begins her role reversal experimentations on David, he asks her, "But how long have you thought about that?" (17). It is *only* in the holograph, however, that she answers, "Ever since we were there [saw the Metamorphosis] that day in the Rodin" (1, 1, bk. 1, ch. 1, 22). "Saw the Metamorphosis" is crossed out in the holograph. Later in the holograph, David declares, "You know the statue moved you and why shouldn't it? Did it not move Rodin?" (1, 1, bk. 1, ch. 1, 23). Rodin's museum, the Hotel Biron, is described elsewhere as the place "where the changeings [sic] had started" (1, 3, bk. 2, ch. 1, typescript 1). The important questions that Catherine asks are, "Are you changing like in the sculpture?" and "Will you be like you were in the statue. . . . Will you change?" And we are told at last that "it was like the statue. The one there are no photographs of and of which no reproductions are sold" (1, 1, bk. 1, ch. 1, typescript 2, page 1). Hemingway's use of "reproductions" here accents his careful suggestion of biological and aesthetic concep-tion as alternatives. All of the above material fails to find its way to the published novel.

What Hemingway makes clear in his holograph is that the idea for David and Catherine's inversions and reversals seems to begin here in art, but he carefully determines that this idea does not end in life, for as David goes on writing and creating while being both agent and victim of such transformations, transformed life begets additional metamor-phoses in art. The omission of the Rodin material from the published novel enormously alters the motivation and determination of action and character, for Hemingway has with it artfully established the intri-cate and multileveled relationships between art and life that determine the fate of his characters.

This is most completely seen by Barbara Solomon, who, in "Hem-ingway's Fiesta at the Prado," writes:

> This particular Rodin obviously fascinated Hemingway because of Rodin's success in conceptualizing a *continuous chain of metamor-phoses*. Ovid shaped from the erotics of real life his creations of his manual on the varieties of love making and his verse "Metamor-phosis." Centuries later, Rodin, as artist, again repeats the process and takes from real life the models for his recreation of Ovid the poet. Catherine and David in their love making, become part of an endless universal chain of love fused with art, in which men and

women fusing and changing sex roles become part of a larger continuum. By totally removing Rodin, the Scribners version loses all connection to Hemingway's "Eden." Not only is Rodin germane to the love making scene, it is the very basis for the novel. (10–11)

As we first read *The Garden of Eden* as given to us by Scribners, we ever hear in the background the voices of the lovers in several early Hemingway short stories. Primarily, of course, we are reading a variation of "The Sea Change"—a term, by the way, used by Hemingway in his *Eden* manuscript (1, 2, bk. 1, ch. 4, 4) but omitted in the published work—but several times we perceive conversations and situations and details already sketched for us in "Hills Like White Elephants," "Cat in the Rain," "Out of Season," and "A Canary for One." The troubled surface that indicates the reef beneath shows readily in all of those stories, as it does in David and Catherine's idyll, in which experimentation with new drinks, perpetual expatriate restlessness, and the search for extravagances and new tastes eventually tire. The exploration of galleries, books, and journals leads David and Catherine (by way of Rodin, in the holograph) to experimentation with their bodies and their lifestyles and the taking on of a live-in companion, ostensibly to keep occupied the wife, who, because of her husband's dedication to *his* art, has nothing to fill her emptiness.

Catherine's boredom is emphasized, as are the surrogate excitements that are meant to complete lives with something "real," lives that are seemingly victimized by the husband's abstract creative excitements. His private fulfillment through his work and its success finally drives the distracted and bored wife to her "madness" and to her charge against him of spilling his seed upon the ground, practicing "solitary vice in a wastebasket full of clippings" (216). Hidden in this accusation is a deeper suspicion-rage, one that emerges only twice in the novel as published although it is extensively developed in the manuscript. It is first seen when Catherine contemplates spending her money, though such spending means putting David's writing aside—"That way we [she and David] can have the fun before I have a baby for one thing. How do I know when I'll have a baby even?" (27). In the significant ending on "even," she creates the ripple on the surface that reveals that the main unspoken question is of her or David's possible sterility. Sterility has kept her "carefree," and carefreeness throughout the book is a synonym for childlessness. Later, there is the second reference:

"I thought if I'd be a girl and stay a girl I'd have a baby at least. Not even that."

"That could be my fault."   ⊛

"Don't let's ever talk about faults. You stay here and I'll bring back the mail." (71)

Mail throughout the novel and holograph is used to introduce its homonym (male). It is Catherine who gets the mail/male while David passively waits, and it is she who grows bored with the process of opening up the mail—another sexual pun—finally doing it as though she were shelling peas, while it is David who says farewell to the mail/male/man.

Mythically, her rage against David's stories and the clippings she burns is justified. Catherine in the novel is named as she is for the same reason Catherine in *A Farewell to Arms* was so named: to link her with her namesake, Saint Catherine, who suffered martyrdom on the wheel. In *A Farewell to Arms*, that wheel was patently the biological wheel of life that was perpetually and inescapably turning from the first page to the last, the "biological trap" that the lovers, however resourceful or imaginative or willful in their wishes, could not escape. It is on that wheel that Frederic Henry's Catherine suffers her martyrdom. In this later novel, a later Catherine similarly tries to deny that wheel, to become, in her challenge to David, a creator-inventor like him: in her stagings of drama and arrangements of life into imaginative patterns that she opposes to its natural patterns, she tries to invent new forms and new postures. Her challenge is essentially a challenge to the God of Eden, for, in bypassing natural reproductive processes, she would remake creation to abolish the penalty for transgression in his garden. But the Father-God who made Eden is the Father who has gifted her with that very problematic fecundity that killed the Catherine of *A Farewell* and that seems to judge the Catherine of *Eden*.

Throughout *The Garden of Eden*, David's art seems dedicated to keeping the legend of his loved and scarcely comprehended father alive, while his mother goes unmentioned. Catherine sees herself as a sacrifice to that art, and it is not surprising that she hates the very father he tries to understand, victim as she is (in her womanhood and in that sterility for which she does not feel responsible) of the treacherous father principle. David's art seems to her dedicated to extolling the primacy of the father-son relationship, one that, so phrased, calls Catherine's very womanhood in question. Although the manuscript is filled with references to sterility and the expressed need for biological fecundity, one of the very few references to birth and begetting that is allowed to remain in the published novel is filled with revulsion toward fatherhood: Catherine describes David's "drunken father staggering around smelling of sour beer and not knowing which ones of the little horrors he had fathered" (189).

The theme of childlessness that activates the novel is only minimally there in the published work, though there is a fully established and finely developed food symbolism that relates to birth or its process. As Barbara Solomon observes in Hemingway's "Fiesta at the Prado," "This has got to be the 'eggiest' novel ever written." The characters in the novel seem to be constantly ordering, eating, and being served eggs, caviar, and chicken. The book focuses upon broken egg yolks, on Catherine's egg on her plate getting cold, on the eating of egg whites and caviar after Catherine's first lesbian experience with Marita, and on Marita's bringing David caviar the next morning. One time, after David has worked, Marita feeds him eggs, and another, when he has similarly worked, Madame Aurol brings him caviar that he reciprocally feeds to her. These eggs that are given to David seem the sacrifice of natural process to his aesthetic creativity. When Madame Aurol tries to turn David's attention to the "charming" gift that Catherine and Marita have given to the bar, a mirror that will "produce" only abstract and illusionistic replications of what already exists, David rejoins that "Everyone's full of . . . charm and sturgeon's eggs." Before he leaves, he warns Madame to "keep the caviar away from Aurol" (131). It is she who, after Catherine's final departure, makes an omelet for David and urges him to eat "some chicken" (235). This constant preparation and eating and destroying of eggs or the egg producer focuses the reader on the engorgement or destruction of the stuff of life; process is seen as an eternal cycle. As when Saturn eats his young or the sow eats its farrow, the life process in this household is uroborically introverted.

It is important to look more carefully at these egg references, for they are one reproductive metaphor from the holograph that remains largely intact in the novel. The moment David confesses to Catherine at Hendaye (Hen-Day) that he wants to start to write, she gratuitously reassures him that he need not worry about her infidelity while he is creatively occupied, thereby suggesting her own available freedom as a result of his solitary creative process. However, the next day, immediately after David does successfully write, they have the first quarrel of their lives. He comes on Catherine, partly drunk from the pernod (or spirits) she has enviously turned to while he has turned to abstract words, and she attacks him, calling him a "clipping reader," and disdains him as a writer. The following morning, he quickly forgets about Catherine while writing, and then he breakfasts alone, eating a beautiful egg with relish after carefully breaking its yolk. When he sees Catherine's egg in danger of getting cold, he eats it, too. David, as successful writer or word creator, seems concomitantly to become David the egg destroyer, one who devours even Catherine's eggs, or takes them unto himself. As Catherine has "gorged" on spirits, David has gorged on eggs. Hemingway obviously wanted these metaphors more visible, for in the holograph he has David refer to the destruction of his manuscripts by saying, "There isn't any use to call in all the King's horses nor all the King's men" (1, 33, bk. 3, ch. 42, 4), by the allusion styling himself concomitantly word and egg producer and affirming that his works of art are his produced eggs.

When Catherine first sees David after she has given herself to lesbian love with Marita, she pours out two of the three martinis he makes for her, throwing away the spirits while eating the garlic olives. The third martini, at his insistence, she drinks, and then she gives David the pit of the olive, exclaiming, in both novel (118) and holograph, "Semiprecious stone. . . . Put it in your pocket" (1, 15, bk. 3, ch. 21, 24–25). Marita's equivalent gift to David is a large tin of caviar, for which egg whites and onions are cut up, and a case of fine champagne. Marita, who admits she has been studying David's needs, gives him the most valued of eggs—for which less esteemed eggs are sacrificed—while simultaneously giving him fine spirits. Unlike Catherine, who finally takes the spirits unto herself while giving David the seed, forcing him to be woman as she seizes male prerogatives, Marita simultaneously offers him egg and spirit. Late in the novel, Marita makes a major point of the fact that she, unlike Catherine, who can be only *either* a boy or a girl, is *at the same time* both. Hemingway was carefully stressing the either/or dynamic of Catherine's world in competition with the both/and synthesis of Marita's.

One effect of Catherine's replacement of heterosexual love with lesbian love seems to be a further movement of David toward the feminine reproductive role she has abandoned. She gives him *her* seed for *his* pocket[4] in a scene where she has denied, poured out the spirit; in another scene, she denies her possible maternity as she holds her glass of spirits against her nipples "so they came erect" (168). Marita, on the other hand, by giving David a gift of eggs balanced with spirit, for which other eggs are willingly destroyed, acknowledges his artist's need to establish a synthesis of both. Most of this spirit/egg metaphoric structure remains intact in the published work, but significant emphases of it are omitted: in the holograph, lest we should miss the fact that the creative process underwrites the destructive eating process, Hemingway has David, served an omelet by Madame Aurol, remark, "You can't *break* an omelet without making eggs" ((1, 34, bk. 3, ch. 43, 9; italics mine).

Even as eggs in the published novel exist to be eaten or broken, not to reproduce, so breasts in the published novel are stylized and celebrated but never suggested as nurturing. Catherine's and Marita's erecting nipples are used as indexes to their thoughts and desires, or their masculinization, but not to nourishing. That the Scribners editor chose to leave in most of the food references—which, as I have tried to indicate, are highly and complexly saturated with productive/reproductive imagery that is closely tied to the creative process of the artist—while omitting, excising, or stripping away the elaborate focus in the holograph on child begetting, seems to deny or neglect their interdependence.

In the original holograph version, Catherine asks Andy, one of the three major characters omitted from the published novel, whether he believes "it about women for breeding, boys for pleasure, and melons for delight" (1, 6, bk. 3, ch. 9, 14), and this Kennedy Library original version, unlike the published novel, focuses fully and hard upon problematic fertility as one of the major reasons for Catherine's flight toward sexual inversion and lesbian love: she seems to seek safety from a process she fears or from feared knowledge of either her or David's sterility. Problematic fertility was a major part of the original conception of the novel.

In the manuscript, Catherine quickly brings a conversation with David to the apparent subject of a rejected, or aborted child: "If we'd had the damned baby. I wouldn't want to have it around any more than my parents wanted me around" (1, 1, bk. 3, ch. 16, 12). Almost immediately, "it" is revealed to be the desired child that they seemingly have been unable to beget, which has become in her escapist pose "the damned baby," which she relates to her sense of her own parents' rejection of her. What becomes the at-once spoken and unspoken question ringing throughout the manuscript is *who* is responsible for the sterility. Catherine rejects David's suggestion that testing might reveal the source of infertility and lets him know he's quite mistaken "if you think we're going to go to a dirty French doctor and have him poke things inside of me and take your juices that belong to me and make slides of them and try to mess up our lives . . ." (1, 1, bk. 3, ch. 16, 12–13). She goes on: "as for that fucking patter of little feet. Probably running to the stables to ask the garage man for an axe to kill mummy" (1, 1, bk. 3, ch. 16, 13). In her mind the child *has* become the monstrous mother killer. When David gently reproves her for rudeness to a "dirty French doctor that we've never met," she answers, "I'd like to have a chance to talk to that miserable faker. That semen stealer. That degrading filthy minded old quack. You'd never make me go to him would you?" When David reassures her, "Never," she continues, "He's obscene. He's my enemy" (1, 1, bk. 3, ch. 16, 16–17). This rather remarkable scene, omitted from the published novel, presents an excessive reaction to a nonexistent doctor. It seems that the very suggestion of his function is what triggers Catherine's violence: his role, unlike that of the similarly feared hypothetical doctor in "Hills Like White Elephants," is not to abort but, rather, to try to solve the mystery of infertility by isolating the source of sterility. It is this role that makes him Catherine's "enemy."

While the source of her infertility is left enigmatic in the quoted exchange with David, it becomes in the holograph one of Catherine's major weapons in her assault on him and goes far toward explaining her motivation. When Marita responds to her reading of David's first story, "I would have been moved by it if I had been made to study it in school," Catherine challenges David's aesthetic creativity with a charge of his biological sterility: "Well maybe your children will have to study it in school unless you take better care of yourself or unless David really is sterile which is quite possible" (1, 20, bk. 3, ch. 26, 13). The speech presciently predicts the immortality of Hemingway/David's work that he is at the very moment writing, while it concomitantly warns Marita against conception and also, contradictorily, suggests David's *biological* sterility. Later, Catherine elaborates this charge against David, telling him, "It may not be your fault that we can't have a baby. It just barely may not, although you admit in that first African book you had the clap when you were fourteen." She will shortly attack his writing as "seen through a little boy's eyes? A little boy who got clap at fourteen." The rage she harbors against David will not let his art, which she declares flawed, be separated from his sexuality, which she also describes as damaged, and, upgrading her attack upon his sexual damage, she admits to him that she had suggested to Marita that "perhaps you had contracted syphilis" (1, 20, bk. 3, ch. 26, 15).

Finally, in the manuscript, Catherine's attempt to deny childbirth itself seems in large part to determine her flight from femininity to masculinity and thence toward fantasy. Her attack, however, upon the very principle of fatherhood as it might be embodied in David expresses itself in a triple attack: first, against his father; second, against David's own manhood and his questionable capacity for fathering children of flesh and blood; and third, against his ability to create fictional children as works of art. Therefore, speaking to Marita, Catherine at once mocks David's father, impugns his fertility/potency, and mocks his art. She must become the castrating woman. Her suppressed rage almost necessarily ends in her gesture of burning the manuscripts, an act that attempts to take potency from the artist while it serves as a form of infanticide that deprives the writer of his "fatherhood." David acknowledges Catherine's seemingly successful castration attempt in part when he reflects, after he has tried to write again after her destructive act: "He had never in his short life been impotent but in an hour standing before the armoire on the top of which he wrote he learned what impotence was" (1, 35, bk. 3, ch. 44, 1). But this is David's realization in the manuscript version. In the novel, it becomes, "He was unable to write the sentence that should follow. . . . It was impossible for him to put down the next sentence. . . . He could not write more than a single sentence. . . . He knew that resolution was powerless" (239). His only inadequacy seems to be a lack of "resolution"; in the manuscript it is, more importantly, a lack of potency.

Coming to Marita with news of his inability to create, he says in the manuscript version, "Wine is fine and bed's our fatherland. But we're burned out. The farm I mean. The barn's burned and the house is burned. The gun's burned and the pictures and the books and the great tusks too. Who burned the Bournes out? Crazy woman burned out the Bournes" (1, 35, bk. 3, ch. 44, 24). In the published novel, this entire passage becomes merely, "'We've been burned out,' he said. 'Crazy woman burned out the Bournes'" (243). It is not accidental that the full imagery strongly invokes the memory of Hemingway's early short story "Now I Lay Me," in which the wife's burning of the husband's guns and collection of treasured relics is powerfully expressed as her symbolic castration of him.

Expressly in the early manuscript, but not in the published novel, David finally labels Catherine the castrating "destroyer" she is, and there he also indulges in a seemingly antic poem—one, however, that studies the need to guard fertility from its enemies:

For who would have his cock or balls shot free so that he could no proper part of England be, nor progeny and wealth acquire, some

Fokker having blasted his desire. Come celebrate with me the thin steel sheet where languidly we park our meat, thus shielding England's tools and seed against our country's future need. (1, 29, bk. 3, ch. 37, insert 30)

In the metaphoric logic of *Green Hills of Africa*, to yield dark life up to its hunters is to consent to the artist's "kill": throughout *Green Hills*, "shots" are equated with the writer's technical means of arresting, or freezing, or getting his quarry, while taxidermically mounted heads are equated with immortality conferred upon living/dying life. Additionally, the brain of the artist is the womb that brings to life or makes live what is otherwise dead. In this logic, the artist kills life to resurrect it into art. David refers to the problems of the story he writes that must be "made to come alive" (108). This motif of life resurrected into its spiritual equivalent in art is taken one step further in *The Garden of Eden* as Hemingway studies the way art also creates life as the Rodin creates the characters' new sexual forms, as David's writing provokes murderous and loving acts, and as spirits (and even ghosts from the past) are made to come alive. At one moment, David is afraid as he mixes a drink that these spirits "might be dead" although "the water bubbled like a spring" (1, 37, bk. 3, ch. 46, 28). At another, he watches the champagne "come alive again" as it is poured (1, 34, bk. 3, ch. 43, 8).

The observations that Hemingway makes on the creative process in the midst of a fertility dilemma, as well as the title and subject of "Hills Like White Elephants"—a story in which the hill becomes the white elephant, or unwanted "gift," the fetus, that the male protagonist would abort—suggest the intricacy of the association of biological child and aesthetic art object in an artist's imagination, and how a burning manuscript, as in Ibsen's *Hedda Gabler*, can indeed be simultaneously the burning of a "child." Surely in *The Garden of Eden*, David's self-concerned creativity or concern with abstractions thwarts or challenges the biological fulfillment of his woman—Hemingway has already told this story in "Cat in the Rain"—and it can readily be seen in such a story how her fulfillment, accomplished in antagonism, might metaphorically be expressed as the burning of his manuscripts. What makes Catherine in *The Garden* interesting—certainly not unique—is her rebellion, her refusal here to accept the cost of David's art.

She is initially one denied fecundity who secondarily becomes one who denies fecundity: she chooses to become a boy, Peter, and she chooses her lesbian alternative to heterosexual love. She then becomes the active killer of the surrogate child, killing the child figuratively when she burns the manuscript. This is made plain in her parting letter to David, when she writes that she feels, by the deed, "worse than hitting someone, a child is the worst I guess although God knows you're not a child—with a car. The thump on the fender or maybe just a small bump and then all the rest of it happening . . . the horror and the guilt. . . . The Frenchwomen screaming *ecrasseuse* even if it was the child's fault" (1, 34, bk. 3, ch. 43, 21–22). I include the manuscript version so that the very minor shifts can be seen. The published version's omission of "although God knows you're not a child" diverts the reader's attention from the fact that in her mind the manuscript has become an extension of David, endowed with his causality, and has run into *her*.

Hemingway, in the manuscript, carefully made the Marita-David relationship one that uniquely upholds the principle of motherhood and fatherhood; and, we must assume, it is Marita's life-concerned interest in motherhood that gives her the ability to supplant Catherine. Marita questions David about his early sexual behavior with his African "fiancée" and the cares they took to avoid pregnancy, and then she says:

> "Can we make love and not care if we make a baby?"
> "Of course," said David.
> "Then let's do it right away," Marita said. (1, 29, bk. 3, ch. 37, 26)

The passage brings back memories of Prudence, the Indian girl who was Nick/Hemingway's earliest sexual partner in the Michigan north woods, who in "Fathers and Sons" had carelessly, eagerly said to him, "Make plenty baby, what the hell" (495). It also opposes Catherine and Marita on what was perhaps the fundamental issue within the love relationships of the manuscript version, the absence or presence of a child in the partnership. Here, after David and Marita make love, she is sure that they have "made the baby." Later, in bed in the dark, their lovemaking again is primarily functional: Marita exclaims, "O I love it so and I love you so, let's be sure and make the baby tonight if we didn't this morning," and, afterward, "We must have, David, this time surely." "I think so, too," he replies. They go on, Marita first:

> "I couldn't feel that way unless we did. I feel as though a whole tree was planted in me."

"I feel as though I love you."

"O I love you so and I love him and everything he does and the miracle he makes."

"I love you." (1, 34, bk. 3, ch. 43, 15)

This exchange is significant for the meaning and resolution of the novel. Marita is focused on David as the way toward the miracle that is made by the divine child, a "miracle" she feels they have together begotten. David's love is not toward the child but toward her. Marita's reconciling love, not a competitive or destructive one like Catherine's, equally worships and supports and participates in the production of the biological child that they must beget and the abstract children of David's brain, the stories he will again, with her support, write. But here, in bed, she is focused on one desire, Motherhood:

"Let's do it one more time to be sure, sure, sure."

"Is this sure?"

"It's so lovely truly sure, David, David my dearest dearest love. I love you so David now please now dearest darling it's so sure and sure and sure."

Sure, David thought. Sure. Nothing is sure. (1, 34, bk. 3, ch. 43, 15–16)

In this early version, "do it" refers explicitly to lovemaking to beget a child, and "sure" is the certainty of conception. In the published novel, as revised, this conversation is reduced to Marita's single remark "I love you, David, and it's so sure now" (235), where the "sure" is made to refer to the now confirmed love. At no point in the Scribners version do David and Marita even mention a child. Toward the end of the first manuscript version, David admits that he could go a long while with Marita without their being married, but Marita's concern is the child:

". . . [married is] better for children."

"I forgot about the children."

"I didn't. That was all I was thinking about yesterday until the fire. I'm sure we started them." (1, 36, bk. 3, ch. 45, 18)

They go on to discuss a hypothetical daughter, her future, her temperament, her training. Marita concludes, "She's having an interesting life already" (1, 36, bk. 3, ch. 45, 18).

The extent to which the absence or presence of the child controls this earliest conception of the novel can be seen in the subplot involving an additional couple, Barbara and Nick, who are fully omitted from the published novel. In this subplot, Barbara Sheldon's infidelity to Nick, Nick's acquiescence under her manipulation of him into what he secretly feels is the image of "some bloody Sodomite" (2, 2, story 1, 5), and her hysteria and perversity are all tied into the hovering theme of childlessness. A conversation between Andy and Nick is revealing:

ANDY: "You should be OK now so she could have a baby."
NICK: "We would have had one always money or not if she could have. It's no use to go into that."
ANDY: "That's rough too."
NICK: "It's a lot more complicated than that."

                              (2, story [2] Redo, insert 3 to 19-1)

In the Catherine-David relationship, Catherine charges David with being sterile and thus the cause of their childlessness; Nick reveals that Barbara's sterility is the cause of theirs. In the original provisional endings for the novel, Hemingway sketches the suicides of *both* women, after experimental infidelities provoked by a boredom carefully related to childlessness, as though to suggest that neither woman is able to forgive herself and survive.

Yes, it is a lot more complicated than that, but the absence or presence of a child is certainly a major and controlling force determining character and action and even sexual inversion in Hemingway's first holograph version of this novel. The theme has been almost totally stripped from the published version, by whatever hand, while it is explicitly the essence of the first holograph account. Marita, in Hemingway's manuscript, is patently the woman to be able to grant David the biological child he lacks with Catherine, whether because of her focus of desire upon the child, her fertility, or her ability to balance David's biological and artistic identities; Catherine, in Hemingway's manuscript, is largely motivated by the presence or absence of a child, and her rage at the trick played upon her is one of the complex forces motivating her attempt to become male, to escape problematic fecundity, to replace biological with imaginative creativity that would manipulate life itself artistically.

Some Hemingway scholars see the published work as the result of an effort to arrive at an editing similar to Hemingway's own, one that places underneath the surface, as the unseen seven-eighths of the iceberg, what is explicit in the early versions—therefore, perhaps, their refusal to respond to Solomon's call to arms. I see Solomon as legitimately provoked by her sense that what remains of the original conception is not one-eighth of an iceberg but far less, and by her lament for the lost great passages and insights of the original. What remains often bewilderingly reaches toward ideas and attitudes and conclusions that have been unacknowledged, if not obliterated, and are hardly implicit in the version we have. Criticism's task should now be to determine whether the tip of the given iceberg, of whosoever's making, is sufficient unto the characters and action it is meant to reveal.

Notes

1. The holograph and typescript materials for *The Garden of Eden* are filed in the Kennedy under the item designations 422 and 422.1–422.9. The vast majority of the holograph manuscript is designated in the collection as Items 422.1 and 422.2, and it is only to materials in these two sets that I make reference in this essay. Throughout the essay, a reference to a holograph quotation will, in parentheses, designate sequentially whether it is item 1 or 2 (of 422), its folder number in the box in which that item is housed, the book and chapter numbers in which it is included, and the page number on which it is to be found. This full reference is necessary, for individual folders often contain separately numbered books and their included chapters. A reference such as (1, 17, bk. 3, ch. 8, 12) would direct one to the 422.1 materials and, within those materials, to folder 17, book 3, chapter 8, page 12. Andy's story is designated "story." Also, occasionally a citation does not follow the usual pattern. In such cases, I have simply transcribed the citation as it is marked on the source.

2. I suggested in "Elephant Hunt in Eden: A Study of New and Old Myths and Other Strange Beasts in Hemingway's Garden" (included in this volume) that David's elephant story, the story he is trying to write throughout *The Garden of Eden*, and finally does write, is *his* ultimate abstract confrontation of the probably lesbian relationship between his mother and her lover and that it finds its physical balance in Catherine's relationship with Marita.

3. Since Jenks has assured us that he worked only with the typescripts and never with the holograph, it might be well to study what typescripts the Kennedy now holds. In an early cataloging of *The Garden of Eden* materials, carried on at the Kennedy Library by Jo August (Hills), four separate typescripts were listed as in the Hemingway collection: (1) a 49-page typescript; (2) a 1,040-page typescript, listed as an "EH Typescript/Manuscript. Heavily pencil-corrected typescript and pencil manuscript"; (3) a partial typescript of the 517-page holograph, including "Book Two, Book Three, Chapters 1–8 and

32–46. Provisional Ending and Story"; and (4) a grouped series (with an unspecified number of pages), each described as "carbon typescript," that comprises book 1, chapters 1 through 28 and 32 through 46; book 2, chapter 1; book 3, chapters 1 through 8; the "provisional ending"; and "Andy's story." A second cataloging of the Kennedy holdings of *The Garden of Eden* manuscripts, apparently carried on later under the auspices of Joan O'Connor, lists, in Box 2, as typescript, a single 36-page chapter from book 2 and, from book 1, chapters 1 through 8 and 32 through 46, as well as the provisional ending to the "story," the total coming to 517 pages. A much more recent cataloguing, carried on by Meagan Desnoyers, lists a "typescript/pencil manuscript," item 422.1, as 1,189 pages. A 460-page typescript, item 422.5, described as "original, triple spaced; pencil corrections, largely typographical, not in EH hand," and typescripts of the "provisional ending" (7 pages) and of the "story" (51 pages) together obviously add up to the 517 pages described in the Hills and O'Connor reports. Also listed is a "photocopy of" a [carbon?] "typescript" of 414 pages. On June 18, 1991, I received by fax from Meagan Desnoyers at the Kennedy the most recent complete new cataloguing of the *Garden of Eden* holdings. It repeats the 1,189-page, 460-page, 414-page, and 517-page described holdings in a more precise, newly ordered listing and adds to these a 62-page typescript described as "photocopy of triple spaced typescript (a carbon?)." Discrepancies among these declared holdings should be noted—though I suspect discrepancies are largely a matter of description—as well as the vast discrepancy between these and the 600-, 800-, and 1,200-page typescripts that Jenks is reputed to have declared he worked with and subsequently mailed to the Kennedy.

4. This inversion has already been expressed in almost the same metaphors in Hemingway's earlier novel *Across the River and Into the Trees* as Renata slips the green emeralds that have passed down matrilinearly in her family—and are coded as a metaphor for feminine reproductive capacity, the family jewels—into Cantwell's pocket.

Works Cited

Burgess, Anthony. "The Joys of a New Marriage." *Life* June 1986: 91–93.

Corn, Charles. "The Fall from Paradise." *San Francisco Chronicle*, 25 May 1986, Book Review section: 1,10.

Doctorow, E. L. "Braver Than We Thought." *New York Times Book Review*, 18 May 1986: 1, 44–45.

Hemingway, Ernest. *The Garden of Eden.* New York: Scribners, 1986.

————. *The Garden of Eden.* Holograph and typescripts. Hemingway Collection, Items 422, 422.1–422.9. Kennedy Library, Boston.

Jenks, Tom. "Editing Hemingway: *The Garden of Eden.*" *Hemingway Review* 7.1 (1987): 30–33.

Jones, Robert B. "Mimesis and Metafiction in Hemingway's *The Garden of Eden*." *Hemingway Review* 7.1 (1987): 2–13.

Josephs, Allen. "In Papa's Garden." *Boston Review* 9.3 (1986): 20–21.

Scafella, Frank. "Clippings from *The Garden of Eden*." *Hemingway Review* 7.1 (1987): 20–29.

Solomon, Barbara Probst. "Hemingway's Fiesta at the Prado." Unpublished manuscript, 1986.

———. "Where's Papa?" *New Republic*, 9 March 1987: 30–34.

Updike, John. "The Sinister Sex." *New Yorker*, 30 June 1986: 85–88.

10

On the Definition
of a Definitive Text
Hemingway

Those of us who could not attend the December 1980 MLA meeting in Houston now read for the first time (in the spring 1981 issue of *Hemingway Notes*) matter that was there voiced, matter that indeed needs extraordinary debate and discussion. In both Michael Reynolds's paper ("Words Killed, Wounded, Missing in Action") and Scott Donaldson's ("The Case of the Vanishing American and Other Puzzlements in Hemingway's Fiction") a strong case is made for "a definitive edition of Hemingway's prose" (Donaldson 19). My admiration for both men is strong, but both articles raise a truly frightening sense of a "purism" that, trying to establish the text on two conflicting bases, may well leave us with an inferior text. Reynolds's article especially is troubling, making ambivalent suggestions: it recommends a close study of existing materials to discover the author's intention (Hurrah!), while at the same time it urges logical bases for ridding the text of apparent confusions (God save us!).

Bryher, in *The Heart to Artemis,* has reported Adrienne Monnier's judgment that "Hemingway will be the best known of you all" and her explanation of the basis of her judgment: "'He cares,' she said, 'for his craft.' (I imagine that she used the word métier.) I then discovered that after a hard day's work and some equally hard drinking, Hemingway went to a printer's shop in the late evening to learn how to set up type so as to know exactly how his manuscripts, to the last comma, would look on the printed page" (213).

We can forget such rare rigor and integrity only at our peril, the peril of critical vanity that we run when we would place our sensibility before Hemingway's when it comes to the question of establishing a definitive text. Analysis and elucidation should be attempts to discover the artist and not to adjust him or accommodate him to our own limited moralities or sense of the rational. Hemingway himself has written, "Many times critics do not understand a work when a writer tries for something he has not attempted before" (qtd. in Breit 58). It is a rare critic who thinks of his or her own limitations, and I am here concerned with the critical tendency to assign to error or absurdity or textual aberration whatever does not fall within our ready apprehension and comprehension.

To challenge an established text, it is not sufficient to have an alternative version in a manuscript in the author's hand, nor is it sufficient to assume that corrections that another unknown editing hand failed to make should have been made, whatever the seeming logic behind the corrections—yet these inadequate tests are urged by Reynolds and Donaldson, respectively. When dealing with a consummate craftsman, whether a Rembrandt or a Hemingway, we owe him more respect than most, as Adrienne Monnier has urged. And in questions of doubt, the artist and his text, as received, are to be preferred before alternative guesses. We have no right, on the basis of *seeming* awkwardness or mystery or obscurity or contradiction, to assume the probability of error—in transcription, typing, typesetting, or whatever. I assume that we are all agreed that after we have done our best to establish a definitive text on the basis of existing correspondence, manuscripts, typescripts, or galleys, in most troubling cases we will still lack any absolute knowledge of the author's final choices. When so faced by enigma in the texts of great writers, it is egocentric to assume that what is there is not what he would have chosen, or that what seems opaque or absurd is necessarily so, and until we can be finally assured that no unrecorded conversation over lunch or unrecorded long-distance telephone call or unseen midnight visit to the press established that text, incorporating or retaining seeming errors, no matter what his intentions were, we really have no right to urge our readings upon posterity. Hemingway was alive and well during long years of his texts in print, and the fact that he, astute as he was, and defensive as he was for the accuracy of a text, chose to ignore such details as Catherine's double nationality and the lost days in the chronology of *The Sun Also Rises* is an argument strongly in favor of their intentionality. It takes far greater temerity, of course, to tamper with a text than to interpret, for the former removes formalized meaning from the world, while the latter still leaves to others the possibility of reassessment or contradiction, yet it is partly on the basis of interpretation that both Reynolds and Donaldson are arguing for a definitive text.

Case in point: Reynolds confronts once again the "impossible chronology" (6) of *The Sun Also Rises*. We surely know enough of Hemingway's art by now not to leap to Reynolds's conclusion that Hemingway "simply made serious mistakes in the chronology which he may have intended to correct but never got around to doing" (6). He continues, "Granting the author license, we shall expect, in the realist tradition, for a week to have seven days" (6). But what has the realist tradition to do with this? Hemingway was writing a symbolic, mythic, and even impressionistic novel where phantom suitcases have as much reality as Cohn's vision of Brett as "absolutely fine and straight" (*Sun Also Rises* 38). One of the major concepts behind the novel is the falsification of reality by the willful or impressed mind: Paris is probably unsatisfying to Cohn because of something he read, and *The Purple Land* becomes a dangerous index to reality for him. People justify their outrages and avoid real responsibilities as they reinterpret reality according to their natures and needs: the peasants' meal is to Mike an "hors d'oeuvre" (157). And time—time is fluid and collapsible. Reynolds writes, "Either Hemingway made serious mistakes in dating with the first draft, mistakes he intended to correct, or he was intentionally collapsing time for artistic reasons. We need to know which tack to take. The chronology can be straightened out without serious revision. If the apparent mistakes are intentional, then we have to read the novel with greater care, for Hemingway is playing a more subtle time game than we have realized" (6).

Of course he is! And how can one read Hemingway over the years without being reinformed a thousand times that when we are most subtle, he is subtler still? The clue is blatant: "Wonderful how one loses track of the days up here in the mountains," says Harris (*Sun Also Rises* 127). But Reynolds continues his discussion of the time question, "I don't have the answer, but an answer is possible. All it takes is a scholar with the patience to collate the manuscript, typescripts, and galleys, along with all the letters" (6). No! That is certainly not enough. The collation will never by itself supply the justification for an established text—the text by itself may—nor is patience a substitute for the kind of attention necessary to fine reading.

Reynolds's recommendations seek to establish logic where the reader falters. Reynolds acknowledges that Hemingway's one use of Bill

Grundy (for Bill Gorton) may, in fact, be intentional, but he goes on, "Perhaps it is, but an equally good argument can be made for it as erratum" (5). But an equally good argument, when considering alteration of a received text, is simply not good enough. He cites other "mistakes": when Mike Campbell says he would like to "go with Bill to the Ledoux fight, and begs off—"but I can't go. I had a date with this thing here. I say, Brett, do get a new hat" (*Sun Also Rises* 79)—Reynolds concludes, "The past tense makes the sentence absurd" (5). Not at all. The past tense enables Hemingway to say more than he could have said with the simple present. What he is saying is I *had* a date, if indeed I still do, given Brett's unpredictability and that of our relationship. The very juxtaposition of the "hat" reference lets us know that Campbell is focused upon Brett's ready alternatives, specifically the donor of that hat ("chap bought it for me" [79]), who may be Robert Cohn. The past tense may not, therefore, necessarily be due to "bad proof reading" (Reynolds 5), whatever the manuscript says, and we may be dealing with a careful authorial revision of that initial manuscript choice. My concern here is not that I may be right and Reynolds wrong in this, but rather that the past tense, whether chosen by Hemingway or not, is not "absurd"—that the test of whether something seems absurd or not is a false test, limited as it is to what a reader at a given time may see or not see in a work of art.

Case in point: Donaldson sees the confused Scotch/English identity of Catherine in *A Farewell to Arms* as probably an overlooked error (19). I think it would take extraordinary condescension toward the creative process of any author to believe that four separate and glaring enunciations of the "split" identity could be accidental, and I believe that there is a relatively simple explanation of this detailed and elaborate confusion. The novel, like other works by Hemingway, is a study of love and war or love in war, so that he may finely analyze the dynamics of opposition and synthesis, dichotomy and dualism, operating in the midst of rival forces urging synthesis and fusion. Throughout the novel, Catherine is an examplar of fusion and recommends the overthrow of personal boundaries and the denial of a fixed position of identity—abdications for which "retreat" and "breakthrough" and Bonello's anarchy are variants on a sociopolitical level. Arguing as she does that "we really are the same one" (Hemingway, *Farewell to Arms* 139) and "there isn't any me" (115), she is wisely presented by Hemingway as without real identity, and the external sign of this is her indeterminate nationality.

However, Donaldson offers the "confusion" of Catherine's ambivalent Scotch/English identity as an example of probable "errata in Hemingway's fiction" (19) and goes on to conclude, "Hemingway was occasionally careless about details, so that his image as a meticulous, eternally vigilant craftsman requires some modification" (19). Whoa! To require the reduction of a reputation because the reader cannot see intention strikes me as among the more terrible injustices.

If we are to extend the approach to errata used by Reynolds and Donaldson, we would end up forcing Hemingway's deliberate and painstakingly confused pronoun references into disastrous agreement. Hemingway gets more mileage out of deliberately obfuscated pronoun reference than any author yet. There is a passage in *Green Hills of Africa:*

> "That's a hell of a literary anecdote," Pop said. "Who's Joyce?"
> "Wonderful guy," I said. "Wrote *Ulysses.*"
> "Homer wrote Ulysses," Pop said.
> "Who wrote *Aeschylus?*"
> "Homer," said Pop. "Don't try to trap me." (195–96)

I can imagine a host of dedicated purists trying to shift the italicization from Aeschylus to Ulysses, thereby obliterating one of the most important aesthetic statements Hemingway makes in that book. In *Across the River and into the Trees*, Hemingway's whole philosophy of the importance of error and his attitude toward it as a structural device can best be seen when he allows Colonel Cantwell to mistake his driver Jackson for Burnham. The meaning of the novel and the significance of its title are held in that simple "mistake."

When Hemingway says that every part of his book depends on every other part, he deserves to be taken seriously; when Max Perkins reassures Hemingway that he would never ask him to change anything "unless it simply had to be done" (qtd. in Reynolds 7), we should listen with care; and when Hemingway writes to Perkins urging, "if someone else wanted to eliminate parts of his writing, then let them sign it as well,"[1] we should so treat all our alterations of text. That these three quotations are taken from Reynolds's article attests to his honesty and care. My point is that even such care must be more scrupulous. When he says that there are "several mistakes in the final books" (Reynolds 5), I suspect that apart from minimal typos there are no "mistakes," not of the sort he has detailed. Throughout all of Hemingway's works, from the first work to the last, there are incongruities, contradictions, seeming omissions, and seeming errors—what might be called "mistakes" if we are presumptuous enough to assume that we are in control of all of

Hemingway's meanings and techniques. But I am convinced that in almost every case where a problem exists—the sixth seat bought for the bullfight (the only way Hemingway acknowledges the unseen presence of Hadley); the lost days at Burguete; the carefully scrambled Scotch-Englishness of Catherine; the switching of the "stagged trousers" and the variation in the number of characters in "The Light of the World" (another of Scott Donaldson's concerns); or the strange alteration of four rhinos to three that takes place on a single page in *Green Hills*—the errors are of a sort that really could not have been missed by Hemingway, not by the Hemingway we know, and that is a far greater argument for leaving them intact than is our own confusion: we have not been obsessed with his manuscript at the level that he was, nor have I yet discerned in any of us a critical intelligence as rigorous and fine as his.

NOTE

1. This is Reynolds's (7) paraphrase from a March 11, 1929, letter.

WORKS CITED

Bryher [Annie Winifred Ellerman]. *The Heart to Artemis*. New York: Harcourt, Brace & World, 1962.

Donaldson, Scott. "The Case of the Vanishing American and Other Puzzlements in Hemingway's Fiction." *Hemingway Notes* 6.2 (1981): 19.

Hemingway, Ernest. *A Farewell to Arms*. 1929. New York: Scribners, 1969.

———. *Green Hills of Africa*. 1935. New York: Scribners, 1963.

———. "Success, It's Wonderful." Harvey Breit, ed., *New York Times Book Review*, 3 December 1950: 58.

———. *The Sun Also Rises*. 1926. New York: Scribners, 1954.

Reynolds, Michael S. "Words, Killed, Wounded, Missing in Action." *Hemingway Notes* 6.2 (1981): 6.

11

Dubliners in Michigan
Joyce's Presence in Hemingway's In Our Time

At the May 1982 Hemingway Conference in Boston, I presented a paper detailing the depth and extent of the Joyce-Hemingway relation and suggesting several ways in which the effects of Hemingway's enduring admiration for and sustained reading of Joyce could be recognized in patterns and metaphors in his prose (Gajdusek, "Hemingway and Joyce"). As I tried to show, the literary influence, which is considerable, rests firmly upon a personal friendship of greater depth and dimension than is generally understood. There is good evidence that Hemingway almost uniquely among his contemporaries recognized Joyce's techniques and early put them to use. Not only did Hemingway read, well understand, and promote Joyce's work, he also hailed Joyce as the one contemporary he truly respected. This respect and appreciation, greater than he gave to any other writer, lasted throughout his lifetime. Joyce, similarly, went on record as acknowledging a deep appreciation of what Hemingway was doing, which he said few people understood (Ellmann 708). (In 1984, I published my monograph *Hemingway and Joyce: A Study in Debt and Payment*, reprinted in this volume, that details the professional relation of the two men.) Here, however, I would like to uniquely study the ways in which Hemingway's first book of short stories, *In Our Time*, recapitulates themes, metaphors, and patterns of Joyce's first book of short stories, *Dubliners*.

Hemingway early "prepared a list of the sixteen titles in fiction which he 'would rather read again for the first time than be assured of a million-dollar annual income'" (Baker 175). This predominantly French and Russian list, which included only two American, two English, and three Irish works, notably included *Dubliners*. He later extended the list, adding *A Portrait of the Artist as a Young Man* and *Ulysses*, but he never lapsed in his respect for *Dubliners*, partly because it was one of the seminal sources of his vision. Certainly, internal evidence in these stories suggests this to be the case.

Preeminently, Joyce's stories in *Dubliners* are concerned to exemplify psychic split and to suggest therapeutic if feared integrations. It is not incidental thematic similarity between these stories and those of *In Our Time* that I affirm, but rather close and deliberate parallelisms. I am not trying to say that Hemingway and Joyce share a style: they do not, but they do share many aspects of technique, and they approach their dissimilar plights and beliefs with similar terminology, strategy, and ritual.

If there is an emphatic thematic and stylistic congruence between the two works, it is first important to note the many ways in which Joyce and Hemingway are thematically unlike. Joyce's *Dubliners* stories are provincially Irish while Hemingway is broadly cosmopolitan. Joyce studies suburban or urban decadence and moral violence; Hemingway, who unlike Joyce had been in the war and had experienced a wounding as well as a crime reporter's beat in Kansas City, the boxing gymnasiums of Chicago, the bullfights of Spain, and probably the hobo jungles of northern Michigan, focuses mostly on itinerant or rootless protagonists who may confront violent death ("The Killers") or unprovoked attack ("The Battler"). Joyce's work ends with exile never or yet to be achieved for his frustrated Dubliners; Hemingway's characters have largely already broken away from their homes and nations. "On the Quai at Smyrna," which Hemingway chose to place as the introductory piece to *In Our Time* in 1930, is not incidentally a study of uprooted people being violently driven from their homeland; they either flee or die, and they frequently die fleeing.[1] Joyce focuses on a world that, however corrupt, was home in his imagination because he knew that whatever relief was to be had would have to be at last socially achieved between husbands and wives and among friends and acquaintances. His work is therefore more filled with the gossip and mundane trivia that are the cock that is owed to Aesculapius, the dance of social man in his milieu. Hemingway's Michigan landscape is more bleak, for it posits relief achieved only in nature at last, in separation from wives, friends, and the social world.[2] Joyce was locked into his culture; Hemingway, in almost atavistic regression, was seeking ways out of his. Hemingway's dislocated soldiers, boxers, revolutionists, jockeys, and expatriates function in relation to foreign or unsupportive environments—even his husbands and wives, who are out of phase (season) with one another, are out of touch with the social or natural worlds around them. In Joyce's world, whatever the conflict and however seemingly disenfranchised the people, Eveline, Little Chandler, Farrington, James Duffy, and even Father Flynn are in the milieu that is their own, that they know, and that accords them advantages, however limited, by virtue of that association. Nick Adams remains the single obsessive presence in Hemingway's work; Joyce's stories—unless the boy of the first three stories is to be taken as a projection of one consciousness—move through a continually changing gallery of Dubliners. There are, of course, innumerable other ways in which the stories of the two men represent two very different sensibilities and beliefs.

But what is of interest to the Hemingway scholar is, indeed, the extent to which the concerns of Hemingway and Joyce are shared, the extent to which their visions reinforce one another. Exile, escape from one's society, or movement toward expatriation from it appear as central themes in most of their stories. Most of them record repressed or real violence, and in almost all works by both writers the focus is on men who are ineffectual, defeated, or lacking in the control they ought to have; in many, fathers are absent or ineffective. The majority of the male protagonists refuse to submit to a world where women and their needs dominate, resent such submission and express fear of women, or sacrifice themselves to women. Many stories record masculine losses and descent for the sake of women. The fear of a dominating mother or maternity is general in both works. Two men together or in league against women, or men alone, or groups of men searching for a lost spiritual or psychic wholeness, populate both books. The portraits of moral failures are largely focused on men, and several of the stories show men attempting to teach one another. Almost all stories by both writers offer portraits of flawed protagonists. In both works competition or competitiveness is high, and the major failure of protagonists in both is a failure to face, admit, or understand reality.[3] The self-destructive or suicidal tendency is greater in Hemingway's work, but it persists in several Joyce stories. Characters in both works struggle to survive in the midst of marked deprivation, and enclosures readily become traps in the work of both men. This is but a very partial list of shared attitudes, but it may begin to indicate the basis for reciprocity and correspondence between the two.

One of the major failures of Hemingway criticism—not of Joyce criticism—is to have looked at such characteristics and to have indicted the author as possessor of the attitudes. Not only is *In Our Time* a work never remotely duplicated in the Hemingway canon, but it also is a work of art, not a diary. Perhaps only Nick of "Big Two-Hearted River" is meant to be admired, as perhaps only the Gabriel of the very end of "The Dead" is to be. The stories generally meticulously record the failures of men; they do not labor to create pity for them. If men are victims, they are also victimizers. Hemingway is not arguing a position; he is, as an historian, the reporter unafraid of facts, making a statement about "our time"—where we "are at." The remedy that he will suggest for this lamentable state he begins to develop in "Big Two-Hearted River" and elaborately develops in all the novels that follow. The unindividuated consciousness of life-shy males is due to their failure to accept their other side, the feminine side of their own natures, death as well as life, love as well as idealism, and this fact he elaborates in great detail in his later work. But that is another matter. *In Our Time* records the condition of the world as he sees it, and that was very much the way Joyce saw it.

The organization of Hemingway's stories is complex and tight. The foreshortened introductory "On the Quai at Smyrna" was only added in 1930, apparently to more perfectly balance the structure of the total work. It seems surely only half a work. Only two other stories, central stories in the group—"A Very Short Story" and "The Revolutionist"— are also radically truncated, and both are, unlike the other stories, extended vignettes. It is structurally of interest that these two equally embrace the middle story of the fifteen, "Soldier's Home," which has seven stories on either side of it (if we consider "Big Two-Hearted River" I and II as one story), and both are about man caught in cycles and victim of them. The pivotal story, "Soldier's Home," is about a man at a point of rest, of stasis, apparently unable to choose direction between masculine and feminine alternatives. Across the street are the attractive girls whom he does not want "badly enough" (*Short Stories* 148) and in the home is the oppressive, dominating mother, who manages her husband and creates nausea in her son; beyond the home is the world of a man's work that the boy does not want to enter, and beyond that world, he is told, is "His Kingdom"—but Krebs says he is not "in His Kingdom" (151). It is of interest that the immediately preceding story, "A Very Short Story," is a portrait of a man victimized through having chosen the feminine direction: the nurse a soldier loves betrays his love, and "a short time after he contracted gonorrhea from a sales girl in a loop department store while riding in a taxicab" (*Short Stories* 142). The absoluteness of the boy's faith for the girl, Luz (light)—who "believed in him absolutely" (142)—is shattered by her cyclical infidelity—her involvement with one man after another means she is a victim of cycles—and he becomes victim of the bridge he has made to a feminine world of casual encounters. The phallus that has done the bridging suffers a species of destruction, gonorrhea, contracted in a taxi (on wheels) when he relates to a girl whose job is one of casual mercantile public contacts and exchanges in a "loop [cycle] department store." The following, ninth, story, "The Revolutionist," is a portrait of a boy equally victimized by men who use him to help establish their revolutionary idealisms. The boy's belief, like that of the soldier in "A Very Short Story," is absolute—"he believed altogether" (*Short Stories* 157)—yet his delights in art, in seeing, and in thinking are all shown to be useless to protect him from the larger external forces that use him. This boy, whose misguided idealism leads him to carry "reproductions" of paintings in September, the ninth month, and who "loved the mountains" (158) in the fall, is caught in ambiguities he does not see and is used by forces to ends not his own. The two stories, the seventh and the ninth, study man as victim of the revolutionary cycles implicit in either direction a man might choose, and Krebs's dilemma in "Soldier's Home" makes that story central, the pivotal story between two apparently opposite but related destructive forces. If we note that the first story, "On the Quai at Smyrna," is about language and about men becoming victims of but surviving through their linguistic strategies, and if we note that the middle stories are about revolution, about men being caught in the prison of cycles, we can speculate that Hemingway deliberately divided his volume with "Soldier's Home." He so gives us the two aborted and destructive halves of the antinomies he studies (word and cycle, or abstractions and realities) in radical and studied separation so that he may ultimately bring them therapeutically together as the systole-diastole of the two-chambered heart that he heals in his composite last story. The six stories that precede "A Very Short Story" have as protagonists men without women, or men radically separated or separating from women; the four stories that follow "The Revolutionist" are focused on married husbands, and in three of them pregnancy or the lack of it is the problem. This organization and movement are very much those of the stories in Joyce's *Dubliners*, and it is not difficult to see that Hemingway, almost concomitantly with his association with Joyce, began to use similar structure and strategy.

A basic thematic opposition that Joyce uses throughout *Dubliners* underlies the progression of the stories. In the first story of Joyce's collection we are given the inheriting sisters, one of whom has trodden-down heels (signifying an association with what is below) and a skirt that is clumsily hooked behind. The boy who lost his spiritual father is revolted by details of sensuality—the priest's ugly mouth—and unable to accept the feminine world, associated for him with the lower chambers and with what is behind and beneath. Seemingly he lacks a physical father as well. He is offered "stirabout" by his aunt, and "cream" crackers by one of the sisters in this world of cycles where there are ashes in the grate but no fire. The story offers no suggestion that this boy without men is able to come to terms with women.

In "Araby," the boy abstractly yearns for his mystical vision of love and moves ecstatically about in attic rooms high above the streets below. His vision is in response to Mangan's sister, who lives in the areaway below, ambivalently spiritual-worldly, and who confronts him from behind the separating railings. Not free to go to Araby herself, she can only turn a bracelet "round and round" her wrist (*Dubliners* 32). The vulgar and sensual bazaar the boy finally goes to for the girl's sake is one that materializes the spiritual. Hugh Kenner sees that great hall—albeit "like . . . a church after a service"—as "a female symbol, entered at last; and it contains sparse goods, the clink of money, and tittering banalities" (43).

In "Eveline," the question is whether Frank, the adventuring young voyager, can reach across the railings to bring animal-faced Eveline, tied to dirty dusty Dublin and the promise to her mother, to that place of good airs, Buenos Aires. He has taken her to see *The Bohemian Girl* ("I dreamt that I dwelt in marble halls") but cannot effect her rescue from the corruptible earth. In "After the Race," the Irish protagonist, Jimmy Doyle, sits with the Hungarian, Villona, in the back seat of the light and graceful racing car that is masterfully controlled by the technique and expertise of the French craftsmen, but as Jimmy strains forward to catch what he can of the wit and wisdom of those technicians who sit in front, Villona keeps up a deep bass hum behind. Jimmy is an Irish provincial son of a shrewd Irish merchant who yearns to but cannot escape his origin or get beyond his mercantile base. In "The Boarding House," the feared but necessary rapprochement with the feminine finally occurs. The question is how to get Bob Doran down from his high attic room to marry the perverse madonna that is Polly; in the last scene, compelled by her mother, Mrs. Mooney, the butcher's daughter, he descends to confront the mother below as Polly's physically intimidating brother comes up from the pantry carrying two bottles of Bass.

Bob longs to "ascend through the roof and fly away to another country" (*Dubliners* 67–68), but he is freighted with responsibility for the over-tures he has made toward Polly and is drawn down towards the earth and the flesh. Little Chandler in "A Little Cloud" is held to the earth and an undesired marriage by the weight of the screaming child in his arms while he yearns for flight to Paris, poetry, and immortality, something "higher than mere tawdry journalism" (*Dubliners* 80). In "Counterparts," Mr. Alleyn, described almost wholly as a head resting upon a pile of papers, maintains authority in his office from upstairs while shouting disembodied orders down through a speaking tube to physical, gross Farrington, who lurches about below. Farrington sees his dreams of challenge and fulfillment frustrated by his bullying wife and his five children. I need not elaborate further these patterns, which insistently unify Joyce's stories. Upper realms, dreams, ideals, and spiritual desires are separated from and unable to be reconciled with their cycling lower-worldly antitheses, just as Gabriel in "The Dead" has not been able to come to terms with Gretta and her origins in the western counties. My point is that Hemingway, in reading these patterns, was instinctively and immediately responsive to their psychic structure, which answered similar needs of his own.

Hemingway's protagonists also, like the boy in "The Sisters" and "An Encounter," or like Stephen in *Ulysses*, often have the need to search for a surrogate father because their own father's cowardice or life-renunciatory aesthetic makes him unsuitable. The father we see in Hemingway's first stories—whether "Indian Camp," "The Doctor and the Doctor's Wife," or "The Three-Day Blow"—is almost irreparably damaged in his son's eyes, yet his son cannot deny him. This son also, like Stephen in *A Portrait* and in *Ulysses*, is in a troubled relationship with women. He is frightened by the potentially destructive omnivo-rousness of sex and the devouring aspects of the Great Mother, whose first appearance to him in Hemingway's stories—in "The Doctor and the Doctor's Wife"—is exactly like that of Molly Bloom in *Ulysses* for Stephen, as a presence behind a drawn blind.

At the beginning of *Ulysses*, priggish Stephen takes part in the arid philosophical vanity of the Martello tower, where he lives in warring harmony with his brother spirit, Buck Mulligan; but he is led to descend that tower and to compromise himself in a journey across the teeming city. At the end, he will urinate with his surrogate father in the garden below the window behind which lies sensual Molly, whose force is like that of a great vortex. How to separate Stephen from Buck and effect this necessary new synthesis is Joyce's problem and strategy. Whether it is Stephen, who must abandon the Jesuit fathers to accept in profane joy a girl wading in the waters as "Heavenly God" (*Portrait* 171) or Frank, Bob, Gabriel, or other Joyce protagonists who must learn to lean across front seats, reach across railings, or leap over the wall of egocentric ascetic idealism to grasp sensual life, or living process, the dynamics are the same: masculine dualisms are contrasted with feared but redemptive integrations, and specious immortalities tied to the spirit and vision— Araby, Jesuitical Catholicism, masculine talk, and the written word— learn to adapt and yield ultimately to vital integrations that are allied with love and death, whether called Gretta or Anna Livia. Buck and Stephen, Shem and Shaun, Corley and Lenehan, Gallagher and Little Chandler are masculine pairs searching for truly creative synthesis.

As originally published, story by story the organization and thematic movement of *Dubliners* and *In Our Time* are strikingly similar. There are fifteen *Dubliners* stories; there are fifteen *In Our Time* stories. "Big Two-Hearted River II" is divided from "Big Two-Hearted River I" by a vignette, "Chapter XV," surely to emphasize its independence and to so make it the fifteenth story. The first few *Dubliners* stories, like those of *In Our Time*, record male isolation or male friendships that are close and defensive though undergoing destruction and disenchantment. Only further in Joyce's series of stories do we find the boy of the early stories—grown at last into Bob Doran of "The Boarding House" or Frank of "Eveline"—descending the stairs or reaching over the railings to try to seize the girl who earlier, in "Araby," was only a visual and mental delight. The boy of "Araby" pursues and is dominated by the image of Mangan's sister, and she exists for him on the other side of the railings he makes no effort to cross. In "Two Gallants," Corley crosses "the chains" to meet his girl, while Lenehan, fearful of such dangerous encounters, remains on the safe side. The moral of "Two Gallants" concerns the girl's surviving and getting the benefits from life without having to step over those dividing chains, and "A Little Cloud" records the cost of the feared rapprochement. Only gradually does Joyce build to a story like "The Dead," which equates death with a new sort of life, a creative victory achieved as Gabriel learns to yield to death through empathy and for the sake of Gretta, as did Michel Furey—and to destroy ego with compassion/acknowledgment of the feminine world.

The organization of Hemingway's *In Our Time* stories (not including "On the Quai at Smyrna")[4] is thematically and structurally parallel to the progression that Joyce developed in *Dubliners*. Certainly it was not Hemingway's intention, in accepting and extending Joyce's vision and progression, to closely duplicate stories within new situations and plots. It was enough to establish the same general outlines and progressions within his own beliefs and forms. Nevertheless, this led to a series of remarkable correspondences.

In "Indian Camp," it is almost with desperation that the boy—who has witnessed his own father's failures of imagination and compassion, and who has seen the death of a father when implicated in the childbirth process of the mother—affirms alliance with the rising sun and with immortality[5]: he still remains under the father's influence, however jeopardized that image. This first story is a close thematic parallel to "The Sisters," Joyce's first story, in which the boy, having lost his spiritual father, first to moral disintegration and decay and then to death, still cannot bring himself to enter into alternative communion with the inheriting sisters. In the second story of In Our Time, "The Doctor and the Doctor's Wife," the son again chooses the direction of and for the father, however overtly masturbatory, suicidal, and dangerous may be the gun that father fondles, and he refuses the request of the mother that he come to her. Joyce's second story, "An Encounter," similarly records the disenchantment a boy comes to feel toward a surrogate father figure whose masturbation creates fear in and signals danger for the boy. In Hemingway's third story, "The End of Something," the boy cuts himself off from his girl, choosing instead Bill. The dangers that the alliance with Marjorie mean are unspoken until the fourth story, "The Three-Day Blow," but are described in the context of a boy's fears of sexual challenge and reduction and the ruins that remain where whirling (cycling) saws had once reduced potent logs. The sense of the boy's entrapment rises with the rising of the moon, even as does Bob Doran's as Mrs. Mooney gains control in Joyce's "The Boarding House." Joyce's third story, "Araby," is similarly a story of youth's painful exposure to and implicit rejection of and by the feminine world he has been courting, and the fourth story, "Eveline," records, like Hemingway's "The End of Something," the broken bond with the feminine. These opening stories are strikingly thematically parallel.

Hemingway's fourth story, "The Three-Day Blow," studies the artificial masculine alternatives to the dangerous bond with the feminine: these alternatives are talk based on drinking daddy's spirits, literary gossip, fictional camaraderie with the heroes of sport or literature, and the attempt to place an imaginary sword on edge between two forest lovers. And it is all vanity. Hemingway's "The Three-Day Blow" and Joyce's next (fifth) story, "After the Race," are remarkably similar studies of men without women, vain young artists at work trying to establish a strategy of survival without recourse to native materials, and both have been preceded by stories—"The End of Something" and "Eveline"—where the native materials, Marjorie and Eveline, have led to disenchantment and disillusion.[6] Nick Adams of "The Three-Day Blow" fears that the device of the sword on edge to separate the forest lovers is unrealistic, for it could not always stay on edge, and when it fell, they "could roll right over it" (*Short Stories* 118). But Nick of "The Three-Day Blow" is like the priggish ascetic young men of Joyce's stories who adolescently dream of a self-sufficient world of male camaraderie based on devices of masculine erection that effectively prevent cycle. The metaphor of the sword that must be kept on edge reveals Hemingway's play: it is a child's vanity to dream of an eternal erection, as it is vain to conceive of life in terms of polarities that will never meet. Masculine and feminine, life and death, form and substance, consciousness and unconsciousness—out of the mingling of these come love and life itself, vision and wisdom, art, and the individuated psyche. Before the story ends, Hemingway insists that we acknowledge Nick's almost unconscious apostasy, the other side of the boy that desires the "roll" he fears and looks forward to reversing an established isolation and plan with a return to the turning girl. How to keep the idealism that is based on psychic split and active polarities and yet bring the lovers together in their love becomes Hemingway's problem[7]—it is Joyce's problem in "Araby"—and it is the central problem in Hemingway because his idealism and his passion as a lover are so pure. Neither would he adulterate.

Going further in *In Our Time*, the reader discovers an older Nick, as, going further in *Dubliners*, he discovers an older protagonist, and what were initially easy adolescent avoidances become desperate life-avoiding strategies. In "The Battler," the dangers of synthesis, the destructive incest gossip that surrounded the Battler when he married, have in part created the alienation and estrangement that have led to the increasingly perverse relation between life-alienated males—Nick and Bill at another remove in time. "The Battler," next after "The Three-Day Blow," where the boys do without girls, studies the perversity of an exclusive male bond carried on into adulthood and carefully duplicates the similar perverse dependencies of Corley and Lenehan of Joyce's next story, "Two Gallants." Corley, of Joyce's story, having played the "Mug's game" (*Dubliners* 53) of sexual reciprocity, is now the "base betrayer" (53) who gets something from a woman for nothing. The conversation between Corley and Lenehan is very much like that between Nick and Bill of Hemingway's "The Three-Day Blow." Bill is, like Lenehan, the less experienced one who is reasonably fastidious in his contacts with women, one who has a strong sense of the dangers of fertility (wetness).[8] The talk between Corley and Lenehan is of getting a girl in "the family way" (51) and therefore of the need to be "up to the dodge" (51). This conversation is about contraception, and Lenehan's "light waterproof" (50) is a contraceptive metaphor. In "The Three-Day Blow," the need for keeping out of the rain under "rubber blankets" immediately follows Bill's attempt to replace water with spirits and precedes his attempt to dry out Nick's wet shoes; his accompanying remark, "It's getting too late to go around without socks" (Hemingway, *Short Stories* 116), includes an ancient "army" euphemism for sex without contraception. Their conversation focuses on the unstated dangers of accidental pregnancy that might bring Nick into an entrapping marriage with Marge, and, as Bill says, "once a man's married he's absolutely bitched. . . . He's done for" (122). The Corley-Lenehan and Nick-Bill conversations are radically related. Such patterns establish Hemingway's fourth story, "The Three-Day Blow," together with "The Battler," his fifth story, as thematically and structurally related to Joyce's sixth and seventh stories, "Two Gallants" and "The Boarding House."

Joyce's "The Boarding House" also has radical correspondences with Hemingway's seventh story, "Soldier's Home." It looks at the entrapment-descent of a young man within a homelike environment dominated by a motherly woman, Mrs. Mooney, and her seductive daughter, Polly. Hemingway's story similarly records the entrapment of Krebs within his home, presided over by his dominant mother, where his sister, like Polly, is apparently the one seductive force keeping him there. The father in both stories is an ineffectual absent presence. Krebs, who does not want any "consequences," is very like Bob Doran, who also fears them but is nevertheless snared.

There are also firm associations between "Soldier's Home" and a later Joyce story, his eleventh, "A Painful Case." The protagonists of both are fiercely determined not to get involved with women. In Hemingway's work, Krebs "did not want any consequences ever again" (*Short Stories* 147)—"the world [the girls] were in was not the world he was in" (148)—and these are certainly the attitudes of Mr. James Duffy of Joyce's story. At one moment in "Soldier's Home," "Krebs looked at the bacon fat hardening on his plate" (151), and in Joyce's story, Mr. Duffy watches as "the cabbage began to deposit a cold white grease on his plate" (*Dubliners* 113). Elsewhere in the same stories Krebs "propped [his newspaper] against the water pitcher" (Hemingway, *Short Stories* 149), and Joyce writes that James Duffy "had propped [his newspaper] against the water-carafe" (*Dubliners* 112). Hemingway, surely trying to impress Joyce as an able student, went him one better: the paper that Krebs's water pitcher supports is the *Star*, and it is additionally steadied by "his cereal dish . . . so he could read while he ate" (*Short Stories* 149). Hemingway had probably been impressed that Joyce had given Mr. Duffy "corned beef[9] and cabbage" for his meal, for Joyce's corned beef is a metaphoric equivalent for the balances created by Hemingway's cereal and *Star*, and reading while eating. Such metaphoric play, the play of poets and artists, is readily understood by Joyce readers, who are alert to what Joyce does as he lets water stabilize paper. Water, which Joyce has used in alliance with fertility, life, and femininity, is used to prop up paper and words, which are used in alliance with abstractness, mentality, and masculinity—this in a story about a sensual woman who tries to enter and give a base to the life of an abstract ascetic man. The synthesis of feminine (corn: Ceres) and masculine (beef)[10] elements that he has Duffy eat is a profound irony. Hemingway scholars should be no less alert to Hemingway's poetry: when Krebs lets water support the *Star*, he reinforces, like Joyce, supernal idealism with its rhythmic fertile base. The irony is that cereal speaks of the feminine cyclical reinforcement of abstractions, a synthesis that Krebs, in this story, cannot make. Hemingway's tomboy sister, who plays indoor baseball, seems the only woman to manifest synthesis (reconciling masculine-feminine and inside and out) in a town filled with girls who are all of "a pattern." In Joyce's story, Mrs. Sinico, whose name braces the "i" of identity with the root sources of syn/thesis and co/operation—Joyce's wordplay with names is evident throughout *Dubliners*—suggests that she with Mr. Duffy might create happiness; but he, in his austerity, sees her as allied with sin and austerely draws back and writes in his journal that "a friendship between man and woman is impossible because there must be sexual intercourse" (112). She subsequently dies of injuries received from the Kingstown train while "attempting to cross the line" (113). Close readers of Joyce might be able to suspect that this victim of patriarchal authority dies of injuries to the head and right side.[11]

Joyce's eighth story, "A Little Cloud," seems to find its extraordinarily parallel recasting in Hemingway's "Cross-Country Snow"—both Nick and Little Chandler are portraits of married protagonists who suffer from the fact of fatherhood and childbirth, while they yearn towards the ideal of a free existence that is based on male camaraderie and conversation and is related to an expertise practiced at heights or distances (the Austrian Alps or Paris) and under absolute conditions. Joyce's tenth and eleventh stories, "Clay" and "A Painful Case," record masculine desire to prohibit and reluctance to accept the descent into life and its cycles, and Hemingway's parallel tenth and eleventh stories, "Cat in the Rain" and "Out of Season," respectively record the same desire and reluctance. "Clay," like "Cat in the Rain," focuses sympathetically on the woman who is victim of masculine, sterilizing dichotomies. When Maria's hand instinctively would choose the earth, clay, in the house of one of two warring antithetical brothers, her hand is redirected and given the choice prepared for her, a prayer book; a convent is prophesied for her within the year. Obviously, the sterilization of the woman whose instinctive nature moves her toward nature is the masculine answer to feminine desire for the earth. This is patently the theme of "Cat in the Rain." The parallelism between the stories of *Dubliners* and *In Our Time* is so distinct that we could argue that "My Old Man" holds its place penultimately preceding the two "Big Two-Hearted River" stories in Hemingway's work in order to balance perfectly the same thematic order in *Dubliners*, where "Grace," a story detailing the final emptiness of the attempt to believe in the spiritual father, precedes "The Dead," which finally resolves the series. "My Old Man" ultimately removes the father as the basis of belief: the last words are, "Seems like when they get started they don't leave a guy nothing" (Hemingway, *Short Stories* 205). This, I propose, is the meaning of Joyce's "Grace," where the spiritual father becomes meaningless.

"Big Two-Hearted River" is an exercise in psychic therapy, probably the greatest story of its kind. I suspect it goes beyond "The Dead" in its total achievement—though both are victories of a very great order—precisely because it ministers to more of human life. "The Dead" teaches us how, through personal metaphoric death, as ego yields to compassion, and as self-justification yields to empathic recognition of otherness, there is a vital rebirth. It details the creative vitalization attendant upon self-transcendence. It also teaches that as Gabriel accepts the reality of the past, as he empathically enters into sympathy with the sleeping Gretta and what she must have felt, and as he understands in part what the lost Michael Furey must have known, he as an artist begins to create, and he as a human being begins to be integral, whole, and able perhaps to love.

"Big Two-Hearted River" intricately, detail by detail, attempts to heal the dichotomized self (which has suffered the death of one half of itself to the natural external world), binding together, putting together what remains of the internal world with the external world, which is the restorer or replenishing source of the lost emotional-unconscious self. The conscious self enters into creative wholeness through a systematic confrontation with its own shadow in a landscape where top and root, light and shadow, body and spirit, flow and fixity, right and left, up and down, seen and unseen, self and the not-self are joined. As Nick enters empathically into the tension of the trout that he watches, which he adjusts to his own inner world through the delicate relations he establishes between line and circle, linear cyclical rod and reel, he grows whole again. Similarly, as Nick recognizes second growth after a fire and relates the bird overhead to its shadow beneath, the high branches of the pine to its past, the fallen circle of pine needles at its base, now larger than the shadow the distant top branches can cast, he learns (like Hart Crane's bridge celebrator) to integrate past and present, life and death, the two poles of conscious and unconscious life that have been dangerously sundered. But the story is, on another level, an Emersonian nature essay; it tells us in human and realistic terms something that we could not readily accept were it baldly stated: that there are, there truly are, mystical relations between one's inner being, and the envelope that encloses one, that one is part of the other, that to harness a physical power, to use a physical craft or technique, to move into action at all, is to set in motion and revitalize an inner world, that we are coextensive with all our actions and our surroundings and that only in such utter wholeness are we truly whole. Hemingway's empathy goes, I suggest, a way beyond Joyce's perception-compassion—goes further and more deeply.

"Big Two-Hearted River," divided into two stories as it is, is, then, an attempt to acknowledge the two halves that have been split and to admit the necessity for them to be joined. If there is to be health, if the badly traumatized boy is to be healed of the almost inadmissible wound, connections must be made, connections as vital as the systole and diastole that permit the human heart to function as an organic whole on a dualistic but integrated base.

The larger vision that Joyce and Hemingway ultimately share in *Dubliners* and *In Our Time* is a vision of the necessity for the reconciliations that take place in "The Dead" and "Big Two-Hearted River." For the sake of life and its natural cycles, the egocentric idealism of man must at last embrace the despised or feared darkness that is on the other side of the dividing chains, walls, barriers, or the psyche's fastidious avoidances, a darkness that is embodied in such masks as woman, nature, and death, or in the cycling rhythms of birth-and-death.

Hemingway goes on to develop and study intricately these psychic dualisms in the protagonists of his later novels. It is for this reason that Harry Morgan, who functions on land and sea and reminds Marie of the loggerhead turtles, has one arm and one "flipper"; that Jake Barnes has desire without the equipment to fulfill it; and that Frederic Henry is himself and not himself to Catherine, being also her lost dead lover. It is for this reason that both Henry and Robert Jordan belong and do not belong to the armies they serve and that Jordan's body must be broken as though in half before he becomes whole just before he dies. Colonel Cantwell of *Across the River and into the Trees* enters that novel as a badly "split" man. He has spent a lifetime dealing with life across battle lines and living by coordinates, and he represents Western man. Not only has he a wounded, "split" hand, but his doctor warns him of the risks that he, as an old warrior, runs as he tries to continue his superannuated mode of life with his cardiac disabilities. His heart twinges on the bridges of Venice, and he tries to hide his increased intracranial and intraocular pressure from his doctor by taking mannitol hexanitrate. The doctor, not fooled, warns him, "They ought to make you drag a chain like a high octane truck" (9). The chain, as it connects the higher essences above with the earth below, connects otherwise sundered opposites; it is therefore another bridge that closes a dangerous gap, and it is also the chain that reduces the freedom and pride (upon which the West is based) as it dissipates the high charge that is the consequence of divorce from the earth—yet there is danger for everyone without it.

When, in *The Old Man and the Sea*, Santiago remembers Indian-wrestling for a full cycle of twenty-four hours, half in darkness, half in light, as his white arm struggles in locked embrace with the black arm of the black man, both elbows on a dividing line, both hands struggling to remain erect or to cross over victoriously into the territory of the other, while he tries to relate the deep marlin to himself in a battle in which one of his hands betrays him and must be restored to health, Joyce's psychic dualisms are active and determine the shape of the narrative. Hemingway has always used this psychic split of Western man as the dominant metaphor of most of his works, and through it he prophetically studies the historical situation of the West. In *Across the River*, the opposition between brother Gordon, who had just "deliquesced" in the Pacific, and the hard frozen corpses of the soldiers in Europe suggests the flow-fixity, cyclical-absolute antitheses that Hemingway relates to East and West. Black M'Cola, with whom Hemingway must finally be reconciled in rites of blood brotherhood in *Green Hills*, is, significantly, the "Black Chinaman." The current that carries Santiago, the old fisherman, eastward, is a mythic drift, and when Harry Morgan in *To Have and Have Not* finally tries to "cross over," he knows he must let the boat "go off" to the East. But Hemingway has always implied that all currents to which man yields himself carry him eastward. It is Western man's greatness to have learned how to face into and against the current and how to hold himself steady there.

In Joyce's work, the boy in "Araby," who carries his "chalice safely through a throng of foes" (*Dubliners* 31), desperately wishes to make his journey to that Eastern bazaar; Farrington, in "Counterparts," dreams of the perfumes and dress of Miss Delacour, "a middle-aged woman of Jewish appearance" (*Dubliners* 90), but the story ends with his infuriating son crying out, "I'll say a Hail Mary for you, pa" (98). Little Chandler in "A Little Cloud" recasts "what Gallaher had said about rich Jewesses. Those dark Oriental eyes, he thought, how full of passion, of voluptuous longing! . . . Why had he married the eyes in the photograph?" (*Dubliners* 83). Those eyes belong to his thin tight-lipped wife, Annie, who, as he dreams, in gathering rage and frustration, of Oriental seductions, has gone out for tea.[12] Joyce's portrayal of Eastern longings in most of his Dubliners will lead to the portrayal of a Jewish Bloom in *Ulysses*. In *Ulysses*, however, it is important that night will bring Bloom, together with his dreams of an Eastern kingdom of enchantments, Agendath Netaim, again to his Irish Molly. In "The Dead," whatever have been Gabriel's dreams of sensuality, his final act of empathically joining himself to Gretta and to "the dead" makes him determined that the time "had come for him to set out on his journey westward" (*Dubliners* 223).

Such studies by Joyce have made Hemingway well aware that the king who is a prisoner of the revolutionists in the story "Envoi" that ends *In Our Time* is no hero. This cycled king, who may have been a force in and a danger to his world, is pathetic as an exiled gardener, but he has been brought back into the garden—where myth would have it we all began—and, unlike the earlier protagonists of Hemingway's and Joyce's works, this king, who looks forward to his journey westward "to America," readily introduces us all to his queen.

NOTES

1. Among Hemingway's later stories, "Old Man at the Bridge," "Under the Ridge," "The Killers," "A Pursuit Race," and even "The Snows of Kilimanjaro" can be seen as studying the possible tragedy of flight. One does not necessarily evade one's fate by fleeing it—flight may be an appointment in Samarra, as *A Farewell to Arms* proves.

2. It is of interest to note how ineffective friends finally are in the stories: Bill, in "The End of Something," in no way assuages Nick's sense of loss, and in "The Three-Day Blow" his inferior knowledge of reality and human relationships is at least partly responsible for leading Nick outside again to look for the father, the man who is both source and active agent of authentic power over life and death in nature. It can be argued that Nick's father is such to Nick in "Indian Camp"—he both bestows life and breath upon the newborn boy child and seemingly bestows death as he seemingly decapitates the Indian—and with him at the oars in the early morning, Nick is given a surety of immortality. In a story such as "The Battler," the friendship is perverse and based on almost sadomasochistic rites, like those of the "I Can Take It-I Can Dish It Out" veterans in *To Have and Have Not*. In "Cross-Country Snow," friendship is merely reinforcement in momentary rites that do little to solve a personal problem. Tutors and teachers often mean more: Wilson in "The Short Happy Life of Francis Macomber," Count Greffi in *A Farewell to Arms*, Anselmo in *For Whom the Bell Tolls*, and Romero in *The Sun Also Rises* are more important for what they teach their companion than Rinaldi, Rafael, Cohn, Mike, or Bill.

3. At no moment is there the suggestion that either Hemingway or Joyce would personally flinch from such acknowledgment: their portraits simply record the dilemma and the problem.

4. I consider the important sequence for our purposes that which was published in 1925 shortly after the stories were written and organized for publication by Hemingway.

5. The position of Nick's hands as he comes upon his feeling of immortality should be noted: one feels warm as he trails it in the dark waters beneath; the other is in the sharp chill of the air. So reconciling in himself both worlds—the watery (uterine) world below, associated with the woman, and the airy (abstract) world above, associated with the masculine—he feels sure he will never die. In Joyce's story "Two Gallants," we note the hands of the harpist standing in the roadway, a man with a spiritual instrument in a common thoroughfare: "One hand played in the bass while the other careered in the treble" (*Dubliners* 54). As a result, the "air" throbs "deep and full" (54). Such synthesis of bass and treble into one deep air was, significantly, learned by Hemingway from Joyce. In "Indian Camp," we might naturally have expected Hemingway to have had a trout establish the leap from darkness (the water world) to light (the air) and again into the watery darkness as it re-enters the water, by so

doing establishing the widening circle of meaning at the end of that story. That he has made it a bass emphasizes the bass to treble mode, rhythm intruding upon and entering the melody or air—Virginia Woolf takes up the same metaphor in *To the Lighthouse*—which is the basis of the wholeness that brings life and immortality together.

6. As the lure of exile becomes very real for Frank in "Eveline" and Jimmy Doyle in "After the Race," we are led to remark that the Irish stories of *Dubliners* and the American stories of *In Our Time* are both written by expatriate writers able to control native materials better at a distance.

7. This can be expressed as how to have and have not, or how to keep love in war, or synthesis amid dialectical oppositions. It becomes the search for the solution of the major problem for Joyce and Hemingway: how not to lose the father, who, historically, has been deprived of his role and power by uxorious capitulations, or how to remain masculine though acknowledging and accepting one's feminine "other" side.

8. It is interesting that Bill, in *The Sun Also Rises*, is the one major character apparently reasonably immune to Brett. His fear of wetness here expands a metaphor that Hemingway is developing and that he received partly from Joyce. The studied dialectics of fire and water and earth and air in Joyce's work are constant throughout *Dubliners*. In "The Sisters," ashes in the grate where there is no fire identify the house where the spiritual father has died. Subsequently, in other stories—in "Ivy Day in the Committee Room" and in "Counterparts," where Farrington's rage rises against the son who has let the fire go out—grates without fire speak of the dilemma of flesh without spirit. Fear of life and death as they are embodied in water and earth is shown by Joyce, as Maria's choice of the soft wet substance (in "Clay") is denied her and is replaced by a prayer book, and as the sailor man (who tries to take Eveline by sea to Buenos Aires, the place of good airs) last sees her "animal" face set against him, and as the boys of "An Encounter," who abandon Catholic school to visit the harbor, find sailors and a green-eyed man whose perversions seem "to circle slowly round and round" (27), whom they fear and finally flee. Corley's girl in "Two Gallants," whom he picked up on Dame Street under Waterhouse's clock, wears a sailor hat, while the description of Lenehan of the same story reveals his inner conflict: he wears a yachting cap but carries a waterproof and wears rubber shoes, and "waves of expression break forth over his face" (*Dubliners* 49) as "jets of laughter" (49) come out of him. When Nick separates from Marjorie in Hemingway's "The End of Something," she pointedly takes the boat out onto the (moon-controlled) waters while he remains with his face by the fire. In "The Three-Day Blow," the boys are proud of their control of and knowledge of whisky (spirits) and fire, and they build the fire as they study ways of remaining immune to women and marriage. We note that the wind that brings that "blow" of the title comes "right off the big lake" (*Short Stories* 61). If,

indeed, the boys fear what the moon and lake almost brought to Nick, eternal domesticity because of the girl and pregnancy, such fatal cycles are foreshadowed in "Chapter II," where, as the waters of the river run "almost to the bridge" (97), there seems to be "no end and no beginning" (97), an eternal cycle.

9. Hemingway notably uses "corned beef" as a compound reconciling antitheses in *The Fifth Column*, where dozens of other similarly syncretic compounds stress opposites forced together. The play is a study of the alien within, of the need to destroy the "enemy" in one's midst, or self. It ends as the hero rids himself of Dorothy Bridges.

10. In "Grace," Mr. Kernan's wife "made beef tea for him and scolded him *roundly*" (*Dubliners* 156). In my essay "Hemingway and Joyce: A Study in Debt and Payment," I developed Joyce and Hemingway's use of tea as T, the tau cross, standing for crucifixion and the spirit of the scapegoat sacrifice. Joyce in this story ironically parodies and recapitulates the fall and resurrection of Tom Kernan, a tea taster, used to tasting tea and spitting it "into the grate," who in his fall has bitten off the tip of his tongue—his "'ongue is hurt" (153). This missing t of a tea taster is the problem that Joyce will elaborate later. Kernan's wife, whom he married in the "Star of the Sea Church," beefs up his tea (makes "beef-tea" for him), thereby drawing him down to the waters—star to sea—and beefing him up with tea. ("Star of the Sea" recapitulates Hemingway's water-propped *Star*.)

11. Hemingway's play with sides and lines or barriers is omnipresent and fundamental to his work—witness the joy of the soldiers of "Chapter IV," who delight in their "absolutely perfect barricade" (*In Our Time* 113)—and it is my suggestion that he was led just as readily by metaphoric needs to the sides and battle lines of his military novels as he was by his war experiences. Central characters, such as Santiago and Cantwell and the Hemingway of *Green Hills*, must reconcile betraying or paralyzed or bad or competitive sides with their other, more life-filled, accommodating, and active good sides. Similarly, Hemingway the hunter and Nick Adams of "Big Two-Hearted River" must carefully adjust right to left, inner to outer, and what is above to what is beneath. This reconciliation of sides is as fundamental to the guerrilla activities (crossing to the other side) of Robert Jordan as it is to the retreat and desertion of Frederic Henry.

12. The journey for tea by Annie makes the woman the one in pursuit of spirit, while her husband becomes the scapegoat sacrifice to her need, as, tied to the wheel, not the cross, he tries to tend the screaming child in his arms. In *A Farewell to Arms*, it is Catherine who undergoes the agony and martyrdom, who strives for the verbal absolutism of "always" against her fate in the rain—she sees herself dead in it. Yet she is the one who manages to effect the triumph of eternity against time, to outwit death, for Frederic last sees her as a statue.

Works Cited

Baker, Carlos. *Hemingway: The Writer as Artist*. Princeton, NJ: Princeton UP, 1963.

Ellmann, Richard. *James Joyce*. New York: Oxford UP, 1959.

Hemingway, Ernest. *Across the River and into the Trees*. New York: Scribners, 1950.

———. *The Short Stories of Ernest Hemingway*. New York: Scribners, 1966.

Joyce, James. *Dubliners*. New York: Viking Press, 1974.

———. *A Portrait of the Artist as a Young Man*. New York: Viking Press, 1956.

Kenner, Hugh. "Dubliners." *Twentieth Century Interpretations of* Dubliners*: A Collection of Critical Essays*. Peter K. Garrett, Ed. Englewood Cliffs, NJ: Prentice Hall, 1968.

Sacrifice and Redemption

The Meaning of the Boy/Son and Man/Father Dialectic in the Work of Ernest Hemingway

My purpose here is to focus on the boy/man and father/son relations in the Hemingway canon, and in so doing to reveal the ubiquity of this dialectic in the works, to suggest the reasons for its presence, and to extricate from those works a pattern or paradigm that seems to emerge out of a complex mythic/psychic necessity.

In chapter 23 of *To Have and Have Not*,[1] as the Coast Guard cutter is coming down the channel between the reef and the keys, her captain and mate go below to "have a look at" (223) the dying Harry Morgan. Harry lies in the captain's cabin on an iron pipe bunk, unspeaking. The captain addresses him, "Can we get you anything, *boy?*" (224)[2] and then, when Harry does not respond, he continues, "Harry, . . . do you want anything, *boy?*" (224). These questions provoke Harry's response, one that is often taken to be the most important speech of the novel. He begins, "A *man*," he says. "Sure," the captain prompts. "Go on." "A *man*," and Harry tries to get out what he means to say: "Ain't got no hasn't got any can't really isn't any way out." The captain, eager to get from him what explanation he can of the tragedy, again urges him: "Go on, Harry. . . . Tell us who did it. How did it happen, *boy?*" "Trying now to tell him," Harry begins again, "A *man*"—but the captain interrupts, "Four *men*," he directs ("helpfully"). But Harry corrects *him:* "A *man*," he urges. "All right. A *man*," the captain says. "A *man*," Harry says ("again . . . very slowly") (224), obviously relieved that he has some sign that he is at last being heard. Then, after further prompting by the captain, Harry lets it all come: "Like trying to pass cars on the top of hills. On that road in Cuba. On any road. Anywhere. Just like that. I mean how things are. The way that they been going. For a while yes sure all right. Maybe with luck. A *man*." And there he stops until, his lips moistened by the captain for the second time, he continues, "A *man* . . . *One man* alone ain't got. No *man* alone now. . . . No matter how a *man* alone ain't got no bloody fucking chance." With this speech he shuts his eyes, for, as Hemingway writes, "it had taken him a long time to get it out and it had taken him all of his life to learn it." He subsides, with his eyes momentarily closed. As the captain prepares to leave the cabin and asks if he wants anything, Harry does not answer, for, as Hemingway notes, "He had told them, but they had not heard." He has this knowledge before they leave, the captain assuring him, "We'll be back. . . . Take it easy, *boy*" (225).

The text focuses repeatedly on Harry's attempt to get one thing especially across, that this is a *man's* knowledge he is trying to impart and a description of a *man's* fate, and very distinctly *not* something that is significantly the province of a boy. The last words that the captain leaves with Harry, "Take it easy, *boy*," are the sign that the captain has surely *not* heard what Harry has been telling. But Harry is finally *not* a boy, and what he imparts is a man's knowledge, the very understanding that distinctly separates him from boyhood. In "The Short Happy Life of Francis Macomber," Francis is described by Wilson as "one of the great American *boymen*" (*Short Stories* 33) "who have softened or gone to pieces" (8). But Francis, like Harry, makes a redemptive crossover from the territory of boyhood into manhood, and this makes in him an emphatic difference, one that leads Margot, who will kill him with her Mannlicher (Man-licker), to look at him "strangely." Hemingway has described Francis as one who, with his face shining, feels "absolutely different" (32). We are talking about fundamental change, and the one great insight of Harry's life, that he has expended his life learning, is the difference between being a boy and being a man. But the captain can't hear—as Harry well knows—probably because *he* is a boy and cannot understand what he would need to be a man to acknowledge.

The three young Cubans who die in the first episode of this novel are never called men or even young men but are described as "three of them"; as this "one" or that "one"; as "young fellows"; just before they are executed, as *kids* (or scapegoats); and, when dead, as "*boys.*" Hemingway most frequently refers to them as "fellows." Even as he shifts to Mr. Johnson, the cowardly deceiver of the next episode, he describes him as "the fellow" who has chartered Harry. Throughout this episode, Johnson is never referred to as a "man." He is to others Mr. Johnson, or a "fellow," or even "this bird"—and Eddy says to him, "The Cap is treating you like you were his own mother" (25). The last words of the first chapter, spoken by Harry to Freddy, are, "Don't you worry either, boy" (29). Captain Willie says of Harry, "That *boy's* got cojones" (78); Roberto asks him, "What you want for the boat, *big boy?*" (100); and Bee-Lips addresses him, "Hello, *Big Boy*" (130). These multiple avoidances of references to men or a man seem awkward, even strained, yet deliberate.

In *To Have and Have Not*, Hemingway outrageously uses the device he began to experiment with in *A Farewell to Arms*, the eradication of the father through the lost patronymic. He gives almost all his characters two first names, abrogating the surname and in so doing disdaining paternal inheritance. Where, in *A Farewell*, the names Frederic *Henry* and Catherine *Henry* demonstrate the device that is calling attention to itself and being played with in the demonstrated inversions of "Frederico *Enrico* or Enrico *Frederico*" (39) and Eduardo *Giovanni* (116)—the device that will later be well used in the name of Robert *Jordan* and that was earlier announced in Nick *Adams*, where Hemingway mythically circumvented the birth process for himself—in *To Have and Have Not*, the debrided patronymic is ubiquitous: Harry *Morgan*, Marie *Morgan*, Richard *Gordon*, Helen *Gordon*, Tommy *Bradley*, Helene *Bradley*, John *Hollis*, Dorothy *Hollis*, Eddie *Marshall*, and Albert *Tracy*. Hemingway goes on to play with parts of first names embedded within surnames: Willie *Adams*, Frieda *Richards*, Nelson *Jacks*, Herman *Fredericks*. Even his allusions are uniquely to such personalities as Babe *Ruth*, Gracie *Allen*, Sylvia *Sidney*, Ginger *Rogers*, and Benny *Sampson*. One of the controlling ideas of the novel is embedded in such naming, and such sexual hybrids, which critics erroneously sense as "new Hemingway" in *The Garden of Eden*, are early being playfully yet seriously studied in such names as Babe *Ruth*, Helen *Gordon*, Catherine *Henry*, and Ginger *Rogers*. This naming, focusing on spurious patronymics, where the individual seems to be trying to make a whole person of him or herself without recourse to paternal inheritance, defines the problem and underwrites the dilemma of a world of lost fathers.

The last words of the twenty-third chapter, "You can't ever tell," ring like fate when we have carefully studied these communications without communication, these attempts to tell in a novel where fear of the mouth and fear of telling have organized the structure of the whole. It is, of course, an enormously bitter realization for one like Harry, an unlettered man who, unlike Richard Gordon in this same novel, is not a writer and must rely at his death on a more primitive oral tradition to carry what truth can be passed on. Characters are not spokesmen for their authors, as Hemingway knew as well as any writer of his time, but he here enunciates a dilemma that his character shares with any author, whose business it is in part to enunciate what his characters discover for him. "You can't ever tell" as terminal logic is a hard insight to have.[3] Just as there seem to be shared relations between Richard Gordon, who looms large in the novel, and Harry, between the writer and the man of action, so there seem to be shared relations in this chapter, as throughout this novel, between the speaking mouth and the words of men, the mouth that eats and the mouth that tells, the belly and the brain, and these are studied together with distinctions between boyhood and manhood.

The three who die in the first episode of the novel, in fear of *lenguas largas*, big mouths and loose talk, undoubtedly die because of them. Eddy is feared and almost executed by his friend Harry because of Harry's fear of his big mouth. Early, the major warning to Harry is a photograph of a man "with his throat cut clear across from ear to ear" (39), and later Harry will execute Mr. Sing—who has threatened Harry that he might "accuse you to them of having betrayed me" (33)—by grasping his throat, getting his fingers "well in behind his talk-box" (54) and cracking "the whole thing" (54). Mr. Sing's name[4] in one of its meanings means to spill secrets, to reveal, to—under pressure or torture—speak out what must not be spoken. Telling may be therefore a fatal act: it may be at once a betrayal and a revelation, what is spoken may be either true or false, and in this novel what may be told is extraordinarily feared.[5] *The Fifth Column* focuses closely on those who spill, who have big or open mouths and, under torture, reveal everything. Not speaking can be the test of manliness, or *cojones*, or mature bravery. *Death in the Afternoon* describes with contempt those bulls who cannot under stress and fear of death keep tight mouths.[6]

Harry, in the "deathbed" speech already studied, leaves his auditors with one other important bit of knowledge as, in the most extended part that I have quoted, he describes the fate of living as less than a man: it is, he implies, like trying to pass cars at the top of hills. For a while, perhaps with luck, you may be all right, but eventually the luck will run out is the warning the Coast Guard men do not hear. What Harry has said is that a man with a knowledge gained from experience, from imagining with empathy what is on the other side, knows what dangers may be there and does not risk either his life or the lives of others foolishly. He has implied that refusing to imagine, and so avoiding knowledge of, the danger that any crossover to the other side may pose is childish and culpable ignorance. This is precisely Francis Macomber's innocence and childishness, and we should note in "The Short Happy Life of Francis Macomber" that Francis becomes a man capable of meeting the threat of death that comes at him from the other side only when he has closely perceived and with detailed observation acknowledged what Wilson has—knowledge of what the animal he hunts, his antagonist at the other end of his reaching rifle, must have felt and would be feeling. Francis, who does not want to "go in there," into the dangerous and perhaps fatal domain of the lion, "had not thought how the lion felt" (*Short Stories* 15) and therefore cannot know what the lion feels, any more than he can know "how his wife felt" or "how Wilson felt" (21). On the other hand, Wilson's "entire occupation had been with the lion" (17). Going forward, however, toward the buffalo, they cross a river to the *other* side and there reach "the rolling country on the far side" (25), and it is there that Francis studies the buffalo with care and sees the precise details of the dangerous life he hunts. In *To Have and Have Not*, the culpability of the "haves" stems from their inability to think about and therefore to imagine how the other half lives and suffers; and a writer like Richard Gordon cannot imagine the truth of a woman like Marie because, as the text tells us, he sees his wife Helen only from the waist up. He fails to see her *other* side—he cannot cross over into the unknown terrain and territory and nature of the other, so he can only exploit and imagine without knowledge, and he cannot be a significant writer, whose truths are imaginatively recovered from experienced knowledge.

In my essay "Bridges: Their Creation and Destruction in the Works of Ernest Hemingway" (included in this volume), I have written about bridges and the way, not only in *For Whom the Bell Tolls*, but in most of the works of Hemingway, they significantly intellectually structure the meaning of his fiction. Here I would like to emphasize the importance of the journey to another side that they provide a Hemingway protagonist. The undertaking of such a journey is a central component of the transition from unindividuated boyhood to mature manhood. Romero in *The Sun Also Rises* teaches this fact as he, an avatar of bravery and manhood, demonstrates the importance of the *torero*'s act, undertaken at risk of death, of crossing to the "other side" by entering the bull's terrain and actually with the sword entering the bull, and so becoming one with the bull. It is the moment in which killer and killed, death and life, meet and join. Later, when Jake retreats, after a species of metaphoric death, for his rebirth to San Sebastian, where at the shore he puts together the sky and the sea depths, the shadowy world beneath and the sun-filled air above, water and air, the depths and the heights, he is described as going to this synthesizing, integrating, individuating encounter at approximately five o'clock, *a las cinco de la tarde*, dressed in his own suit (of lights) and walking out across the sand to meet the bull of the sea—all of this phrased in description that repeats that of Romero entering the arena at the same hour and approaching his own deadly bull. When Jake then almost immediately goes to meet Brett in Madrid, he does so as a changed man, one who is no longer a devoted acolyte and servitor of the goddess but a fairly cynical *man* who is now able to hold his own line of self-definition. Hemingway's point is that Jake, by exposure to and entry into the domain of "the other," has become more authentically a *man*. A story like "The Three-Day Blow" studies boyhood's fear of such an encounter and the penalties for inexperience. The young men, terrified of the consequences of significantly or profoundly relating to the "other"—Marjorie in Nick's case—try to get what information they can from an antiseptic and safe distance. *A Farewell to Arms*, a novel multiply structured by significant bridgings and crossovers, and with a great number of actual bridges, studies with exquisite care and detail the boyish ill-preparedness of Frederic Henry for manhood and therefore for fatherhood. Finally, Catherine's death, we are led to believe, adequately disciplines this man of multiple cowardly retreats, desertions, and failures so that he may finally tell his self-incriminating story. The novel is also a story of a son without a father who must learn how to become a man without one, and it is therefore a story of a search for the surrogate father—whether Rinaldi, the priest, or Count Greffi—who may lead him to manhood. As I have noted, Frederic's absent patronymic—like that of Harry Morgan or Robert Jordan—reinforces a sense of the absent or incompetent or non-functional biological father throughout. His crossings of the bridges at Codroipo and Latisana, his water crossing of the Tagliamento and later of Lago Maggiore from Italy to Switzerland, and even the metaphoric crossing that he undergoes when he is wounded, as he becomes for a brief time an inhabitant of the kingdom of death before returning to the world of the living, are rites of passage that help to bring him toward manhood. Hemingway, at the end of the first book, shows Frederic as a helpless, vomiting child cared for in the hospital by others and fleeing before any conversational pressure from any fixed, defensive intellectual position. At the end of the novel, he, as changed as Jake and a failed actual father, goes forward toward his role as abstract father—teller and controller of the words that master fate with knowledge.

Hemingway throughout his work has studied the realm of the feminine as the *other* side for the man as is the realm of the masculine for the woman, and he has repeatedly and consistently studied the multiple evasions and cowardices that have kept men like Francis Macomber, Mr. Elliot, the husband in "Cat in the Rain," and the young man of "Hills Like White Elephants" from committing themselves to an intimacy with this reality. Without such knowledge, men remain unintegrated, unindividuated, and undeveloped boys or boy-men whose words must forever be hollow and false, their knowledge only partial. What prepares Frederic for love and has given him partial knowledge is his wounding, which brings him into the kingdom of death before releasing him to life again, but his subsequent detachment within his relationship to Catherine keeps him from ultimate knowledge and manhood. It was Jake's missing phallus in *The Sun Also Rises* that enforced a stultifying physical detachment in that first novel, one as fatal for biological creativity as may be the aesthetic detachment of the artist in his creative work. The doctor-father's linguistic and racial distance in "Indian Camp," like the linguistic distance of the officer in "On the Quai at Smyrna" and that of the husband in "Cat in the Rain"—who remains detached by virtue of the words he attends to—all are analyzed as the incompletenesses of unformed men. In *The Garden of Eden*, Hemingway carefully studies how the artist in his detachment needs the experience of "the other side" to put him in touch with his sources and to make him sufficiently fertile to be capable of dealing with the profound and true material that is his subject. This is another way of saying that the feminization of the masculine psyche is the necessary act of integration that makes a man a man and an artist a complete artist. The sexual inversions of the novel, which catapult David into the realm of the feminine, bring him through Catherine's agency to the manhood that is necessary to the mature artist.

It is not accidental that the controlling metaphor of *To Have and Have Not* is the *crossover* and that the abiding question is whether it is a good or "nice night to *cross*" (165). This crossover brings Harry at last to his experience of "the other": as he confronts his death, he confronts the fact that "the moon was up" (173) and that the moonlight "came in" (174). "Hung against the wheel"[7] and unable any longer to hold off the "other"—"If the bitch wouldn't only roll" (173–74)—he finally accepts "the roll . . . and took it" (175). He has at last accepted the necessity for the other half he had repressed and denied: "No matter how a man alone ain't got no bloody fucking chance" (225).

Hemingway's first important work, *In Our Time*, a carefully integrated study of patriarchal failure, moves unerringly to its last vignette, "Envoi," the portrait of the imprisoned and impotent, cowardly *(father)* king in his garden. In contrast, the penultimate vignette of the collection focuses on the boy/son. Showing the execution of Sam Cardinella, it highlights the failure of spiritual *fathers*, the priests, and also the self-contamination of Sam—the inability of the *son*, or *boy*, to be a *man*. *Five men* are to be hanged, and Hemingway four times calls them *"men,"* but Sam, unable to support himself, must, like a child, be carried to his execution. "Be a *man*, my son" (193), says the younger *father/priest*, as he himself skips neatly to his own safety when the trapdoor for Sam is sprung. The admonition is bitter for one who dies without grace or genuine support, for how is a *boy* or *son* to become a *man* when there are no acceptable biological or spiritual fathers? "Big Two-Hearted River," which brackets those vignettes, is in part an answer.

Hemingway's attention to the perimeters and definitions of boyhood and manhood is constant. The first chapter of *Across the River* ends as Cantwell styles himself a boy: "Keep your temper, *boy*, he told himself" (7). Then, to emphasize the important insight of this work, so that no one should miss the distinctions, Hemingway emphatically begins the next chapter: "But he was *not a boy*. He was fifty and a Colonel of Infantry in the Army of the United States" (8). Nadine DeVost has brought close attention to the boy/man vocabulary.[8] Throughout the novel these distinctions are intricately and painstakingly studied: "*Boy*, he said, you certainly are a beat-up, old-looking bastard. You're a Colonel of Infantry, *boy*" (169). "Cheer up, *boy*, he said. . . . So don't be gloomy, *boy or man*, or busted General" (189). Generally, his emphasis is revealing—"He was not a *boy* anymore, of course" (233)—as is Renata's "That *boy*, he is a *man* now, of course" (96). Elsewhere, Cantwell notes a *man* who "was really only a *boy*" (183).

Arnold Sabatelli has studied Hemingway's complex use of *boy* in *Islands in the Stream*. In the first section, "Bimini," there are *"the boys"* who are Hudson's three *"sons"*; in the middle section, "Cuba," there is *Boise*, the cat, whose name suggests the role of surrogate for the lost dead "boys"; and finally, in the last episode, there are the machine guns that Hudson calls *"niños,"* Spanish for *"boys"* or *"sons,"* as the protection and security he cradles and clings to. Sabatelli brilliantly studies the implications of their role in constant support of the inadequate artist *man/father*.

Throughout Hemingway's works, scenes place boy against man, son against father, immaturity against maturity, ignorance against knowledge, and unfamiliarity against expertise. The purpose is to get at something more important than rites of passage and individuation—rather to enunciate, as Hemingway knew he should (ever since his association with Joyce and Pound), myths for the uncreated conscience of Western culture, regenerative myths that he felt, as they did, were necessary for his time. The necessity for the definition of manhood and the rejection of boyhood undoubtedly, on a psychological level, rested on Hemingway's perception of his own father's, Clarence Hemingway's, inadequacy as man and father—insufficiencies that his first stories, like "Indian Camp" and "The Doctor and the Doctor's Wife," well studied. Both Frederic Henry of *A Farewell to Arms* and Robert Jordan of *For Whom the Bell Tolls*, men who lack patronymics, have seemingly rejected their biological fathers. Their pursuit of valid father surrogates structures their lives and casts upon them responsibilities that they, too ill equipped for the demands of maturity, must exercise. Robert Jordan's memory of when he said farewell to his father at the train station is one where the father becomes the child, and the boy, saying farewell to boyhood, becomes the man. Such fictional paternal relations undoubtedly in these cases rest on the author's own history, as does Hemingway's need at too early an age to style himself Papa and to call his women acquaintances "daughter."

My point, however, is that Hemingway's art gained its impetus and its mission as he understood his own dilemma as central to the West and the problems *in our time*. His book of that name is a complex study of the inadequacy of the father in the Western world, of manhood itself. It is a great manual on the failure of the patriarchate and the dilemma of a world without adequate rites of passage or role models for sons, who must, like Nick, in the early stories of the collection, go off alone with the father or, in the last stories, go *off alone* into the wilderness to perfect their own rituals for personal and cultural survival.

Where does this search and perception take Hemingway? I think it led him unerringly to the perfection of a paradigm to express his need, one that, being also concomitantly the need of his world in his time, made him into more than a writer—into a mythmaker simultaneously becoming the mythic figure, Papa, that he could not avoid becoming. It is one in which the false father is bypassed, renounced, and replaced by the good father, who must be discovered or recreated, one in which the boy or son must, under the pressure of necessity, be sacrificed to fatherhood. The cost of the restoration of a valid father principle is the sacrificed son.

Let me suggest this pattern in outline. Again and again in the Hemingway oeuvre there is, in fact or metaphor, a son figure who, to support the father, tries to assume his place, as substitute or usurper. Inevitably this son becomes a sacrifice who must be eliminated or transcended so that the true father, not in personal authority but in abstract mythic and godlike authority, may be restored to power. This pattern, one that surely drew on Pound but even more on Joyce, suggests how complicit the three were in deliberate mythmaking. Finnegan and Bloom dominate Joyce's major works, and Joyce made no secret of his ironical treatment of Stephen in his *A Portrait of the Artist as a Young Man*—Hemingway well understood Joyce. In a letter to Dos Passos on March 26, 1932, he wrote, "Don't get any perfect characters in [your novel]—no Stephen Daedeluses—remember it was Bloom and Mrs. Bloom saved Joyce" (*Selected Letters* 354). Hemingway—I think by virtue of his personal familial dilemma *as* a young man—was instantly an acolyte of both Pound and Joyce and instantly accepted by both. He saw, as did Joyce, that in the Christian Trinity the son's power was inadequate to a restoration of spiritual authority, and therefore he elevated to the center of his belief a re-empowered father. Joyce re-empowered his cuckolded Bloom, and Hemingway avowed that *The Sun Also Rises* celebrated the earlier chapters of the Old Testament. In a letter written on August 9, 1932, to Paul Romaine, Hemingway insisted that he had written his book "to show the superiority of the earlier Hebrew writers over the later quoted Ecclesiastes versus G. Stein" (*Selected Letters* 365–66). The danger, as these men well understood, was to the entire patriarchal dispensation of the West. For them, therefore, the Father and the Word had to be restored to power for civilization, as we know it, and for literature to continue. And if the son was to be a sacrifice, as he was initially meant to be, to reaffirm the authority of the Father, the son would have to be consumed in the sacrifice—so that he might not himself be venerated, so that he might disappear within the reinstituted authority and power of the Father.

Hemingway saw and understood the business he was about—his imagery affirms it. One of the great errors that is made by critics of *The Sun Also Rises* is a misreading of Cohn as an anti-Semitic portrait.

Rather, Hemingway excoriates scapegoat psychology, and Cohn is a parody of the suffering Jew, Christ, who is, as scapegoat, pilloried by others. Early described as "a nice *boy*, a friendly *boy*" (4), Cohn is later, to Harvey Stone, "a case of arrested development" (44), someone with a "a boyish quality that had never been trained out of him" (34). He is the ineffective boy-man, cast as a son, who lacks experience and knowledge and depends on Jake to show him the way. Jake is the one the others go to with their confessions, their problems, and it is he who leads and looks out for them and prays for them. At the end, still a paternal figure, he goes to aid Brett and help her in her impasse. One might read his dephallused state as the condition of a father who must be removed beyond incest, and of a father God, whose son may be the necessary scapegoat sacrifice, but whose personal detachment is demanded.

The need for a re-empowered validated father or man is the center of *The Torrents of Spring*. Scripps is a boy-man, without father, mother, wife, daughter, or home, on the road and suffering. His original home, destroyed by *Sherman* on his march to the sea, is lost because, without Scripps's father there, as the general says, there can be no "*man to man*" (16). Scripps, now from *Mancelona* and learning from "that *man* Mencken," finds the waitress Diana, who chants, "You are *my man and more than my man*" (33)—"She had a *man* now. A *man* of her own" (42). Unable to hold Scripps, however, even with the *Man*chester Guardian and the Book*man* from the post*man*, Diana loses Scripps to her replacement waitress *Man*dy. Enough. The book is a romp, a satire, an aesthetics, and a personal document. It is also a *man*ual of manners for *man*hood.

In *A Farewell to Arms*, Frederic Henry is a boy lacking any visible father: he volunteers in a war that is not his own to do a man's work for which he is ill equipped. The religious symbolism is there, as it was in *Sun*, to highlight what is mythically happening. Frederic, the son without a father, has, in his wounding, been described as having died and then been reborn. This resurrection—and the book is based on several metaphoric deaths and resurrections, as well as on imagery of crucifixion—is followed by Catherine's pregnancy. Catherine, based on Saint Catherine, after her torture crucifixion on the biological wheel, gives birth to a dead son. The couple await their child's birth in the Swiss Alps above Montreux, and there snow begins to fall "three days before Christmas" (281). Later, after it has "rained for three days" (291), it is "on the morning of the third day" (291) that they descend to Lausanne to prepare for their child's imminent arrival. This placing of a suggestion of divine birth with Easter crucifixion-death-resurrection imagery codes the son as Christ, the son of the father God, and this is further reinforced as the child is being born when the waiter pronounces the *consummatum est*, "It is finished." Frederic, in constant pursuit of a surrogate father, is himself, however, early styled "Baby" by Rinaldi. Given his many inadequacies, he logically fails as a biological father, but as he walks off in the rain, he walks toward the writing of the book we have just read, which is to make him father of the Word, a legitimizer of the spirits of the dead. His own dead, even denied, son is the sacrifice who underwrites the emergence of a valid Father. Hemingway in his other work similarly validates fatherhood as the function of the writer/artist who resurrects life through the Word, and in *The Garden of Eden*, David, the writer rebuked by his wife Catherine for spilling his seed in a wastebasket—for denying her the child she desires—is suggested as doing so because of his greater dedication to the word or his work as a writer.

In *Green Hills*, Hemingway, though an adult writer-husband-man, becomes the *son* figure to *Pop)*, the true hunter, and P.O.M., Poor Old Mama. A son without a discernible biological father, he learns to function as a man without Pop, leaving Pop back at the camp-hearth with P.O.M., and he goes through rites of passage and performance that eventually establish his authority, but not before the trinity of M'Cola, the old man, and himself have undergone their Calvary: under their burdens, they fall several times while going through the thorns, and they finally acknowledge meat on a stick overblown with ashes, or crucifixion without resurrection. As the novel ends on the Sea of Galilee, Hemingway promises with the last words of the book to resurrect Pop by writing "a piece some time" that he will "put him in" (295)—the very book we have just read. Throughout *Green Hills*, Hemingway has reviled Garrick, who is several times metaphorically identified as Christ,[10] and he says of him as we first meet him, "I had never liked him and I liked him less now" (3). The book therefore is an abstract restoration of the spiritual Father, the spirit behind the hunt, a restoration based on a sacrifice of the son.

In *For Whom the Bell Tolls*, Robert Jordan has psychologically separated himself from his biological father and, by enlisting in a foreign war, seems to be acting as surrogate for his cowardly father—but this is a role for which he must discover maturity. Initially, he is the son who enters the cave and, in primal rites of overthrow of the old king, participates in Pablo's cowing. The significant act of the book is his refusal to kill Pablo, who, allowed the opportunity to reverse and redeem himself, does so. The son is the sacrifice left behind as Pablo, the re-empowered father, goes on over the hill toward posterity. Coming to terms with surrogate fathers, Jordan at last awaits his death as the to-be-crucified and resurrected Christ who, in three days, will suffer death and resurrection, sacrificing his life for others. The point is made that in his death-immolation in battle as the son, he perfects the resurrected life of the spirit as he remains spiritually active in those who remember, and is replaced by the written book we have read, while the mature man/father is resurrected through his Christlike sacrifice, the cowardly suicide of the unmanly father being replaced by the manly death of his son. The trinity that goes on over the hill into posterity at the novel's end pointedly has Maria braced on each side by father and mother, Pablo and Pilar, the son being excised from the trinity, as he was in Green Hills.

Sacrificed sons in Hemingway are by symbolism iconographically established as mythic son/Christs—the boy/child who dies in A Farewell while "It is finished" (311) is pronounced; Garrick in Green Hills, who spreads his arms wide and intones, "It is finished" (3); the ineffectual "small" electrician who is killed in The Fifth Column, whom nobody believes, who spreads his arms wide and declares, "No hay luz . . . there isn't any light" (17); and Robert Cohn. All are necessary mythic son sacrifices.

Son figures not only are sacrificed in the works to enable a man to come into being, the father to be re-empowered, but are seemingly executed. In The Fifth Column, Wilkinson, presented as the "young boy" who takes the place of Philip Rawlings, dies because he has assumed that role. His executioner "shoots the boy in the back of his head" (51). Philip at the end is a man alive because of the surrogate death of the boy/son figure. In For Whom the Bell Tolls, the boy Joaquín dies as he is "shot . . . in the back of the head" (322) by Lieutenant Berrendo. His death prepares for the sacrificial death of Robert Jordan, who is left behind as the Father is re-empowered in the shape of the written work, the book we have read and that we all take on over the hill with us toward posterity. In To Have and Have Not, it is the boy revolutionary Emilio, carefully described as "the boy," in contradistinction to the "men," who is first executed by Harry—"he sighted carefully on the base of the back of the boy's head" (170). Later, Emilio will be described by the sheriff as "the one that looked like a kid" (250). Albert Tracy's death—of another "boy"—is seen metaphorically as the crucifixion death of Christ. That Margot Macomber's shot, which hits her husband in the *back* of the head, is allowed to be read ambiguously as perhaps an execution reveals Hemingway's own careful coding of this back-of-the-head killing, a killing that takes place at the moment when the *boy* threatens to usurp the powers of the Father. This is carefully enunciated as Wilson's danger—that Francis will "blow the *back* of my head off" (25)—and is averted as Margot's shot slams into "the *base* of [Francis'] skull" (36). In *Islands in the Stream,* a work that studies the necessary regeneration-redemption of the biological and spiritual father, Thomas Hudson must yield up to death his trinity of sons.

This pattern of the necessary deaths of boy-son figures in the Hemingway canon is extraordinary, and the fact they are shot in the back of their heads suggests the execution of the son as a necessity underwriting the reinstitution of the abstract power of the Father. We might see a lost boyhood as the sacrifice accepted by the son who responsibly tries to validate the ineffectual failing father. For Hemingway, the cost of becoming Papa was great, and we must wonder whether Nick in "The Doctor and the Doctor's Wife" knows what that cost may be as, promising to show his father where "the black squirrels are," he leads the way.

NOTES

1. All references in this introduction will be from one brief chapter of *To Have and Have Not;* the inclusive pages are 223–26.

2. Throughout this essay, italics in Hemingway quotes are mine.

3. I like to think of Hemingway's writer's realization here as sharing greatly the despair of Cantwell in *Across the River.* Cantwell, like Hemingway, apparently knows just how impossible are the hopes of the writer, since he knows, as Hemingway does, how unperceptive are readers and critics. At one moment Cantwell describes himself as speaking "to no one, except, perhaps, posterity" (168), assured as he is that what he has to say will go over the heads of his immediate audience. Like the Coast Guard captain, most of his critics, if not "angleworms in a bottle" (*Green Hills of Africa* 21), are boys ill equipped to hear a man's knowledge or the terms of its knowing.

4. Hemingway, for whom song had been coded as his mother, Grace Hemingway's, métier, probably could not avoid that association. Undoubtedly, some of the associations of *Sing* and *song* are for him so influenced.

5. Similarly, for a writer who compares a literary work to an iceberg with its bulk remaining unseen beneath the surface, and who thereby remands the significant to absence and silence, not telling can be the test of a writer. Hem-

ingway, perhaps more than any writer of his time, well knew what was *not* to be told.

6. Importantly, it should be observed that speaking is a *bridging* device: it connects people while connecting what is inside with what is outside, and a closed mouth is not unlike the "perfect" barrier that was thrown across the bridge in "Chapter IV" of *In Our Time*, or the garden wall barrier of "Chapter III." The attempt to cross either of those is, as Hemingway portrays them, to risk death, and only brave men can do it.

7. Harry's hanging on the wheel should be seen as Hemingway meant it to be seen—as his crucifixion on the wheel. He is here playing this against Catherine's death in childbirth in *A Farewell to Arms*, where she, like her namesake, is martyred on the wheel, for her the biological wheel of a pregnancy that cannot be taken from her. Harry's accepting the "roll" of "the bitch" is his recognition and acceptance of a nature he had tried to dominate. Despite Frederic Henry's metaphoric assumption of morning sickness the morning after Catherine has told him of her pregnancy, one cannot take another's place.

8. The title of her essay, "Hemingway's Girls: Unnaming and Renaming Hemingway's Female Characters," may obscure the fact that in a footnote, where good authors often place some of their most significant insights, she has dealt with masculine naming.

9. In my essay "A Brief Safari into the Religious Terrain of *Green Hills of Africa*" (included in this volume), I studied some of the intense overlays and religious iconography in the Hemingway texts. Garrick, who overtly pronounces the *consummatum est* at the beginning of this novel, thrice in the novel throws his arms wide: once when he predicts the dying of the light, once when he despairingly confronts the sky, and once when he falsely prophesies the coming of the great bull that they pursue with dwindling faith. Elsewhere, when he appears, posturing, and is acknowledged with "Look, what we have," the response is "Christ."

WORKS CITED

DeVost, Nadine. "Hemingway's Girls: Unnaming and Renaming Hemingway's Female Characters." *Hemingway Review* 14.1 (1994): 46–59.

Hemingway, Ernest. *Across the River and into the Trees.* New York: Scribners, 1950.

———. *Ernest Hemingway: Selected Letters, 1917–1961.* Ed. Carlos Baker. New York: Scribners, 1981.

———. *A Farewell to Arms.* 1929. New York: Scribners, 1957.

———. *The Fifth Column.* 1938. New York: Bantam Books, 1969.

———. *For Whom the Bell Tolls.* 1940. New York: Scribners, 1968.

————. *Green Hills of Africa.* 1935. New York: Scribners, 1963.

————. *In Our Time.* 1925. New York: Scribners, 1958.

————. *The Short Stories of Ernest Hemingway.* 1938. New York: Scribners, 1966.

————. *The Sun Also Rises.* 1926. New York: Scribners, 1954.

————. *To Have and Have Not.* 1937. New York: Scribners, 1965.

————. *The Torrents of Spring.* 1926. New York: Scribners, 1972.

Sabatelli, Arnold. "The Re-forming of Word and Meaning in *Islands in the Stream.*" Paper presented at the American Literature Association's Symposium on Realism and Naturalism, Cabo San Lucas, Mexico, November 1993.

"Is He Building a Bridge or Blowing One?"

The Repossession of Text by the Author in For Whom the Bell Tolls

As Robert Jordan crosses over to work behind the lines, he enters immediately into his plans to complete his mission, one that will be fulfilled only when the bridge is blown. What is fascinating to observe is that the preparations for his destruction of the bridge are the very strategies and devices that Hemingway the writer must forge for himself in order to write the book that can only be completed as he brings his protagonist and cast of characters to the successful completion of their task.

As Jordan reflects on the way Karkov prepared him for the work he is to do, he remembers Karkov telling him of the "many things" he will need to read to "understand" what he needs to know. Karkov said that "out of this will come a book"—which at this point Jordan hopes he will be the one to write—a book that is "very necessary" and that "will explain many things which it is necessary to know" (264). Before these reminiscent reflections end, however, Jordan has thought about the book he has himself already written, and he has decided also to write the book on what he is about to undergo. He acknowledges that he will "have to be a much better writer than I am now" (268).

During his few days with the guerilla band, he trains himself for the task ahead, and his training is composed of lessons that at once address a bridge blower's needs and a writer's needs. Occasionally, when his senses are being refined, as they are when Pilar talks of the smell of death, and Jordan urges her on—"If it is necessary for one to learn, let us learn" (275)—the training seems more directed toward the writer than the bridge blower, but more frequently what is learned by Jordan is a sharpening of faculties, knowledge, and attitudes that might simultaneously serve writer or guerilla leader. Thinking of how he has misrepresented the killing urge, he thinks, "Don't lie to yourself . . . nor make up literature about it" (309). The cold detachment he studies in himself, the discipline he demands—"There must be discipline" (315)—and the observations he makes—"There are a few things to observe" (294)—all serve both creator and destroyer. Jordan many times alludes to the book he has to write, and the alert reader may see that techniques, strategies, devices, and styles that seemingly relate to the problem of the bridge or to cultural or language differences aptly apply to a writer's stock in trade. But these are stages along the way toward a yet imagined act and book in a book, at the moment of Jordan's training, actually being written by Hemingway (and read by us), where the frequent discussions of necessary techniques and tools are inextricable from the demonstrated sense of them in the prose we read.

Jordan knows that he has "only started his education" (250) but that he "liked to know how it really was, not how it was supposed to be" (250) and that when he gets it straight, he is going well and as he is supposed to proceed. His notebook entries for the task ahead of bridge blowing are carefully ambiguous in that they suggest as well the task of the novelist.

"Thinking closely and well" (245), he is pleased by what he writes; he writes and reads over what he has written and observes, "It's perfectly clear. I do not think there are any holes in it" (250). Toward the end of the novel, he is able to observe, "I don't know whether anyone has ever done it before, but there will always be people who will do it from now on given a similar jam. If we do it and if they hear about it. If they hear about it, yes. If they do not just wonder how it was we did it" (401). That speech, like the preceding ones, points at once to Jordan the bridge blower's pride in his resourcefulness and also to Hemingway's pride in his accomplishment and in his solutions to problems of style, and it looks forward to readers who will study the technical solutions to problems of prose, not just of demolition, to see and understand the victory they represent. It is simultaneously Robert Jordan's reflection and Hemingway's.

At many moments, Pilar helps Jordan in his learning process. At one, she insists, "*Ingles*, learn. That's the thing. Learn" (275); at another, she lets him see that in their situation "one cannot say what one feels"

(324); and at another, she teaches him how to tell a tale and establish sensory values in the prose he might wish to use in his telling—she says, "I must tell certain details so that you will see it" (202). From Anselmo's speech Jordan learns a style, "neither the English pose of understatement nor any Latin bravado" (47). Also, Maria stands at his side—"Can I help thee with thy work?" (186)—and reassures him, "You must not worry about your work because I will not bother you or interfere" (186). The careful way Hemingway has left the "work" unspecified in her speech builds the ambiguity. When Maria does intrude on his actions, he warns her back and out of the way: "She had no place in his life now" (288), so he tells her, "Get thee back now" (291). Jordan knows that the plan for this "Headache Bridge" (171) of his is, as Karkov has ironically described the attack, "a very complicated and beautiful plan" (9), but as he develops it, he almost apologizes to El Sordo for the part of himself that is only abstractly involved: "Paper bleeds little," he says, as he explains his complicated ideas that are "on paper very simple"; and Hemingway's character El Sordo laments that he and his band are not allowed such abstract creativity "that we should conceive and execute something on paper" (166).

These are singularly fascinating pages in literature, where an author who is in the act of creating a character, and who is in a very real way standing in for him, has his characters aid him in the creation/destruction of themselves, attentive to and sharing the creative job in which their creator is engaged. Jordan acknowledges their distance from him and says that he is "compelled to use the people whom he liked as you would use troops towards whom you have no feeling at all" (177). Jordan's acts, as Fidel Castro noted, are almost an essay on the use of irregular troops in behind-the-line operations, and Jordan's struggle to succeed and Hemingway's struggle to present this are together an essay on the very act of writing such an essay.

In guerilla territory, Jordan is almost immediately dealing with those "who cannot read"; with those, like Agustín, who are focused almost completely on the "unprintable"; with those, like Pilar and the gypsy, whose mysticisms suggest another kind of communication; and with those, like El Sordo, who are deaf. A cold-headed logician, Jordan studies the problems he faces, makes notes in his notebook, and makes sketches and drawings to plan his procedure. Meanwhile, he familiarizes himself with his cast of characters, always learning more about them, as he plans to dispose of them objectively and coldly and use them to his best advantage. As he proceeds, he knows he is "learning very fast," and is "trying to think his problem out clearly," for "you have only one thing to do and you must do it" (62). He celebrates his work and his belief in it, knows that "it is very difficult and important" (37), and knows that his "obligation" lies in his task, "and to fulfill that I must take no useless risk of myself" (68). He is "very preoccupied with [his] work" (100), for "that is my business. . . . It will all be written" (47) and thus be "for everyone's knowledge so that all should know" (47). Agustín judges, "He must know his business or they would not have him doing this" (104).

Jordan as character and Jordan as Hemingway, the writer of the book, are increasingly fused and take on a common identity, so that there is a nightmarish secondary story, almost a horror story, of the identity of one submerged within and desperately struggling to surface, to have its features emerge from the enclosing fictions of the other. From the very beginning, Jordan the bridge blower projects himself as the eventual writer of the tale, which is the very life that he is living, not realizing that he is only the creature already enveloped and prisoner in the story another tells by means of him, that another man within him is through him building a bridge to posterity and using him to accomplish his own contradictory ends. The two fused identities of bridge builder and bridge blower do not immediately separate, nor does Jordan immediately come to consciousness of the schism within him, but it gradually and incrementally makes itself felt.

Early on, Jordan is deceived into believing that after the war he will eventually be the one to tell the tale he is living and recording, but we learn how false that is as he becomes at last sacrifice to and abandoned within the action and landscape of the tale, while the author is inhabiting him and using him to accomplish his own apotheosis. Jordan tells himself "you ought to write" (96) and later asserts, "He would try to write it . . . perhaps he would. I wish I could write well enough" (147). He goes on speciously and myopically for a character in an enveloping fiction, "Nobody owned his mind, nor his faculties for seeing and hearing" (147). When he finally exultantly crows, "I'm going to write a true book," he is immediately sarcastically answered by the other, now more realistic, more informed, and newly conscious side of himself, "I'll bet that will be easy" (179). By the time of this outburst, he has witnessed seeing his thoughts as fictions and has realized how readily "one man can make a bureaucracy with his mouth" (239), how far paper is from bleeding wounds, how painful it is to treat people you love as abstractions, and how readily clichéd and propagandistic phrases and slogans inhabit his mind. These are all stages in the humbling of an embryonic writer.

Therefore, his comment on his ambitions—"I'll bet that will be easy"—comes from the other side of himself, the sarcastic side that observes him and looks on, and Jordan begins the split that will gradually widen until he has been almost overtly separated out as the two distinct selves, the bridge blower and the bridge builder, Jordan and Hemingway. After he has made love to Maria in the heather, and the earth has moved, Jordan quickly detaches himself into the "clear and hard and sharp" (177) focus of his mind, and his thoughts lead him to consideration of the book he must write. However, he now notes that "thinking by yourself," you tend to think "rot" and that this reprimanding other side of himself is the part to discipline the radically detached observer. Thinking of how he might exorcise his demons by writing about them, he muses, "It will be a good book if you can write it" (181), but his other side takes him in hand: "Don't lie to yourself" (183). It is at this point in the novel that Jordan enters into internal colloquy with that other part of the self that has now gained dominance, "the other of him" that speaks to him, refutes him, and mocks him. Later, we get such passages as "It's all right, he told himself. . . . Then himself said back to him" (327).

The ending of the novel witnesses the acknowledgment and integration of the two discrete selves, the protagonist fulfilling his own fictive mission that is simultaneously the author's fulfillment of the aesthetic quest, art as therapy overthrowing and curing schizophrenia.

Anselmo lets us see how fully Hemingway has made the fictive bridge and the novel being written—the thing to be destroyed and the thing being created—become one and the same, as he replies to Pilar's exasperation at Jordan's laborious slowness ("Is he building a bridge or blowing one?") with "Patience, woman . . . he is terminating his work" (478). This remark, given to us near the end of what has been a long journey through a long novel, draws us up short, for, indeed, we clearly see that both the character who is completing his task and the character's creator, the author Hemingway, are equally and together terminating their work, and we, as readers, are forced to exist both inside and outside of Hemingway's creation, inside both the writer (Hemingway) and his character/creature (Jordan). The reader has been brought to a point of transcendence, lifted from his imaginative immersion in fiction to rise above it, to be in it yet beyond it at the same moment. This kind of transcendence the whole book and Hemingway's developed philosophy in it exist to achieve. Jordan has been brought to a recognition of the fusion of dramatic opposites in transcendent synthesis in his love-making with Maria/Rabbit, who has taught him how, through love, the sacred instant of orgasmic "now" can be eternity and "now" simultaneously, just as Pilar has taught him how 72 hours can be a lifetime and how there is always something mystical and unknown within the logical and the known. Jordan has systematically learned, so that at the end he speaks at once to Maria and to us, the readers.

The Anselmo/Pilar exchange has disengaged Hemingway from Jordan sufficiently so that the creature and creator are both identifiable together and at once. But then, as Jordan lays his charges and wires the bridge for destruction and is nearing the end of his mission, Hemingway simultaneously splits Maria, so that she, recipient of Jordan's love, the one partly for whom he lives and dies, is obviously at once the fictional Maria/Rabbit and also the reader, and they receive instructions that are clearly instructions from the bridge blower and the author: "Each one must do it alone. But if thou goest then I go with thee. It is in that way that I go too. . . . Thou wilt go now, I know. . . . Thou wilt go now for us both" (498). As Jordan sends Maria on to life beyond him, he, we realize, is Hemingway sending us on also into the safety-dangers of our unpredictable lives, carrying inside us the memory of his acts and love and sacrifice, so that he does not die but remains there and has immortality only in and through us who are affected and remember and have been changed in the reading encounter. Jordan and Hemingway and Maria and the reader have been precipitated out and been atoned. Pronouncing the benediction at the end and the proof of the atonement that all great writing in the aesthetic experience of reading exists to achieve, Jordan cries out in what we hear as at once his voice and Hemingway the author's voice: "I am thee also now. . . . You are me now. . . . Now you go for us both. Truly. We both go in thee now" (499) and "Thou art all there will be of me. . . . I am with thee" (500). Hemingway not only has invested us with his work, creating an inseparable, undeniable, and intense reader-author bond but has perfectly placed the charges to blow the bridge, destroy the fiction, and allow the novel at the end to end, so that he is finally left behind, as he must be, and exists only in the silence, the space he has created, the hidden depths below the tip of his iceberg. The blowing of the bridge that is the completion of Jordan's mission must be almost simultaneous with the ending of the written novel, and all that remains is explanation of the process: the injunction to the reader to carry the experience within him safely; the celebration of his, the writer's, own achievement; and the rites he prepares for the death of the writer/bridge blower who must be consumed within his work. Hemingway does all this in religious imagery and rites, and in the person of his own dying protagonist, who is sacrificed to the fiction that encloses him and that gives him existence, he pronounces his own *consummatum est* upon his own work. There are few greater moments in all of fiction. The artist, Hemingway tells us over and over—with Harry of "The Snows of Kilimanjaro" as with David of *The Garden of Eden*—must purchase his work at the cost of life, and Jordan's many forays into cold, clear planning for his great task have illustrated carefully the way the bridge blower extricates himself from his love and his life relations in order to have the clarity and isolation in which he prepares to fulfill his life's mission. The blowing of a bridge is the supremely apt metaphor for the meaning and cost of the creative process, which makes connections only at the cost of a disengaged breaking of connections. Bridge blowing, the destruction of bridges, lies at the heart of art, which is a bridge from the past to the future, from one person to all others. "Is he building a bridge or blowing one?" (478) Pilar rages. The answer is, of course, both. He is simultaneously doing both. After the bridge is blown and Jordan has received his death wound, Hemingway still does not let us go beyond without understanding fully the fusion of art and life, life and death, time and eternity, mortality and immortality that he has structured. He has Robert Jordan prepare for his end:

> He looked down the hill slope again and he thought, "I hate to leave it is all. I hate to leave it very much and I hope I have done some good in it—I have tried with what talent I had. Have, you mean. All right, have." (502)

The "talent," we see, is preeminently that of a writer who must simultaneously be a bridge builder and destroyer in order to remain a writer. When in his reflections Hemingway-Jordan refuses the past tense and insists upon "have," we as readers are further forced to continue to exist at our high point of transcendence while still being within the fictive world. As Hemingway rejects his death with his character's death, so that he can (in a unique way) survive to go on to write another masterpiece, we are made to exist both in and outside the fiction. The author inside the creature he has created for destruction insists upon the survival of his own talent, although the very means through which he lives in and through us, Jordan the character, must die. Also, we witness a deeply moving sight as Jordan expresses his reluctance to leave the land he lovingly appraises: we see not Jordan so much as the author within his own created work appraising and loving the fictive landscape of his dream, so involved and within his fiction that he hates to "leave it." His expressed lament at the end is, "I wish there was some way to pass on what I've learned though. Christ, I was learning fast there at the end" (503). Yes, Hemingway was so learning, and only as we see and study what he has given us the transcendence and detachment to see, in seeing the way the craftsmanship and style are inseparable from its created creation, the way the accomplishment rests on the process—the message, by the way, of the whole book as well as of the artist—is his stylistic aesthetic victory able to survive.

WORKS CITED

Hemingway, Ernest. *For Whom the Bell Tolls*. New York: Scribners, 1968.

14

False Fathers, Doctors, and the Caesarean Dilemma

Metaphor as Structure in Hemingway's In Our Time

What Ernest Hemingway brought to the short story was a new style, emerging from his work as a journalist and his excitement over the "new language" of telegraphy that he used in his métier, influenced by Anderson, Turgenev, Flaubert, Maupassant, Lawrence, and others but developed under Joyce. In Paris, he had time to read and experiment and study, and his new discoveries in prose were begun and perfected in his 1922 efforts in the crafting of a sentence and subsequently in his spare structuring of his vignettes: these brought an absolute of lyrical hardness and economy to his short story form. Additionally bringing the aesthetics of Cézanne and then Cubism to bear on prose, he made the pages of a short story a charged canvas where geometric and mathematically structured forms, as in music, established the undercurrent of significant movement and meaning. More important still, he concomitantly, as a result of his deep studies with both Pound and Joyce—as I have emphasized in my several essays studying especially Joyce's profound influence upon him[1]—embedded the full range of modernist techniques and attitudes in his work. A Hemingway story is usually prominently a modernist work, and I consider Hemingway—notwithstanding the rich allusiveness, inclusiveness, and strategies of Joyce and the mythologies of Pound—probably the supreme modernist prose writer, whose multileveled intellectual structures, unlike those of Eliot, Pound, and Joyce, had the sophisticated forbearance to conceal themselves.

Hemingway took pride in masteries, in knowing what he knew and knowing the world about him, and especially in being responsible to his métier. However, the basic pride of Hemingway, the writer that Wyndham Lewis styled the "dumb ox" (for his apparent anti-intellectualism), was his *self*-knowledge—after all, what is more central to the virtue of a Hemingway protagonist finally than his own knowledge and judgment of *his own* performance and behavior? What is moral is what one feels good after; morality refuses external definitions. It is this internalization of morality that should let us understand what violence we were doing to Hemingway texts by such critical nonsense terminology as "the code hero" or "the macho hero" when we should have immediately seen that they may have applied to characters but never to the author. He carefully defined his attitude toward his work: in his Nobel Prize speech, he says, "Writing, at its best, is a *lonely life*. . . . [A writer] does his work *alone* and if he is a good enough writer he must face eternity, or the lack of it, each day. . . . [The writer] should always try for something that *has never been done*" and "It is because we have had such great writers in the past that a writer is driven far out past where he can go, out to *where no one can help him*" (qtd. in Baker 528–29; italics mine). Hemingway's pride was in this isolate self-knowledge, purchased at the cost of remaining essentially unread and unknown, except as the absurd parody of a persona that the public was given—partially in contempt by Hemingway and partially by the journalism of his time. As he many times said, he looked to posterity for his legitimization. We are that posterity, and we have so far in many ways failed him.

If we are to attempt to newly, freshly read Hemingway, what could be more salutary and necessary than a return to his early work? This essay goes back to the first three stories of his collected book of short stories *In Our Time*—not to exhaustively read them (that is impossible here given the depths and dimensions of his art) but merely to suggest overlooked structural techniques brought to his earliest short story writing.

It was in 1930, with the Scribners reissue of *In Our Time*, that the introductory very short story (or "miniature") "On the Quai at Smyrna" was added to the collection. Hemingway had undoubtedly been unconsciously seeking for some time for a keystone to tightly finish off and lock together the arch of his archetype, to give total structural integrity to his first volume, and "On the Quai" was it. "On the Quai," though partly originating in current events and Hemingway's journalism, transcends them; thematically, structurally, and metaphorically, it seems essential to the collection. It is saturated with the same obsessions and deep concerns that were forming the early *In Our Time* stories that he was also writing in Paris during those years. As one looks at its mysterious implication and involvement with the other two stories that follow it, "Indian Camp" and "The Doctor and the Doctor's Wife," it is apparent that the three, each deeply, amazingly implicated in the other two, form a rigorous triadic introduction.

A controlling metaphor of this trio of stories is birth—appropriate to a book's beginning—but a complicated and unnatural birth process, in which, on the surface in the first two stories and metaphorically in all three, birth and death are inextricable. The young Nick Adams of "Indian Camp," freshly given to us as a child observing birth, is directly studied in the emotional/psychological complications of his origins and the handicaps of the violent world he has entered, but all three of these introductory stories relentlessly focus on overt or latent violence, questionable origins, and, as I will show, the birth process itself. That the two stories that follow the three, "The End of Something" and "The Three-Day Blow," are stories driven by a fear of pregnancy but further embeds the theme.

The thematically joined introductory three stories seem very different, having unshared settings and drama: an emergency evacuation procedure at the quai in the harbor at Smyrna during the Graeco-Turkish conflict there; a Michigan Indian camp by night where an emergency Caesarean operation must be performed with inadequate medical equipment; and Nick's home at the lake's edge, where, during a log-collecting operation at the shore, complex sexual challenges from an Indian laborer and subsequently in his home from his wife suicidally challenge the doctor in his identity as husband and father and man.

Despite these radical differences, the stories are radically similar. Indeed, the second and third stories are in reality mirror image reversals of one another. In the first of these, three men—a father, his son, and another man—come from the highly technologically developed literate, verbal, mental, rational white world to help the Indian world, bringing their tools with them to assist in prying loose a child, questionably the child of the given father, unnaturally locked in the womb of the mother. In the next story, a similar male trio—a father, his son, and another man—journey from the dark and intuitive, physical and instinctive Indian world to help the white world, bringing with them the tools to pry loose the logs, metaphorically established as the children of the claiming but false father, logs that seem mired in the placental shores of the amniotic waters of the womblike lake. In both stories, *apparently* legitimate paternity is questioned, and the father whose claim to fatherhood is made suspect seems the sacrifice to the birth process, while the interloper, the outsider, who functions in the responsible role of aiding the birth process, although acting to restore unnaturally presented life to its natural relations, is portrayed as detached and alienated from natural life. All these stories put an outsider in the role of the one who negotiates between life and death in a birth process in which legitimate fathers are sequentially absent ("On the Quai"), incapacitated ("Indian Camp"), or challenged as unvirile ("The Doctor and the Doctor's Wife").

In all three stories the major metaphors are not just birth but also death and rebirth. "Indian Camp" overtly looks at the birth process, and its connection there to death lets the reader know that this childbirth is a traumatic stage in a rebirth rite of passage for Nick, who will be, we feel, fundamentally changed as a result of what he has seen and heard and learned of both life and death. Out of his immersion in a situation where birth seems inextricable from death—as though in mythic death-journey initiatory rites—will be reborn a new Nick whose father-son relation is being recreated. The doctor father's failures are not lost on the boy. The Indian father in the story is ineffectual and impotent to help, and the suicide death of this father (whose very paternity is called in question in the story when he commits suicide and when it is Uncle George who gives out the celebratory cigars) is heard against the suffering of the violated mother and the arrogance, if necessity, of those who intrude to help while taking the father's power from him.

In "On the Quai," the absence of declared or identified fathers is central, given the witnessed suffering of children and women and beasts, so that alien officials acting in guiding paternal roles seem, like the doctor of "Indian Camp," to have replaced the absent real or ineffectual fathers. Here, too, in the midst of birth is death; babies are seen as at once alive *and* dead and as extricated from a place of dying and death. The major action of the story, however, is focused on a rescue *rebirth* operation to restore life to the dead victims of war.

In the third story, the logs are metaphorically portrayed as the children claimed as belonging to a morally questionable and sexually intimidated and humiliated father/husband. His ownership of the logs, which have been lying unclaimed and are locked in deathlike trance until released, is called in question, and at the end it is suggested that the responsibility has devolved upon the story's largely disregarded son to save his father by leading him on a death journey through the hemlock (death-associated) woods to the place of genuine life/sexuality.[2] The suggested necessary death/rebirth journey of the father, following the story's focus on the immersed and unclaimed logs that need to be rescued/reborn, ends with a son thrust into a new guiding/teaching paternal role.

In all three stories, those who officiate in a paternal role are mocked. In "On the Quai," the speaking voice of the negotiating officer is mocked and mocks itself; in "Indian Camp," the presiding doctor (also a father) is remorselessly exposed in his vanities; and in "The Doctor and the Doctor's Wife," the father's cowardice, lies, and impotence are painfully revealed.

All three stories focus on linguistic strategies of avoidance and defense. In "On the Quai," the British officer's linguistic detachment and the almost insane impropriety of his diction and language seem necessary, even if callous, buffers against unbearable reality; in "Indian Camp," the doctor's inappropriate diction and fastidious linguistic distance seem a temperamental liability, even if a chosen professional strategy, connected to the fatality; and in the third story, the defensive linguistic controls of the doctor/father and the wife/mother—those of the father to avoid the recognition of his immoral pilfering and his sexual/physical inadequacy, and those of his wife, to gain a Christian fundamentalist manipulation of reality while revealing in diction a loveless and distanced detachment from both husband and son—suggest the enormity of the son's dilemma and estrangement. Language in all three stories is central: it violates as it functions.

All three stories, interestingly enough, offer the imagery not only of childbirth but of necessary *Caesarean* obstetric techniques that must be brought to the aid of dangerously thwarted unnatural nature. The described Smyrna harbor in "On the Quai," where reality is unnatural because of war, is patently a womb; at the end of the pier in the harbor that is enrounded by its amniotic sea, the to-be-born children and their mothers are seen as though attached to the placental wall of the harbor. Helpless as the Indian mother and her child, they must depend upon the strategies and techniques and technology of others—clinically detached alien figures introduced to serve in this unnatural birth/rebirth process—to be pried loose and brought out through the narrow vaginal channel to the possibility of life beyond. The officiating "obstetric" official, at once alien, detached, and aloof in his manner, seems to bestow (and be simultaneously allied with) both birth and death. This behavior is precisely like that of the doctor of "Indian Camp," who, if he brings life out of the mother, is seen by his son as bringing death to the Indian father: Nick sees his father, one of his hands holding the light, the other seemingly decapitating the Indian.

In "Indian Camp," the obstetric process and doctor need not be metaphorical, but the Caesarean operation itself takes us into an inner darkness and the mystery of otherness as it demands a journey into the visceral, physical inner life of another. It is a journey both into the instinctual Indian culture, essentially alien to the detached doctor, and into the unseen inner mysteries of the Indian woman, to which the doctor tries to introduce his son. In "The Doctor and the Doctor's Wife," the darkened inner world of the wife/mother is elaborately screened from the doctor, but the lake shore in which the logs are embedded, if carefully read, is again here given as a placental wall from which the logs need to be detached and then rocked and carried free so that they may be subsequently named, claimed, and acknowledged. The scene in which the doctor/father's ownership of them—his paternity of them— is questioned is one filled with vivid sexual taunt and denial of the doctor's potency. Dick Boulton's ejaculated spit that runs off the log is a sexual metaphor as filled with sexual challenge and paternal vaunt in this story, as is Uncle George's distribution of cigars as he arrives for the birth at the Indian camp. "Don't go off at half-cock, Doc, Dick said" (27) is a hilariously contrived line. If in "Indian Camp" the paternity of the child being brought into the world with Caesarean section is questioned, and the suicide of the reputed Indian father is made to seem somehow related, in this third story, as the doctor father fondles and plays with his gun, not only a masturbatory but also a suicidal undercurrent is well established that is implemented by the direction he finally takes toward the hemlock woods. Gun and hemlock are the two means: one suggests death in defeat, the other death as victory, leading to rebirth. The latter, in a Freudian/mythic way, is tied to the resurrecting son.

All three stories study the dereliction and failure of fathers, unnatural birth processes, and flawed nurturing; all three study alien "others," who, in intrusive detachment, bring their tools and techniques to guard a threatened natural process; and all three equally, with harrowing insistence, implicate childhood and examine the danger that the child creates as he presents himself in the world. Those dangers are obvious in "On the Quai," given the inopportuneness of the births and the hazards and handicaps they present, and are also obvious in "Indian Camp," but they are hidden in the third story until the reader sees that it is the extrication/birth of the logs that is the act that brings the father into confrontation, defeat, and potential suicide.

In "On the Quai," the very cycles of the life process are seen as the cause of terror. The question is asked why the women scream every night just at midnight. The answer to that unanswered question is that midnight, unlike noon, is the end of one cycle and the beginning of another. Like the life/death on the pier here and the birth/suicide death of "Indian Camp," the metaphoric problematic birth of the otherwise submerged and slowly decomposing logs, and the suggested suicide of the questionable father, these enforced oxymoronic joinings of birth and death are uroboric, the mouth eating the tail, and the process never-ending: they are troubling in the extreme. In "On the Quai," the arrest of this eternal uroboric cycle is seen when the mothers keep their dead babies at their breasts and refuse to give them up. In that unmoving frozen image of new life become death feasting on life, and again in the image of the old woman whose feet draw up at the moment of death, in fetal position, as though she were about to be born, death locked to life is the expressed problem. This image is reinforced in "Indian Camp" by the fatal urgency created by the child who needs to be but cannot be born—an emergency in which the unnatural use of Caesarean techniques *is* the remedy. In "The Doctor and the Doctor's Wife," the logs will remain in a state of slow decay if they cannot be extricated, and again it is the alien intruder with his special potency and equipment whose power breaks life from death.

The resolution of the problem, the act of breaking the uroboric round and separating life and death, is left to the surrogate fathers, those who bring obstetric process and detachment to the situation—shutting their eyes to the "nice things floating in [the harbor]" (11), refusing to hear the mother's screams, and having no inhibiting moral scruples to get in the way—as they take the dead babies away from the mothers' breasts ("On the Quai"), or with Caesarean expertise cut loose the unnaturally presented fetus ("Indian Camp"), or rock and roll the mired logs free ("The Doctor and the Doctor's Wife"). Their detachment and their function recommend our consideration of their larger historical/aesthetic meaning. The detached, cool discipline of their emotional involvement in the material in which they are forced to deal—using a distancing language that allows them at once disengagement and ambiguities that might be called lies—suggests that in these very first stories (of a writer who is to become a consummate artist), the real subject is the complex and simultaneous pride and guilt that the artist cannot escape. Nick, at the end of "Indian Camp" feeling quite sure that he will "never die," is a sure indication of the outsetting artist's assurance and clear perception of the way toward immortality.

Artists must confront again and again the need to attain, through a hard objectivity and at great cost—running the risk of a judgment of inhumanity for their function—the role of the culture's heroic challengers, the ones who break the pagan preliterate world's control. Essentially this is the role of the writers who heroically help their culture escape the eternal uroboric round of birth and death in which one eternally comes out of and returns into the other. The artist legitimizes the dualistic aesthetic terms whereby the word on the page permits the detachment necessary to civilization. Hemingway, aware of Joyce as we know he was, well understood from Joyce's *A Portrait of the Artist as a Young Man* that the further role of the artist was "to forge in the smithy of [his] soul the uncreated conscience of [the] race" (299). He well knew the artist's further role as priest of the unconscious and *Kulturträger*. The young Nick at the end of "Indian Camp," who is discovering how he might "never die," and the young Nick at the end of "The Doctor and the Doctor's Wife," who is leading the father back into the darkness of the forest toward the sacred vitalistic mysteries with which he has failed to connect, is indeed setting out on his life's journey. "Big Two-Hearted River," at the end of *In Our Time*, defines the sacred place and the rites of psychic restoration, while "Indian Camp," at its beginning, clearly delineates the essential vital role of the father as well as his yet "uncreated conscience," one that Nick is studying to forge.

I have for many years been a student of the sculptural art of the portals, modillons, and capitals of the early Romanesque churches of the Saintonge area of France. I have always been exhilarated to see in these sculptures a sculptured image of a man standing on a circling snake that is trying to swallow its own tail while the man prevents this by holding by sheer force the head and tail apart. I well recognize that in very early Romanesque churches, where you will uniquely see this image, it means the end of the pagan round, broken by the light of civilization; it means the introduction of that challenge to the Romanesque arch that will eventually create the Gothic lancets and spires. It means the overthrow of holistic prehistoric night by the split psyche and idealistic mode of modern thought; and it means the victory of the spirit over the flesh, of consciousness over unconsciousness, and the Word triumphant over organic life. And, I posit, it means the same victory in Hemingway's protagonists, those that both he and we may judge harshly (and perhaps sentimentally) for being disengaged while tampering with natural process, for their intrusion in the natural fact of inextricable birth and death. They are the technicians, the word makers, who, in detachment and difference and distance, are able to comment on and record the natural scene they serve and witness. They are the artists whose very art is our glory and, when they are as sensitive as Hemingway, their shame. We can understand why the young Nick Adams—returning across the water with the returning day, having seen his father fail and succeed as doctor/priest at a service of both birth and death (that Nick as acolyte attended)—will trail one hand in the warm, deep waters, while the other reconciles him to the upper cool and life-giving air.

As one proceeds through the *In Our Time* stories, the protagonists in "The End of Something" and in "The Three-Day Blow" see themselves as victimized by pregnancy and the facts of birth, as subsequently will be Hubert Elliot and the husbands in "Cat in the Rain" and "Cross-Country Snow." The later "Hills Like White Elephants" certainly belongs with these stories. But this ambiguous pregnancy danger is immediately declared, if mockingly and covertly, at the very beginning of "On the Quai" as Hemingway examines in detail the danger of the ship "coming in," coming down a narrow channel into a harbor. In the antepenultimate paragraph, it is a sexual joke, and he elaborately develops it. In that one paragraph Hemingway tells us that they were ordered "not to come in" but that they "came in" and were going to dangerously "come in." The result of all that "coming in" is predicted catastrophe and leads to the next paragraph's description of an amniotic harbor with "plenty of nice things floating in it" together with the imagery of bestial birth. This danger of "coming in" is the basis of discussion by the life-fearful boys in "The Three-Day Blow." In that story the classic sexual joke is extended to the dangers of having and not having "socks on" and the boys' need for rubber blankets to keep them safe from the wet. (Water and wetness have been identified with the dangers of Marjorie and her moon-driven powers in the preceding story.) Such prophylactic imagery importantly underwrites the interlocked themes of death and birth in the first three stories.

Death that cannot be separated from birth, or birth from suffering, leads the sensitive writer-artist into his pursuit of responsible surrogate aesthetic strategies of detachment. The uroboric situation is, as I have implied, the state of unconfronted nature, and the conferred or seized distance that allows for detachment concomitantly brings language, art, and civilization—but *at a price*. Caesarean obstetric strategies in all three introductory stories, tied as they are to an overthrow of guardianship and the paternity of fathers, as well as to detached linguistic modes, suggest that Hemingway was from the very beginning of his career alert to technique and the "price," the costs of the writer's aesthetic distance when dealing with life, and—and this is the important point—inordinately sensitive to the violences of art and the occasionally almost fatal meaning of art's surrogate role. What happens to Catherine as a would-be creator and to David as writer in *The Garden of Eden* is but a further development of the argument begun at the very beginning of Hemingway's career in his first published book of stories. Yes, it is all about Eve's apple and Nick Adams's sharing of it. We are not dealing with Nick Adams, but with Nick's Adam.

NOTES

1. In several of my writings I have studied the Joyce/Hemingway connection, most notably in two essays included in this volume: "Hemingway and Joyce: A Study in Debt and Payment" and "Dubliners in Michigan: Joyce's Presence in Hemingway's *In Our Time*."

2. In "Fathers and Sons," the place where the black squirrels are is heavily coded as the place of primitive and potent sexuality.

WORKS CITED

Baker, Carlos. *Ernest Hemingway: A Life Story*. New York: Scribners, 1969.
Hemingway, Ernest. *In Our Time*. 1925. New York: Scribners, 1930.
Joyce, James. *A Portrait of the Artist as a Young Man*. London: Egoist, 1916.

15

A Farewell to Arms

The Psychodynamics of Integrity

A Farewell to Arms studies the psychodynamics of integrity—whether of the lover, the soldier, the physician, the artist, the priest, or the anarchist—and it does so at a fundamental level, considering all relations between individuals as efforts at Being, caught in the pressures of life, where one either establishes identity or may be reduced to Unbeingness or absurdity. In this novel Hemingway is concerned with the alternative bondage or freedom of the self; false or authentic selves or false or authentic commitments are scrutinized, and the failure to hold a defined line—in love or war—is seen as potentially fatal. Arms bind, as do hearts and words, in the world of love, just as duties, conventions, obligations, and a sense of camaraderie and responsibility bind in battle. To be so bound, to disdain and break such bonds, and to wish to break such bonds are some of the psychological positions intricately, subtly studied in the novel.

The lovers are seen as, initially, disengaged; they play their "game" with one another and with themselves. Catherine is well aware of her willingness to use the illusion of love (in the illusion of attachment to a nonexistent "other," her dead boy lover) as a hysterical mode of excitement; and Frederic is opportunistically willing to use her masturbatory need as a means to his own real sexual fulfillment. Later, when Frederic finds himself "in" love, he must recognize that it means attachment within the sunderings of war. He has already discovered the way freedom is imaginatively expanded by the abstract reality of the "other": in chapter 7, shortly after he has entered into his "game" of love with Catherine, he is able, apart from her, to visualize an interlude in a hotel in Milan that is far more sensually precise and erotically detailed than any of his actual moments with her have been. When he concludes his revery with the observation "That was how it ought to be" (38), the reader observes that for Frederic at this time imaginative fulfillment is superior to actual experience. In Milan, and with the lovers "in" love in chapter 20, Hemingway carefully focuses upon the details that suggest the burden of reality and on how realistically limited their love is by the fact of possession: at the racetrack with Catherine, Frederic neglects her, and though he tries to pacify her, he has been seen going through elaborate strategies of avoidance.

The priest has, however, defined love as the desire to do something "for" another, as an internal imperative that conditions external action and demands the virtue of selfless gestures. The gifts he brings to Frederic in the hospital—the mosquito netting, the English magazines, and the vermouth that Frederic likes—are examples of such self-transcendence and thinking into the other, while the gift of Rinaldi, the cognac that he largely consumes himself, is just the opposite.[1] Catherine's strategy that she uses against time and reality is to erect an illusionary "we" or "us" (134), with which she would destroy the I/Thou of their separate identities. She justifies the eradication of her Self and establishes her illusion as a means of perfecting a stronger "we" against "them" (134), those who might otherwise "get" them, destroy them. Thereafter, a host of real details and situations ironically comment on such a bond and show it to be both spurious and a form of bondage. The lovers cannot descend the stairs together at the Milan hotel, for one must precede the other; Catherine cannot "be" with Frederic as she wills, for her duties refuse her that as surely as do his; they will not fall asleep together, however nice it may be to think that they may. Their "always" (121) must be accommodated to the rain and reality and shown to be a fake absolute caught on a spinning wheel of season, time, and Fortune.

The perfected Self, the lost Self, the perjured Self, and the Not Self are Hemingway's subjects, as are the hysteria, lies, illusions, and falsifications that immediately enter a life based on such unreal constructions. As Gertrude Stein might say, "There is no 'I' there," and consequently there may be no true "there" there either. Hemingway demonstrates how the "I" is generally lost in society, so that as it ceases to exist, a narcissistic infantilism, dependent and hollow, takes its place. Visited in the hospital by the major and Rinaldi, anxious to please and agree with them, and willing to do so at whatever cost to the self, Frederic destroys his integrity. The result of his too-great willingness to accept an external reality, the "other," and his unwillingness to defend the integrity of the self by acknowledging the necessity for dialectical interchange across boundaries—conversation!—is absurdity: feminine Roma becomes "the mother and father of nations" (74), and Romulus, one of the suck-led founders of Rome, becomes the maternal suckler. That is the point. Desperately anxious to create a "we" in war on the model given to him by Catherine in love, and perhaps subtly conditioned by his "death" experience of being wounded, which has powerfully influenced his sense of what lies "on the other side," he now verbally shifts between false and created identities and ends up becoming, to Rinaldi, "Baby" (75). Book 1 ends by showing him as a helpless and dependent child, sick and vom-iting, cared for in a hospital by others.

Hemingway begins book 2 with chapter 13's portrayal of a domi-nant "they" who manipulate the questionable "I" that lost its identity at the end of book 1. Now, at a new beginning, he meticulously studies the consolidation and establishment of a new "I" that Frederic pointedly brings into being by his demand for answers to *his* questions when he finds himself surrounded by incompetents and unrespectable and irre-sponsible "others." His extrication of his Self from "them" is central to the possibilities for the new "we" that he almost immediately establishes with Catherine. However, by the opening paragraph of chapter 18, Hemingway is, in intricate counterpoint, ironically studying the va-lidity of this new "we," and by the end of the chapter it has been legiti-mately called in question. Catherine's accepted offer to do anything to please Frederic, and "to play" (112), must pointedly acknowledge the constraints within which it is made: "I'll go and see the patients first" (112), she tells him. Chapter 19 begins with a chant where, in the first fourteen lines, the pronoun "I" sings out twelve times, but this is the chapter where Frederic discards Catherine for the "boys" (115). Chap-ter 20 examines the reestablished but totally spurious "we," and Heming-way allows the reader to witness its falseness as it shifts its referent out from under Catherine in midparagraph. He begins the paragraph with "We four drove out to San Siro" (124). The four have been carefully identified as Frederic, Catherine, Ferguson, and Crowell Rodgers, and Hemingway steadily orchestrates and controls the paragraph with this same "we" as subject—there is no point at which it shifts in any fashion away from its antecedent. But the last sentence of the paragraph ends, "We saw people we knew and got chairs for Ferguson and Catherine and watched the horses" (124). The reader witnesses a tour de force of Hem-ingway's style as he lets Frederic "lose" the girls and notably cut himself off from Catherine without anyone seeing how it happened, let alone Catherine; his subsequent actions express his desire to be restored to his own devices. In the next chapter, chapter 21, before Frederic receives the news of Catherine's pregnancy, he has thrown his allegiance to an alternative "they" and reconstituted another new "we" that again excludes her, and as he returns to the hospital to meet Catherine, he is totally dominated by a selfish "I" that only finally relinquishes its obsession with the self and its interests when he finally reflects on "our horse, Japalac" (131). The irony of this is bitter: *their* horse was Light For Me, the losing horse they had chosen *together* to be able to be free of such disguised phonies offering tips as Mr. Myers, a man who shares nothing with his wife. Such minutely studied relations of "I" and "we" and "they," carried in pronoun dominance or shift, express the meaning of the novel in miniature.[2]

To George, the barman, Frederic presents Catherine and himself as a new "we," but George is perceptive: like other barmen and other hoteliers later in the novel, he refuses to believe in the false union. He argues against the wine Catherine has chosen for them to drink: "You try it, lady, . . . if you want to. But let me bring a little bottle of margaux *for the Tenente*" (109, italics mine). When Frederic says, "I'll try it, too" (109), George responds, "Sir, I can't recommend you to" (you two?) and finally says, "I'll bring it . . . and when *the lady* is satisfied, I'll take it away" (109, italics mine). Carefully, Hemingway extends his analysis as he has George lend Frederic money, give him that which is not his own: "That's all right, Tenente . . . I know how a man gets short. If you *or* the lady need money I've always got money" (109, italics mine). His refusal to accept the false union offered by Frederic Henry is a warning: he well knows the sources of castration—"how a man gets short"—that are related to a loss of the Self.

In war, the inability to maintain identity, and thus the loss of integrity, is studied as the cost of disguise, desertion, permitted breakthroughs, anarchy, and the casting off of significant duties, roles, and established definitions. Hemingway lets us know how utterly a self depends upon gestures or acts of acknowledgment of the "other." The self exists on one side, and it must come into awareness of, acknowledgment of, what exists on the other side—not to capitulate to it, but to experientially know it so that "it" may be respected—so that both may be integrally respectable. This is the lesson Romero teaches in *The Sun Also Rises*, as he shows how a crossing can be made into the territory of the feared "other," so that the two if only momentarily become one:

such knowledge and daring strengthen the self at no expense to the self. A self insulated against the other, like that of the anarchist Passini, who would only "convert" others to *his* point of view, or like that of Rinaldi, who cannot afford to listen to the priest, is not truly an "I," just as a Self that surrenders and capitulates to the "enemy," or the beloved or the "Other" on the other side, ceases to be a Self. With real selves in real situations, there is a firm sense of recognition of the other, of shared and unshared reality, and each in the interchange crosses over into the terrain of the other while remaining in his other own identity and returning to his other "Self."[3] This is fully illustrated in Frederic's reciprocal and shared relations with the barman at Stresa with whom he goes fishing, a man who will later save his life, and in his game of billiards with Count Greffi, an avatar of male integrity. In these relations there is disciplined and controlled physical and linguistic crossover into terrain of the other *and* return.[4]

Hemingway's metaphoric extensions of his insights into the psychology of Being are projected in exempla of identity and loss of identity: in Rinaldi gesturing to bring the priest into the brothel, as if the differences between the spirit and the flesh could be ignored *without penalty*, in the anarchist Bonello's desire to sleep with the queen, and in Passini's desire to throw down his arms and go home, as though class lines or battlelines could be treated as if they did not exist, *without penalty*. On the other hand, Japalac, the "painted" horse—like Frederic Henry in Italian uniform, or like Edouardo Giovanni, an American singer who performs under an assumed Italian identity—is at once what he is and what he is not, and those who recognize this profit from the recognition, however limited their gains. Japalac exists in part to illustrate that one cannot ignore the reality beneath the disguise *without penalty*. When one of Frederic's cars comes to rest on its "differential" (194), distinctions are lost between one side and the other, and immediately a man dies: an Italian is killed as if he were an enemy Austrian. The ignoring of distinctions creates ignorance and death. Those who jokingly call the madam of the brothel "the Mother Superior" (181) ironically practice eradication of distinctions, but a real self makes real distinctions between reality and illusion, the "Self" and the "Other," the one side and the other. When Rinaldi waves the priest into the brothel, he playfully would treat the priest's emphatic moral boundaries as insignificant, and he is, in fact, irritated by such careful definition of the Self, which seems a judgment on his own inconsequence. Passini, who argues for the dissolution of boundaries between the self and its enemies, dies calling out simultaneously upon the Virgin Mary and "Mama mia." The bad doctors cannot tell an X-ray of the left foot from the right; the carabinieri, satisfied with insufficient evidence regarding identity—who belongs to which side—arbitrarily kill patriots, infiltrators, and deserters as they attempt to establish lines of meaning against chaotic flow. It is the silhouette maker, who carefully separates one side of his creation from the other so that both may be seen, who addresses himself and Frederic as "I" and "thee" (130). The whirling world of Milan and the big cities, where distinctions between the self and the not-self are lost, is poised in the novel against the priest's world of the Abruzzi, the high, cold, clear world where distinctions and conventions are rigidly respected: one is a world of cycles and enveloping darkness, the other a world of high, clear, paternal spiritual authority.

In the novel, isolate identities are opposed to broken, destroyed, and invaded identities: such integrities as the mountains and towns that cannot be taken, walled gardens, and the priest's unchanging belief under the fire of the men's mockery are opposed to captured and occupied towns, crossed bridges and rivers, clouds that come over the mountain, the almost shameful spectacle of the interiors of smashed houses that have lost walls and have plaster and rubble in their gardens, and a car "disgraced and empty" (16) with its engine open and parts spread about. The point is that most of these inert specified details enter the novel less to express verisimilitude than to underwrite intellectually the struggle for identity under stress and in seasonal time that the novel is studying. Hemingway examines the losses to wounds, bridgeheads, and philosophies and the demands of perverse love, which break down such vital perimeters. Ruptured forms, abandoned positions, cast-off hernial trusses, breakthroughs, capitulations in love and war—all speak philosophically. It is recognized that "anybody may crack," and the narrative line thereafter is the illustration of the mode and effects of such cracking or breaking of essential walls or vital perimeters.

Youth, of course, covets experience and disdains reactionary conservative entrenchment. Although the priest is mocked as having yielded his identity—"priest today with girls" (7)—the irritation he provokes is rather caused by his virtue among the unvirtuous. He is therefore assailed: "priest wants us never to attack," and priest "every night five against one" (7). The charges are of an insularity and a masturbatory refusal to readily yield to, or an unwillingness to explore, the "other side." Frederic acknowledges distinctions—the "difference between the night and the day" (13)—and he well knows the difference between the Abruzzi, where he did not go, though he wanted to, and the centers of culture, where he nevertheless went for his sexual debauch. But in Milan, he undergoes loss of identity and dissolution of the integral boundaries of the Self when he exposes himself to rapid repetitive cycles—"One thing had led to another" (12)—and his recitation of places visited is like "a timetable" (11) as he tries to respond to Rinaldi's twice-expressed wish for "everything at once" (11). In such a conglomerate world, of going everywhere but nowhere, of "waking and not knowing who it was with you" (13), of "uncaring" and "not caring in the night" (13), people are lost and life is lost. It is right that he should note upon his return from leave that "it did not matter whether I was there or not" (16), for in a cyclical world where differences are negated, individuality is lost, and there are only replaceable, because noninte-gral, parts. The soldiers wish that the girls in the brothel might be rotated more frequently so that they might *not* become comrades: they are not after an I/Thou relationship, rather just the opposite. With Frederic, inner reality is sacrificed to the flesh, but he has been one who deals in charades, where the inner implied reality is a sham: therefore, his world is one where holsters are stuffed with toilet paper, where the semblances of real injuries are recommended to cowards who fear the line of genuine encounter, and thus he is at once prepared for and con-ditioned by the decadence of his initial relations with Catherine.

Frederic's sexual advances toward Catherine in the garden are care-fully paralleled with the military advances to be made up river, where a bridgehead is sought on the other side. The hard, bright burst and flash of an exploding shell upriver in war is echoed by the sharp, stinging flash in the garden when he is hit by Catherine as he tries to cross to the other side, in love. Initially, he makes his "bridgehead": "her lips opened" (26). Italians on the Austrian side upriver are balanced by the Ameri-can making inroads on British terrain. To underline how carefully this study (in love) of the subversion/invasion of identity is paralleled with military aggression, Hemingway has Frederic say, "I did not care what I was getting *into*" (30) and say that it was "a game like *bridge*" (30, italics mine). Bridges are being built and crossings made, but, after all, it is a battlefront where, the reader is told, the battery is "in the garden" (15), where death is in paradise, or the place of birth, where there are strate-gies of war in love, and where subversion precedes capitulation. Ignor-ing internal subversion, Frederic pretends to himself that the war "did not have anything to do with me," and he allows Catherine to place inside him the words he has not said or felt, all in the interest of the spoils of the "game" played for unfelt, and therefore supposedly imaginary, stakes.

Such invasion or admission of the unacknowledged "other" within the perimeter of Self to function as though it were the self inside the Self, Hemingway suggests, is fatal to our Western conception of integrity or identity. In that way, illusions become reality; people die as a result. Under the influence of this invasion, Frederic in the next chapter is corrupt: his "dream" of a rendezvous with Catherine, in which he clearly is not interested in whether he is acknowledged by her as a Self in the encounter, seems more real than any meeting that he actually has had with her. It is in this same chapter that, as he watches distinctions being made in the external world—the wounded being sorted at the *smistimento* to be sent to "different" hospitals—he is the one to think "about nothing" (33), and it is here that he creates for the straggler who has a "rupture"—the man who has fled the line and thrown away the truss that keeps the inside from the outside—the lies and disguises that are to reward cowardice with safety. Before the chapter ends, after a drinking bout in which it no longer really matters whether he is Federico Enrico or Enrico Federico, he readily replaces his God with Bacchus. Few have noted that something extraordinary has happened to Frederic's voice, his mind, between the earlier chapters and chapter 7: both his thought and his expression have become absurd, and *post hoc ergo propter hoc*, they have become so as a result of the Self that was "lost" in the garden. If this suggests a biblical parallel, it is because Hemingway meant that it should. The chapter ends with Frederic properly feeling "hollow" (41): he has lost both his God and his girl as he has lost the Self. Seen in this light, narrative incidents and details in the chapter owe almost nothing to memory or history or an attempt at verisimilitude: they are propositions, geometrical and mathematical forms in a philosophical debate.

A Farewell to Arms is not about war per se, and it is not about love per se. It is a highly intellectual novel that studies the psychodynamics of integrity, of what it is to be wholly human, and it does it as resolutely and philosophically as *The Confessions of Saint Augustine* or the essays of Montaigne. It is important to note this, for it is the continuing and controlling subject of Hemingway's entire work, and we have in our literature few treatises on the nature of morality and the costs and strategies of remaining human that are as rigorously precise and unsentimentally demanding. As Suzanne Langer would affirm, art *is not* discursive. Good art is not didactic, but it is always an intelligent projection and externalization of intricate perceptions. A good novel says more about the psychodynamics of human perception than any scientific treatise or text can say, and a *great* novel has systematized, mastered, and reconstituted those recognitions and placed them in the framework of history.

I have diluted Hemingway's intricate study immeasurably in order to make a point. Were we to trace the delicate line of psychic distinctions that he draws, or follow the vectors of force that he defines as existing in human relations, we would be witnessing an unbelievably subtle analysis of the workings of sensibility in culture and history. His novel is perfectly aware of the sentimentalities of "make love not war" rhetoric, as it is equally aware of the barbarism of those who remain encastelated within their uncompromising armies or attitudes. He is also rigorously aware of where we are historically—he was as conscious of what is called "the decline of the West" as was Spengler or Fitzgerald or Joyce—but he chooses to study the dynamics of that shift in the consciousness of the reduced self, the perjured or lost self, while he equally studies and advocates the therapies and strategies for the restoration of Being.

NOTES

1. Thinking into the other becomes a talent that Hemingway increasingly respects; his later novels are filled with admiration for those who exhibit the ability to imaginatively inhabit the experience of another or empathically and sensitively project into another's needs. This quality is elaborately studied in *Across the River* and *Islands in the Stream*. In Hemingway's early work, as a story like "Big Two-Hearted River" makes clear, the Hemingway protagonist is systematically developing a sensitive reciprocity with nature; in his later works, the emphasis shifts more to human relations, and the delicacy of recognition of the needs of another becomes an accurate indicator of humanity.

2. Those who speculate about numerology in Hemingway and see him "playing games" with chapter numbers might be interested to observe that chapter 19, which in its Roman numbers (XIX) separates the two would-be identical lovers, X and X, with an "I," is the chapter in which Frederic introduces an "I" that comes between Catherine and himself. The following chapter (XX) is the one in which he creates a false, spurious "we" and in which he and Catherine, impelled by Catherine, try to separate themselves, in their bond, from the others. The next chapter (XXI) is the one in which the announcement of "one" to be added to the two, Catherine's pregnancy announcement, begins to create problems.

3. It can be argued that in "The Short Happy Life of Francis Macomber" Francis is the "boy" who shamefully suggests leaving the wounded lion in the bush. The suggestion is that he has not developed the ability to imagine what the lion is feeling, that he lacks the ability to project empathically into the "other," and that only after he truly sees and feels with the buffalo is he prepared for manhood. Most of Hemingway's unrespectable and morally delinquent characters, like the young waiter in "A Clean, Well-Lighted Place," like Mike in *The Sun Also Rises,* and like Richard Gordon and the unimaginative "haves" in *To Have and Have Not,* lack the ability to, or do not choose to, imagine what is really happening in another.

4. Rowing to the island with the barman, Frederic rows while the barman trolls. On their return, Frederic trolls and the barman rows. That evening, playing billiards, Frederic and Count Greffi speak "American" as they play the first 50 points in 100; for the last 50 points they "change over" and speak Italian.

Works Cited

Hemingway, Ernest. *A Farewell to Arms.* 1929. New York: Scribners, 1957.

16

"Where Did Uncle George Go?"

A Study of Debridement and Purgation Rituals in the Works of Ernest Hemingway

Students of Hemingway perhaps too quickly accept the "iceberg" theory to explain Hemingway's omissions and technique of composition. We all use it because of its convenience and aptness: it so fully seems to provide answers to the bedeviling sense in his work of a story beyond a story, of obscure antecedents for indefinite pronouns, of significant scenes occurring offstage, and of the levels of profundity the reader senses or with study finds. But the theory too readily and easily becomes explanation that forestalls further inquiry, and that is a shame, for the more interesting questions would lead beyond the fact of style to the sources of style, beyond the method to the philosophical basis of it. It is not enough to say that an absent principle or agent acts like a present fact. Why and how it does so, and why ellipsis and reticence are preferable— these are still interesting and unanswered questions.

Not only leaving out, but cutting away, debriding, jettisoning, purging, and shedding of significant contents are constant thematic stylistic devices of Hemingway's work. A complicating fact is the recognition that for Hemingway the written work of art itself might be a purgation: in "Fathers and Sons" we learn that writing was an act of ridding oneself of troubling realities—"If he wrote it he could get rid of it. He had gotten rid of many things by writing them" (*Short Stories* 491). And in

Hemingway's work, which itself may be a purgation, the additional phenomenon of the hero who has suffered amputations or the protagonist who casts away parts of himself is so consistent as to be a stylistic constant. Explanation of why this insistent pattern exists ought to be sought.

Perhaps the supreme example of an absent principle driving a major novel is Jake Barnes's missing phallus in *The Sun Also Rises*. It is this absent but ever-present fact—balanced in the narrative line by the active need to cast off and excise the scapegoat—that determines the action and focus of the work. But if the excision in this case occurred before the story began, in most of Hemingway's work we witness within the frame of the work the ritual act of excision itself, a purgation, or the rites of exclusion and omission—and these rites are often practiced as cleansings, as psychic denials or renunciations, or as therapeutic reconstitutions of the self. Such acts, most frequently creating health where there was disease, or freedom where there was compulsion or dependency, are significantly related to the aesthetic that chooses to omit. These gestures are, partly, the visible exemplification of the aesthetics operative during composition: if the craftsman artist, driven by cunning strategies of forbearance, fashions a form that omits significant parts, and the man at work, always discovering in the act of composition more than he can anticipate, is in rereading repeatedly confronted with the need to rid himself of spoiling contents, of what might rot and go bad, his protagonists frequently share the same fastidious moral and aesthetic standards. Robert Cohn's need to be cleansed from self-contamination by being forgiven, Brett's need to cleanse herself of Cohn with another lover, and Romero's use of his expert commitment to his craft in the corrida to wipe out the contamination he has suffered in his contact with Cohn—all echo against Jake's San Sebastian cleansing rites. Renata, in *Across the River and into the Trees*, brings her love to "purge" (240) Cantwell of his hate, and Maria in *For Whom the Bell Tolls* pleads with Jordan to "do quickly what it is we do so that the other is all gone" (73). The Francis Macomber who begs for forgiveness for his self-contamination but learns "to clear away that lion business" by "fixing it up on buffalo" is exemplary (*Short Stories* 11).

The typical story would be "The Snows of Kilimanjaro," an exercise in psychic therapy that ends in death. It is probable that all such exercises, if absolute enough, necessarily end in a species of suicidal death as the real self measured by the idealistic self suffers and must at least in part be sloughed. The rotting part of Harry, his gangrened leg, is left below in the devouring jungles at the foot of Kilimanjaro; it is only in imaginative flight, as the mind is cut free from the body, that he moves towards immortality. We learn in the epigraph to that story that if a beast of the jungle tried to ascend to that "House of God," there would be at last only the undecaying carcass of the animal to remain as testimony to its unnatural aspiration. If it is a sign of the boldness of the aspiration, it is also a warning of the possible price. The variations on this theme are everywhere in Hemingway's work. Ironically, death is where absolute idealism leads. Life also, of course, leads to death, but if a living part uniquely subject to rot and decay were to be cut away, the living remaining part might, without contamination, have a chance to reconstitute itself, at least temporarily, cleanly. Surely this was basic knowledge that Dr. Hemingway might have taught his son—that same doctor-father who fastidiously demanded that all soiled things must be boiled antiseptically clean, that same projected doctor who, in "Indian Camp," carefully sterilized his instruments but was also portrayed as out of touch with the fecund dark world. The unnaturally presented baby in that story must by a Caesarean operation be cut free so that its mother, and it, should have a natural chance to live. In "On the Quai at Smyrna," the dead babies are torn from the mothers' holding arms so that the mothers can be saved, and in *A Farewell to Arms*, the baby that is unable to breathe must by Caesarean be cut away from Catherine if she herself is to have a chance to live. The assumption is that the dead, paralyzed, or dying part that is going bad is a form of rot that must be debrided, cut away. This is the "something worthless," Santiago's hand, which he would willingly sacrifice: "If he cramps again let the line cut him off" (*Old Man and the Sea* 85). The boy in "God Rest You Merry, Gentlemen" hysterically pleads for castration and finally operates upon himself to rid himself of the part that offends.

Another assumption seems to be that the one-armed, seemingly handicapped man might be enabled by the sacrifice, might become "strong at the broken place" (*Farewell to Arms* 249), even as the sentence from which elements, even vital elements, have been pruned, might be more powerful. The quadriplegic Indian in *The Torrents of Spring* readily beats Yogi Johnson at pool, and Francis Macomber, when his fear is gone "like an operation," has "something else [that] grew in its place" that "made him into a man" (*Short Stories* 33). Frederic Henry, in *A Farewell*, exasperated with the incompetent doctors who discuss the treatment of his leg, retorts, "I want it cut off . . . so I can wear a hook on it" (97). He is joking, as the house doctor affirms, but there is more than joke here. Harry Morgan, in *To Have and Have Not*, indeed does have his arm cut off and at last *has* a hook. The stump of his arm becomes his "flipper" (113), which brings him closer to the seas and those dependencies that humanize him and lead him toward the lesson he at last learns. As he jettisons the compromising sacks of liquor, after he is wounded because of them, the loss of his arm and the casting away of the ham-shaped sacks of liquor-pig-encircled spirits seem metaphorical equivalents. (We should remember that in *Across the River and into the Trees* we are told the tale of the smuggling of the body of St. Mark into Venice "under a load of fresh pork") (29). The surgical teeth of the sharks strip away the flesh, the decaying part, of Santiago's great fish, and what he brings back at last is the skeletal undying part; and we learn that as the sharks debride or amputate the flesh, "it was as though he himself were hit" (*Old Man and the Sea* 103). In *Across the River*, we are told of the watch, a Rolex Oyster Perpetual, which apparently has not the vicissitudes and liabilities of Cantwell's failing heart that brings him down into love and life—and therefore death. He dies because of the part of himself that betrays him, that he refuses to further harden or deny but rather risks in love. He, however, purges himself through confession of destructive memories, even as, through ritual defecation, he rids himself of the psychic hold his old wounding has had upon him. The boatman in the same novel flings out the decoys "as though he were ridding himself of something obscene" (4). In *The Fifth Column*, Philip Rawlings throws out all his black market luxuries that compromise him after one who takes his place, a son figure, is sacrificed for his sake. In that play there is no question that Dorothy Bridges is the infecting, contaminating part, the "commodity" that Philip Rawlings can do without, and he relentlessly practices rites of personal hygiene in cutting her off. The play itself in its very title and subject speaks of the ramifications of the infecting or contaminating part inside the citadel of self that is inseparable from the body social and that must be extirpated. Such purgation and rites of cleansing in *Green Hills of Africa* rid Hemingway the hunter of his morally stultifying nature; he casts away part of himself, the selfish, competitive, jealous part. The Hemingway of *Death in the Afternoon*, who rids himself at last of the little old lady he has suffered and entertained, is judged callous in his exclusion. Yet he is finally cutting away the unendurable sentimental and clichéd part of the self that he has labored to humanize, that he has tried to educate and redeem with facts and anecdotes of death. It should be noted how similar this is to the ostracism of Cohn in *The Sun Also Rises*. As Nick rids himself of Marjorie in "The End of Something," we sense a similar revulsion against her unearned and fundamentally unpossessed knowledge, and we want very much to know the full dimensions of the "something" that Nick must shed, or "end." Robert Jordan tries to cast off his sentimental father and to absorb the stress (caused by the loss) by placing extra weight on the realistic warrior grandfather. Frederic Henry has cast off *his* father, and even Catherine readily disposes of her own: "You won't ever have to meet him" (*Farewell to Arms* 154). (Indeed, the use of last names that are first names throughout the Hemingway cast of characters suggests that cast-off patronymics are the debridement of the father.) Truth seems to be the hard core that Hemingway defends, and in *Across the River and into the Trees* Cantwell judges illusions to be the suspect part that must be excised: "You can cut out everything phony about the illusion as though you would cut it with a straight-edged razor" (232), he says. And whether something is cut away by the flensing knives of conscience, to strip the "fat" from Harry's soul in "Snows," or stripped away by the teeth of sharks or by a three-day blow is probably less important than the fact that it is cast off.

Occasionally, there is a resuscitation or resurrection of a dead or dying part that has been denied. In "The Three-Day Blow," Nick dreams of reviving, resurrecting, Marjorie, a part of himself he cast away in "The End of Something." In *Across the River*, the insensitive and wounded part of Cantwell, his hand, must be forced into feeling by the Renata whose name speaks of resurrections; and the betraying paralyzed left hand of Santiago, in *The Old Man and the Sea*, must be resurrected— come alive again to cooperate with his right hand—if he is to survive to be the great fisherman he aspires to be. The reader can see Pablo of *For Whom the Bell Tolls* as the selfish part that is rotten and fast going bad: at first sloughed, or taken out of the action or narrative, he is at last restored to life and returned to service as he learns to feel what the rest of the whole organic body feels.

The scapegoat represents another aspect of purgation. It is that upon which the communal sins may be loaded so that in its sacrifice the body social may be cleansed. Cohn is the scapegoat in *The Sun Also Rises*, the sentimental part of the self cast out first by Brett and subsequently by others. Hemingway understood from the beginning, however, the inhumanity and ugliness of scapegoat psychology. He pilories the attitude and rituals in *The Sun Also Rises* and subsequently derides all scapegoat sacrifices. One does not, he seems to say, deal with personal rot by imagining it onto another, who dies for our sins; each of us must deal with it alone and relentlessly inside the self.

What is the significance of this obsession with purgation carried to the point of stylistic mannerism? The inability to accept the imperfect or compromising part of the self and to cut it away—"if thine eye offend thee pluck it out"—is almost a postulate of classical American literature, rooted as it is in Old Testament fundamentalist idealism. Poe's heroes bury the telltale hearts that bind them to mankind, or bury the troubling living body itself, or try to wall out the ungovernable tide of bloody crimson that is their human heritage. Similarly, Hawthorne's Ethan Brand and Man of Adamant substitute hearts of marble for the human heart; Aylmer in "The Birthmark" destroys life when it contradicts absolute idealisms; Ahab's missing leg in Melville's work is that part sacrificed to his inhuman pursuit. Such patterns make Hemingway's debridements more comprehensible. Fertility itself—children, wives, lovers, and mothers—creates those human ties that are "hostages to Fortune" and difficult for an absolutist to sustain. The Indian father's suicide in "Indian Camp" warns how destructive such bonds of the heart may be. Therefore, thereafter, the vulnerable parts are often sloughed.

A life connection is, in Hemingway's works, the part that is purged. Those things jettisoned—the ham-shaped sacked spirits in *To Have and Have Not*, the corned beef and eau de cologne and the temperament and role of Dorothy Bridges in *The Fifth Column*—exemplify joiners or connectors of opposites. Jake Barnes's missing phallus is such a lost connector. Uncle George is the white man in "Indian Camp" who has made authentic connections with the fertile dark world; after he disappears, Nick feels that he himself will never die. Love, of course, is always such a connection, and in Hemingway's works, those who establish the love or life bonds for the idealist heroes are most frequently conveniently lost to them or sundered or cast from them, whether they are children, wives, mothers, or lovers: Frederic Henry's and Thomas Hudson's sons, Brett, Catherine, Renata, Maria, Helen, Margot, Marie Morgan, Helen Gordon, or Dorothy. The men are subsequently, in each work, without their women as they practice inner rites of lonely individuation. This is true at or toward the ends of *A Farewell, Green Hills, To Have and Have Not, The Fifth Column, For Whom the Bell Tolls, Across the River,* "The Short Happy Life of Francis Macomber," "The Snows of Kilimanjaro," *Islands in the Stream,* and *The Old Man and the Sea.*

Although Hawthorne goes on to record the criminality/absurdity of his idealists who sacrifice life to art, and Poe frequently judges the inhumanity of his madmen by having them betray themselves into the hands of the law, Hemingway ordinarily goes further: he studies the costs of his protagonists' isolation, a result of their debridements—what they have been cut off from and been reduced to—and then he has them use their alienation to learn rites of reintegration into the world. Frederic Henry walks away in the rain but compulsively tells his tale; Thomas Hudson learns how to survive with grief; Harry Morgan learns what it has taken him a lifetime to learn; Robert Jordan at the end is "completely integrated now" (471); and Cantwell acknowledges that love means death but is worth it. When Cantwell thinks, "Cut it out and be a human being," Hemingway is focusing on the necessary debridement operation and also on the alternative atonement. In Hemingway's stories, the men who sacrifice life to art, or human imperfection to their idealism, are finally presented as culpable or absurd if they do not manage to genuinely atone for the crime. It is the atonement that makes the difference. Harry atones; Richard Gordon does not.

Hemingway's life connectors are sloughed so that the lonely godlike protagonists, who have denied their feet of clay, may, in disciplined and hard-learned roles of individuation rebuild inside themselves whole, life- and death-accepting human beings.

Robert Jordan does not die when he blows the bridge but later and because the packhorse impedes him when he tries to make another crossing. The packhorse signifies a desire to take it all—the world—with him, and such attempts to bridge or simultaneously have idealism and materialism create the bond with process that, pat like the catastrophe, devours those who would look to the yet-unassimilated world for solutions to internal problems. That was Frederic Henry's mistake, to let Catherine convince him that *she* could be his other half. Jordan, however, at the novel's end a broken man stripped of his beloved, still dies complete, having atoned: the victory is, as with all Hemingway's injured protagonists, achieved inside the self.

It is the human heart and the world itself that creates problems for the classical American writer. But Hemingway's heroes by and large risk their deaths to be at last reconciled with that private heart and that inner nature that had early been the betraying and therefore debrided part. The way a reader creates a whole story out of partial information, recreating what has been deliberately omitted or excised, is the way a character makes a whole integral self where amputations have been suffered. Feeling must be restored to the unfeeling part. The reader has a part that he depends on cast away, and thereafter, forced to imaginatively compensate for it, he becomes stronger at the broken place. Purgation and debridement in Hemingway are the external stylistic and thematic rituals that create the need for internal healing: such healing is achieved as the incomplete character at last realizes an individuated state and as the uninformed reader simultaneously creates his imaginative reconstitution of the omitted or cast-off part. Hemingway has fashioned in his narrative line the visible externalized dynamics of his aesthetics.

Uncle George is just one of several integrators removed at the beginning of In Our Time, and it is their purgation that places on Nick the need for a personally reconstituted self: the rituals for such individuation are practiced at Big Two-Hearted River. Purgation or omission is a moral-aesthetic device in Hemingway: it establishes the need for a responsible response on the part of both writer and reader, joining them at last in shared rites of fulfillment.

WORKS CITED

Hemingway, Ernest. *Across the River and into the Trees.* 1950. New York: Scribners, 1970.

———. *A Farewell to Arms.* 1929. New York: Scribners, 1969.

———. *For Whom the Bell Tolls.* 1940. New York: Scribners, 1968.

———. *The Old Man and the Sea.* New York: Scribners, 1952.

———. *The Short Stories of Ernest Hemingway.* New York: Scribners, 1966.

———. *To Have and Have Not.* 1937. New York: Scribners, 1965.

17

Gender and Role Reversal in Fitzgerald and Hemingway

Dick Diver's Metamorphosis
and Its Hemingway Analogues

F. Scott Fitzgerald's *Tender Is the Night* was born after a nine-year gestation period, during which it went through several elaborate metaphoric stages. It seemed to resist its realization, perhaps because the author was embroiled during these troubled years with the desperate personal circumstances that found their fictive expression in the novel. In that book, Fitzgerald was dealing with his own alcoholism and moral disequilibrium, his wife's mental illness, and the complex lives and situations of Sara and Gerald Murphy and other friends who appear thinly veiled in the fiction. Set against the background of the Paris, Switzerland, and Riviera settings of the 1920s and 1930s, the characters were painfully close to Fitzgerald's own tragedy. Indeed, it was this "closeness" of the material to the fiction that troubled Hemingway, and he so told Fitzgerald (Hemingway, *Selected Letters* 407–09).

In Hemingway's career, one of his last great works, *The Garden of Eden*, underwent an equally extended series of metamorphoses and a difficult birth process, consuming—as did *Tender* for Fitzgerald—many creative years. Remarkably, it was focused on a writer and his wife living on the Riviera during this same time and in about the same location as Fitzgerald's characters. Hemingway's couple, David and Catherine, bear a remarkable resemblance to Fitzgerald, the then-successful writer, and his bored and unfulfilled wife, Zelda, whose competitive sense, like

Catherine's, attacks the creative process of the artist-husband. Indeed, the Catherine of *Garden* has many traits Hemingway observed in Zelda—even the tales of lesbian interludes and the facts of mental disease are shared—and although unquestionably Hemingway's heroine was based, as closely as was Fitzgerald's Nicole, on his own wife and other loves, Zelda's imago lurks behind Hemingway's Catherine just as completely as does Fitzgerald's own image behind his fictionalized Gerald Murphy. It is fascinating to note that in Zelda's account, *Save Me the Waltz* (1932), which used, as Fitzgerald affirmed, the same and "his" material—covering as it did the same period and many of the same incidents as Fitzgerald had with his Nicole and Dick Diver—her self-projection as her heroine, Alabama, is married to her thinly veiled portrait of her husband, David. Hemingway's choice of David for his protagonist's name undoubtedly suggests an additional level of allusive sophistication in his work.

It is not an arbitrary relationship between the two novels that I define here but one essential to an understanding of the deeper levels of meaning within the texts. As Fitzgerald makes his characters draw, to a great extent, on their real perceptible historical analogues, he seems almost to be crying out for a reader's understanding that the biographies and lives so transparently overlaid should imaginatively be brought to bear as another level of meaning to be added to the fate of his characters. It is really almost impossible for a literate reader to avoid Gerald and Sara Murphy, who are concomitantly F. Scott and Zelda Fitzgerald as they all inhabit the fates of Nicole and Dick Diver, but in fact Fitzgerald wished to be Gerald, even as he wished his wife to be Sara. André Le Vot, one of Fitzgerald's finer biographers, readily saw this and described them as "Gerald-Scott, Sara-Zelda, Scott-Sara in juxtaposition, permutation, fascination with themselves and each other" (208). Le Vot saw that the "subject" of *Tender Is the Night* was really the "degradation of the Murphys in Fitzgerald" and that their relations were "an impossible romance in which the beloved's face was sometimes Gerald's, sometimes Sara's, seen in shifting moods of admiration and despite and defiance" (208). Le Vot recognized that Gerald thoroughly understood "that process of symbiosis that would form the composite character of the Divers in *Tender Is the Night*" (209). Murphy described the four of them in a letter to the Fitzgeralds of September 19, 1925: "Currents run between us regardless: Scott will uncover for me values in Sara, just as Sara has known them in Zelda through her affection for Scott" (Miller 19).

Fitzgerald's novel at last would be his exposition of this, his process of transformation and metamorphosis.

Hemingway seems to make a similar demand, calling up to the sophisticated reader the menage à trois of his first wife, Hadley, his second wife, Pauline, and himself, while simultaneously almost insisting on applying over these an imagery taken from the Fitzgeralds' lives as well as other allusions to his own. He had very early found the advantages of this style for mythmaking, so that his persona looms large and inescapable behind and within his fictive scenarios and scenes. Of course, a concomitant liability of this process was for Hemingway the participation of his texts in the creation of the Hemingway persona that has enveloped his fiction and obsessively drawn to itself the criticism and attention that should have been focused on the texts and their casts of characters.

I am here suggesting, however, that these particular novels do not merely use personal experience as the base of their fiction—as all writers do—but use it deliberately so that history, biography, and myth may play against and together with the fictive details to establish a more complex genre elucidating a more complex myth. What both novels (and the other works of both men) ask us to perceive in their alluded-to lives as well as in their fictions is a composite in which the two are intricately and inextricably interwoven, so that the mysteries of role and sex inversion in the lives and concerns of both authors can be more profoundly and finely explored. It is these metamorphic transformations that will here be explored.

Fitzgerald's novel, showing the effect of a new historical consciousness and of his early excitement for Spengler's *Decline of the West* (published sequentially in two volumes in 1918 and 1922 and in one volume in 1932),[1] is, like his earlier *The Great Gatsby* (1925), aiming at greater range than mere psychological portraiture. It attempts to study the great subject of the great books of its time—Joyce's *Ulysses* (1922), Hemingway's *In Our Time* (1925), Ford's tetralogy *Parade's End* (published as four novels sequentially in 1924, 1925, 1926, and 1928),[2] Eliot's *The Waste Land* (1922), and D. H. Lawrence's *Women in Love* (1920)—namely the decline and fall of the patriarchal tradition. As Dick Diver has softened and as the women about him have concomitantly hardened or seized male prerogatives and even costume, a historical change is being studied, especially in the declining powers of its spoiled "high priest." When Dick says his own farewell over his father's grave, "Good-by, my father—good-by, all my fathers" (*Tender* 205), the larger sense of a farewell to a lost male-centered world is inescapably there, for the speech echoes against his reflections over other graves, when, earlier in the novel near Amiens, in the falling rain over the indistinguishable fallen heroes, he historically considered the end of an age. Diver, however, has long ago abandoned the old virtues of this fallen world, and he has laid down his weapons: his own "spear had been blunted," he had "let himself be "swallowed up like a gigolo" and had "permitted his arsenal to be locked up in the Warren safety-deposit vaults" (201). Going on about him in his world is an acknowledged "obscure yielding up of swords" (298). Such almost blatantly obvious Freudian imagery belongs to a novel where a psychiatrist, unable to maintain the detachment of a surrogate father—indeed, the detachment upon which the Western patriarchal tradition is based—has in incestuous self-projection overthrown the guardian father in himself for the indulgent lover and by the indulgence lost whatever paternal authority he might have had. Therefore, the simplistic Freudian symbolism is itself a statement about complexity reduced to simplicity and about clichés and sentimentalities that have replaced the sophistications upon which real cultural authority rests. Fitzgerald accents this: "The cloudy waters of unfamiliar ports, the lost girl on the shore, the moon of popular songs. . . . A part of Dick's mind was made up of the tawdry souvenirs of his boyhood" (196). This imagery also, however, expresses with this disempowerment a setting aside of male attributes. When Maria Wallis kills a man in the Gare St. Lazare, we are told that he can scarcely be identified because she had neatly "shot him through his identification card" (84): In the act she is described as having, like a warrior, a "helmet" of hair, while his ineffectual cardboard identity is her target.

The protagonists of both *Tender Is the Night* and *The Garden of Eden*, however autobiographically based, intriguingly illustrate at once their unique individual fates and the historical fate of their age as it is examined and understood by their authors; and both writers demand a shared group of symbols elucidating a common threat to their protagonists that they believe is unique *in our time*—therefore, a word about historical transformations.

Fitzgerald's perceptions in *Tender Is the Night* grew out of the situation he observed in the world about him. The Paris that both he and Hemingway shared in the 1920s strongly exhibited the situations he fictively defines. That Paris not only gave a stage to and flaunted the mannerisms of the homosexual world so vividly portrayed at the Bal Musette in Hemingway's *The Sun Also Rises*, and in the scene in the "house hewn from the frame of Cardinal Retz's palace in the Rue Monsieur" (71) in Fitzgerald's *Tender Is the Night*, but also in multiple ways brought women into masculine roles while stripping men of their prewar authoritative posture. These were basic social transformations, taking place everywhere in the postwar world, but more actively and readily and visibly in Paris, which did not attempt to hide the process or its mode. Dress, as in the *Bal des Quatre Arts* or in Natalie Barney's *Ecole des Amazons*, was often flagrantly cross-dressing; and the styles of Dolly Wilde, Romaine Brooks, and others exhibited on the street the sexual shifts being explored. "Women like these women I have never seen before" (306), exclaims old Gausse, the hotel owner in *Tender Is the Night*; and Hemingway's audience could just as well have said that about the Brett of his first novel and the Catherine of his last.

That postwar world was forced to acknowledge transfers of power from the patriarchs to their wives and daughters. The leisures of the American educational scene provided the children of the robber barons—who themselves were too preoccupied by their practical affairs and businesses to be so distracted—with the seductions of history and culture that were European based. Millionaires like Cunard and Ellerman, Loeb and Guggenheim, Singer, Cross, and J. P. Morgan were able to underwrite the salons and presses and Paris experiences and power of women like the Princess de Polignac (Winaretta Singer), Natalie Barney, Nancy Cunard, and Caresse Crosby of Paris. And the apparently self-sufficient authorities of Gertrude Stein's salon and Sylvia Beach's Shakespeare and Company owed themselves to money sent from lesser fortunes to sustain such daughters and inheriting women. Even Robert McAlmon's Contact Publishing Company was an alimony spin-off from Bryher's fortune, amassed by her father, Sir John Ellerman, the heaviest taxpayer in England; and Harold Loeb's magazine *Broom* owed itself to the Loeb/Guggenheim fortune just as much as Harry and Caresse Crosby's Black Sun Press owed itself to Harry's uncle, J. P. Morgan, Jr. The profits of American entrepreneurial genius, accumulated by men who were too consumed by business, or too aged or too ill, or ill equipped by temperament to be gallivanting about Europe, or who were now dead, frequently passed into the hands of the active, energetic, and adventuring and inheriting wives and daughters. Fitzgerald throughout his novel records the phenomenon: "The hostess—she was another tall rich American girl, promenading insouciantly upon the national prosperity" (*Tender Is the Night* 73).

This usurpation of power or transfer of it from men to women Fitzgerald studied, and he developed his observations in his work through the metaphoric or actual masculinization of women and an attendant effeminization of men. Both Nicole and Baby Warren of *Tender Is the Night* are classical portraits of the process, in which the women not only finally break ties to the sources of their power, pretending self-sufficiency, but also often break the spirits of the men that they submit to their wealth and subdue with its power. "We own you, and you'll admit it sooner or later. It is absurd to keep up the pretense of independence" (177) is Baby Warren's unspoken thought. Fitzgerald, pronouncing on Nicole, writes that she, "wanting to own him, wanting him to stand still forever, encouraged any slackness on his part, and in multiplying ways he was constantly inundated by a trickling of goods and money" (170). The danger to the male of this power shift was also a theme of Hemingway's work—well illustrated in "The Snows of Kilimanjaro" but earlier studied in Robert Cohn of *The Sun Also Rises* (1926), a man dependent upon money given by his mother.

The dominant undercurrent of the surface action of *Tender Is the Night* is a state of undeclared war. Newly equipped and armored women were everywhere about Hemingway and Fitzgerald in Paris, and as they often "hardened" to the practicalities and necessities of the work they had assumed, their more inert, less engaged men, no longer in the lists of financial combat, were often, in being deprived of their usual weapons, unmanned—made impotent or essentially castrated. Lovely, still dewy-eyed Rosemary Hoyt is nonetheless a warrior: "It was good to be hard, then; all nice people were hard on themselves" (55), Rosemary reasons, already well trained for combat by her mother. As noted earlier, Maria Wallis, shooting a man in the Gare St. Lazare, is a woman with hair "like a helmet" who hits "her target" (83). Dick "scented battle from afar" with Nicole and has been "hardening and arming himself" for that encounter (100), yet earlier, when Dick is being defeated by Baby Warren in a preliminary skirmish, Fitzgerald reflects, "It would be hundreds of years before any emergent Amazons would ever grasp the fact that a man is vulnerable only in his pride, but delicate as Humpty-Dumpty once that is meddled with" (177).[3] This sense that the battles are those of masculinized women defying an established patriarchate is voiced by one of Dick's patients, who cries out in her suffering, "I'm sharing the

fate of the women of my time who challenged men to battle" (184). Trying to ease her pain, he urges that "many women suffered before they
mistook themselves for men" (184).

The great fact of the matter was that a major cataclysmic event had
stripped from the French a generation of its men, for whom there was
no replacement. The multiple deaths of fathers that Fitzgerald records
in his novel were historical facts as well as symbols. Fathers themselves,
whether indicted for causing the war or through not surviving it, left
the future to undiscerned, unknown inheritors, and a cynicism as deep
as their seldom-visited or unknown graves suggested that whatever
forms a new world might take, whatever transformations of old styles to
new there might be, they would not be borrowed from the old patriarchal past. The postwar revulsion against the dealing of death extended
itself—as it did after World War II—to the weapons that sustained it,
and the putting aside of guns and male symbols of power in the postwar
world was to be expected. Put aside with them was the temper and philosophy and the skills that had shaped them and used them, the attitudes that had trained generations in their use—a general loss of male
equipment for male lists of honor. In Dick's own encounters, Nicole is
described as "disarming" him (188). The "blunted" spears, the "yielded
up" swords, the "locked up" arsenals spell out a belatedly recognized
lack of male preparation for battle.

In Fitzgerald's novel, the personal and historical situation, which
records in multiple ways the mode of overthrow of phallic and paternal
power—as surely as does Jake's missing phallus in *The Sun Also Rises*—
is answered by an equivalent symbolism (which runs throughout *Tender
Is the Night*) of the inversion-effeminization of Dick Diver. This occurs
simultaneously with the inversion-masculinization of such women as
Nicole and Baby Warren, Mrs. Speers (Rosemary's mother), Lady Caroline, and Mary North. Even as Mrs. Speers in her name bears the missing male weapons, so Dick's spear is "blunted,"[4] and Dick Diver in his
name drowns his masculinity in the feminine depths and waters that he
explores but from which, as the novel ends, he cannot emerge. These
waters are characterized in the novel, like the moon and cycle—from
which "cycling" takes its metaphoric meaning: on the last page of the
book, Dick's fate is described as one in which he is cycling "a lot"—as
essentially feminine.

What is especially fascinating to study in Fitzgerald's novel is the
actual and metaphoric sexual metamorphosis of Dick Diver. After
Fitzgerald chose the title of his novel from Keats's "Ode to a Nightingale,"

he carefully omitted two of the vital lines of that poem from his epigraph: "And haply the Queen Moon is on her throne / Cluster'd about
by all her starry fays." Fitzgerald was well aware of the effeminate overtones of *fay* or fairy, and these omitted lines, as in most Hemingway
works where the omitted part is crucial or the point of it all, establish
the major concern: Who is enthroned and who has taken power, and
just what are the conditions of "her" servitors? That Fitzgerald's first version of the novel was a tale of matricide suggests the enormous mythic
distance the book came as its author realized that the more interesting
story lay not in recording the attempt to hold off the Great Mother but
rather in visualizing the mode and stages by which her enthronement
was inevitably achieved and at what cost. An elaborate symbolic system
throughout the novel elevates the action to a divine cosmological level,
where gods and goddesses battle for power. Early in the book, the setting
in the Villa Diana and events "managed" by the Moon are but indica-
tions of this overlay. Although at one moment Nicole declares, "I am
Pallas Athene" (*Tender Is the Night* 160), her consistent profane identification is with "the night from which she had come" and with the dark
woods from which she emerged "into clear moonlight" when "the
unknown yielded her up" (135). Her witchery and Dick's early controlling divinity are strongly suggested in the novel, though Dick is at the
beginning given to the reader as a godlike figure with his consort and is
only later seen as a god captive and destroyed. Mrs. Speers, intent upon
sharpening her daughter into a masculinized competitor in what is still a
man's world, and knowing her daughter's need to use both masculine
and feminine weapons to win advantage in that world, is a typical Great
Mother.

   As the novel begins, Dick Diver is centered as a principle of belief
for all those who "believe in" (29) his world: he is adored (31, 112), he is
listened to with "wild worship" (112) by Rosemary who sees him as
"something fixed and godlike" (104); he makes an "apostolic gesture"
(27) while Nicole brings "everything to his feet, gifts of sacrificed
ambrosia, of worshipping myrtle" (137). Tommy Barban defends the
Divers against those like Mrs. McKisco, who can ask, "Are they so
sacred?" (43). Indeed, they are, in the mythos of the novel, where Dick is
described as one who "evaporated before their eyes" (28), as appearing
and disappearing in an instant (35). At one moment Rosemary tells her
mother that the Divers "really are divine" (95). The reader is told that,
like a god in the mind of a believer, "so long as [everyone] subscribed
to [his world] completely," it existed within its "intensely calculated

perfection," but "at the first flicker of a doubt . . . he [Dick] evaporated before their eyes" (28). Early, as the children sing *"Ouvre-moi ta porte/ Pour l'amour de Dieu,"* the gate to Dick's garden opens to admit the "body" of the other guests (29). Rosemary, who has been "in adoration" and "believed in him," feels the cloth of Dick's coat "like a chasuble" and is "about to fall to her knees before him" (38). In the prison where he has gone to help Mary North and Lady Caroline, he is described as being "like a priest in the confessional" (304). At the end of the novel, before he leaves, though already proven a "spoiled priest," he nevertheless appears "with a papal blessing" "blessing the beach"; and Nicole, even at that moment raised by him—she gets "to her knees," saying, "I'm going to him" (314)—is pulled down by Tommy Barban. But if this is the Nicole to whom Dick earlier has "devoted" himself—that profane believer who later "crossed herself reverently with Chanel Sixteen" (291)—part of Dick's metamorphosis is from a godlike principle of belief into the priest who finally cannot sustain devotion or compel belief.

The world of *Tender Is the Night* is also a world where the gold star "muzzers" come to "mourn for their dead" sons (101), where the graves of heroes cannot be found, where Dick's father's death seems the death of all fathers. It is a world where one father whips and punishes his son to drive him toward "manliness," and another, trying to protect his "nervous brood," succeeds "merely in preventing them from developing powers of adjustment to life's inevitable surprises" (186)—parental failures both. Focused on parental incest, the supreme cultural paternal abdication, and set in a milieu where the need for fathers is the primary fact, the novel belabors the patriarchal failures of the time. Fitzgerald himself, who had been embarrassed by his own father's failures and weaknesses, was constantly attentive to and advising his daughter or offering her lists and strategies for development and success, obviously trying to avoid such parental failure.

"Death by Water," a theme that T. S. Eliot had enunciated in *The Waste Land*, is the patriarchal fate being explored here. Nicole's father's dying, during which he can take in "nothing except liquids" (*Tender Is the Night* 247), will be, the reader is told, "a sinking" (248). This seems natural for what is throughout carefully described as a world drowning in enveloping waters, with "lavish liquidations taking place under the aegis of American splendor" (133). Rosemary, who embraces these waters and wallows in them (5) where they reach up for her and pull her down into them (5), and who seems in alliance and league with them, yearns "to surround [Dick] and engulf him" (66). The "entirely liquid"

(73) Abe North's dying, it is predicted, will seem like "the wreck of a galleon" (82) as voices that come to say farewell to him mimic "the cadence of water" (83). It is a world "already undergoing a sea-change" (83): "Full fathom five my father lies" is the unquoted but understood new condition under which life is lived. It is on a "watery day" that, near Amiens, Dick and those who listen to his lecture on the meaning of history face the "dissolutions" of soldiers under the rain (59).

These are the carefully defined feminine waters that will surround and engulf Dick, until, with "the ethics of his profession dissolving" (256), his life "inundated by a trickling of goods" (170), he will at last be unable to aquaplane, to walk on the water, but rather will lie floating exhausted on those very waters that he cannot master and above which he can no longer redemptively raise another (285). Nicole's schizophrenia has its own hydrodynamics: Considering her madness, Dick reflects that "the versatility of madness is akin to the resourcefulness of water seeping through" (191). The irony is that Dick takes on the water of Nicole's dissolution that Fitzgerald has associated with her, and that, as he consequently declines, her fortunes rise. Dick, earlier in the novel, had been reunited with Nicole by means of a funicular. Fitzgerald makes the point there that for one car to rise, the other must take on water and consequently, inevitably, by natural law descend.

As Dick downplays the danger of his son's possible exposure to dirty infected water, he can no longer serve as a protective father, for to that son he has become the betraying father. The point is made that, in having failed the office, he has forfeited a father's rights and privileges. This is certainly true with Rosemary, the fatherless girl he met on the beach and with whom he metaphorically assumed the role of father and teacher—and genuine fathers subsequently flee him, while more forthright men, like Earl Brady, refuse "the fatherly office" Dick has assumed and then betrayed (31). The dissolutions and drownings define another transformation in the Fitzgerald male: becoming the victim of waters that he once dominated, fluidity and its attendant flaccidities and macerations replace the fixity and firmness of the earlier heroic world.

The subtitle of the novel might well have been "The Cycling of Dick Diver": Engulfed and encircled, Dick predictably ends up as the victimized cyclist. Fitzgerald openly tells the reader that Rosemary wanted to "devour him . . . to surround and engulf him" (66). As she turns "round and round" (5) in the water, her advice to McKisko is to "roll." "Round and round in a corkscrew" (149) goes the funicular that brings Dick and Nicole together. When Dick early meets Nicole, it is under the moon with his bicycle. Again she meets him coming from a wood into the moonlight on "a rolling night" (135). When she plays a revolving record for him, it is "Lay a silver dollar / On the ground / And watch it roll / Because it's round" (136). Later Dick watches as she "curved into the half-moon entrance" of the Palace Hotel in a "Rolls" while "the air around him was loud with the circlings of all the goblins on the Gross-Münster" (145). Significantly, when Dick meets her again, he is cycling into Montreux.

Married to her at last, having shifted his devotion to this cyclical moon-endorsed principle, he has metamorphosed from a dominating sun god—the reader is explicitly told that Nicole "had played planet to Dick's sun" (289)—to an attendant to the moon. Fitzgerald elevates his analysis to a historical dimension as he tells the reader that from where Dick meets Nicole, on the slopes above Lake Geneva, one confronts the "cyclorama" that reveals "the true center of the Western world" (147). He admits to Franz that "we're beginning to turn in a circle" (179), and he describes the mentally disturbed as those "beginning . . . another ceaseless round of ratiocination, not in a line as with normal people but in the same circle. Round, round, and round. Around forever" (182). Nicole is similarly described in her madness as being "like one condemned to endless parades around the circumference of a medal" (277). Out of control in Italy, Dick's world "reels" (226). It is at the Agiri Fair—which they approach through "mammoth steam rollers"—that mad Nicole flees from him; then, in desperate pursuit of her, Dick "wheels" and, leaving the children with a woman beside the lottery wheel, circles the merry-go-round to find Nicole atop a revolving Ferris wheel (189). Retrieved, Nicole, with her mad hand clutching the steering wheel, nearly kills them all (192). No wonder that at the end, as the legend of the upstate New York cyclist, Dick can arbitrarily be found "in one town or another" (315): once the principle of firmness and absoluteness, he has had his solar fixity stripped from him forever.

Dick's first name suggests his phallic potential, and his last describes his envelopment by and commitment to the very principle of his dissolution. His alteration from hard to soft, from firm to fluid, and from fixed and straight to cyclical, can best be studied in his transformation as he relates to Rosemary and especially to her mother. To Rosemary, Dick, to whom she prays, is "perfect"—but to her, her mother is "forever perfect," too, and "Mother is perfect, she prayed" (37). Rosemary's mother has assumed the father's role of guardian and teacher, and she is now the enlightener who advises Rosemary in the ways of the world. At last she casts Rosemary adrift to be self-sufficient, even as Dick will seem to cast Nicole adrift to be self-sufficient and cured. Rosemary intones to Dick, "I think you're the most wonderful person I ever met—except my mother" (38), and in one breath she recites, "I love mother and I love you" (65). Even as Rosemary is Mrs. Speer's child, so, to Dick, Rosemary is "child" and "baby." In one chapter Dick is "with her in her heart" while her mother is "with her in her heart." Redundantly she declares, "You like to help everybody" and "Mother likes to help everybody" (84). After her quarrel with Dick, she says, "I feel as if I'd quarreled with mother" (219). This enforced linkage of the mother and Dick, even as he is himself overthrowing his paternal role, receives its obvious inevitable summation as Nicole becomes afraid "of what the stricken man . . . would feed on while she must still continue her dry suckling at his lean chest" (279). When Nicole finally leaves Dick, she has "cut the cord forever" (302). Such specific maternal imagery, associated with Dick but here emerging from Nicole as she sees him as the unsatis-factory nurturing breast, finally comes from Dick himself when he is "uneasy about what he had to give to the ever-climbing, ever-clinging, breast-searching young" (311).

Dick is changed from phallocentric man to ineffectual breast nur-turer. As the whore's pink "step-ins" (undergarments) become a flag and are alluded to in a parodic national anthem—"Oh say can you see the tender color of remembered flesh" (297)—the imagery speaks of a lost heroic world based on principle, now seduced by sensation: feminine sexu-ality represented in the lower-body undergarments now dominates the sky. Mary North and Lady Caroline in male costume trying to pick up two girls authorize the sexual inversion, one that is studied on another level in the transfer of financial power from Devereux Warren to Baby Warren. Devereux's incest with Nicole merely prepares for Dick's mul-tiple incestuous inversions, and incest itself in this novel is the uroboric overthrow of the basis of civilization, so that time is made eternally to circle about a past center, no longer capable of linear historical progres-sion.[5] That is what incest means: stopped, unprogressive time. It is, there-fore, metaphorically appropriate that Dick, yielding the world to its inheriting masculinized women, should accept his metaphoric effemi-nized death by water, while concomitantly becoming the cyclist.

What of the Fitzgerald behind this portrait? Evidence suggests his excessive castration anxiety, his ready fear of being stripped of his mas-culine authority and power. He fled repeatedly from the feminine in himself, which undoubtedly supported his genius. Feeling threatened and intimidated by its emergence, he coevally, however, played with those very feminine attributes that caused his embarrassment. If Zelda's desire for creative success as a writer threatened her husband, the latter was equally painfully susceptible and vulnerable to her suggestions of his unmanliness, masculine deficiency, or femininity. Nancy Milford, in *Zelda*, records Fitzgerald's confession to his wife's physician, Dr. Rennie, in later years—"In the last analysis she is a stronger person than I am. I have creative fire, but I am a weak individual. She knows this and really looks upon me as a woman" (261)—and Andre Le Vot repeats Sheilah Graham's comment that Zelda "tried to emasculate Scott" (237). Zelda terrorized her husband by implying or stating that she believed that he and Hemingway were in a homosexual relationship, and Fitzgerald challenged her in a long letter, "Written with Zelda gone to the Clinique": "The nearest I ever came to leaving you was when you told me you [thought] I was a fairy" (qtd. in Milford 181). A letter from Fitzgerald to Maxwell Perkins on November 15, 1929, reveals how tortured he was by knowing McAlmon had "assured Ernest I was a fairy" (Kuehl and Bryer 159). That there was a basis for Fitzgerald's fear of Hemingway's perception can be seen in the latter's portrait in *A Moveable Feast* of the Fitzgerald he met in Paris:

> Scott was a man then who looked like a boy with a face between handsome and pretty. He had very fair wavy hair, a high forehead, excited and friendly eyes and a delicate long-lipped Irish mouth that, on a girl, would have been the mouth of a beauty. His chin was well built and he had good ears and a handsome, almost beautiful, unmarked nose. This should not have added up to a pretty face, but that came from the coloring, the very fair hair and the mouth. The mouth worried you until you knew him and then it worried you more. (149)

Fitzgerald himself developed the basis of his own fear by projecting feminine attributes and mannerisms on his self-projections in his work. As the reader meets Dick Diver on the beach near Cannes in the first book of the novel, he appears for a moment "clad in transparent black lace drawers. Close inspection revealed that they were lined with flesh-colored cloth. "'Well, if that isn't a pansy's trick!' exclaimed Mr. McKisco contemptuously'" (*Tender Is the Night* 21).

Fitzgerald's fears allowed him readier access than most of his contemporaries (except perhaps Hemingway) to signs of the effeminization of the Western psyche. Ernest Hemingway spent his childhood in a home governed by his masterful and dominating mother—see the biographies and the autobiographical revelations of "Now I Lay Me" (*Short Stories* 363–71)—who was only gradually found by her son to be in a long-standing, probably lesbian liaison with one of the maids in the Hemingway household, Ruth Arnold. As a result, Hemingway was extraordinarily susceptible to role reversals and was gifted with an unconscious sympathetic understanding of the lesbian world. Lesbians were among Hemingway's closest friends throughout his life, and in Paris they gravitated to him—Gertrude Stein, Janet Flanner, Sylvia Beach, Jane Heap, and Margaret Anderson, among others. We also know that they were occasionally among his staunchest supporters (Sylvia Beach) and that he was attracted to them: Gertrude Stein, Margaret Anderson, and Djuna Barnes.

In Hemingway's works, gender inversion has been well studied, from the masculinized image of Brett in *The Sun Also Rises* (1926) as one of the "chaps" (22, 32), to Pilar of *For Whom the Bell Tolls* (1940) as stirring spoon/baton wielder of power in the cave once Pablo has been "cowed," and on to *The Garden of Eden*, where such inversion is overt and central to the novel. What has not been adequately noted is that the sex role inversions in Hemingway's works link up in a consistent pattern, one that reveals a need for therapeutic gender inversions: male to female and female to male. Indeed, *Across the River and into the Trees* (1950) is an extended essay on the historical necessity for such inversion, while *The Garden of Eden* is an example of it.

In *The Sun Also Rises*—where we are told, "Caffeine puts a man on her horse and a woman in his grave" (115), that Abraham Lincoln ("a faggot") "was in love with General Grant" and that "the Colonel's Lady and Judy O'Grady are Lesbians under their skin" (116), and where the order of drumstick and egg in Bill and Jake's meal is reversed—readers should be well prepared for mysteries of sexual inversion. It is no accident that the women in the novel all bear suggestively masculine names: Brett, Edna, Jo, Frances, and Georgette. Brett, in her hairstyle, her manner of speaking, and her aggressive behavior, flaunts a masculinized image and seized power, but the reader must be equally alert to Jake's inversion: his inability to make love to Brett is due not only to his lacking male equipment but to his having been physically remade into an unsatisfactory image of a woman, a man bearing a wound where he might wear his potency. In an early scene in the novel in Jake's apartment, Hemingway is careful to let it seem that he passively lets Brett make love to him—this is the "getting something for nothing" (148) that he alludes to later. His inadequacy as customer to the prostitute Georgette leads him to jest about her buying him his dinner, a jest that throws him into the female role, a role he takes upon himself. Later, at Burguete, it will be Bill who tries to marry irony and pity to the tune of "The Bells Are Ringing for Me and My Gal" (114), casting Jake as the bride—this shortly after Jake has been diligently searching for worms and urging Bill into "getting up," in a chapter subsequently rich with sexual inversions where men without women, as in other Hemingway works—"The Three-Day Blow" and "A Simple Enquiry," for example— enter into elaborate sex role reversal play. Such metamorphosis into feminine identity has been with Hemingway from the start. Many of the boys and men of *In Our Time* assume what were earlier considered femi- ninely passive positions—in "Cat in the Rain" and "The Doctor and the Doctor's Wife," for example—and in "The End of Something," "Sol- dier's Home," and "Mr. and Mrs. Elliot," power and authority shift to the woman.

Jake's alteration in *Sun* is mimicked in *A Farewell to Arms* (1929) in Frederic Henry's metaphoric assumption of pregnancy and its morn- ing sickness. In *Across the River and into the Trees*, as Colonel Cantwell permits Renata to slip into *his* "pocket" her matrilineally inherited green emeralds, coded as the feminine family jewels, and also as he mo- mentarily creates and tastes the blood in *his* mouth with pleasure immediately after Renata declares her sexual dysfunction due to men- struation, he also puts on feminine identity. For him, before the novel ends, the "shooting's over" (294), the guns put down. Such metamor- phic movement away from male identity, as I have tried to indicate, begins well before this. In *To Have and Have Not* (1937), scores of char- acters lack a patronymic, and even allusions to public figures—those like Sylvia Sidney, Ginger Rogers, Gracie Allen, or Babe Ruth—refer to a world of lost fathers, for all of these discard surnames or patro- nymics and bear only what seem to be doubled "given" names. This stripping away of paternal authority is true throughout Hemingway's work, whether we note the names of the "heroes" of the major novels or stories—Nick Adams, Jake Barnes, Frederic Henry, Henry Morgan, Robert Jordan, Thomas Hudson—or simply note the dephallused hero of *The Sun Also Rises*.

In *The Garden of Eden*, Hemingway's last novel, sodomy is the meta- phor for Catherine's assumption of masculine identity and David's as- sumption of feminine identity. This fact may retrospectively say something about the real source of Jake's aversion to and dislike of the "superiority" of the homosexuals, to whom he is joined by virtue of his "wound" in Hemingway's first novel, *The Sun Also Rises*. That Catherine in *The Garden of Eden* seems to get little satisfaction from "opening up the mail [male]," finally doing it "like someone shelling peas," suggests that the described gender inversion, however desired, may be no more satisfying for Catherine than it was for David. The "opening up of the [male]," however—when it is meant as Hemingway meant it, the breaking down of the protective barriers of the male ego that insularly refuses to risk itself in exposure to what lies beyond itself—is something Hemingway has been about since the beginning: it can stand as metaphor for his texts.

The return of Pablo in *For Whom the Bell Tolls* has been described as the turning point of that novel. Indeed, many have speculated that his return, based as it is on Saint Paul's revelation on the road to Damascus, which led him to reverse his direction, is the "miracle" that changes everything—the future of humanity. That reversal, related to such a fine and seemingly incidental act as the blowing of a bridge, can indeed alter everything.[6] Pablo's patriarchal mode, supporting laissez-faire economics, individualism, and private property as well as proprietary sexuality, is under pressure to change, and Hemingway belabors the point that everything may hinge upon Pablo's willingness and ability "to change": "Forced to a change, he will be smart in the change" (95). Jordan's reconciliation with the returned and altered Pablo is described by Pilar as a homosexual encounter: "What are you two doing? Becoming maricones? . . . Cut thy goodbyes short before this one steals the rest of thy explosive" (404). The necessity for Pablo's "change" is given by Hemingway as due to the fact that "the river is rising" (95). This rising of the waters, which in Fitzgerald is a concomitant of the overthrow of patriarchal power and the emergence of matriarchal power, can be seen as a metaphor related to the effeminization of the masculine that Fitzgerald and Hemingway shared.

As the river is high and the moon is full in *The Sun Also Rises*, Brett, the feminine vortex about which men dance, makes her successful appeal to her acolyte Jake to help her capture Romero, who, as *torero*, is, in the mythos of the bullfight, solar hero. In *For Whom the Bell Tolls*, as "the river" rises, Pablo's change is forced upon him; in *A Farewell to Arms*, it is as the river has risen almost to the bridge that Frederic Henry, about to be executed, dives into those waters in a carefully structured rebirth/transformation rite of escape from which he emerges no longer a warrior but a significantly altered dependent man. In "The End of Something," with the moon rising over the waters of the lake, Marjorie is revealed as the competition and threat that Nick fears. When, in "The Three-Day Blow" he and Bill on a wet day attempt regression to an insular masculine world where the threat of the feminine is excluded, Hemingway carefully codes the feminine world as allied with the cycles and the waters from which they contraceptively and carefully guard themselves as they turn instead indoors to fire and spirits. In the last story of *In Our Time*, "Big Two-Hearted River," Nick Adams finally knows that the days are coming when he will be able to fish the swamp, where the fishing is tragic and the waters rise dangerously against you. Harry Morgan's, Santiago's, and Thomas Hudson's transformative encounters were dangerous and fatal sea journeys, but that way lay their manhood. Only as Harry Morgan, dying, not only accepts but also yields himself to and takes the "roll" of the moon-driven sea does he come to terms with, and accept an alliance with, the feminine powers of the world: "No matter how a man alone ain't got no bloody fucking chance" (225) is his dying wisdom. It is, however, only in his late-published work *The Garden of Eden* that Hemingway intricately explains in sexual metaphor and psychic shift the inner dynamics he has advocated throughout his career: the crossover inversion into the territory of the other sex that is necessary for the full individuated wholeness of a human being.

The Garden of Eden begins with David fishing in the canal on the Mediterranean, and in its penultimate chapter David goes to the sea on the Riviera and high-dives into the "circle of milling water . . . making a boil in the water that a porpoise might have made reentering slickly into the hole that he had made in rising" (241). Joining together his diving and his rising, the sea and the sky, he places his salty mouth against Marita's and says, *"Elle est bonne, la mer. . . . Toi aussi,"* then kisses first the tip of her left breast and then the right. Such reconciliations of opposites, pairings, and integrations that bring masculine and feminine, male and female, into new creative combinations, are everywhere in the novel. In one instance, David studies the nipple of the female breast as masculine in its erectile response while being circular and maternally milk providing. As David, at the novel's end, reconciles Marita's two breasts, he is accepting and reconciling the dualities hidden in gender. This reconciliation of opposites, this joining of the sea and the woman, this acceptance of the dark depths of the sea and the bright heights of the sunstruck air, and of the dualisms hidden within a single sex—a strategy similarly used by Jake Barnes at San Sebastian in *The Sun Also Rises* to bring himself to wholeness—is Hemingway's strategy here for victory over the very watery conditions that drowned and cycled Dick Diver. I do not think it fanciful to assume that Hemingway structured his David's successful diving scene to echo against Fitzgerald's failed Diver and made his David's mode of masculine and feminine integrative reconciliation a reproof for Fitzgerald's Diver, who had not learned how to master his necessary immersions in and commitments to the feminine fluid medium in which he was metaphorically cycled and drowned.

What conclusions can be drawn from this brief overview of symbolism germane to gender inversion in the work of both writers? I think we can see gender inversion at the very heart of Hemingway's and Fitzgerald's shared perception of the altering nature of the West. Both writers saw clearly the role inversion and effeminization of the masculine psyche taking place in their time, and both clearly saw the end of the patriarchate. Hemingway's *Across the River and into the Trees* is his major analysis of the dynamics of this psychic crossover, and Fitzgerald's *Tender Is the Night* is his historical recognition of the situation in which we find ourselves. Dick Diver's "Good-by my father—good-by, all my fathers" finds its literary mythic equivalent in Colonel Cantwell's "The shooting is over." What is especially interesting is the shared nature of their special language, its imagery and symbolism. Both use water in its relation to cycles and the moon and the feminine with its classical burden of associations, but both additionally emphasize its association with matriarchal threats to the male world. Both recognize as well the dangers of male submission to rolling, cycling, submersion, and immersion in fluid process, and such are portents of and agents of masculine death. This imagery itself readily explains that this fear is a fear of regression to the womb, to the undifferentiated fetal state from which the male ego had been extricated and risen to consciousness. The aptness of the incestuous basis of Fitzgerald's novel is immediately apparent as one reflects that incest usually culturally identifies such regression. Yet each author takes a remarkably different stance with respect to this knowledge: Fitzgerald studies uxoriousness in action and the overthrow of or damage to the male in his encounters with women, waters, the moon, and cycling; while Hemingway consistently throughout his work—though he as fully as Fitzgerald recognizes the risks and dangers—nonetheless advocates male mastery through submission to these forces as the only way to acceptable or full or worthy manhood.

Throughout Fitzgerald's works is lament, whether for Gatsby or Diver, whose uxorious dependencies leave them both fatally floating on waters that master them. His summary attitude can be well seen as Dick leaves the field to victorious Baby Warren: "The American Woman, aroused, stood over him: the clean-sweeping irrational temper that had broken the back of a race and made a nursery out of a continent, was too much for him" (*Tender Is the Night* 232).

Increasingly, throughout Hemingway's texts, there is an acceptance of an inevitable new dynamics for a reconstituted male identity achieved by healing immersion in the experience of feminine identity. One of the signs of this is the command "Roll!" that repetitively occurs throughout his texts. We find it as early as *A Farewell to Arms*. In that novel, however, it is ambivalently understood: Frederic and Catherine flee for safety and their luxurious idyll out of war to Switzerland, where, they are told, there are "no rolls" (265). It is a weak pun, to translate croissants as cycles, but the continuing novel exists to prove that biological "rolls" are inescapable—Catherine dies in her ninth-month roll on the inescapable wheel of her pregnancy, and Frederic walks off at the very end "in the rain" (314) that is earlier described as "the permanent rain" (4). If rolls, the cycles implicit in rain and birth, are indeed the concomitants of tragedy, it is increasingly in the Hemingway text the man who yields to them, who runs the risk of feared death as he accepts his feared feminine side—like Cantwell, Harry Morgan, and the Frances Macomber who have gone over to the "rolling" other side to accept and acknowledge the feared "other"—who is worthy at last of our respect and his own true manliness.

Fitzgerald's Dick Diver dissolves in or becomes a cycled victim of waters he cannot master; the effeminization he well understands yet fears is his undoing. Gatsby lies dead, floating at last on the waters destined to claim him. In Hemingway's works, the rains are indeed coming— see *Green Hills of Africa*—and although Hemingway knows as well as Fitzgerald what that means mythically, culturally, and psychically, his strategies of survival in a time of the rising of the waters include accommodation and male transformation.

Notes

1. Oswald Spengler's *Decline of the West* was introduced to Fitzgerald early by his famous Princeton professor Christian Gauss, but throughout his life he

returned to the work, citing it, quoting from it, and obviously still strongly influenced by it (see Le Vot 37).

2. *Parade's End* is the cumulative title given to the Christopher Tietjen novels, which make up the four-volume tetralogy of Ford Madox Ford (Hueffer). The novels were published singly and in succession as *Some Do Not* (1924), *No More Parades* (1925), *A Man Could Stand Up* (1926), and *The Last Post* (1928).

3. The identification of the male Humpty Dumpty with the egg is a fascinating sexual confusion that hides the rhyme and reason of the fairy tale, as, I suspect, it here hides the effeminization of Dick Diver. The insensitive manipulation of male pride can well be seen elsewhere as Mrs. Speers advises her daughter, "Wound yourself or him—whatever happens it can't spoil you because economically you're a boy, not a girl" (40). Dick later well perceives how callously Mrs. Speers has used him to promote her daughter's sexual education, even as he well sees how Baby Warren has similarly discarded consideration of him in her concern for her sister.

4. Hemingway also often deliberately and flagrantly played sexual jokes. His story of sexual challenge, "The Doctor and the Doctor's Wife," where Dick Boulton demonstrates his phallic contempt for the impotent father, begins with the name of the powerful Indian "Dick," who later will taunt the doctor father: 'Don't go off at half cock, Doc,' Dick said" (*Short Stories* 100).

5. See Neumann and my article "Death, Incest, and the Triple Bond in the Later Plays of William Shakespeare," where I conclude:

> Incest seems to be itself a metaphor for the dissolution of consciousness, the breakdown and yielding of the ego to the primal material from which it once emerged. Incest is the fundamental pan-humanistic metaphor for regression to the original state of undifferentiated unconsciousness in uroboric introversion in the womb of the Great Mother. The incest taboo is the transcultural device, the alarm, embedded in the psyche of man to alert him to the dangers of the loss of ego, of selfhood, of consciousness itself, once it has been seized or rescued as the original light breaking in upon the great and primal darkness. (Gajdusek 158)

6. Aborted, blown, incomplete, and destroyed or crossed bridges determine the significant action in most Hemingway works—see my essay "Bridges: Their Creation and Destruction in the Works of Ernest Hemingway," included in this volume. I ask the reader to acknowledge Jake's missing phallus as the blown bridge of that first novel. Were he intact, the space could be crossed: a crossover would be possible into the other and inner terrain of the "other."

WORKS CITED

Fitzgerald, F. Scott. *Tender Is the Night.* 1934. New York: Scribners, 1983.

Fitzgerald, Zelda. *Save Me the Waltz.* 1932. New York: New American Library, 1968.

Gajdusek, Robert. "Death, Incest, and the Triple Bond in the Later Plays of William Shakespeare." *American Imago* 31.2 (1974): 109–58.

Hemingway, Ernest. *Across the River and into the Trees.* 1950. New York: Scribners, 1970.

———. *A Farewell to Arms.* 1929. New York: Scribners, 1957.

———. *Ernest Hemingway: Selected Letters, 1917–1961.* Ed. Carlos Baker. New York: Scribners, 1981.

———. *For Whom the Bell Tolls.* New York: Scribners, 1940.

———. *The Garden of Eden.* New York: Scribners, 1986.

———. *A Moveable Feast.* New York: Scribners, 1964.

———. *The Short Stories of Ernest Hemingway.* 1938. New York: Scribners, 1966.

———. *The Sun Also Rises.* 1926. New York: Scribners, 1954.

———. *To Have and Have Not.* 1937. New York: Scribners, 1965.

Kuehl, John, and Jackson R. Bryer, eds. *Dear Scott/Dear Max: The Fitzgerald-Perkins Correspondence.* New York: Scribners, 1971.

Le Vot, Andre. *F. Scott Fitzgerald.* Trans. William Byron. New York: Warner Books, 1984.

Miller, Linda Patterson, ed. *Letters from the Lost Generation: Gerald and Sara Murphy and Friends.* New Brunswick, NJ: Rutgers UP, 1991.

Mitford, Nancy. *Zelda: A Biography.* New York: Harper and Row, 1970.

Neumann, Erich. *Art and the Creative Unconscious.* New York: Harper and Row, 1959.

18

Elephant Hunt in Eden

A Study of New and Old Myths and Other Strange Beasts in Hemingway's Garden

In James Thurber's tale "The Unicorn in the Garden" a man encounters an imaginary beast in a real garden. When he tries to tell his wife, he is excoriated by her for concern with fiction, not fact; but when she, to get him out of the way, takes over his role and tells *his* tale, she is the one considered to be mad and carted off to the asylum. The wife in bed, whose concern is seemingly with the flesh, resents her husband's imaginative fictions, which exclude her, and her resentment/retaliation ends in her own "madness." It may be of interest that only a virginal maid, the Edenic Eve, can entrap the mythical beast. What Thurber implies about the relations between sexuality and innocence, practicality and imagination, and real and fictive beasts is of the essence in Hemingway's *The Garden of Eden*, where a writer's imaginative pursuit of a real beast is related to his wife's "madness," and the elephant hunt in Eden is indeed an important and necessary part of Hemingway's novel.

Hemingway was hunting big game in this work, and though most of it was game he had shot before in familiar terrain, in *The Garden* he entered some new territory where the beasts are exotic indeed, some that he had, I think, for personal reasons earlier avoided hunting. Many of the book's critics say it reveals a startlingly more human and vulnerable Hemingway, yet in most ways it is classic Hemingway, and different largely in being more revealed. The author's reluctance to finish and publish it *might* have been due to his recognition that its ostensible subject, however much a metaphor, was too close to its real subject, the story he had never been able to write, or he may have recognized that in a *technical sense* it too overtly reused the themes, metaphors, and devices of the other works. Throughout *The Garden of Eden* one hears echoes, from the "crazy" Catherine of *A Farewell* to the inadequate hunter/teacher/father of the short stories, and the subject of sexual role reversal in Hemingway is well-tilled ground. Readers are familiar not only with the woman's desire to cut her hair short while the man is to become more like her but with the Brett who in *The Sun Also Rises* was one of "the chaps" (22) and with the Catherine who entered *A Farewell* carrying a swagger stick to manipulate Frederic into doing as she wished, to play her "crazy" game (30). The Helen of "The Snows of Kiliman-jaro," who unmanned her man through her monied control of his cre-ative gifts, and the Pilar of *For Whom the Bell Tolls*, who "cowed" her man as she seized the baton of authority within the cave, are only two further examples of similar role reversal and seizure of phallic power. Most frequently, such action is covert. Frederic in *A Farewell*, the morn-ing after Catherine announces her pregnancy, awakens with morning sickness and metaphorically takes on feminine physical attributes—the sack of empty bottles that Miss Van Campen removes from his room is, metaphorically, a womb-sack that must be stripped from him before the chapter ends. Colonel Cantwell in *Across the River and into the Trees*, as he is considering Renata's menstrual cycle, is kissed by her hard so that he can then taste his own blood in his own mouth, which he enjoys (111). He takes the matrilinearly inherited green emeralds into his own "pocket" to experience the sensation. Such metaphoric assumption of pregnancy, menstruation, and feminine fertility by the male has been covert—in other works, breasts are concealed in an imagery of two stuffed upper breast pockets (*Across the River*), and wombs in sacks attached to waists ("Big Two-Hearted River")—and the sense has been that feminine attributes have been male appropriations. However, in *The Garden*, it is the man who is cajoled into becoming recipient of the woman's desired experiments and her desired transformations: the focus is importantly upon *her* "wants," and David overtly, not metaphorically, assumes the feminine position. Androgyny and bisexuality are openly explored here, even as they were widely explored in the literature and lifestyles of the Paris of the twenties that Hemingway's original manu-script more systematically included.[1] His use of sexual inversion here merely records and participates in this major theme of the time that he studies. His constant use of it as theme elsewhere, however, makes it importantly our concern.

Hemingway is fundamentally here, as he was in his other work, concerned with psychic shift in his time. M. Aurol early announces that "not only the weather" but "everything was changed and what was not changed was changing fast" (94). The Aurols, who set the stage for the Bournes, are the ones who wish "to move with the change" (167). David knows that he and Catherine are "pioneers" in opening up the "new season" (167) but that he need not be "such a pioneer" (168) as to openly shave only one side of his face. He learns at last just how greatly he has been "divided and separated" (183), and he also finally understands that what he always believed *could not* be shared can be shared.

The Garden of Eden is a study in male relinquishment of power and in a new male posture. In almost all his major novels, Hemingway focuses on the changes that are necessary, that must be undergone in the male psyche for there to be genuinely new accommodation. This is the struggle in Hemingway's important works: an incomplete or vain or egocentric man learns that he must alter and achieve a new stance that balances masculine and feminine parts, his dark side with his light side. The major subject of *In Our Time* is the ineffectuality and failure of masculine authority in a world that desperately needs a new ordering principle. The men supposedly in control on the quai at Smyrna and at Indian Camp are *not* authentically in control, and that book ends with the king in the garden as an impotent prisoner of the encircling revolutionists. The dynamics of its concluding story, "Big Two-Hearted River," suggest that a man can become whole only through an accommodation between himself and nature that balances internal and external realities and both sides of his conflicting being. In later works this becomes "A man alone ain't got no bloody fucking chance" (*To Have and Have Not* 225) and "No man is an *Iland*" (the epigraph to *For Whom the Bell Tolls*).[2]

The Garden of Eden is concomitantly a study of the dissatisfaction of contemporary woman in her role and her attempt to seize the attributes and authority of the male. One question being asked, however, is whether modern man eats of the new fruit offered by this willful and rebellious Eve for her sake or for his own sake. He certainly does act to please her, but the holograph version of the manuscript makes much indeed of David's participatory desire to be altered. Catherine's acts are an attempt to reverse her role and to assume denied prerogatives of control, but then she uses given power to destroy whatever David has made that does not include her and that *she* now defines as useless. She has finally come to desire not balance but unilateral power: "I'll do anything I want to you" (223), she declares. But ignoring the will of the world, other people's desires or nature's desires, Hemingway implies, is a madness that can be fatal. As hunter, fisherman, and explorer of landscapes, he has always studied personality as a delicate balance between the human being and nature. Now he presents Catherine, who seemingly believes she need but do what *she* wants to "be" herself. This is culpable innocence if it ignores remorse and "others." Hemingway has warned against such simplifications: "Make love, not war" was not a solution in *A Farewell*, nor was the imposition of one's will on another or anarchy a way to identity, or the laying down of one's arms a guarantee of peace. To cross over and attempt to join the other side, in sexuality or politics, he seems to say, is not a simple but a highly complex psychic maneuver.

David clearly sees, and sees with guilt, the source of Catherine's dilemma in his exclusionary art. The imaginary world of his art does exclude her—he is the creator whose creative act seems to replace her own biological creative function—and only his "narrative" of their life together gives her what she feels is a participatory role. She, in retaliation, becomes creator in the real, unnaturally manipulating life into fictive postures, creating drama. I've "invented you" (191), she says of David and Marita, reciprocally trying to control destiny.

The metaphoric action in *The Garden* has therefore much to do with these redefined perimeters of identity. But this is not new. Colonel Cantwell in *Across the River* is explicitly preparing "the best way to be overrun" (104), and in *The Garden* David Bourne is at last directly told, "You've been overrun with girls" (244). In *A Farewell to Arms*, Frederic Henry's defenses, personal and public, are similarly "down," as the retreat from Caporetto mirrors a larger psychic defeat and breakthrough, and as the battle lines and the lines of his identity are both overrun. Historically and mythically, Hemingway is alert in *The Garden of Eden*: "There aren't any sides any more" (243), David finally announces. He has learned that what could not be shared can be shared and that his father does not need to kill elephants to live. He also knows that Catherine is driven to excesses of destructive behavior by historical time—she fails because she is "hurried"—trying to seize too quickly what she wishes to have. With Marita, however, David goes beyond the competitive relationship he had with Catherine. He finally knows the new balance required for the future: "You're my partner. . . . Be with me" (245), he adjures Marita, and she replies, "I'm with you" (245). He can write "the Bournes" in the sand at last to mean the new alliance with Marita because it acknowledges that they and birth and the word itself accept cyclical death. He dives into the sea like a porpoise, the mythic creature who reconciles the worlds of life and death, uroborically diving back into the very hole he made in rising—so affirming that in his end is his beginning, death meets birth. For a moment before he dives he seems "to hang . . . without falling" (241); then he gives himself to the "circle of milling water" (241).³ This icon of eternal return allows him to accept both sides equally, the heights and depths. David now can kiss the tips of both Marita's breasts as they rise above the water. Acknowledging them both with love, he has, as completely as Harry Morgan, accepted the moon-driven waters that rock him and control him, and as completely as Robert Jordan he has put both sides together and gotten himself turned over.

Hemingway's novel is an attempt to remodel the soul and technique of modern man and artist into that of a sharer: as David puts his arm "around the girl" (203) while "they together read the writing" (203), he knows it is something he has never done before—and he who wrote it now reads it *as* she reads it. Marita is the new wife for the new man: having received his words, she puts her arms around him and kisses him so hard she draws blood from *his* lip (203), balancing spirit and flesh, word and blood. She exacts from him what he has taken from life. But now David has at last written the story he held off all his life, that of the necessary replacement of the father hero with the elephant hero. He has moved from identification with killer to identification with killed, and in so doing has undergone the very shift that made Francis Macomber into a man. David only began to grow to become a man within the elephant's moon-thrown shadow when he became one with his dog Kibo. It was only thus that he could distinguish the elephant's other side, and it is only as he becomes one with the elephant that he defies his father at last.

The story that David tries to write is a memory that hides a double guilt, his betrayal of the killer and the killed, of both the elephant and his father. If in his past he has deceived and cast off both sides, betraying his relationship with the great beast by yielding his visionary experience of him to others who then kill him, and giving up his trusting relationship with his father, who may never trust him again and whom he never so trusts again, he desperately needs to write the story, to make it art that integrates the experience and makes it whole. Exploring that history, he reveals the dynamics of his subsequent relationship not only with his art but also with Catherine. In Africa, he betrayed to others his moonlight vision of the double-sided, equally greatly right- and left-tusked mystery elephant. The penalty for such revelation of the secret source of individuated wholeness is the provoked destructive pursuit by others, their need to acquire what he has discovered and revealed. This, in miniature, is a study of the dynamics of art itself: the public avidity for the artist's art is that very provoked voracity for the experience behind the story, the life behind the words that the artist has signaled in his composition. The audience follows the linearly defined trail to try to get what has come within its ken only by virtue of *his* daring and venturing within the dark and moonlit forests of the mind, by his "telling," but their possession leads to its destruction. Hemingway often repeated his belief that to write anything was to lose it, or kill it, so that an artist kills the thing he loves.

David's story explains for us the psychic necessity to acquire the revealed synthesis that the elephant is. It is also precisely the story of Catherine's envy of David's art, the mystery and "other side" she has looked upon, and a foreshadowing of the way in which her covetousness leads toward its destruction. David's tale is an abstract exemplification of her acted-upon desires; it is the paradigm of the process that Catherine follows, and as it tells of the transformation of life lived into art, it tells of the conversion of creative love to destructive love. As David has revealed to Catherine his own authentic vision as artist, she now covets that "ivory" (181) and tries to make herself over into the individuated object—she wants to be at once dark and light (or African, "ivory") and also bisexual, at once balanced dark fluid mystery and tusked killer, at once creator of herself and of that which she pursues, hunter and hunted in the same flesh, girl-lusting "boy" who is yet the very girl she lusts for. (Although she becomes Peter, David becomes, revealingly, Catherine.) In this way she seeks the integration and the self-sufficiency that the artist, David, has. The psychic integrations that the artist undergoes to become artist and that take him to the vision in the darkness are simultaneously the reward and the way: they establish the authority of belief that gives life meaning, if it be only belief in one's talent or art. When vision and the seizure of vision in form are fulfilled, when David has guaranteed through his search that the right and left tusks of the sought beast are equally great, and then when the elephant tusks are finally placed together—like the trinity of animal horns at the end of *Green Hills*—"no one could believe them even when they touched them" (202). What is sought is the redemptive belief that can be acquired only through the arduous journey and the skilled craft. The hunter and the hunted must be similarly joined, as in "The Short Happy Life" the master hunter and guide Wilson profoundly understood the lions he killed as in the hunt they were totally focused on and joined to him. Here even the elephant makes his own journey to death to reconcile himself with his dead partner, the lost part of the self, before he himself is slain.

The Garden of Eden also, on one level at least, is Hemingway's variation on one theme that all artists explore: the eternally retold story of the guilt the artist feels for his frustration/betrayal of life as he brings to his abstract medium of art the passion that he takes from or diverts from his beloved. Henry James wrote it as "Maude Evelyn," D. H. Lawrence as Sons and Lovers, and every great artist writes it at least once—to expiate his otherwise "useless" activity purchased at too great a price. Edgar Allan Poe in "The Oval Portrait" lets us see that as each tint of color is placed on the canvas, the beloved model who sits for her portrait gets paler: as the canvas is complete—Voila!—the sitter is dead.

There are, of course, other fabulous beasts being hunted in this novel, especially the beast of whom David has never been able to tell. Much needs to be finally exorcised about the autobiographical Hadley and Pauline menage à trois situation that we recognize behind the details of the plot, as well as the compelled twinning of Hemingway and Marcelline as children, but there is bigger game yet: the story that is basic to the breakdown in relations with his father and the reason for the absence (once again) of the protestingly "hated" mother. Mike Reynolds explores the real but hidden story in his recent biography The Young Hemingway as he focuses on the Ruth Arnold/Grace Hemingway relation, which he identifies as one source of the poisoning of the parents' relationship. I think The Garden of Eden covertly yet strongly tells us that the Arnold/Hemingway relationship was far more destructive and perhaps more creative than we have realized: it helped destroy the son-mother relation, though it may have contributed to the making of an artist. In a dark forest, a boy covertly explores to spy upon the great elephant—he comes upon it where it is hidden and then, daringly stalking, he follows it into the intimate depths of the forest to become voyeur to whatever primal scene reveals the elephant's "other side." Fleeing with this knowledge back to his father, he sets in motion the forces of what becomes now his father's hunt, a vengeance hunt, that at last strips from him his vision, the great two-sided elephant he loved, and the honesty of his relationship with his father. In other words, the story David writes and the life he lives both tell of the dangers and costs of feared yet desired, destructive and creative androgyny. An artist's art, which is nothing if not the exemplified holistic fusion of two opposite unnaturally wedded worlds, is one way to resolve the problem of such desperate knowledge.

NOTES

1. That was the Paris of Nathalie Barney's Ecole des Amazons and Eliot's *Waste Land*, where bisexual Tiresias is the seer for the "Unreal City"—there are *Waste Land* allusions in *The Garden of Eden*—and of Djuna Barnes's *Nightwood*, where Dr. Matthew Dante O'Connor is the Tiresian bisexual "bearded lady." Hemingway's multiple allusions to Scott and Zelda Fitzgerald's struggle for sexual identity are close to the surface in his *Garden*, as are those to Scott's *Tender Is the Night* and its increasingly ineffectual bisexual protagonist, whose masculinity is stripped from him and whose breasts are described as no longer nurturing or sustaining the "breast-seeking" young (311).

2. Hemingway's male protagonists most often learn only late how they should have lived, how they might have balanced their lives. Dephallused Jake can never wholly relate beyond himself, Frederic learns humility too late, and Cantwell, Jordan, and Harry Morgan recognize the necessary capitulation or need to "get turned over" just before their deaths. It has taken Santiago many years to get to his final victory/defeat, and it takes the Hemingway of *Green Hills* most of the book to learn how to seize victory out of defeat, how to come to terms with "the other side." Francis Macomber and Harry of "The Snows of Kilimanjaro" have been victims to their own uxoriousness and childishness and have found no viable alternative, for they die as they learn at last what they should have known. On the whole, Hemingway's protagonists are men who, significantly, learn late how to accept, explore, and bind themselves to the other and unknown dark side of their natures, to acknowledge and love the "other." David, in *The Garden*, is learning throughout how to accept his repressed side, and in doing so, is learning how to truly love a woman.

3. This repeated figure is everywhere in Hemingway's work but perhaps best seen in Harry Morgan hanging on the wheel before accepting the roll of the moon-driven sea that is to be his couch of death.

WORKS CITED

Fitzgerald, F. Scott. *Tender Is the Night.* 1934. New York: Scribners, 1983.
Hemingway, Ernest. *Across the River and into the Trees.* 1950. New York: Scribners, 1970.

————. *A Farewell to Arms*. 1929. New York: Scribners, 1957.

————. *For Whom the Bell Tolls*. 1940. New York: Scribners, 1968.

————. *The Garden of Eden*. New York: Scribners, 1986.

————. *To Have and Have Not*. 1937. New York: Scribners, 1962.

————. *The Sun Also Rises*. 1926. New York: Scribners, 1954.

Reynolds, Michael. *The Young Hemingway*. Oxford, UK: Basil Blackwell, 1986.

19

The Oxymoronic Compound and the Ambiguous Noun

Paradox as Paradigm in A Farewell to Arms

Hemingway began his life in Paris in the twenties as a short story writer, poet, and journalist, but by mid-decade he had successfully made himself into the novelist he wished to be. His arrival on the scene as a novelist was sufficiently spectacular to impress most—even his first novel was anticipated by some with great expectation—and therefore we must look at his later years in the twenties *after* the publication of *The Sun Also Rises*, when he was mainly writing and publishing only short stories—*Men without Women* came out in 1927—as years during which he was not only consolidating his literary and social relations with other leading writers of the period but also perfecting his technique and his own image of himself as the serious novelist he wished to become. In letters about *The Sun Also Rises* written shortly after its publication, we find him occasionally self-denigrating, explaining that first remarkable novel as not exactly what he would like to be able to do. Allowing for the need to pose before his recipient, we nevertheless find him explaining to Sherwood Anderson that "it's Christ's own distance from the kind of novel I want to write and hope I'll learn how to write," while in letter after letter he is already looking forward to his next and subsequent novels (*Selected Letters* 218). Surely, therefore, if we set aside *The Torrents of Spring* as a literary tour de force that interrupted the composition of *The Sun Also Rises*, we must imagine him in these post-*Sun* early years as casting and recasting in his mind for the subject that would inevitably and rightly serve him for his second novel. From 1925 on, Hemingway must have been reviewing as a craftsman and artist his available materials, the experiences he had to build on that gave him a certain familiarity with a subject, a drama, and a landscape that might serve his needs. He had proven himself enough of an artist with *The Sun Also Rises* so we can imagine the vast intellectual labor of getting his imagery and metaphors right, of finding the exact vehicle for the content he wished to confront. That he delayed the beginning as long as he did, says, I believe, something important about the intensity of that search, for the exact setting and complication and the precisely articulated set of events, the inevitable narrative, that might do what he needed done. Everything declares the seriousness of the young man in his high conception of the artist's task (undoubtedly learned from Joyce; see my essay "Hemingway and Joyce: A Study in Debt and Payment" in this volume) and the meticulousness of his choice of images (learned from Pound)[1] and his search for the right plot for the right subject. He found it at last. We have the heart of it given to us in the short poetic title that he also subsequently labored to find, *A Farewell to Arms*.[2]

"A Farewell to Arms" as a title hides inside itself the very creative-destructive bonding that its author wished to study. The title needs careful examination, for in it is held the primary vision of the novel and the key to the form and narrative structure of the whole. As a farewell to arms it is the renunciation of the tools of death and also a farewell to the métier, the soldier's profession, that bound this protagonist in bonds of faith, camaraderie, and commitment to those administering death. It therefore looks forward to the desertion that takes him toward his beloved and love and away from his comrades and war. As a farewell to arms, it is simultaneously the renunciation or loss of the arms of the beloved that hold him captive or lover in love. The ending of book 2 exemplifies or witnesses the latter, as Frederic Henry leaves Catherine Barkley in Milan to return to the front; the ending of book 3 demonstrates the former, for in diving into the Tagliamento River he deserts the army and is on his way to find Catherine. Literary allusions in the work emphasize this dualistic basing of the title. In the title of the novel are coevally the two bound and related commitments of Frederic Henry's life, and insofar as the situations of the novel suggest that denial of one seems release to other, there is a yet greater irony brought to bear in which denial of one proves to be finally coevally the loss of the other, so that the tragic outcome of the novel, the loss of Catherine after renunciation of the army in order to then, naturally, have her, is answered by the unnatural birth in which he loses her as well. Both the

beloved and the army, implicated in one another, seem necessarily concomitantly if not causally lost: honor and love, duty and desire. This
emphatic forcing of opposites together and upon one another determines the structure of the novel, a novel that begins with men of death
(soldiers) seen as childbearing women and ends with a woman in childbirth finding death.

But titles have been, throughout Hemingway's work, indices to this
very enforced synthesis or bonding of opposites; whether we consider
the obvious antitheses being studied in such titles as *Winner Take Nothing,* or *To Have and Have Not,* or those that are so readily implicit in
titles like *Across the River and into the Trees* or *Islands in the Stream*—in
which the opposing sides of the river, or shade or no shade, or stasis
in flow is the concern—Hemingway names his fascination. A *Moveable
Feast* speaks of the interaction of the secular and the sacred, the fixed
and the cyclical, as readily as *The Sun Also Rises* insists that we recognize
the absolute sun implicated in planetary cycles. It takes but a moment's
reflection to see that Hemingway's narratives similarly have a fundamentally oxymoronic structure. *Death in the Afternoon* studies the intricate relations of *torero* and *toro* in which the two eventually become
one, all taking place in *sol y sombra; The Fifth Column* defines those
inside Madrid who are invisibly part of those outside the city; *The Garden of Eden* studies the attempt to be both sexes at once; and a story like
"The Short Happy Life of Francis Macomber" focuses closely on the
moment of real life that is indistinguishable from the moment of
received death. The undecaying carcass of the leopard, which from the
epigraph on dominates and oversees the action of "The Snows of Kilimanjaro," is death in the semblance of life; what would normally be
decaying dead flesh is instead held in a species of eternal suspension
near the western summit of the mountain called the House of God.
Such binding together of the flesh and the spirit, the temporal and the
immortal, is typical.

The conceptual paradigm implicit in the title of Hemingway's second major novel seems to dictate the dynamics of the first short chapter
in which the soldiers going to war, looking as if they are "six months
gone with child" (4), ironically carry very real destruction in the cartridges in their clips in the cartridge boxes under the rain capes they
wear. Their vows and dedications as soldiers commit them to hate or
destroy the life of their enemy, yet they will do so with those bullets,
which are first seen in this novel of war as though the enwombed fetus,
created out of the vows and commitments of love. Not only are creation

and destruction and the making and taking of life simultaneously suggested, but the image so implicates one in the other that the child itself seems to be that which kills as it becomes the bullets that will destroy the bodies of soldiers, who are here seen as inseparable from the child. The identification of fetal life with the body of the soldier who will both administer and receive death unearths a profound suicidal metaphor.

Throughout his work Hemingway associates birth with the number nine, nine being the number of lunar cycles that produce a child. Indeed, it is at nine o'clock in September, the ninth month, that Catherine will announce her pregnancy to Frederic. However, it is in the ninth chapter that he is wounded and experiences a "death" before he is subsequently reborn; and, as I studied in my essay "The Ritualization of Death and Rebirth" (included in this volume), the very events of his experience of wounding and death in the hole in the bank and his subsequent revival and extrication from that hole are given in an elaborate imagery and description of an obstetrically assisted birth. Subsequent metaphoric rebirths that are concomitantly deaths—like Frederic's diving into the Tagliamento (and crawling out of it like an emerging baby through the willow branches) and then later rowing across Lago Maggiore (described in the iconography of a crucifixion) lead him through fictive death to a real new life that awaits him: they are elaborate constructs of simultaneous birth and death.[3]

The dust on the leaves of the trees in the first paragraph of the novel places death cosmetically upon life, and soon rain, which ordinarily vivifies and is the very metaphor of cyclical process, will bring death as it brings "the cholera" (4); Catherine, as the rain falls at the end, will contrarily be seen as absolute statue. The cyclical, normally life-affirming rain, identified here with the death it brings and, presciently, so feared by Catherine, opposed here to the marmoreal fixity of the statue that Catherine seems, places life against death, flow against fixity, or mortality against immortality.

Multiple details, some prominent and others minuscule, insist on oxymoronic bonds throughout the novel until they become a stylistic convention. Hemingway's deliberate obfuscation of Catherine's nationality so that she can be at one and the same time Scotch and English (20–21, 64–65, 111, 122, 236) is a little like the treatment of Frederic, who is equally styled Enrico Federico and Federico Enrico (39). War ruins in Gorizia are described to reveal at once both the insides and outsides of houses, and the retreat from Caporetto—significantly due to the breakthrough when the line is erased that has separated and defined opposites and enemies—may fatally make enemy and ally indistinguishable: Frederic Henry is in danger of being shot for being the enemy he is not. The other side of the bridge, which should mean safety and alliance with one's own, means danger of execution, of being shot for being the other. Forces everywhere in the novel labor to eradicate distinctions so that opposites are confused with one another: whether this is due to a haircutting ritual, a conversation where differences of thought are repudiated (73–74), the bringing of an anarchist to the king's bed by virtue of the overthrow of instituted authorities (184), or a fancifully considered operation in which Rinaldi, who early claims that Frederic is "really an Italian," would take out Frederic's liver and put in "a good Italian liver" (162), Hemingway's intent is constant throughout—to focus attention on the oxymoronic compound being forced toward becoming the ambiguous noun. In "A Farewell to Arms": The War of the Words, Robert W. Lewis calls attention to the priest's Abruzzi as a "timeless place where nature and people exist in harmony" (112) and urges attention to the seeming/being duality in this novel, where roles are being played "on a stage of real blood and death" (107–8). He asks the reader's awareness of what Frederic has learned: "the awful divergence between action and language and the unconscionable hypocrisy of acting on . . . corrupted words" (148). The forcing together of "corrupted" abstract words and physical acts is related to the seeming/being dichotomy that loses its integrity when the distinctions are lost or indiscernible, caught in an oxymoronic bond that increasingly masks the dualities. Overtones of religious allusions—"In the beginning was the Word," heard against "the corruption of the flesh"—help the reader interpret the inversions in these linkages.[4]

    The reader discovers quickly that the novel is based on a profound intellectual and mystical study of the inseparability of ultimate and antithetical dimensions and experiences of life, that the writer is almost obsessively illustrating the irony that life is death and death is life, that to beget life is to beget death, and that love kills. Hemingway is not so much tracking the irony of the oxymoron, which implicates one thing in its opposite, usually in an epithet—as in "cruel kindness"—as he is fastidiously studying the attempt by one thing to take over the identity of or to become one with the identity of its opposite so that the two become one and inseparably the same. It is as the bound or joined opposites labor to annul, disguise, or eradicate their opposition that a single and highly ambiguous entity begins to replace or be suggested as replacement for the former fused antitheses. The dominant example of this is, of course, the love bond between the two protagonists, Frederic and Catherine, who strive to become one, but it can readily be seen in such minor characters as Bonello and Piani, the two anarchists who dream of sleeping in the king's bed and who, by doing so, would create anarchy. The reader might note that as one of Frederic's cars comes to rest upon its differential (194), which normally lies between and affirms the distance between the two similar but *opposite* joined sides, the car is lost.

Hemingway's deeper studies of discreteness, identity, and the loss of these in bondings with antitheses drive the dynamics and structures and forms of the novel: Catherine imaginatively imposes her lost lover upon Frederic—two time-separated, life-and-death–separated rivals—so that one seems to disappear into and become the other; later, she will urge hair styling and imaginative excesses to try to make herself into Frederic and Frederic into herself. Frederic, who has put on an Italian uniform, seems by that strategy to be Italian; American opera singers like Ralph Simmons, who becomes Enrico DelCredo in Italy, take unto themselves Italian names so that their audiences will see and accept them as Italians, and Frederic in chapter 22 will even metaphorically seem to assume Catherine's morning sickness in order to be the pregnant woman *he cannot be*. Frederic, talking with Rinaldi and the major in the hospital, will invert masculinity and femininity and express ideas and thoughts that are not his own in order to be accepted as and identified with those he speaks with (74). The "anarchists" Piani and Bonello would make king into commoner and commoner into king, and Passini, who urges the dissolution of boundaries between enemies, the insignificance of opposites, the making of love rather than war (50), is the one who dies crying out concomitantly to Maria, Mother of God and "mama mia" (54).

This enforced reconciliation of the warring sides of a dualism seems to excite a concomitant distinct counter-reformation that tries in the works to reestablish the lost distinctions. The sorting of the fleeing army at the bridge at Codroipo is an attempt to unmask the enemies going disguised as Italians; the furor at the racetrack in Milan is about identifying a disguised horse (Japalac); and the ejecting of the machine-gunner from the seat he tries to claim for Frederic by assuming Frederic's place is another case in point (140, 152). Pointedly, Bonello and Piani are neither the king nor the queen whose places they try to take, and the novel builds a revulsion against those who pretend to be what they are not, by that revulsion extricating characters from seized and pretended roles: Frederic from his role as Catherine's lost fiancé, from his metaphorically assumed pregnancy as Catherine, and, later at the hospital in Lausanne, from his seeming role as false doctor—all the duplicities masked in single roles that they *cannot* assume.

The implications of the systematic identification of opposites, which throughout this novel imposes love upon war and life upon death, are profound. They undoubtedly help explain the inextricability of love and war in Hemingway's novels and probably also the meaning of the simultaneous rites of killing and rites of love throughout Hemingway's work. "Fathers and Sons" carefully establishes the relation between killing and lovemaking and the gun and the phallus, but it would be foolishness to simplistically judge Hemingway a war lover or one who sought in the excitement of war an equivalent for the orgasm of love. His pursuits were always far more intellectually underpinned. When, in "The Snows of Kilimanjaro," Harry plays with language, reciting "Rot and poetry. Rotten poetry" (*Short Stories* 58), he is engaging in the sort of verbal play the writer himself goes through in *The Sun Also Rises* when he has Jake note that the serving girl brings in buttered toast, "or, rather, it was bread toasted and buttered" (114). In both instances there is an intentness to observe the way antitheses create ironies: rot is the antithesis—mythically, intellectually, and poetically—of word, just as toast and butter, relating to sequential exposure to fire and grease, one the spirit, the other the flesh, suggest similar associations of radically disparate things. It is one thing when opposites exist in oxymoronic proximity and opposition but quite another when they are focused upon one another to form a compound, suggesting inseparability and unity. Hemingway seems to be saying that if you put rot and poetry together, you get "rotten poetry," or that in accepting the compound one destroys dualism, the way, in love or in marriage, a "couple" may obscure the disparate identities it unites.

But all of this begs the question, which must be the critic's attempt to understand Hemingway's profound and constant study of the shifting relations between the oxymoronic paradox and the ambiguous noun. What I mean by this is the way Hemingway's art seems to be based on the definition of a dualistic situation that is then placed in a struggle complicated by a desire for a resolution in an impossible synthesis. Hemingway frequently invests a character or thing with a paradoxical duality—so that Catherine in *The Garden of Eden* can seemingly be both a boy and a girl, so that Frederic can seemingly be both an American and an Italian, so that destructive soldiers can seemingly be procreative women, and so that Frederic can seemingly be to Catherine her lost soldier lover while yet being himself. This fictional complication is most often caused by an attempt to make the two together become one, which forces a species of madness into life—for example, as Catherine labors to dissolve her and Frederic's separate identities, as Rinaldi tries to prove to Frederic that Frederic is really Italian, and as Frederic tries to prove to Rinaldi and the major in the hospital that he is really one of them. These are very basic or simple illustrations of far more complex oppositions and syntheses at work. One might speculate that the fundamental deep polar struggle that this pattern implies is, as it always is in a work of art, one between form and content, between the material and the conception, one in which the artist's imagination idealistically or fictively tries to do battle with the dragon of reality by addressing and metaphorically arranging the gross factual material. The paradigm for this struggle is the paradox of language itself, and it is this paradox that the self-reflexive artist makes visible. It is my contention that Hemingway was unusually fascinated by the aesthetic encounter, one that he saw as an almost fatal engagement between imagination and reality, or between fiction and truth, and yet one in which the struggle through fiction toward truth became the supreme battle, and that this concern was in very large part the source of the oxymoronic pattern.

As *A Farewell* ends, Frederic walks away in the rain, leaving behind him his last vision of Catherine as a statue. The image of the cyclical rain against which is seen the whitened image of the fixed and undecaying statue is a fine example of the enforced opposition of time and eternity, death and life. For a *moment*, Catherine seems to be an absolute that outwits seasonal change, yet she is caught in seasonal change. The writer has made us firmly aware that the statue is a fiction and the rain is real, however they may be joined. (We see this same metaphor being developed in "The End of Something" as the real white stones seen through second-growth woods, a metaphor of an absolute caught in cycle, become to Marjorie "our ruin" (108), her and Nick's castle, while Hemingway lets us strongly feel Nick's withdrawal from her romanticism within his skeptical and, at that moment, destructive mind, which is intent upon reducing and annihilating such fictions.) The ending image of *A Farewell* balances the image of the soldiers that began the novel, whose "pregnancy" was fictive while their impending deaths were very real, with a Catherine whose real death is counterpoint to the unreal births that are not allowed to happen. Catherine herself throughout the novel has argued for imaginary or wishful conditions that might resist reality and that Frederic again and again reproves as he brings facts against her fictions: she may profess that she will do whatever he wishes, but she herself admits that she must first see the patients; she may wish herself and Frederic always together, but he reminds her that he must leave at midnight; she may urge that they fall asleep at the same instant, but he tells us that after she fell asleep he lay awake; however she may wish that they may be one, he tells us that he goes to the front whereas she stays in Milan.

The point is that in Catherine Hemingway embodies the fictive principle attempting to elevate itself into reality, while in Frederic he embodies a basic realism whose destructive temptation is toward desired escape into fictions. In *The Sun Also Rises*, Cohn is the sentimentalist who tries to force his conceptions into absolutes—to him Brett is "absolutely fine and straight" (38)—while Jake is the realist, made so in part by injuries gained in a real war that has brought him hard against reality: he faces his wounds in the mirror. Though he tries to discipline Cohn's illusions with reality, he contrarily wishes to escape into fictions himself. Hemingway makes this ironic pattern more emphatic by making Jake a journalist who wishes ardently to write a novel, to be a fictionalist. His final "Isn't it pretty to think so?" (247) is the reader's reassuring concluding knowledge that Jake understands the vanity and contradiction of his desires. Such basic oxymoronic joinings of fictional or imaginative conceptions and hard facts underwrite most of Hemingway's oppositions. In his novels, when someone like Romero, who normally necessarily deals with life factually and realistically, whose medium is that very reality that must be contained and mastered or understood, begins to wish to be led into fiction, tragedy is imminent. As Romero places his hand in Brett's and asks her to tell him his fortune, he asks for reassuring lies. Jake similarly asks Brett for lies early in the novel, and she refuses to accommodate his sentimentality. The interplay of fiction and fact in the first novel almost demands Jake's last words in which the separation between fiction and fact that he makes lets us leave the novel.

In *A Farewell*, Frederic's Italian appearance and identity are an adopted fiction, as are those of the American students of Italian opera. Various held beliefs—of Frederic's ambulance crew, that to lay down one's arms does not entail consequences; of the lovers, that love can be played as a game without stakes; of the soldiers, that a combatant can pretend a sustained injury, like the man with a hernia, yet remain a true soldier—are fictions that life will reprove. Catherine, like the Catherine of *The Garden of Eden*, tries to become the creator in the finite, the fictionalist who creates reality, as she forces her desired state of being "always" in love against the real conditions of the eternally cycling rain. The reader, given "the permanent rain" (4) in the first chapter, is confronted with the oxymoronic bond that will structure the novel: rain is no more permanent than love, or life. Yet of course the victory is Catherine's, for it is through fiction that we know of her, that her sufferings are real to us, and *that* created reality is a factor of the trace that remains within the mind of the abandoned Frederic who walks away in the real rain as the novel ends: he carries with him the fiction of a woman become statue who remains absolute enough within him in her fictive nature to compel him to the act that entraps the truth of the real—the fiction that he, like the Ancient Mariner, is compelled to tell.

I have looked at only a very few aspects of Hemingway's structuring devices in *A Farewell to Arms*, notably the oxymoronic bond and its desire to shift into a more fundamentally ambiguous noun. As Hemingway's plots seem to reprove this desire, he seems to be insisting on the clear difference between fiction and reality, between truth and illusion; nevertheless, his plots outwit his logic and finally seem to suggest that his real acknowledgment is the greater wisdom of the paradoxical nature of art in which truth in fiction becomes truth indeed.

NOTES

1. This is my own conclusion from research, in the summer of 1994, on the intertwined lives of Pound and Hemingway and the sources of their imagery in Paris and in the cities and landscapes of Italy. Also see Wilhelm's *Ezra Pound in London and Paris: 1908–1925*.

2. In *Hemingway's Hidden Craft: The Writing of "A Farewell to Arms,"* Bernard Oldsey has well studied the full range of titles Hemingway considered for his novel. *A Farewell to Arms* seems to have been taken from a line of verse in George Peele's "Polyhymnia" (1590). Carlos Baker (199) says that Hemingway told his family in December 1928 that he had recently found his title as that of the Peele poem in *The Oxford Book of English Verse*.

3. In several of my essays I have looked at the Christian iconography that invests this lake crossing: see "Hemingway and Joyce: A Study in Debt and Payment" (included in this volume).

4. I have discussed many of these forms at greater length in "*A Farewell to Arms*: The Psychodynamics of Integrity" (included in this volume).

Works Cited

Baker, Carlos. *Ernest Hemingway: A Life Story*. New York: Scribners, 1969.

Hemingway, Ernest. *Ernest Hemingway: Selected Letters, 1917–1961*. Ed. Carlos Baker. New York: Scribners, 1981.

———. *A Farewell to Arms*. 1929. New York: Scribners, 1957.

———. *The Short Stories of Ernest Hemingway*. New York: Scribners, 1966.

———. *The Sun Also Rises*. 1926. New York: Scribners, 1954.

Lewis, Robert W. *"A Farewell to Arms": The War of the Words*. New York: Twayne, 1992.

Oldsey, Bernard. *Hemingway's Hidden Craft: The Writing of "A Farewell to Arms."* University Park: Pennsylvania State UP, 1979.

Wilhelm, J. J. *Ezra Pound in London and Paris: 1908–1925*. University Park: Pennsylvania State UP, 1990.

20

"Road to Hell Paved with Unbought Stuffed Dogs"

Prefigurations of David Bourne in Hemingway's Earlier Work

It is immensely important to re-examine Hemingway's early work in the light of his recent *The Garden of Eden*, because too much is being made, by unperceptive readers, of the "newness" of the last work: everywhere we hear that it reveals a new Hemingway, heretofore unguessed at, unknown, a never-before-imagined Hemingway. Well, that is nonsense. What we find in *The Garden* and what we discover in its artist protagonist David Bourne has been there in Hemingway's work from the beginning but is suddenly highlighted so that it can be at last seen with a clarity that was missing when in the earlier decades we read without the informing perspective of time. One of the wonderful aspects of *Eden* is that beyond it, innocence has fallen away and man can be seen in all his nakedness, his full and human dimensions, and this late novel of Ernest Hemingway—declaring overtly the themes and attitudes that it does— permits us to re-examine with similarly informed sight and to see as though for the first time with new comprehension.

David Bourne, as avatar of the writer, is clearly established in *The Garden* as the artist who, dedicated to his art, inadvertently creates by that very dedication dramatic and fatal scenarios for his wife, Catherine. Not only is she jealous of his detachment and his ability to isolate himself emotionally and in some ways practically from the real world that they inhabit in love together, but she is, because of him, a partially abandoned woman who, in desperation, is forced to find her own substitute gratifications in order to explore the possibilities of creativity that remain open to her.[1] Creator in reality rather than illusion, she attempts to restructure God's given genders. Normal heterosexual love seems a sacrifice on the altar of necessity, sacrificed by Catherine to the vanity, arrogance, and masculine self-sufficiency that seem necessary to her husband's creative process and its needs and its concomitant aesthetic detachment for aesthetic abstract ends. If we read the early manuscript versions of this novel, we quickly see that Catherine's rage there was against the male appropriation of the creative functions in a home lamentably lacking a child. David's successful and acclaimed published works seem even a mockery of her own fertile reproductive capacity— the ignored but desired biological child becoming the cost of David's metaphoric abstract "children."[2]

An auxiliary and necessarily related theme in this late work is the masculinization of Catherine and the effeminization of David, as gender switching and transgression become modes of actively striking at the unacceptable marital stance of the artist. The book seems driven by the artist's struggle to perfect his necessary aesthetic stance (while feeling guilt for the restricted terms of life that he seems to impose upon his wife) as much as it is driven by her avid pursuit of alternatives to her enforced loneliness and isolation. Defeminization seems an unavoidable response to the abrogation of her role and function. Hemingway is explicit in A Moveable Feast, discussing what it is like "when the husband is a writer and doing difficult work so that he is occupied much of the time and is not a good companion or partner to his wife for a big part of the day" (209–10).

Based as The Garden of Eden is in the time, place, and situation of Zelda and Scott Fitzgerald on the French Riviera in the twenties, there is much in Catherine of what has been biographically well studied as Zelda's boredom—much of her competitiveness, her threats of retaliation, and even her madness—that seemed to grow as she found herself bypassed, set aside, and even "ripped off" by Scott's art. There is also even a portrait of Fitzgerald's coeval effeminization, hinted at by Hemingway in A Moveable Feast,[3] that he himself so well developed in the Dick Diver of Tender Is the Night.

All of this seems shocking and new. But is it new? Not at all: these themes have been Hemingway's subject and concern since he began to write, and his clear statement here at the end of his life allows us the gift of new sight, the ability to read freshly the old texts.

It is important to perceive accurately the basis of the struggle in *The Garden of Eden*. It is on one level a showdown battle in a heterosexual love bond between the different priorities and interests of the man and the woman. It is a classic study of the woman's—Eve's—legitimate demand for Adam's focused consideration: after all, God placed them in Eden together, and in their creation myth Adam is implicated in Eve's creation. God, however, did not create Adam and then give him his art; he rather gave him Eve as his companion in that ideal bourne, and as far as she is concerned, Adam's personal interests are alternative substitute gratifications and distractions. The idea that his interests should focus elsewhere than on her or on them and their lonely dilemma beyond Eden is the outrage. The strategies used in order to challenge man's alternative desires are at the heart of the piece, and her challenge is legitimately the subject matter of a good part of the world's literature: "hell hath no fury like a woman scorned," and however man may argue his aesthetic dedication as artist/writer, to her his métier is but a power-ful rival and elicits a comprehensible rage.

The artist's dedication and the frustration of his wife or lover have been from the beginning and throughout Hemingway's career one of his subjects. He has thoroughly understood the irony of such dedication in a male, which can seemingly set aside love, and he has well understood the insult it carries to his partner. Unlike the forbearance of the wives of young men in such stories as "Cross-Country Snow," who seemingly absorb their husbands' neglect in favor of sport, artists' wives must con-front a competitive, challenging male creative process, one that is poten-tially intimidating. "The Snows of Kilimanjaro" could be styled a study of this human comedy, though it is framed in a fatal setting, where we are asked to accept as tragic Harry's deathbed lamentation for having placed his métier second to his uxoriousness. "Snows" is a wonderful piece in the total puzzle of Hemingway's "subject matter," focusing as it does uniquely on the male who has, unlike David, allowed his Catherine—in this case Helène, correctly classically named—to usurp his attentions and distract him from his own otherwise perhaps excessive concern for himself as writer/creator.

The perfect foil to this portrait in Hemingway's oeuvre would be Richard Gordon of *To Have and Have Not*, who is comically led to plead for his adulterous sexual indulgences the justification of his art. Helène Bradley is argued as the subject matter he must study for knowledge— "She interests me both as a woman and as a social phenomenon"

(140)—but Helène's rejoinder is the real challenge of the book: "Do people go to bed with a social phenomenon?" (140). Hemingway carefully lets us know that Helène, however, is herself inadequately "studied" and, lonely in her isolation, is neglected by her husband for others who accommodate his *furor poeticus* or lust. In *The Garden of Eden*, Catherine challenges her husband to give preeminence to their narrative and not to put it aside (as he does) for his own more dedicated memoir of his childhood with his father. In *To Have and Have Not*, Hemingway lets us see that Richard Gordon is a bad artist to begin with—he does not comprehend his wife or Harry Morgan's wife or Helène, his paramour, the subject of his purported studies, while they all are the cost of his presumption as he justifies marital neglect as necessary to art. It is important in this novel to recognize how general is the portrait of male neglect, legitimized by whatever logic: Harry Morgan sets Marie aside—he has to do what he does alone—until death, staring him in the face, brings him to what is a telling recognition in many of Hemingway's great works: "A man alone ain't got no bloody fucking chance" (225) (with its resonance of "No man is an *Iland*," the epigraph to *For Whom the Bell Tolls*[4]). In this novel, the veterans set aside their women, as do the Chinese laborers, the homosexuals, and several of the ambiguously distracted yachtsmen, as politics, economics, and natural predisposition all are argued, however spuriously, as causes of male isolation within the heterosexual bond. The creator of Eden, however, created two sexes for that garden.

Detached Krebs in "Soldier's Home" justifies his sundered bond with his mother and his detachment from the girls, but however adroitly he justifies his dislike of "consequences"—his revulsion is real, and we feel it in part—those consequences are implicit in the human contract. The husbands in "Cat in the Rain," "Out of Season," and "Cross-Country Snow" cavalierly step aside from responsibilities in marriage, while Nick in "The End of Something" and "The Three-Day Blow" tries to hide from "consequences" by divesting himself of the dangerous Marjorie.

Hemingway often offers war and idealism as alternative responsibilities of men that subordinate love and marriage. The soldier's role is one that demands his estrangement and separation from his woman and creates her abandonment and loneliness. Dedication to war or its logics means the dissatisfaction of the woman. When in *The Fifth Column* Philip Rawlings sees himself as having signed on for fifty years of undeclared war, it means destruction of the metaphoric bridges of

Dorothy Bridges.[5] To make the point of an uncompelled alternative male commitment (and perhaps to highlight the artifice of such idealisms), Hemingway shows Robert Jordan of *For Whom the Bell Tolls*, Frederic Henry of *A Farewell to Arms*, and Philip of *The Fifth Column* as all unnaturally serving as soldiers in chosen wars—not in their own land, not with their own armies, and not thrust upon them. In two of these works, the military imperatives would argue for warriors before lovers, and Jordan and Rawlings, though tempted by love and life's domestic alternatives, remain firm within their ideal commitments; in the third work, Frederic flees from war, from the obscene military slo-gans and patriotic lies, and back toward Catherine to support life and pregnancy, in what still remains an incomplete commitment. "I could not love thee, dear, so much, loved I not Honour more"[6] may indeed be an unironic Cavalier sentiment, but it isn't honor that drives Jordan or Frederic or Philip—Hemingway is not that simplistic. It is rather the many complex commitments that Hemingway acknowledges move heterosexual love aside, to place it behind or nowhere. (My book *Hem-ingway's Paris* and Hemingway's *A Moveable Feast* well illustrate the multiple allegiances and distractions that usurped and surrounded Hemingway from his early years as a writer.)

In *The Sun Also Rises*, dephallused Jake is certainly as shocking as sodomized David, yet his specific wound moves the book inevitably from tragedy to human comedy. We quickly are led to believe that Jake's debility, which keeps him from entering a woman, estranges him from a biological reproductive role. The supposedly sterile David of the holo-graph manuscripts of Hemingway's last novel seems equally unable to beget the child for whom Catherine, in that version of *The Garden*, yearns, and he is taunted by Catherine for the supposed excesses in his youth that might be the cause of his sterility. It was, however, Jake's role as flier in his war that was responsible for the lovers' insoluble problem; and it is the world of masculine camaraderie and interaction among warriors that breaks connections with that shared fertile arena and earth, as *A Farewell to Arms* so fully reveals, where women are left behind. Yet the Burguete episode and others in *Sun* readily show that this disassociative male camaraderie is just as operative in peace as in war, suggesting that the war is scapegoat for a more profound force work-ing to frustrate biological scenarios.

A Farewell to Arms, read in this sense, is also a comedy, one of the greatest of the Western literary canon, as it explores, in intricate detail, the scores of alternative substitute gratifications thrown up by the male to legitimize his distraction from God's duty: playing billiards with Count Greffi, going to the races, fishing with the boatman, reading the newspapers, gossiping with the "heroes," working out in the gymnasium, skiing, and the war itself. Hemingway is a rigorous thinker: he knows how even the best of motivations, to "blow the bridge," can take its place finally beside various other adulteries. He has too good a mind to fail to see that even the highest of all commitments, when brought to final judgment, is still pleading. And he is too great an artist not to see that his real job is to hold God's scheme up for judgment as well: Do we really want Philip to "cave in" to Dorothy Bridges?

There is surely no place for the gratifications of domestic love in war, but additionally there is a compounded feminine price: Brett, as we learn her past history, deprived by war of her beloved, has grown ever more estranged from a valid love relationship and has become ever more "one of the chaps," so that her increasing masculinization (and an increasing kind of madness or bizarreness of behavior) seem unavoidable concomitants of the frustration of her femininity and her biological role. This masculinization of women—the early equivalent of Catherine's lesbian and role-switching experiments in *The Garden*—is readily elsewhere seen in "The Sea Change," in Pilar in *For Whom the Bell Tolls*, in "Mr. and Mrs. Elliot," and in the shifting of the gun to Helen's hands in "Snows" and to those of dangerous Margot in "The Short Happy Life." It is superbly studied in *Across the River* in Cantwell's placement of male power, authority, knowledge, and command in Renata's hands for the future.

Catherine Barkeley's craziness in *A Farewell* is also a function of the dynamics of war, and her victimization is, like Brett's, due to its capture, use, and destruction of her beloved. Both *The Sun Also Rises* and *A Farewell* are as much about Brett's and Catherine's shared dilemma (as inheritors of the problem of such divorce in heterosexual love) as they are about Jake's physical tragedy and Frederic's loss. Jake as war victim is the late cause sufficient for Brett's pain and dilemma; Frederic, in his army duties and in his distracted desires for male camaraderie and masculine rites that take him away from Catherine, is equally the source of her dilemma and pain. Both works, like *The Garden of Eden*, study the neglected or deprived woman, the radical alterations she undergoes, and the cost of this neglect. *The Garden of Eden*, in its portrayal of Catherine Bourne, who in her own way is deprived of her lover, and consequently crazed, only provides a more sophisticated examination of the problem. In *The Sun Also Rises*, Jake puts the central fact into words: thinking of himself and Brett, he muses, "I had been getting something for nothing. . . . I thought I had paid for everything. Not like the woman pays and pays and pays" (148).

Hemingway knows well that his best major metaphor for male apostasy is the artist's commitment to his art—God's commitment to his essence and his power that precedes his responsibility to his Eden and his created creatures. Yes, Hemingway argues, his artist/God is saying, "I precede my subject, which does not exist without me." "However," says Eve, "having created me and my passions, you are not only responsible for but subject to my actions—and should I wish, I can give to Satan power over your dominion. And never forget, Adam, you are not God but my consort."[7] In *A Moveable Feast*, we find in the Hemingway of the apartment home on rue Cardinal Lemoine and the studio on rue Descartes another tragicomedy based on man's usurpation of God's role, and Hemingway acknowledges this as he puts Hadley aside with a gesture that reminds us of Richard Gordon's insipid plea to Helen: "'Don't talk to me,' he said. 'I'm going back to work. I have it all in my head'" (176). In *A Moveable Feast*, Hemingway acknowledges that "the one who is doing his work and getting satisfaction from it is not the one the poverty bothers" (50).

For Hemingway's artists, carnal flesh is not an adequate adulterous justification—that is partly why Richard Gordon will later plead that his passions are really aesthetic and that erotic sex is but explorative geography in the services of Apollo. And that is why what really possesses the men in "On the Quai at Smyrna"—and the doctor in "Indian Camp" and "The Doctor and the Doctor's Wife" and the boys in "The Three-Day Blow"—is the need for detachment, sight, distance, disengagement, preeminently within their languages or words: "In the beginning was the Word." What apparently short-phallused fastidious Mr. Elliot does in the dark is not "the dirty," like Jim Gilmore of "Up in Michigan," but the writing of long poems. Robert Cohn and Jake Barnes are—like David Bourne, and Richard Gordon, and Harry of "Snows," and even Robert Jordan—writers; or, like the idealist of "The Revolutionist" or the husband of "Cat in the Rain," able to set aside the heterosexual world for words and slogans or books or conceptions of reality. Words on luggage labels and words that distantly, abstractly justify the unspoken abortion and expatriate detachment in "Hills Like White Elephants" replace human attachments and biological birth. In

"Indian Camp," the doctor-father's dreams of immortality, as he envisions himself published, rapidly disengage him from the Indian mother, whose screams of anguish he does not earlier hear.

It is soon apparent in Hemingway's works that the deeper metaphoric meaning of skiing, fishing, hunting, war, writing, and many of the commitments of men—in which they give themselves to alternative fascinations at the cost of undeveloped, sidestepped, abandoned, denied, or frustrated heterosexual loves—stand in for one another as seductive alternatives to domestic biological commitment: they evade the commitment and responsibility that is so massively feared in the word *consequences*.

Many of these various activities of men seem far indeed from the solitary craft of the writer, but, looked at with care, the early stories of *In Our Time* and other stories readily reveal their masks of difference that hide the common face. In "On the Quai at Smyrna," the cost of the war seems not only the pier filled with women but biological life itself, immersed in the biological facts of birth and death and its bestial connections. Husbands and fathers are absent, off somewhere in their war, while their women and children seem the sacrifice to whatever fatal commitments justify their absence. Dead babies held to the living maternal breasts are—as emphatically as twelve o'clock midnight (as distinct from twelve noon) and as the woman who in dying goes into fetal position—uroboric expressions[8] of the wheel of life arrested in its natural cycles. The women in this tale and their dying and being-born children seem sacrifices to the dominant overriding and controlling threnody of the narrator, whose bizarre speech and detachment and estrangement from the suffering are the primary madness. He comments madly on a world he observes as an outsider: as he oversees it and brings light to it, he highlights its horror, but his neutrality and disengagement seem somehow allied with the very source of the suffering. As emphatically as any other work, "On the Quai" studies life as the cost of language.

In "Indian Camp," again, it is the doctor's detachment and estrangement, his role as outsider, as one not belonging to what he oversees and comprehends, that is largely the cause of his linguistic distance. The voice and logics of that doctor father, treating life—viscera, flesh, the feminine womb, and pain—objectively, can be heard against his son's lament, "Can't you give her something to make her stop screaming?" (92). Verbally exultant, he seems to rest his hope of immortality on the primitive suffering maternal world. Immortality or never dying seems the sophisticated masculine desire that is opposed to the bloody bath of primitive fatal birth. The doctor father seems willing, in his arrogant language, to sacrifice the woman to his skill and verbal command. His lecture to Nick reveals the significance of sight, demanding that his son see and comprehend what Nick cannot any longer stomach. In his disengaged stance, Nick's father oversees with linguistic control what cannot even be enunciated by the primitive world. He exemplifies the detachment of the author, like David in *The Garden*, who gains victories in his abstract craft while he fails to see the depth of Catherine's suffering. This is a world where fears of the reproductive process (legitimized after the Indian father's suicide) seem to demand the sacrifice.

In "The Doctor and the Doctor's Wife," again the verbal power and intellectual detached realm of the doctor father is opposed to the physical primitive world of instinctive sexuality of the Indians. The barrier between the husband and wife emphasizes how they exist for one another radically severed and distinct—the woman superstitious and sealed off in darkness from the man of sight and knowledge. The story enunciates a heterosexual breakdown that seems a concomitant of an impotent, masturbatory father whose energies are directed inwards and not out into physical engagement with and mastery of the vivid, teeming world.

Whether we look at Marjorie in "The End of Something" and "The Three-Day Blow," the pregnant girl and the unseen wife of "Cross-Country Snow," the young wife of "Out of Season," or the whole feminine world that is biologically discarded by the boy's catastrophic attempt to transcend sexuality through self-emasculation in "God Rest You Merry, Gentlemen," biological process is opposed in the stories to male talk, word, detachment, ascent to heights, and broken ties with the earth; and skill and craft are often abstractly exercised at the cost of heterosexual love and reproductive process. The transcendent yearning implicit in the portrayal of the undecaying leopard of "The Snows of Kilimanjaro" and in Harry's self-contempt for his betrayal of his craft focuses on masculine rites of death and need for immortality as these relate to the male artist's attempt to extricate himself from the otherwise eternally demeaning, rotting processes of gangrenous life. Helen's pain and suffering on that African plain seem inevitable concomitants of masculine aesthetics and idealism.

Hemingway profoundly recognizes the price paid by women for the male creative process. Paper relics, books, and frozen icons—worlds outside of natural process that attempt to circumvent it—are readily created by and sought by artists or by men who either fear or disregard deeper engagement with life. In *The Sun Also Rises*, the desire to be a writer, to freeze the imagery and stuff of life in abstract forms, relates to imagery of stuffed dogs and hard-boiled eggs, and such suspensions of life in abstract facsimiles of life ironically observe the sacrifice of natural creative process to abstract creative process. The revolutionist in the short story of that name is only ironically justified and completed in his solitary idealisms by the rolled reproduced images of the virgin that he carries with him. Such sterile cycles celebrating divine inhuman and unnatural feminine reproduction and the moment of immaculate conception replace other conceivable natural heterosexual reproductions. The title of the story is of course an additional major irony.

Hemingway has long studied fear of natural cycles and what they inevitably bring—death as well as birth—and has also studied the creative artist who sets himself to reveal, confront, outwit, and transcend that process. (This eternal battle between the patriarchal Word and feminine Cycles I have studied in depth in my essay "Death, Incest, and the Triple Bond in the Later Plays of William Shakespeare.") The beloved will die in the turning of time, but, as the bard says, "So long as men can breathe, or eyes can see, / So long lives this, and this gives life to thee" (Sonnet 18, lines 13–14). The poem, the book, the statue, the work of art strive for their immortality and transcendence within the cycles of repetitive birth and death, decay and rot; but as process itself carries within it the overthrow of anything that would arrest it, the artist is again and again led to the unveiling of his vanity. Hemingway's themes, concerns, plots, and metaphors, from his first work to his last, place him in the forefront of those who face death in a magnificent battle against it. He is a mythic artist signed on for the duration of his life in a battle against the gods—that is to say, against the received terms of creation that are God's gift and man's inheritance. His young men in his early works fear pregnancy and birth as fully as his later warriors fear and knowingly face (in their reductions and deaths) the inevitable defeat they know lies before them. What makes Hemingway so great is his intelligence and courage, his repeated and knowing engagement with an unbeatable enemy, life itself.

In stories like "The End of Something" and "The Three-Day Blow," the metaphors of this battle are close to the surface. In the first story, Nick flees from a Marjorie who envelops him in the chthonic powers and moon-driven cycles that are the inevitable concomitants (in the birth process) of any profound embrace of life. This heterosexual relation drives him into his alternative stance within an apparent absolutism of renunciation and denial—male camaraderie within its idealistic vanities. In the succeeding story, "The Three-Day Blow," Nick clearly sees the inadequacies of his absolute stand but finds eventual solace in recognizing that the days, being part of a weekly cycle, inevitably bring him back to a renunciation of his monastic vows and to the possibility of Marjorie once again. The two stories, taken together—as they must be, since the second deals with the problem of the first, and studies in intricate detail its cost—tell us that Hemingway knew well the terrors of the life of man both within and outside Eden. He also knew the guilt Adam would suffer within it were he to allow Eve to pay the penalty for the transgression in the garden. Hemingway understood from his earliest years that life would defeat him, as it must and should, and that whatever his strategies of avoidance, they placed upon him responsibility for the suffering they caused. Ultimately, to be a frozen leopard on the mountain of God is a victory of sorts, perhaps better than to resign himself to his death overseen by his caretaker Helen. The continuing battle of Ernest Hemingway, hunter, warrior, artist, and lover, carried on in the face of inevitable defeat, is a very great spectacle indeed.

In *The Sun Also Rises*, stuffed dogs and hard-boiled eggs, metaphors of life arrested in process, leave us with an ambiguous victory over time. Such facsimile effigies of frozen life are meant to amuse us as ironic commentaries on the strategies of art and the vanities of transcendence. Such devices, attempting to outwit death at the cost of love, are magnificently elaborated in the works of Nathaniel Hawthorne; and such attempts to avoid the connection with life I have explored in my essay "Bridges: Their Creation and Destruction in the Works of Ernest Hemingway" (included in this volume). In Hemingway's logic, fish taken out of their fluid medium to be mounted, and the mounted heads of beasts removed from their jungle—like the words of poems and novels on their pages, carrying within them the visible enacting film of the life they record—have only seemingly outwitted inevitable decay. How can the escape to Burgete, where Jake and Bill lose track of time, exist as a uniquely male strategy while suffering Brett remains, metaphorically, tied to the wheel of her journeys by taxi through of Paris and Madrid?

It is right that Frederic's last image of Catherine before he walks away in the rain is of her as statue because he walks not only through the cycles and death that rain means and that he can no more than Catherine ultimately escape—but toward the writing of the very book we have just read. In "On the Quai at Smyrna," mothers with dead babies at their breasts would arrest the natural cycle and be held in suspension forever. It is this recognition that brings the tale-telling English officer to his job in that harbor, to play his obstetric role. The Indian mother's agonized inability to give birth in "Indian Camp" is a metaphor for life denying life, and it takes a caesarean to restore the cycles to their rhythm. The *Kulturträger* must journey to darkness for the sake of life, and the mythic hero, confronting a frozen world, must restore it to its cycles. It is not just whimsicality that gives the title to Hemingway's first novel, *The Torrents of Spring*, nor is it in that book incidental landscape painting that gives us at its beginning a frozen world sealed in ice. The resurrecting Chinook wind that begins to blow again restores the pumps, connecting the flow beneath and the world above, and sets the cycling wheels in motion. Hemingway has signaled to his close readers what will follow: a very joyful and sophisticated discussion/dramatization of the creative process and its subject matter.

"Roll" is the command that both Frederic Henry of *A Farewell* and Colonel Cantwell of *Across the River* give to their drivers. Frederic, after the insult of war, tries to bring his nine-month's cyclically dependent love—she tied to the nine-month cycle of her pregnancy—to the heights of Switzerland, to a frozen kingdom set apart where, at unmelting heights, the lovers can live within the illusion of stopped process. They have been told that in Switzerland "we haven't any rolls" (265). However, spring rain and melting outwit any illusions of eternal life or life apart, and Catherine necessarily dies giving birth—that's what cycles mean, birth and death, and time, which turns and reconciles them. In *To Have and Have Not*, Harry Morgan tries to ignore the necessary compromises of life and, consequently wounded unto death, lies in his boat on the rolling moon-driven waves and cries out, "If only the bitch wouldn't roll" (175). Then, humbled by his return to dependency in the world as it is, and reconciled to the death he has defied, he finally accepts its victory: having early (and throughout his life) braced himself "against the roll, . . . he lay quietly and took it" (175). In "Snows," the leopard of the epigraph, out of its medium and beyond its limits, is driven to seek whatever brings it beyond decay and to its frozen state of sought arrest; it is to us, the readers, that the author offers the questioning of the possible absurdities in a natural quest for the unnatural.

The *corrida* and the *torero* fascinated Hemingway and led him to *Death in the Afternoon* because they focused on the artist as culture hero, defying death and attempting within his art—not just his craft and technique—to master it, in those linked-up and gorgeous and incomparable passes that seem within their flow to stop time. The "detachment" of the matador is what he loves—"the measure of his detachment of course the measure of his imagination" (56). The perfect technician awaiting the perfect bull is joined with the bull in a primal and magnificent encounter. As Hemingway describes the bull in the arena as being like the canvas the artist paints, the marble a sculptor cuts, or the snow a skier's skis cut through (99) and allies bullfighting with all impermanent arts—like singing or dancing, which are arts consumed in their performance—Hemingway lets us know that he is there, exploring again, where he always was, on the living, dying, defiant edge of man confronting his destiny and possibility.

Notes

1. Since presentation of this paper at the International Hemingway Conference in Saintes-Maries-de-la-Mer and its publication here, Hemingway's *True at First Light* has been published. From it, we are able to see that Mary's desperate need to get her own lion on her own terms is a similar demand made by a Hemingway wife who is jealous of her husband's detachment and achievement.

2. The holograph manuscript at the Kennedy Library in Boston reveals that Catherine's inability to beget a child, due to whomever's fault, is a major problem existing throughout Hemingway's manuscript version of *The Garden of Eden*, though stripped from it apparently by Tom Jenks, its editor at Scribners. See my essay "The Cost of Sin in the Garden: A Study of an Amended Theme in *The Garden of Eden*," included in this volume.

3. Hemingway wrote in *A Moveable Feast*, in the first description of F. Scott Fitzgerald: "He had . . . a delicate long-lipped Irish mouth that, on a girl, would have been the mouth of a beauty. His chin was well built and he had good ears and a handsome, almost beautiful unmarked nose. This should not have added up to a pretty face, but that came from the coloring, the very fair hair and the mouth. The mouth worried you until you knew him and then it worried you more" (149).

4. The passage is from a sermon by John Donne, and, continued, it is that from which Hemingway extracted his title *For Whom the Bell Tolls*.

5. In my essay "Bridges: Their Creation and Destruction in the Works of Ernest Hemingway" (included in this volume), I have traced this metaphor throughout Hemingway's art.

6. A frequent sentiment of the seventeenth-century Cavalier poets, but quoted here from a poem by Richard Lovelace (1618–1657), "To Lucasta, Going to the Wars."

7. These religious structures in Hemingway's works are everywhere. An example of such a structure pursued at length can best be seen in my essay "A Brief Safari into the Religious Terrain of *Green Hills of Africa*" (included in this volume).

8. Uroboric imagery, here expressed in the icon of the snake that eats its own tail, is central to Hemingway's psychosomatic structures. See my essay "The Oxymoronic Compound and the Ambiguous Noun: Paradox as Paradigm in *A Farewell to Arms*" (included in this volume). I expand upon such paradigms in my psychoanalytic essay "Death, Incest and the Triple Bond in the Later Plays of William Shakespeare."

Works Cited

Gajdusek, Robert. "Death, Incest and the Triple Bond in the Later Plays of William Shakespeare." *American Imago* 31.2 (1974): 109–58.

Hemingway, Ernest. *Death in the Afternoon*. 1932. New York: Scribners, 1957.

———. *For Whom the Bell Tolls*. 1940. New York: Scribners, 1968.

———. *A Moveable Feast*. New York: Scribners, 1964.

———. *Short Stories of Ernest Hemingway*. New York: Scribners, 1966.

———. *The Sun Also Rises*. 1926. New York: Scribners, 1954.

———. *To Have and Have Not*. 1937. New York: Scribners, 1968.

———. *True at First Light*. New York: Scribners, 1999.

The Mad Sad Bad Misreading of Hemingway's Gender Politics/Aesthetics

In his preface to Mina Loy's *Lost Lunar Baedeker*, Roger Conover writes, "In order to read her, we not only have to get past neglect; we have to get past legend" (xviii). This is true. It is equally a troubling fact that in order to read Hemingway, we most frequently have to get past attention as well as legend: most versions of the marketed legend are shameless false appraisals, and attention that has been paid has most often been scurrilously paid to the myths of the man, while the texts have languished, superficially read. It is a lamentable fact that Hemingway's journalistic image, his own often scornfully projected persona, and our avidity for the sensational distracted Hemingway criticism for many years from what the texts were so patently saying. The image of the man—so male, so brash, so energetic, so in the midst of violent life and love and of war and mating—seemed to insist that what he was about was justifying macho and patriarchal ideals. How could he have so fully insisted upon his role of Papa otherwise? How could he have used guns and rods as he did? How could he have walked so forcefully in the companionship of Marlene Dietrich, Ingrid Bergman, Jane Mason, and those beauties who almost seemed created to endorse the romantic and Freudian myths of the trophies that beauty holds in store for the virile male? Taking things at face value—always a bad idea when we are dealing with art, not kitsch—led us culturally to enthrone him where he did not belong, somewhere among the product endorsers of the American Dream, as if his message were that simple hardihood and bravery earned one the fair, that beauty and honor belonged to those who had won them in tests of fire and gallantry, of standing up to the guns or to charging lions or buffalo. We both unconsciously *and* deliberately misread him, reading our image of him over his texts and not letting the texts have their say.

Today we need, with some exasperation, to ask why we could not see that his first major protagonist was a *dephallused* male—and what writer in the history of prose had ever had the courage to give us *that?*—who was eventually able to assess his sporadic treacheries and weaknesses and that Frederic Henry of his second novel, *A Farewell to Arms*, though placed in what might have been a hero's position as the novel began, was revealed in that novel to be a callow young man, opportunistically finding his way through the spoils of war, at various times a fraudulent lover, an unconvincing liar, a bad officer, a deserter. Couldn't we recognize that Hemingway's self-projection in Nick Adams was of an often frightened, often mistaken and bewildered young man and that his other male protagonists of *In Our Time* and of the other stories were often vain and self-justifying, superficial young men struggling in the midst of massive fears and uncertainties to find a valid way?

Even as we began to move away from our biographical obsession and have our vision cleared to read the texts, we began putting on the blinders of postmodernist modes, removing one determining filter by replacing it with another. If it wasn't Marxism, or feminism, it was poststructuralist aesthetics or any one of a number of critical new languages, each having built within it its predisposing bias, alert to receive answers uniquely relevant to the methodology chosen. It is rare that criticism hasn't loaded onto the Hemingway texts the massive baggage of established attitudes, biases, and hopes, while the texts have lingered there, aging unconscionably, waiting to be rescued, or captured, like the unicorn, by the innocence of virginal sight.

I offer no presumption of virginal reading, but I am here to suggest that cobwebs do need to be brushed from our eyes and that a lot of established attitudes—such rubbish as "the code hero" and "the macho Hemingway"—need to be washed away so that the basic and relatively clear narrative line of the stories and novels may be more readily seen.

Let me chronologically range, surely too swiftly, through a number of Hemingway texts, emphasizing not so much meaning as poise, the stance taken by the protagonists, their placement in their situations, and their informing or saving recognitions. I am not arguing for any selected reading, only enunciating patterns that Hemingway has given us from the beginning to the ending of his life and that clearly offer an unremitting message to his male readers: that individuated male consciousness must be purchased through a daring act of surrender to the feminine and that only through the effeminization of his consciousness and psyche does a boy become a man.

The high school stories—whether "Judgment of Manitou" or "Sepi Jingan"—readily reveal an adolescent fear of the "other," the threat that lurks in an untamed and dangerous nature, one that must be managed, held off, or mastered. In these stories a dialogue is constant between opposing forces, where darkness and threats out of that darkness dangerously oppose the ill-informed and poorly prepared idealistic forces of the light. The message is jejune and conventional, however embedded in patterns and situations and attitudes that belong uniquely to Hemingway.

By the time Hemingway has become a veteran living in Paris, the protagonists of his stories have come to be differently portrayed. Now no longer avatars of virtue in a battle with evil, they are themselves seen to have become the distinctly troubling central subject of concern. Whereas in the high school stories Pierre, the wolves, and Paul Black Bird were malign forces seeking to destroy the forces of good, and whereas heroes like Dick Haywood were largely unquestioned, in these later stories the focus has shifted to a critique of the nature of the protagonists themselves, whatever dramatic complication they may face. In "On the Quai at Smyrna," we are *meant* to regard the troubling voices that comment on the disaster in the Graeco-Turkish War as the real subject of the very short story: it is the tone, the voice itself, that makes it a short story and not another journalist's filed report on a war. In "Indian Camp" we recognize that the unnatural childbirth and suicide largely function to focus the readers on the doctor's imperfect strategies of defense, his fastidious inability to meet the world of the "other" that he serves, and his son's vulnerabilities and defenses. "The Doctor and the Doctor's Wife" similarly is structured to admit us into the imperfect marriage of the parents; we clearly see the mother behind the screen in the darkness as a threat to the father, and we see the father's weaknesses and impotence and the son's vulnerabilities in that household. "The End of Something" vividly shows us Nick's inability to deal with Marjorie and what are for him the emotional complexity and dangers of engaging her. "The Three-Day Blow" skillfully portrays the glibnesses, the avoidances and defenses, of life-shy and imperfectly life-informed young men, who have only abstract information about what they confront in life from their privileged position at a distance and who are too afraid of the heterosexual world to face it. "Cat in the Rain" reveals, as perfectly as "Hills Like White Elephants" will in a later collection, the callow self-defensive and domineering strategies of young men imperfectly prepared for love or life. "Cross-Country Snow" similarly reveals boys becoming fathers who are unprepared for that role because of their masculine fear of the full meaning and responsibilities of love. And so it is throughout the collection.

Where, I ask, in all this, is *anything*, anything at all of the macho Hemingway we are asked to believe he supports and affirms? Nowhere. He has instead given us a magnificent analysis of the fears, uncertainties, vanities, and disguises of males poorly educated to come to terms with women and occasionally retreating in cowardice into macho strategies of defense. In the last two stories, those of "Big Two-Hearted River" I and II, he lays down an aesthetic suggesting that the river and life journey into the wilderness is a psychic necessity for the emotionally damaged and psychologically injured male, who must learn how to join nature to himself, and the unconscious to his conscious being, in a healing individuation process. How could we ever have become so vicious as to attribute to Hemingway the callousness and cowardices and self-defensive strategies that he is actually pillorying in his representation of them?

Implicit in *In Our Time* is a metaphoric assumption that nature, darkness, the moon, the unknown, and "the other" are all somehow related to the feminine. This is not politics, it is rather the statement by a suddenly quickly mature Hemingway that *immature* boys or *immature* boy-men have simultaneously alienated themselves from love and life, from "the other" and the feminine, and the desperate situation in our time, a psychic dilemma in a patriarchal culture, prompts the imagery: men *must* first be able to face up to the feared "other" before they are in any way prepared for a full heterosexual union. Boy-men like Hubert Elliot and Francis Macomber know almost nothing about the natural world beyond them. What does Francis know about what the lion is suffering, let alone thinking; what does he really know about Margot, for that matter? That these boy-men fear engagement with the feminine, as do Nick of "The End of Something," the boys of "The Three-Day Blow," and Krebs of "Soldier's Home," is not a denigration of the feminine. It is Hemingway's very mature analysis of the way boys, egocentrically terrified of the loss of self in orgasmic or passional overthrow or in love, devise life-avoiding strategies that mask their fears. The salvation from this lies in the daring journey into the heart of darkness where one is made to cross over to "the other side" and to gain there the necessarily humanizing understanding of and acceptance of the other part of the self.

"The Three-Day Blow" is about prophylaxis and detachment and ways of dealing with life abstractly rather than authentically, and at an antiseptic (safe!) distance. It is about being able to pick the horses without being at the track or too close to the action. It is about building moats and drawbridges, but especially about using abstractions and ideas, information and texts, to distance oneself from too dangerous a troubling relationship with reality. It focuses on fastidious safety devices that allow observation from a detached distance. It is a study of male cowardice and strategies for insularity. The implicit message—and Hemingway's messages are always implicit—is that the life-and-death journey, the crossing over to vulnerably confront the "other," at whatever risk, must be made.

This philosophy is one that makes the acceptance of the feared parts of the self the acceptance of the feminine "other," suggesting that Hemingway does not isolate, alienate, or set off women but rather knows deeply that the male way to heterosexual love is through recognition that this "otherness" is part of oneself and that the supremely necessary male act is to dismember and eradicate what is essentially the very young masculine fear of it. To see this, I will briefly look at the heavily embedded apparatus in the major Hemingway texts that argues for the creation of a necessary psychic balance or rites of restoration of a male-female psychic integration within alienated, detached, and self-justifyingly insulated boys, boy-men, and men.

In Hemingway's first novel, *The Sun Also Rises*, dephallused Jake— his wound the highlighted dilemma—emblematically reveals that the problem is modern man's inability to cross over to that other side, his inability to penetrate and advance, empathically or actually, into the territory of the other. Jake's unique wound is the unavoidable reminder of a masculine incapacity for that act. When the metaphors of penetration and invasion of or by the other are lifted to as high a metaphoric level as they are in *Sun*, it is important to look at variants of essentially the same metaphor and their highly charged function in later novels. In *The Garden of Eden*, David's acquiescence before his own sodomitic penetration by Catherine is an example of this; in *A Farewell to Arms*, when Frederic Henry assumes a morning sickness the morning after Catherine announces her pregnancy, there is a similar echo; and in *Across the River and into the Trees*, as Cantwell metaphorically assumes menstruation, blood in the mouth, as he reflectively considers Renata's monthly period, there is yet another.

All the men in *The Sun Also Rises* are wounded in one way or another—Cohn's and Mike's nose injuries are a phallic comment—but it is Romero who teaches them the lesson (that Jake acts on at last at San Sebastian) that without the crossover into the always dangerous territory of the other, and a moment of psychic integration with the other, without the daring and surrender of self that takes place when *two become one*, there is no possible redemption or cure. At San Sebastian, in chapter 19, toward the novel's end, Jake's mimicry of Romero—as he in his "suit" advances across the level sand to meet his own bulls (of the sea), at the hour of the corrida—brings him into elaborate rites of integrative relationship with sea and sun. Diving to the bottom and then rising to the top, pulling up and then diving again, dealing with both shadow and sun, Jake deals with the "rollers" of the sea.

Indeed, throughout Hemingway's texts, the "other side," because of its suggestive relationship to the unknown feminine and the world of biological creative process, is opposed to the abstract creative act of the male writer and is more related to the cycles of the moon than to the absoluteness of the Apollonian sun-drenched world. It is therefore most frequently a "rolling" other side. When Harry, in *To Have and Have Not*, lies wounded almost to death, a victim of his attempt to make a crossing, he is at last able to acknowledge the other side that he has dominated and neglected and can only finally accept. Given who he is, an isolated, proud man, his final acquiescence is wrung from him in grudging acknowledgment. "If the bitch wouldn't only roll. If she'd only quit rolling. . . . I wish this bitch wouldn't roll," he cries in pain (174–75), but then, at last, looking at the moonlight, accepting the sea, after trying "to brace himself against the roll," he acknowledges how things truly are and "lay quietly and took it" (175). So driven by the moon-driven sea, he is led toward his great final integrative pronouncement: "A man alone ain't got no bloody fucking chance" (225).

In *A Farewell to Arms*, it is to Switzerland that the lovers flee to be beyond war, to be safe from death, to exist in a frozen fixed idyll in the mountains above the lake. It is in Switzerland that they are told "we haven't any rolls in wartime" (265)—one of many philosophically sensitive lines in the book!—and Catherine (named after Saint Catherine martyred on the Catherine wheel) hilariously says, "I don't mind there not being rolls. . . . I thought about them all night. But I don't mind it,

I don't mind it at all" (266). After all, she has made the *crossing* with her lover of the wounded hands who, "sacrilegious," says, "There's no hole in my side" (271). The unavoidable, unarrestable seasonal cycles and those of the rain and its process and of Catherine's pregnancy (which they try to suspend or outwit) bring them down at last to the flowing waters and to their necessary acknowledgment of integrated birth and death.

In almost all Hemingway works, the necessary demand to enter into the cyclical world, that uroboric world where cycles bring life to death, death to life, and man to woman, is the command to roll. "We'll roll" (193), says Frederic Henry to his men, shortly before they are trapped by their mud-enmired "spinning" wheels. "Let's roll" (30), says Cantwell to his driver in *Across the River*, and when he sees a man cycling in the road while reading, paying attention only to the paper words above that he reads while doing so and failing to heed the wheels beneath him, Cantwell asks his driver to "give that cyclist some horn" (13), so demanding a crossover akin to that the bull makes into the perhaps vanity-filled detached terrain of the *torero*, to perhaps startle him with the fact of death. The cyclist, so warned, and given his lesson, "moved over to the [other] side" (13). In Biarritz, toward the end of *The Sun Also Rises*, when all accounts are being settled, the bankrupt men are revealed for what they are as they "roll for it" (229). They roll rounds of poker dice: "Let's roll. . . . We rolled. . . . We had another round. . . . We had another round. . . . I went out on the first roll. . . . Bill and Mike rolled. Mike won the first roll. . . . On the final roll Bill rolled" (229). It isn't, however, until Jake responsibly goes down to the "rollers" of the sea in San Sebastian that he creatively rather than destructively uses the process he accepts there for his redemption.

Chapter 12 of *The Sun Also Rises*, the Burguete chapter, is a river journey that similarly emphasizes the rites and rituals of crossover inversion that can psychically heal. Though here it is a healing rite for Jake and Bill, preparing them for their waiting encounters, it reiterates the psychic stance necessary to bring boy-men and cowards to the bravery that permits heterosexual risk and finally love. The Burguete chapter of *Sun* is one of the great intellectual games of modern literature, where "Henry's bicycle" (115) and how to "put a man on her horse" (115) and getting "cockeyed on wine" (122) are rare and wonderful intellectual aesthetic/psychic problems.

In this Burguete chapter, Jake, arising to descend to dig worms that the trout will later rise to take, urges Bill to "get up," to go down to eat, and Bill makes a distinction between "getting up . . . for fun" and "getting up" to "be right down" (113). Bill follows this with his morning song of marital rites, "For Me and My Gal," and speaks of *marrying* irony and pity (114). At breakfast, his chant of praise for coffee equally celebrates a gender/sexual synthesis—it "puts a man on her horse and a woman in his grave" (115)—and the thought leads him to an analysis of an artist's failure when he is "an expatriate": "Nobody who ever left their own country ever wrote anything worth printing" (115). His logic is that loss of connection with the seminal base, with the native earth, is the danger, and he immediately challenges Jake that his wound has two alternative sexual implications: his inability to connect must mean either that women support him or that he is impotent. In either case, he is out of vital contact. This connection of the writer's failure of his art and the writer's wound is too important to be overlooked in this first novel.

Jake's defense, that he "just had an accident" (115), is, we are told, like the mystery of Henry's bicycle: it is a fairly obscure reference to Henry James's sexual wound and disqualification, a way of avoiding explicit acknowledgment of his inability to support or fuck women. Such a metaphor allows Bill and Jake to relate that disabling bicycle to a tricycle and the tricycle to a plane, where, we are told, "the joystick works the same way" (116): raised up or down, it permits rising or descending, a connecting to heavens or to the earth. The difference is that one does not pedal a plane—one does not, in riding it, make a connection beneath to the cycles and the earth. Jake, in "standing up"—a phallic irony—for the tricycle, supports what connects the two opposites or antitheses as, in the connection—in bringing the feet beneath to the cycle—it permits cyclical progression through engagement that amends the male/female breakdown and the divorce between the sexes. Granted, this is all pretty "heady" stuff, but it is necessary to clarify it for a writer who has been read as anything but heady—indeed, he has been described as a "dumb ox."[1]

Continuing their discussion in this chapter, Bill and Jake playfully suggest that civil war—a war between two normally otherwise united parts of one whole, in which one side refuses to accept the other—is due to either homosexuality or lesbianism, similar refusals of one sex to accept, engage, the other, which imply, as Bill says, that "sex explains it all" (116).

The two men go fishing in what is an essentially redemptive landscape, where dust rises and cattle are in the hills. To get to this chosen land, they go "across" a meadow to where a path "crossed" the fields. They walk "across" the "rolling" fields, and where a path has "crossed" a stream, there is a sapling bent "across." They go up a bank and again "across . . . rolling fields." Then, having "crossed" yet another field, where the path "crossed the stream," they go into a beech wood where the tree roots bulk above the ground. Bill says, "This is country" (116–17).

Their expedition, in which they carry both rod and bag, records a journey where the land itself compels multiple acts of integrative crossing over to the "rolling" other side. Going to where dust rises, where cattle and roots ascend, their journey takes them to an early example of "the chosen place," the "last good place," the land on the other side, a magic country that must be celebrated as such and that will become a persistent theme in Hemingway's work: it is the place where the individuating experience can take place and the rites of celebration of it can be performed. We see it magnificently revealed in "Big Two-Hearted River" and *Green Hills of Africa*.

It is predictably there that they joint up the rods and put on the reels, and that they connect above and below, fishing both above and below the dam that divides the two. In their fishing, it is Jake who, fishing above, uses worms of the earth for bait, while Bill, below, fishes with flies. Jake connects both sides of the river, separating/dividing his catch by throwing the shucked insides of his cleaned trout "across the river" (119) to the other side. Leaning against the trunk of two trees that have grown together, Jake reads A. E. W. Mason's novel of a separated couple who—the "bride" in life, her husband in death; one above frozen in the glacier, the other below waiting on the moraine; one in flow, the other in fixity; one in time, the other taken out of it—fruitlessly await a reconciliation, their unification that will be able, however, to again start the arrested cycles of life, but with the wife's new-found new "true love."

Playfully opposing the drumstick and the egg, the male and female principles, Bill relates these icons to William Jennings Bryan (and the alternative myths or theories of creationism and Darwinian selection, spirit and cycles), and they eat and drink in elaborate rites of reconciliation of spirit and flesh. Bill first stands "sucking the drumstick" (121) and then, with the drumstick in one hand and the bottle of wine in the other, like an emblem of a reconciling fertility god, pronounces the sermon in the wilderness. Together they celebrate the importance of understanding the ironies in "being cockeyed on wine" (122), in being able to hold Apollo and Dionysus together in one bond. Such mythic oppositions are developed by acknowledging the difference in going to Loyola with Bishop *Manning*, or to Notre *Dame* with Wayne B. *Wheeler*.

After eating, they reconcilingly lie with their heads against the earth in the shade, looking up into the trees above them and at the skies beyond. This dense chapter ends with joined rods and reels being disengaged— the rod put in the rod case, the reel in the tackle bag: the very sexual divorce and separation that the chapter has studied ways of outwitting. It is poetically right that the Burguete interlude is followed by the need to descend from the integrative heights in the hills to Pamplona on the plain, where the two men can be joined with Brett.

In work after work, such psychic crossover, essential to modern man (if he is to mature and become a whole man worthy and capable of love) is studied. In *Death in the Afternoon*, in *For Whom the Bell Tolls*, in *Green Hills of Africa*, in "The Short Happy Life of Francis Macomber," in *The Fifth Column*, and in *To Have and Have Not*, the crossing over is one of the major metaphors and structural devices of the work. To cross over the lines (*For Whom the Bell Tolls* and *The Fifth Column*), to cross over the horns (*Death in the Afternoon* and *The Sun Also Rises*), to cross from island to mainland (*To Have and Have Not*), to cross over into the unexplored unhunted virgin territory (*Green Hills of Africa* and "The Short Happy Life"), to enter the unknown other land, to learn how to inhabit and live in and succeed in the territory of the "other" and to there find one's *virtu* and an understanding of what is the *not*-self—all this *must* take place before individuated selfhood permits the creation of a whole man, at last worthy of sexual and love relations with a woman. Never doubt that the act and experience of individuation is the fusing of the bipolar idealistic male self under the cautery and in the crucible of uroboric psychic regression so that in that experience the male self experiences and takes unto itself the imprinting understanding of the feminine self. That's what male initiation rites are for (see my essay "The Oxymoronic Compound and the Ambiguous Noun in the Works of Ernest Hemingway," included in this volume).

If Hemingway is able to conceive of the phallus as a bridge, one that allows the male in whom it is anchored to cross over into the unknown and hidden territory of the "other," the feminine, then we can understand why major works by him are elaborate descriptions of and analyses of the need for and the danger of bridges: an attempt to cross over a wall into a garden; the construction of an "absolutely perfect barricade" to a bridge (as in the "Chapter III" and "Chapter IV" vignettes of *In Our Time*); a death at a bridge; the inability to cross a bridge; or the need to blow a bridge. Indeed, it was back in 1983 that I delivered and subsequently had published a paper titled "Bridges: Their Creation and

Destruction in the Works of Ernest Hemingway" (included in this volume) in which this major—I believe perhaps *the* major—metaphor of Hemingway's work was tracked in its two variant forms: sides that refuse to connect or negotiate and sides that meet and bond.

In *The Fifth Column*, Philip needs to locate and root out and destroy those who have a foot in either camp, on both sides of the line, and Hemingway with enormous political sophistication in this work analyzes well the cost of war, which rests upon polarized antitheses. This same fascination in *A Farewell to Arms* draws Hemingway to study literally hundreds of variations of what is implicit in war and love, enemies and lovers, dialectic and synthesis. There, Americans and Germans dressed in Italian uniforms, and soldiers, lovers, and even horses assume the identities and the roles of others: the anarchist sleeps in the queen's bed. One tries to take the place of and *be* the other, or exchange roles with another, *or* one tries to establish and defend and rigorously manufacture boundaries. In *The Fifth Column*, there is no room for a valid heterosexual bond when one has signed on "for the duration"—that's what ideology and war do to love—and how to get rid of Dorothy *Bridges* is the *warrior's* question. "The Snows of Kilimanjaro" emphasizes and vividly reveals its philosophical thesis in its epigraph: Whatever *was* the leopard seeking at that altitude? What *is* a creature of the jungle plains doing on the slopes of the Mountain of God? The dilemma of the men is the same in "An Alpine Idyll," in "Cross-Country Snow," and in "A Simple Enquiry": they have all been *up* in the high mountains and near the sun too long, and it is time indeed to descend the slopes into the valleys where death, decay, process, and heterosexual love await them.

The examples are as many as there are Hemingway works, but who—in those falsely reassuring years between two wars when the public need was for an heroic image, the bravado of the journalistically provided Hemingway—*could* have called in question the dominant image of Hemingway as macho male that we had locked in our journalistically conceived mythology? Who, indeed, would have believed, against the massive weight of the claque and the critical bias affirming him the patriarchal male, that indeed it was he, almost alone and far out beyond others and with enormous artistry, who was writing texts demanding sexual inversion and the effeminization of the male psyche and arguing that in any artist or man of action there had to be a necessary exploration of the feared feminine part of nature and the self? The vast majority of American writers didn't get the message until the late sixties, well after Hemingway's death. While Scott Fitzgerald was still lamenting the costs of uxoriousness, Hemingway was writing tracts describing *with love* the necessary and systematic dismemberment of the patriarchal perimeters.

That's what *The Garden of Eden* and *Across the River* are all about. *The Garden of Eden* urges the necessity for sexual inversion and "other-gender" experience for the artist as it does for the man of action, and *Across the River* tells us loud and clear that the hour is late: the old Colonel, like Santiago, must bring sensation into the paralyzed and dysfunctional other side of the self. When, at the end, Cantwell, the military man of rigorous dialectical engagements, places himself at great risk in the hands of Renata and, as her name suggests, allows himself, under her orders, to be reborn, and gets into the *back* seat of his car to accept his death, he has indeed accepted the union of birth and death in uroboric synthesis and crossed over into the kingdom of death where sensual love abides. He has chosen love, not war, and has crossed over the river to lie down under the trees on the other side. On his way to his death, coming back from his last shoot, Cantwell says, "The shooting's over" (294). As he is at last reconciled with his "enemy" boatman in the stern, the ducks are carefully placed on the bow of his boat, "breasts up," and the guns are relinquished. The story, after all, is exquisitely placed in the city of art that rests on the moon-driven waters—in Venice, the city of bridges.

Across the River and into the Trees announces the omnipresent subject in its title. It spells out that the journey to the other side is always a death journey and at the risk of everything, and it is in this novel that Hemingway articulates that indeed the controls and masteries must be reversed: that patriarchal control must be placed in the hands of the woman. It must be at last Renata who orders the meal, who commands the gondolier, who officiates at the rites of lovemaking. At the end of this novel, as "The shooting's over" is cried out and the guns are handed over, the translation of power from the patriarchate to the matriarchate is magnificently ritually observed. This had earlier been portrayed iconically as Cantwell had allowed Renata to slip the matrilineally inherited family jewels, the green emeralds, into *his* "pocket." In *The Garden of Eden*, Hemingway explicitly at last outlines the transformative and healing rituals of sexual inversion upon which rest the hope for mankind: the reversals into the "other" that cure because they ultimately acknowledge and accept. He is careful to enunciate what anyone but a sentimentalist must assert, that return from that healing journey is return to one's own identity, that one journeys to become whole, and that only in being whole through the acquisition of an effeminized psyche is a man worthy of the love of a whole woman. A whole man is one who has become so through symbolic capitulation, inversion, the yielding of himself into the hands of the "other." Consequently, only in recognition, understanding, acceptance, and brave empowerment of his adolescently feared "other" does he authentically become a man.

Many don't like Hemingway's use of what has often been a patriarchal arsenal of "feminine" emblems and signs—the moon, water, rhythm, darkness, the instinctive and the intuitive—that are attached to women. Women today wish themselves Apollonially empowered: "Why not the sun?" they cry. But Hemingway is there long before we ever dreamed he was, understanding and sympathizing with this need, sensitized by his role in a family where his mother's lover had throughout his childhood been a maid in his own household.[2] In *Across the River*, he assures Renata that indeed she *does* want power, she *does* want authority and control, and this is what Cantwell has been teaching himself to yield and what he has been training Renata—whose name tells us that she is also being reborn—to accept.

Notes

1. It was Wyndham Lewis who so described Hemingway in a massively unperceptive and dishonest reading of him in an article titled "The Dumb Ox."

2. All evidence—as I read the biographies—suggests that Hemingway came at last at age nineteen to a full and shocked awareness of his mother's troubling relationship with Ruth Arnold. (I know that the use of the term *lesbian* may be prejudging the relationship without greater evidence. But what am I to do with letters from Ruth to Grace lamenting their inability to lie holding one another in their arms when "the doctor" is there?) Hemingway, understanding the effects and implications of this in his own household, and sensitively juggling his initially repressed response, was undoubtedly imprinted with a sensitive awareness of lesbians that characterized his subsequent relations: he was either close to, friendly with, or in frequent relations with Gertrude Stein, Janet Flanner, Djuna Barnes, Margaret Anderson, Sylvia Beach, and Ginny Pfeiffer, among others. His hair fetishism, the *gamine* nature of both Pauline and Mary, and what seems his sexual predilection for women like Pauline and Mary whose figures, hairstyles, and dress emphasize their boyish attributes suggest a profound gender ambivalence that has been carelessly read by some as repressed homosexuality.

WORKS CITED

Conover, Roger. Preface. *Lost Lunar Baedeker*. By Mina Loy. New York: Farrar, 1996.

Hemingway, Ernest. *Across the River and into the Trees*. New York: Scribners, 1950.

———. *A Farewell to Arms*. 1929. New York: Scribners, 1957.

———. *The Sun Also Rises*. 1926. New York: Scribners, 1954.

———. *To Have and Have Not*. 1937. New York: Scribners, 1965.

Lewis, Wyndham. "The Dumb Ox." *Life and Letters*, April 1934.

22

Bridges

Their Creation and Destruction
in the Works of Ernest Hemingway

In the work of Ernest Hemingway the image of the bridge becomes the central, dominating, and obsessive metaphor. In all of the novels, crossing over to the other side or making connections, bridging to another side, is the most significant act, controlling the larger action and determining the outcome: the novels cannot be resolved until the proper connections are made or the proper integrative bridging is achieved. In many of the works the image of the bridge is overt, needing no metaphoric vehicle; in others it is thinly masked.

In *The Sun Also Rises*, dephallused Jake Barnes lacks the sexual bridge to connect him with the opposite sex, and that is the urgent fact. It is Romero, the solar hero, who confronts the bull of darkness, who teaches bridgeless Jake how to "cross over" as, in the corrida, he becomes one with the bull. In *Green Hills*, Hemingway succeeds in becoming whole and getting his kudu—*kudo* means glory or fame—only after he has made a "crossing" (229) into new and virgin territory where he hunts in a new way. It is there that the "Black Chinaman" M'Cola, the Mama worshipper, and the white Western hunter, who idolizes Pop, become one in intricate rites of crossover or joining. Macomber in "The Short Happy Life" makes a similar crossover to "the far side" (*Short Stories* 25) before he is ready to live and to die. In *To Have and Have Not*, Harry Morgan is patently a boatman who plies a ferry between two shores, island and mainland. He dies after he is forced into being such a bridge for the revolutionaries and when he aborts that function. (Key

West itself, where the action takes place and where Hemingway for many years chose to live, is the butt end of a long bridge connecting mainland and island.) In *For Whom the Bell Tolls*, Robert Jordan's mission, which dominates all action throughout, is the destruction of a bridge, and as the bridge goes, so goes Jordan. In *The Fifth Column*, Philip Rawlings, who crosses over by night behind the lines and so risks his death, at last gets rid of his reconciling mistress, Dorothy Bridges. His mission is to capture the man outside Madrid who is uniquely connected with all those who betray it inside; in effect, he has, like Robert Jordan, crossed over to the other side and come there to destroy a bridge.

In *Across the River*, Colonel Cantwell, who is trying to move from being a warrior to being a lover, from being an irascible military bastard to being kind and gentle, to bring feeling into his unfeeling side, has a double-chambered heart that twinges on the bridges of Venice; and just before he finally dies, he crosses over from the front seat to the back seat of his car. The problem that his physician has early spotted, his greatly increased intraocular and intracranial pressure, needs to be solved: "They ought to make you drag a chain like a high-octane truck" (9) is his prescription. What he recommends is a bridge that would remove the danger of the radical difference between the two sides, and it is exactly this bridge that Cantwell perfects before his death. The title of the novel, one pointedly about the movement toward death, uses the bridge symbol, a crossing over a river, to describe the desire for final rest under trees on the other side. The moon-driven waters on which the art city of Venice rests, and out of which stepped Renata as Venus reborn, suggest the biological cycles of life and death that are placed against the death-defying techniques of the skillful old warrior who has spent a lifetime in dialectical exchange across boundaries. Hemingway's novel and the old warrior end together as love, concern for others, and kindness heal the psychic split at the cost of life. But this novel began as Cantwell broke the ice between the air above and the water below so that the birds might come down to the water and meet their deaths. Santiago, the old man of the sea, is one who has spent his lifetime connecting fish and fisherman, what is above with what is below in the depths, by delicate adjustments of his lines. As he does so in this novel, we see him practicing the rituals and disciplines of connecting his right side with his betraying partially paralyzed left side. Thomas Hudson of *Islands in the Stream* dies at last on the flying bridge of his sub chaser.

Studied in one work in more detail, the complexity of the pattern may emerge. *A Farewell to Arms* deals with an American in Italian service and uniform who takes the place of a bereaved girl's lover—connects her to her vision—in the midst of a war that has established radical and fatal lines of separation between warring enemies. It equally deals with her attempt to become him, to dissolve the indissoluble, real differences between them, to cross over to have his experiences with the women he has known, to wish her hair short and his long—rhetorically and physically to remove the barriers to utter synthesis.

It also deals with the destruction of the spaces between opposing forces, of lovers and of warring countries. In the loving, as the lovers mix or join and so lose their identities in one another, Catherine is the real sacrifice, and Frederic the survivor who lives to tell the tale; and in the fighting after breakthrough, as Germans mix with Italians and Italians are taken for Germans, Aymo is the real sacrifice, killed as he tries to cross over a railroad line, and Frederic again only the metaphoric victim. Frederic is first wounded as a bridgehead is established—the troops crossed the river "enormously" (62), Rinaldi tells Frederic in the hospital—and Frederic can no longer, in his conversation with Rinaldi and the major, stay on his own side in a conversational exchange, can no longer defend his own distinct point of view. Later, when battle lines are bridged, distinctions are everywhere erased: Piani and Bonello dream of anarchy and sleeping with the queen; and an American in an Italian uniform, who has already been the bridge to connect Catherine with the ghost of her lost dead lover, seems indistinguishable from the Germans and is nearly shot at the bridge. It is at this bridge crossing that Frederic, who has already in his wounding known death and been restored to life, and who has therefore already been on the other side, dives into the Tagliamento and crosses over from being a soldier under sentence of death to being a reborn deserter. He saves himself again later by making another successful bridge crossing over the railroad bridge at Latisana on his way to join Catherine at Stresa, and here the two cross over from Italy to Switzerland, from the land of war to the island of peace. These are only several of the crossovers that structure the novel.

As Michael Reynolds has suggested, a fear of bridges also runs throughout the work (172). In Milan, one of the most desolate scenes is when Frederic Henry and Catherine are on a bridge in the fog (150). "Why haven't they blown the bridge up?" (211) is Frederic Henry's later concern, and a real sense of true danger and encirclement comes as he and his men watch Germans crossing a bridge. The novel began as birth and death seemed reconciled: the soldiers going perhaps to death and carrying their gear under their bulky capes are described as looking pregnant, the inorganic guns that bestow death are covered with vines that suggest life—opposites are joined, as they are by bridges. And the novel continues as Rinaldi, inside the brothel, beckons to the priest to come inside as well. To bring the priest into the brothel would be to connect the spirit and the flesh, eliminating their distinctions. The novel ends as childbirth (life producing) becomes death (death causing) and as the body of Catherine seems transfigured to a statue, life in time become immortal, flesh become art. Such perverse reconciliations embrace all intervening action between the interacting poles of war (opposing sides in conflict) and love (opposing sides meeting and joining). War and love, or warriors and lovers, are in all of Hemingway's novels less his ways of talking about love and war than modes for considering dichotomy and synthesis, the problems of psychic dissociation and integration, of unbridged (unconnected) or bridged (joined) sides.

Not only are the plots of Hemingway's novels about bridging or bridges to be built or destroyed; throughout the works, bridge references, metaphors, and puns abound. Monuments are built to bridges: In *The Sun Also Rises*, Jake Barnes remembers "what was perhaps a statue of Ponte" at the hospital "where the liaison colonel came to visit me" (31). A few pages later he rounds the "statue of the inventor of the semaphore engaged in doing same" (41), connecting one side with another across an interval or gap. There are jokes made about them: in *For Whom the Bell Tolls*, Robert Jordan reflects, "A good life is not measured by any biblical span" (169). In *A Farewell*, Frederic Henry considers that the love-game he plays with Catherine is a little "like bridge" (30). And in *The Sun Also Rises*, Robert Cohn risks "higher stakes than he could afford" in "bridge games with his New York connections"(9). He asserts that "a man could always make a living at bridge" (9), yet the bridge of his nose, like that of the noses of Harry Morgan and Cantwell, has been broken.

Hunting and fishing to Hemingway and his protagonists were basically rites of bridge building, means of crossing over. All fishermen in Hemingway must learn that the bridge between the fisherman and his prey can be successfully created only by one who knows how to relate opposites to one another, to connect them. The dynamics of the reel and the terms of the line—the cycle and the line—embody the same sexual dynamics as the butt of the rod in the socket. In *To Have and Have Not*, Mr. Johnson loses Harry's equipment through failure to keep the butt in the socket, to connect masculine and feminine elements. This man, who disappears into the air, betrays the sea, and such a man can build no successful bridge to his desire. The sea, however, as Santiago early makes clear in *The Old Man and the Sea*, is feminine to all those who love and respect her and therefore receive gifts and perhaps their deaths from her. Johnson, an apparently wifeless, loveless man, wants to do everything all by himself, like Manolin's father in *The Old Man and the Sea*, and he suffers the penalties of one who refuses to make a bridge of sympathy or empathy to the world beyond. "Big Two-Hearted River" is two hearted, diastolic and systolic in its double nature, and Nick puts those two sides together again: knowledge and feeling, nature and man. He learns to relate the fish to the fisherman by coordinating/relating right hand and left, consciousness and unconsciousness. The internal and external worlds are bridged as any transcendentalist might wish, and the two parts of this double story are joined so that a whole and integral crossover can be made.

There is an important revelation in the fact that "Big Two-Hearted River" is split into "Part I" and "Part II"—that the stories are twinned but are nonetheless kept separate, two joined yet integral parts of a whole. The technique of Hemingway's hunters is the sexually charged one of putting the wedge of the foresight into the slot of the rear, and this connection of the gunsight's two parts helps connect killer and killed, hunter and prey. The rifle and its extended bullet are the bridge. It is Macomber's failure to know what the lion is thinking, his inability to unite with the object of his quest, that makes it impossible for him to cross over from boyhood to manhood: Only after he has connected himself to the buffalo and has seen them closely and clearly and accurately is he able to live and to die.

That these rites, the preparation for integral and individuated wholeness, or manhood, are also a preparation for death is one of Hemingway's profound insights. It saves his work from any sentimentality. We must note that desired and necessary bridges are built by all Hemingway heroes, but the building of the bridge, which connects opposites, may also be a fatal act releasing a man to mortality, exposing him to the death he has perhaps feared.

In Our Time records people unable to cross over to another side without dying or being injured. This is the problem for those on the pier in "On the Quai at Smyrna." In "Indian Camp," to cross the lake to the other side, to unite mental and instinctive worlds, means to experience death/birth and trauma. The joining of Indians and the white world in "The Doctor and the Doctor's Wife" means destruction for the father; at the end it is Nick who would show his father how a vital and successful crossover can be made. In "Chapter II," the terror of the evacuation is shown in the context of water coming almost up to the bridge. In "Chapter III" and "Chapter IV," soldiers die as they try to cross over a barrier and a bridge. "The End of Something," "The Three-Day Blow," "The Revolutionist," "Soldier's Home," and "A Very Short Story" all record the damage and fear of the damage of crossover, while later stories like "Mr. and Mrs. Elliot," "Out of Season," "Cross-Country Snow," and "Cat in the Rain" record fastidious avoidance of or withdrawal from it.

Fear of death and the overcoming of this fear explain in part the psychological necessity of coming to terms with the other side. The *torero* in crossing over between the horns risks his death, and that is the point. The coward fakes it. Romero and the bull, life and death, become one: that is his achievement; and, of course, as the two otherwise carefully opposed sides become at last one, a bridge is built of perhaps fatal reconciliation. What makes Romero supremely important is that he teaches how to connect with the "other" without losing the self, the most difficult of all arts: how to have synthesis without loss of discrete identity. Hemingway lets us see that the *torero*'s sword completes a bridge of which the *torero* himself is part: in *Death in the Afternoon*, he describes the moment "when bull and man form one figure, as the sword goes all the way in, the man leaning after it, death uniting the two" (234). An important thing to notice about the *torero* is the way he springs back away from the bull, quickly destroying the bridge, so that the bull may die alone with the *torero*'s abandoned sword in him.

This is not the case with almost all Hemingway heroes who successfully connect with the "other," the opposite part of life or themselves with which they hold dialogue: they do not spring away, and they die. They die basically because it is exact and right that death should enter the world as paradise is abandoned: death is what one chooses when one fully chooses life. Life means death also; it is only the fastidious avoidance of death through fear of it or rebellion against it—or adolescent devices of immortality, or art itself—that pretends man is not man but God. The bridge is the place where death is possible, where immortality or the egocentric and isolating dream is yielded up to mortality. It is no accident that Anselmo is killed by the bridge and by Robert Jordan's mission to destroy it; that Thomas Hudson dies on his boat's bridge; that the old man of the short story waits for his death at the bridge; that "My Old Man" dies at the bridging crossover; and that Jake begins to destroy himself as he becomes the bridge to serve Brett when he, as translator, brings Romero across the gap to her.

In *Across the River*, Hemingway warns, "Don't ever build yourself a country house, or a church, or have Giotto to paint you any frescoes, if you've got a church eight hundred yards away from any bridge" (19). After Frederic Henry emerges from his experience at the bridge where he is taken to be killed, he takes the stars off his uniform. Cantwell, who has lost his stars before the novel begins, thinks of those soldiers who lose their sense of personal immortality through having been wounded, through having crossed over briefly to death's other kingdom. In "My Old Man," the boy loses his father and a sort of absolute faith as his father dies at the steeplechase jump, at the crossing. In the "Chapter III" vignette of *In Our Time*, as the Germans who cross the wall die and fall down into the garden, their garden fall suggests the loss of Eden or immortality as a result of the crossing, and "Chapter IV" records the dream of absolute perfection that refuses the crossover to soldiers on a bridge. The bridge is therefore in Hemingway that which man must fear even as it is what he must build, for through it he loses immortality, Edenic bliss, and all absolutes but joins mankind.

Hemingway examines closely those who fail or refuse to cross over. There are the soldiers in *Across the River* who, in order to avoid combat, infect themselves with gonorrheal pus that they have stored in a matchbox. They obviously do not have the courage to risk contact with or to cross over to and make a "match" with "the other," whether the potentially destructive infectious woman or death itself in the front lines. They are the ones who "did not wish to die" (59). There are those like Passini, who would abandon the line or refuse to confront what lies on the other side. They believe that refusing the encounter and retreating acquiescently and passively back to their homes will provide peace. But they are like the trout that is unable to face into the current and is carried instead where the current wills. There are the cowards, like Pablo, who, in running away from battle, avoiding death, because of selfish desire to enjoy their own possessions, betray themselves and those who depend upon them. In *Across the River*, Cantwell deplores the generals who operate far behind their own lines and without experience of the deaths they deal, the men they kill. Cantwell's respect is for the infantry, and his contempt is for all who remain removed or insulated from, or who flee from, the antagonist with whom they ostensibly deal.

The aborted or abandoned bridge finds its expression variously in Hemingway's works. In the "Chapter V" vignette of *In Our Time*, he records the self-congratulatory tone of the English narrator in describing the "absolutely perfect" (*Short Stories* 113) barricade that has been erected across a bridge. It gives those who erect it an advantage in death dealing, not dying. They are able to dispense death like gods, controlling its terms. From their side of this barrier, having radically divided one side from the other, they have advantages of sight and knowledge and objective distance that permit them, like the doctor father of "Indian Camp" and the observer in "On the Quai at Smyrna," the tone of dispassionate disengagement and a species of inhumanity. With verbal and technical controls, they remain out of contact with the life to which they must descend to gain their victories. This image helps explain the part of Hemingway that refuses and denies the individuating crossover, that would destroy and blow bridges, not build them. It is patently a desire for immortality and absolute conditions or controls over human life. For Harry in "The Snows of Kilamanjaro" to renounce the bridges that destroyed him as an artist, he must renounce his connections with life itself, which he does while he yearns for the square top of the Mountain of God. He effectively returns himself to the condition of dephallused Jake Barnes as he leaves behind the rotting gangrenous leg that was the bridge to connect him with the earth and its cycles of death and corruption, and he jettisons the world for the sake of the vision of the mountain. Helen is being exorcised, as is the money, the materiel, and his mode of life that have been the means to his decadence. When Philip in *The Fifth Column* casts off Dorothy Bridges, he is dedicating himself to the battle that keeps love, its soporific bliss and its reproductive processes, at bay, while he fights to establish ideals against time and in perpetual war.

To these aborted, blown, or abandoned bridges should be added the children who are denied or killed in Hemingway's works, since a child is perhaps the most obvious symbol of the successful bridge built by two opposed sides. Jake Barnes cannot beget a child, Frederic and Catherine's son dies, Thomas Hudson's three sons die, and the women in "Cat in the Rain," "Mr. and Mrs. Elliot," and "Hills Like White Elephants" are denied their children. The cost of a child in "Indian Camp" seems to be the father himself, who dies making a symbolic connection, cutting his throat "ear to ear" (*Short Stories* 20), as a result of his inability to be as detached as Nick's cool father.

The supreme example of a destroyed real bridge is, of course, the one in *For Whom the Bell Tolls*. But a novel proclaiming that each is a part of the main, that no man is an island, that focuses on an American crossing over to another side of the lines to join a Spanish cause, should have the building of a bridge, not the destruction of one, as its central metaphor. Toward the end, Pilar cries out, "Is he building a bridge or blowing one?" (444), and of course the former is the case. We are carefully permitted to see that to wire the bridge for destruction is to connect both sides and to interweave between sunlight and shadow, uniting the above world of the sky with the dark world of the ravine. Indeed, as the bridge goes, that which was cut off above is united with that below; Pilar (above) and Pablo (below) join one another and, at the end, bracing Maria between them, disappear over the hill. The significant bridging has been made—"I am with thee now," thinks Jordan, "We both go in thee now" (463–64). And Maria and the reader have become the other side of Jordan/Hemingway and carry toward posterity his fame.

There are in Hemingway also the homosexuals who are in Jake Barnes's vocabulary—not Hemingway's—those who refuse to or do not care or dare to run the risk of crossover. Such choice, perhaps seen by Jake in *The Sun Also Rises* as fastidious avoidance of the risk of the loss of the self in the territory of "the other," the other sex in this case, seems an insult to his incapacity, however gained in service to his country. Their apparently willful refusal to cross over to where he, disqualified and incapable of so crossing, would wish to be explains in part his attitude toward them. Similarly, in "The Battler," "A Sea Change," and "Mr. and Mrs. Elliot," Hemingway studies the homosexual/lesbian choice that discards heterosexual love and so abandons the bridge to "the other" side. The stories record the damaged or altered sensibilities of people who, unlike Nick in "Big Two-Hearted River," fail to struggle to connect and to "become whole."

As a result, in Hemingway's works there are many devices of sexual crossover so that the male or female psyche may be therapeutically immersed in the nature of the other sex. We could readily use a vocabulary of anima and animus to explain the psychic therapy being practiced. Not only are male lovers exhorted to grow their hair long while their women cut theirs, but full sexual crossover is attempted. I have elsewhere described the male assumption of pregnancy in *A Farewell to Arms* and male appropriation of feminine fertility as well as menstruation in *Across the River*. *The Garden of Eden* plot involves transvestitism and sexual crossover of a much more developed kind, but sexual crossover or role reversal has been a constant theme for Hemingway. In *The Torrents of Spring*, he honors the general who assumes the mother's place in her bed as one "who always seemed to us like a pretty brave man" (107), and Scripps O'Neill himself, as he cradles the bird against his body (in mimicry of his memories of nestling against his mother's side) calls his sexual identity in question with the telegrapher and the drummer. Chapter 12 of *The Sun Also Rises*, a chapter in which Bill jokingly speaks of "putting a man on her horse and a woman in his grave" (115) and marrying irony to pity (114), and in which the mention of drumsticks before eggs reverses female-male priorities, intricately enacts rites and rituals of crossover and sexual reversal. At one place in this chapter, in sixteen lines there are ten references to bridging or crossing over to another side.

Those Hemingway heroes who pass through individuating rites that put them psychically together become in Hemingway's language "atoned." Atonement is the most important ritual in Hemingway: joining themselves wholly together, they are prepared for full life and also for their deaths, which frequently they immediately receive. It is on the bridge that Anselmo achieves his fulfillment, and as the bridge is destroyed, he, now inseparable from its destruction, dies. It is only later, after Jordan has gotten himself all together at last, that he is ready for death. In *A Farewell to Arms*, the soldiers in the first chapter and Catherine in the last all force birth and death imagery, opposites, together and are sanctified for their deaths. In *Across the River*, when Cantwell's soldiers cheer d'Annunzio (the living) when they should be observing a moment of silence for the dead, their leader cheers, too, so that he may be atoned with them and "share their guilt" (51), and it is only after Cantwell has gone through rites of communion-atonement with his boatman that he is ready to die. Similarly, only after Harry Morgan joins himself to mankind is he also prepared for death. Morgan, Cantwell, Thomas Hudson, and Catherine die on their bridges or in the act of crossover. The same can be said of all dying Hemingway heroes, including Macomber, who at last connects himself with what he kills.

It was this compulsive necessity for crossover that made Hemingway's heroes into the humanists they are. He himself was never narrowly sectarian and he was apolitical because he could always readily be on the other side of the fence, feel and see the position and belief of, or make a bridge to "the other." Empathically, he inhabited the territory of his adversary. In *For Whom the Bell Tolls*, he compassionately has Pilar describe in detail what "we" did to them, to the fascists, because, as Jordan later explains, we already know and only too well what was done to us. In *Across the River*, Cantwell speaks of the Germans whom he fought against but whom he liked. When Renata objects, "But they were in the wrong," he responds, "Of course. But who has not been." He goes on to observe, "When we have killed so many we can afford to be kind" (132).

Later he confesses, "I love my enemies, sometimes, more than my friends" (286). With this same mental crossover or inhabitation of the other side, Robert Jordan in *For Whom the Bell Tolls* observes the fascist planes high above and sees them as beautiful "whether they are ours or theirs" (467). His immediate reversal, "The hell they are," shows that he nevertheless recognizes the imperatives of battle, but this follows his remarkably syncretic belief: "There's no one thing that's true. It's all true" (467).

When Hemingway writes, in *Death in the Afternoon*, "Do you know the sin it would be to ruffle the arrangement of the feathers on a hawk's neck if they could never be replaced as they were?" (151), the reader is aware that this is Hemingway the hunter speaking, a man who desperately loves the beauty of the nature he struggles against. The deep admiration and respect that he evinces in that book for the noble bulls is equivalent to that which he has for the noble *torero*. It makes this Hemingway a brother to Santiago, the old fisherman who knows that he kills the thing that he loves and in killing becomes inextricable from— at last he cannot tell who is bringing in whom. Wilson of "The Short Happy Life" knows not only what the lion was probably thinking but also what he was feeling and suffering. And, responsibly, he knows what the smash of a .505 "with a muzzle velocity of two tons" (21) would be to receive, not merely to dispense. As Thomas Hudson lies dying on the bridge, he says to Henry, "It doesn't hurt any worse than things hurt that you and I have shot together" (461–62). That remarkable ability to be on the other side, to cross the bridge from one's own self to inhabit the other—whether by inhabiting Catherine's pregnancy, Renata's menstrual cycle, or the lion's death—is to cross the bridge that Hemingway knew a man had to imaginatively build, at whatever cost.

In Hemingway's works, a host of linguistic tricks and devices and compound images conceal deliberate bridge building and destroying. Water mixed with spirits is not the same as straight spirits and mixers on the side. When pronouns his lovers labor to perfect, *we* and *us*, are pointedly broken into "Monsieur and Madam" (*A Farewell to Arms* 151), *him* and *her*, or "Sir" and "the lady" (113), bridges are deliberately destroyed. Such casual remarks as "really perfect," "Really?" "Absolutely," "talking rot," "Rot and poetry. Rotten poetry," "perfectly natural," or "I love you now and always," though seemingly innocent, are not. When a character offers to give someone a "lift down" or is described as someone who "turned to the right as he left the dock," there is careful contrivance: reconciled dialectical oppositions. Readers should have been alerted to such nuance early by the studiously crafted revision in *The Sun Also Rises*, "The girl came in with the coffee and the buttered toast. Or, rather, it was bread toasted and buttered," (114), or by the description of small animals in "The Snows of Kilimanjaro" as having "quick dropping heads and switching tails" (58). The fallen pine needles that begin and end *For Whom the Bell Tolls* are a consummate bridge symbol, the antitheses of death in cycle and immortality forced together or expertly joined. That Maria is also "Rabbit" tells us that she is, like Renata, a priestess of spirit and flesh, of heavenly transcendence (immaculate conception) and biological reproductive cycle, that she at one and the same moment abandons and establishes the terms of nature.

In work after work, an integration of opposites precedes resolution: Robert Jordan, though broken in body, at last is "completely integrated now" (471), after he has gotten himself turned over and has accepted his approaching death while acknowledging both the sky and earth. His two balancing elbows evenly brace the gun whose wedge-shaped fore-sight and notched rear sight create the linear bridge between Lt. Berendo and himself. Joined to his enemy, the killer with the killed, his victim, he celebrates life as he awaits death at the place where cyclical meadows meet evergreen forests. In *Green Hills*, the cry is "Come on, let's pull ourselves together" (85), and in *Across the River* and *The Old Man and the Sea*, the protagonists do just that: they efficiently connect or join their paralyzed or betraying sides with their good sides to effect the internal wholeness that at last gives them their victories. In *Old Man*, Santiago remembers Indian wrestling with "the black" for a full night and day, light and dark cycle of twenty-four hours, until he gains the victory at last by crossing over into the territory of the "other," of the dark man. The memory is a preparation for his necessary final rites.

But what are the major functions of such bridges in Hemingway? Hemingway's bridges seem to join the shores of life and death, of con-sciousness and unconsciousness, and of masculinity and femininity. His novels are studies of the individuation process or are studies of those who flee from such necessary integration and the knowledge to be gained in the journey to the other side. He repeatedly implicitly urges the necessity for the death journey that he in World War I, and Frederic Henry in *A Farewell*, undertook, and partially for this reason war is his major subject. He draws a gallery of portraits of those who pass over to that other side: "A man alone ain't got no bloody fucking chance" (*To Have and Have Not* 225); "No man is an *Island*" (epigraph to *For Whom the Bell Tolls*). The spoken pronouncements are almost a litany, but he also paints those who fastidiously avoid the perhaps fatal Stygian waters, flee the encounter, or refuse to cross over.

Early, the Hemingway hero is often like Harry in "The Snows of Kilimanjaro," renouncing the bridges that destroyed him as an artist. In the later Hemingway, however—in *Green Hills* and *To Have and Have Not* and in *For Whom the Bell Tolls* and *Across the River*—the dangerous bridge is affirmed, celebrated, and crossed.

Hemingway lets us see that to cross a bridge is a very ambivalent act: it may be heroic acceptance of what lies on the other side, it may mean health and acquiescence before unfeared death, but it is also a releasing of oneself into the maw of process, the vagina dentata, regression into the dark night of the eternal Mother; and he knows that the victories of art and the spirit can be achieved only in dialectical battle with, not in acquiescence before, life and death. His driven men who must hold off the darkness or keep the light burning throughout the night, though driven against the wall, "do not go gentle into that good night."

Bridges seem to be the supreme metaphoric expression of the "both/and" that challenges the sensibility of the Hemingway hero who moves through an either/or world. They embody the principle of total ambiguity, for they force together into uroboric bonding those antitheses that are the opposing and antithetical shores. If to cross a bridge can be a ritual of atonement and be the humanizing individuating experience or death journey that ultimately integrates a man, that crossing can also be the abandonment of the self, the relinquishment of belief, and the denial of all absolutes. Similarly, to refuse such crossover can be cowardice and insularity, provincialism and childishness, or the position of the absolute idealist, the purist and the saint. Hemingway's work is a vast analysis/study of the alternative choices—love or war, if you will—their ambiguous meanings, their costs and rewards, and their necessary rituals. He knows that art is a bridge and that the artist is someone who loses the self in those surrogate abstract forms of perpetual reintegration and individuation that are works of art. He also knows that prehistory was timeless because it rested on a uroboric base that refused to permit the mind extrication from process. He was a culture hero, one who rescued and defended the mind by teaching it its rituals of survival and creation, even as he was a primitive who, having early and traumatically crossed over, totally understood and desired the dark night on the other side. One could say he was enough of a divinely divided man to know full well the gap that sundered and had to be healed, or that he was enough of a poet to know that the truth was never single and simple and required a crossover from concept to fact, immersion in the nature of its opposite. He was also enough of an individualist and idealist to honor the gap, the separation, that established identity.

As Nick Adams moves away from the parallel and unmeeting train tracks at the beginning of part I of "Big Two-Hearted River," he walks to the bridge over the river and looks down to see the trout who keep themselves steady against the opposing current of the "fast water" (*Short Stories* 209). Looking down further into the depths, he sees the big trout at the bottom also trying to "hold themselves" in the current. He sees clearly the fish that breaks the surface of the water and, so doing, loses in that other medium of air, on the other side to which he has crossed over, his normally accompanying shadow. Nick observes that the cost of crossover is the loss of the dualism and resistance, for as the fish re-enters the stream, he now seems to be no longer fish and shadow but only shadow, and that shadow is borne "unresisting" (216) by the current until it reaches a position under the bridge where, now, like a soldier at "his post," the fish is able to tighten and face again upstream and against the current. The fish is separated out from his shadow, becoming himself, as he reassumes dialectical opposition.

There is a lesson here at the beginning of this big two-hearted adventure to prepare the reader for the therapy that follows. Bridging crossovers observed from a bridge teach the loss of, the envelopment by, and the extrication from the shadow part of the self that one normally keeps in delicate dialectical balance. Such lessons taught at the end of *In Our Time* echo back to those of "Indian Camp," which began the book. There, Nick, as a younger boy, recognizes the surety of immortality as, one hand connecting him with the warm depths, the other in the cold air, he recrosses the lake to the white world and back from shadow experience on the dark side. As he does so, he, too, watches a fish that leaps into the air and then re-enters its own medium. Caught within cycles of time within returning day, he watches the widening rings that are testimony to the bridging crossover that has been made. Delicately poised himself, balanced like a bridge between the worlds of water and air, victim of neither, he feels quite sure he will never die. Hemingway's life was this delicate balance on the boundary between love and war: he could contemplate as one figure birth and death and recognize that immortality might at last belong to him, the detached observer vitally connected to the process.

Works Cited

Hemingway, Ernest. *Across the River and into the Trees*. 1950. New York: Scribners, 1970.

——. *Death in the Afternoon*. 1932. New York: Scribners, 1957.

——. *A Farewell to Arms*. 1929. New York: Scribners, 1969.

——. *The Fifth Column*. 1938. New York: Bantam Books, 1969.

——. *For Whom the Bell Tolls*. New York: Scribners, 1968.

——. *Green Hills of Africa*. 1935. New York: Scribners, 1963.

——. *Islands in the Stream*. New York: Scribners, 1970.

——. *The Old Man and the Sea*. New York: Scribners, 1952.

——. *The Short Stories of Ernest Hemingway*. New York: Scribners, 1953.

——. *The Sun Also Rises*. 1926. New York: Scribners, 1954.

——. *To Have and Have Not*. 1937. New York: Scribners, 1965.

Reynolds, Michael. *Hemingway's First War: The Making of "A Farewell to Arms."* Princeton, NJ: Princeton UP, 1976.

Harder on Himself Than Most

A Study of Hemingway's Self-Evaluation and Self-Projection in His Work

It would be too great fortune to have the time here to go through a rereading of stories from *In Our Time*, one in which I would emphasize the ironies and judgmental overtones that go into the moral groundwork of a Hemingway portrait. I would like to do so to suggest the moral persuasion that a character in a Hemingway work bears and especially the way the moral energy of a Hemingway work derives from the character most invested with Hemingway's own background and history. Of course, any character in a literary work is a fiction—art is not mirror—but some characters strongly gather to themselves significant aspects of the author and his or her story. I will call such a character a self-projection.

What is abundantly clear in Hemingway's early stories is that he does not hesitate to work extraordinarily close to reality; in some, like "The Doctor and the Doctor's Wife" and "Up in Michigan," he uses the actual names or backgrounds and details of the lives of people he has known. In instances where he has created projections of his own family as well as of himself, he has been merciless in his moral judgment and accounting. Rigorous in self-examination, relentless in indictment, he pursues through his characters, especially those based on himself, his own moral failings. What becomes apparent as the reader goes further in *In Our Time* is that in most stories where the protagonist seems to be in many ways standing in for Hemingway as a young man, he is harshly treated.

In the early stories of Hemingway, what fascinates is the extent to which the Hemingway projections are singled out for excoriation, vilification, and scorn. A case in point would be "the young gentleman" of "Out of Season," identified by Hemingway as a self-portrait: Hemingway admitted to Fitzgerald that this story was "an almost literal transcription of what happened" (*Selected Letters* 180) in Cortina d'Ampezzo, and this makes the fact that the young man is mocked as he is especially revealing: He is insincere, cowardly, ineffectual, imperceptive, ignorant of the language and customs of the country, and, at the end, too much of a coward to deal honestly with the corrupt gardener who cons and mockingly manipulates him. Yet he is but one of many Hemingway projections in *In Our Time*, and whether we are studying George in "Cat in the Rain," Nick and Bill in "The Three-Day Blow," or Nick and George in "Cross-Country Snow," there is both pain and high humor in these portraits, the humor that goes with the exposure of the absurdities and lies and hypocrisies that they so thoroughly illustrate. Though Nick at the end, in "Big Two-Hearted River," is indeed a young man gravely wounded who desperately is in search of amendment and health, these final stories leave us with the necessary paradigm, a Hemingway projection who is seriously injured where it does not show: that is, he carries within him the problem that is in search of resolution, the wound to be healed.

That these stories draw heavily on the author's self-examination, that they delineate moral and spiritual deficiency, and especially that, as organized, they suggest a larger historical and cultural statement means that Hemingway indeed does "lay it all on the line"—that he lets himself in this work, as also in all his subsequent works, stand in for the failures and delinquencies of twentieth-century man, that he descends into his own unconscious to gain what insight he has into and what evidence he has for the basic moral failures of his age.

Malcolm Cowley, speaking of such Hemingway stories as "A Way You'll Never Be" and "Now I Lay Me," is quoted as saying, "Candor about his inner life is one of the great things about his early stories" (Brian 200). He goes on to say, "Part of Hemingway's do-it-yourself psychotherapy in controlling his fears of death and his nightmares of going insane was to put them down on paper, to write about them obliquely in his fiction" (Brian 200). Cowley here is merely verbalizing what Hemingway himself has told us many times: how necessary it was to write "things" to be rid of them, how thoroughly the telling or writing of a tale or even just writing must often have been a therapeutic acknowledgment of an otherwise seemingly hidden inner fault, as well as an

exorcism and an amputation of a rotten part. Feeling corrupt in his relationship with Pauline because of his treachery to Hadley, Hemingway
writes Pauline (on November 12, 1926), "I might as well write it out
now and maybe get rid of it that way" (Brian 220). Arnold Gingrich
noted the tendency and explained, "He wrote things out of his life, got
rid of them by writing about them" (Brian 74). And Denis Brian, speaking of this technique of exorcism, writes, "He took his fears and weaknesses to the fire as if to cauterize them" (Brian 318). Writing, then,
even before a plot was chosen or chose itself to illustrate or enact
redemption or absolution, for Hemingway served a moral function of
absolving, purging, amending, getting beyond, or putting to rest the
sense of imperfection, sin, or personal failure that needed to be
addressed—by the very act of moving into abstraction and aesthetic
resolution what had been inner psychological problems. Hemingway
exonerated himself from nothing. Critics who focus on his moral short-
comings, as many do, to the exclusion of the texts, are latecomers to his
inner terrain. Hemingway has been there before them and far more
thoroughly and with infinitely greater integrity overseen that psychic
landscape.

"The Short Happy Life of Francis Macomber" is biographically
based on Philip Percival (or Colonel Richard Cooper or Count Bror von
Blixen), and Jane and Grant Mason, and, of course, himself; in it, as in
"The Snows of Kilimanjaro," moral delinquencies, such as cowardice
and corruption, are studied, as are attempts at moral reconstitution. It
is important to see how clearly Hemingway's African stories focus on
the male's deficiencies or failures. This is especially true in "Snows,"
where Harry is patently a Hemingway projection, but it is also important
to note that in both stories the accomplished, purged, cleansed, or
redeemed state seems to be purchased at the cost of death. Harry's
merely imagined dream vision of his arrival at the summit of Kilimanjaro is, like the story itself, only a fictionalized realization and stands, I
would say, as metaphor for Hemingway's process of using fiction itself as
the mode of purgation and cleansing. To consider writing as almost an
avenging angel that somehow exists to punish evil and redeem the bad
or cleanse the psyche is to give it a strongly prominent role in life.
Therefore, we are not surprised to discover Hemingway writing to
Fitzgerald (on March 31, 1927) shortly after the publication of *The Sun
Also Rises*, that "there was a story around that I had gone to switzerland
[sic] to avoid being shot by demented characters out of my books"

(*Selected Letters* 249). Here it is almost as though the author sees himself as pursued beyond the fiction and into life for further justice by the abstract Furies he has awakened.

Jake Barnes is a not only physically but morally flawed man who learns to acknowledge his moral failures and to find ways to rid himself of them. Frederic Henry is a corrupt young man, often callow, insensitive, cowardly, who only after the death of Catherine and his son has enough insight and overview to arrive at the exculpatory act of self-confession that is the story that he subsequently writes and that we read. The Hemingway of *Green Hills of Africa* is competitive, vain, argumentative, quick-tempered, and petulant, but he learns in time to amend his faults and be reconciled to humanity. Colonel Cantwell of *Across the River and into the Trees* is frequently a hard-nosed, vain and arrogant, loud-mouthed "sonofabitch," as he in his amended nature would readily admit, but the entire novel exists, not as self-exoneration, but as a self-confession in a desperate attempt before his death to set himself morally right, through a self-inversion and a justice that demand nothing less than a psychic restructuring, an effeminization of the psyche, and an exchange of the sensibility of the warrior for that of the lover. These characters are all, as most critics agree, extremely close projections of Hemingway, and all are as Hemingway meant to make them: they are initially corrupt not because the mirror of art so exposes the reality of the instinctively projected psyche of the artist but because the work of art has structured them consciously to be exemplars of their vices, already severely judged and presented, long before we, the often officious and vain readers, intrude upon the scene to imply that *we* have discovered such deficiencies in the unconscious sensibility of their creator. Most Hemingway works examine and present moral failure and inadequacy, and also—and this is where Hemingway differs from Fitzgerald and why Hemingway finally realized that association with Fitzgerald was bad for him—study amendment of and victory over moral dereliction and vice. Fitzgerald exquisitely presents and recognizes moral failure; he presents uxoriousness in action and moral failures as victims. Hemingway, on the other hand, presents immorality in action and the stages of moral reconstitution and cleansing. His protagonists are never meant to be approved or heeded as presented, nor are their attitudes meant to be taken for those of their maker; rather, they are to be noted in their struggle to get beyond and master their deficiencies, deficiencies Hemingway in self-projection minutely studies. Santiago must get rid of the betraying part within himself, Cantwell must have feeling driven into his insensate side, and Robert Jordan must get "turned over" and must hold off the cowardly suicidal impulse within him that is his paternal inheritance.

To see how Hemingway used self-projection to arrive at the moral passion play that is his every novel, we can perhaps best look at *To Have and Have Not*. In that work, Harry Morgan seems a long way from Ernest Hemingway, but Harry gains exoneration from too great moral incrimination through his underdog ethics, which seem products of the very environment that makes him. Nevertheless, we finally see heroism and a deathbed conversion in his dying confession, in which he renounces the very isolating and isolated psychic dynamics that have led to his insensitivity, crimes, and death. It is in Richard Gordon in that novel, however, by too many readers too hastily read as a portrait of John Dos Passos, that the Hemingway projection superbly functions. Gordon is less a projection of Dos Passos than he is of Hemingway himself, and he is the character in the novel most set up for attack and vilification. His insensitivity toward his wife, Helen, is a close projection of Hemingway's guilt toward Hadley and Pauline for his dedication to his art—better studied in *The Garden of Eden*—and for his infidelities. Gordon's dismissal of Helen's needs for those of the story in his head— "Don't talk to me. . . . I'm going to work. I have it all in my head" (176)—literally reenacts Hemingway's own historically verified morning exchanges with Hadley, and Helen's references to swimming at Cap d'Antibes and skiing in Switzerland are from the Hemingways' own history. Therefore when, in probably the most vitriolic and damning speech in all Hemingway's work, Helen attacks him as lover and writer (concluding, "I'm through with you. . . . Your kind of picknose love. You writer" [186]), the attack is self-directed remorse and guilt-driven self-flagellation. Additionally, Gordon's relationship with Helene and Tommy Bradley is an acknowledged portrait of Hemingway's relationship with Jane and Grant Mason.

In the original holograph version of the novel,[1] in passages deleted from the published work, Hemingway fascinatingly allowed his projection in Gordon to confront his own historical image:

> "There's a writer lives here," someone said. "Hemingway. You know him?"
> "He's a big slob," Richard Gordon said.
> "I guess so," the man said.
> "You know him?" Freddy asked Richard Gordon.

> "No. But I know he's a big slob."
> Somebody laughed. (Folder 7, p. 59)

I think we can know who laughs, and why. Later, in the text:

> "Hemingway makes money," somebody said.
> "That big bastard is shot in the ass with luck," someone else said. "I've never seen him working yet." (Folder 8, p. 60)

Hemingway allows one of his characters to defend him: "He works. . . . He's a friend of mine," says Freddy. When, still later in the novel, Richard Gordon passes what is clearly and carefully described as Hemingway's own house in Key West, he says to himself, "That's where the big slob lives, what did he ever write after that one novel, it was a tour de force, all he writes now is that tripe in *Esquire*, what did he quit for? He's let us all down, easy living softened him up, I guess" (Folder 9, p. 61). Evaluating Hemingway as "too drunk" to write anything worthwhile now, Gordon reflects, "Well that's the way they go when they get in the money. He stinks and his stuff stinks."

What is fascinating about this are the split halves of the creative psyche of Hemingway, the fictive and the real, in antagonistic destructive interaction, as they were in Cohn and Jake in the first novel. The careful reader can see the outlines of Harry in "Snows" being formed just shortly before the actual composition of that story.

Hemingway has occasionally been described as a "counterpuncher," one who, when struck, would instantly retaliate and flash back his own response to the received blow. There is some truth in this, but what has more seldom been noted is his own subsequent remorse and shame that he had to absorb for his often intemperate or hasty reaction. He was thin-skinned indeed, often as raw as one flayed, and criticism of his work readily drew blood, but he was especially morally hypersensitive, supremely alert to his own faults, which he understood far better and explored far more deeply than even the most vicious of his critics. We have ample biographical evidence of how readily he became the victim to the pleas of others once he felt that, in defending himself initially, he might have hurt them. He was therefore finally unable to remain steadfast in his opposition to the requests of Philip Young and James Fenton and others, largely out of guilt, guilt that less sensitive writers would not have felt. As Philip Young acknowledged to Brian, "He said I was still free to call him a son-of-a-bitch if I wanted to" (210). His remorse showed especially after acts of intemperance: The night after his verbal attack on Harold Loeb in Pamplona—the basis of an important scene between Jake and Robert Cohn in *The Sun Also Rises*—Loeb received the following note: "I was terribly tight and nasty to you last night and I don't want you to go away with that nasty insulting lousiness as the last thing of the fiesta. . . . I'm thoroughly ashamed of the way I acted and the stinking, unjust uncalled for things I said" (*Selected Letters* 166).

Hemingway in Paris, after a dinner table argument with Nathan Asch that ended with their exchanged blows in the street, appeared in the middle of the night at Asch's apartment door. By Asch's account in a letter to Cowley, "I couldn't sleep until you forgave me," he said. "You know, of course, that I was wrong in the argument. You've got a lot of talent. You've got more of everything than any of us" (Brian 54). This fundamental decency, however delayed, is representative, and it emerges from an exquisitely alert conscience that cannot rest if in the sense of a state of wrong or error or sin. Speaking of Harold Stearns, Hemingway confessed to Fitzgerald (in a letter on December 24, 1925): "I couldn't sleep if I hurt his feelings. Christ nose [sic] that when I cant [sic] sleep I have enough sons of bitching things I've done to look back on without adding any ornamental gloss" (*Selected Letters* 181).

Hemingway's son Gregory said, "My father had a terribly powerful remorseful conscience. It would give him no rest when he made a mistake" (Meyers 345–46). His first son, John, remarked, "My father was a person of inner turmoil about anything he did to hurt anybody . . . he really suffered" (Brian 73). Denis Brian focuses on Hemingway's black moods of depression based on his remorse, and Jeffrey Meyers studies these. Peter Viertel, writing in *Dangerous Friends*, records Hemingway's pattern of instant "abject apologies" for intemperate moments (87), and Mike Reynolds, writing in *Hemingway: The Paris Years*, also records the frequently dropped "bitter remark to be regretted later" (303) and Hemingway's "keen and well-honed sense of remorse after behaving badly" (305). He also describes a pattern of apologies, retractions, and incredible unmailed letters. Archibald MacLeish paraphrases a letter he received from Hemingway in which he wrote that "he always beshat his friends. He suffered for it—knew he'd done it, and suffered" (qtd. in Brian 92). This temperamental inability to escape guilt and remorse persisted throughout his life, and, of course, one can see suicide as a final self-judgment. Biographical evidence readily reveals how desperately guilty Hemingway felt for his abandonment of Hadley, and then subsequently for his divorce from Pauline, but Meyers writes that

"Hemingway . . . had a more tender conscience and was more sensitive to moral nuance than Pauline," and therefore "suffered much more" (181). When asked by Bill Bird in Paris the reason for his divorce from Hadley, he responded, "Because I am a son of a bitch" (qtd. in Brian 79). In a letter to Pauline at the time, Hemingway speaks of his betrayals and killing and destroying (*Selected Letters* 220–25, November 12, 1926), and in a letter to Hadley he focuses on his cruelty and the "great hurt" (*Selected Letters* 228, November 18, 1926) he has given. He signs a letter to Scott in this year "Ernest M. Shit" (*Selected Letters*, to FSF, 20 May 1926, p. 205). This kind of self-judgment persists: in a letter as late as 1957, to Rupert Bellville, his signature is "Ernesto the super-shit" (December 7 [actually 26] 1957).[2] Writing to Scott, he accepts everything as "completely my fault" and concludes, "As we make our hell we certainly should like it" (*Selected Letters* 217). Later, describing Pauline as having turned "mean," he hastily concludes, "Although it is your own actions that turn her mean. Mine, I mean" (qtd. in Meyers 347), and in a deleted passage originally intended for *A Moveable Feast*, he speaks of how "where we went and what we did and the unbelievable wrenching, killing happiness, selfishness and treachery of everything we did" created in him "a terrible remorse." In one letter to Pauline (November 12, 1926), he writes:

> In the nights it is simply unbelievably terrible . . . all the world just being made into the figure representing sin and I get the horrors . . . so I know this is a lousy terribly self pitying letter just wallowing in bathos . . . and so it is . . . I'm not a saint, nor built like one. . . . I had to get this poison out and I've just been stewed in it. . . . Please forgive this letter. It is everything contemptible. But that is the way I get. (*Selected Letters* 221–22)

Here again the letter, the writing, is given as the way to absolution or to at least release of the "poison." November 1926 was the terrible month, and on the 24th, Ernest wrote to Fitzgerald:

> Anyway I'm now all through with the general bumping off phase and will only bump off now under certain special circumstances which I don't think will arise. Have refrained from any half turnings on of the gas or slitting of the wrists with sterilized safety razor blades. Am continuing my life in original role of son of a bitch sans peur et sans rapproche. The only thing in life I've ever had any luck being decent

about is money so am very splendid and punctilious about that. Also I have been sucked in by ambition. (*Selected Letters* 232)

I am not describing a youthful hypersensitivity. It never abated. The letters he wrote to Adriana Ivancich between 1950 and 1954 are filled with his sense of self-condemnation and guilt: He acknowledges, "I have every fault that you know and probably others" (March 18, 1951), and in a letter on May 8, 1952, he confesses:

Since I started my campaign against being stupid, conceited, opinionated, bigotted and boreing [sic] we always get along wonderfully in dreams and you think I am as fine a man as I hope to be if this great campaign against my general worthlessness succeeds. Wish you were here to direct the campaign. It needs a director of higher moral qualities than me. Black Dog does his best. But he is too kind.[3]

It is entirely possible that had his relationship with Adriana not cast her into the role he here describes of confessor and leader of a campaign of absolution, *Across the River and into the Trees* might never have been written, recounting as it does almost this exact relationship between Renata and the corrupt Colonel who seeks his psychic and moral rebirth through her, a priestess who hears his confession, permits him purgation, and grants him his absolution. Quotations can be almost endlessly supplied to demonstrate Hemingway's hyperalertness to moral faults that most writers would neither consider faults nor suffer for.

Perhaps one last group of letters should be noted, those exchanged with Robert Morgan Brown in 1954 (now in the Harry Ransom manuscript collection at Texas University in Austin), offering answers to religious questions. In one letter dated July 14, 1954, he writes:

Human beings are not perfect and I have certainly lived more of my life in a state of sin than in a state of grace. I am living in the present time, in a state of sin, according to the church, but I have no feeling of sin.

Privately I could not make an act of contrition at the hour of my death since I know if I lived I would repeat the sin again. . . . If there is a hell I shall certainly go to it if the rules are applied like The Immigration Act. Might get to it anyway to see how my friends are doing. . . . I could possibly be weak enough to make a false confession. I hope not. But who knows?

. . . Please do not try to make me out a good man. I have tried to be and I have failed. But I try to be a good writer and it is difficult enough under the circumstances. . . . My last advice to you as of religion is to call me a son of a bitch.

In another letter, on May 25, 1956, he writes, "Let me know if there is anything I can do myself and if my low-grade conscience permits, it will comply."

In still another letter (September 24, 1954), he writes,

But the toughest thing is to be any form of hero to anyone. I always try to make it believable and sure that I am not any form of hero, so that afterwards people do not have to decide that their hero was a bum. This sounds conceited but if you had to be the official hero of Archie MacLeish and poor Scott Fitzgerald over a period of years only for them to find that their hero was worthless, you would understand the obligations of being a non-hero of any type.

Finally, in a letter on July 22, 1956, he states, "Don't see how my prayers can help anybody because they must be canceled out by my blasphemies. I remember Joyce telling me, 'But remember, Hemingway, blasphemy is not a sin. Heresy is the sin!'"

What is valuable here is Hemingway's compulsive necessity to face his own moral failures with extraordinary completeness and rigorous honesty, and the necessity to somehow gain absolution from or amendment of them. I really am suggesting that Hemingway's writing was his mode of moral purgation; that through it, in abstract projection, he did not exonerate but held his life morally accountable; and that, holding up to life a far more rigorous moral standard than most, he avoided absolution or forgiveness that was not based on his best efforts toward fundamental moral amendment or psychic reconstitution.

Notes

1. The holograph version of *To Have and Have Not* is in the Hemingway Collection in the John F. Kennedy Library in Boston: *THHN* ms, item 212, folder 3 and folders 8 and 9, pp. 59–61.

2. In the Harry Ransom MS Collection, Texas University, Austin, Texas.

3. EH's letters to Adriana Ivancich are also in the Harry Ransom MS Collection.

Works Cited

Brian, Denis. *The True Gen: An Intimate Portrait of Hemingway by Those Who Knew Him*. New York: Grove Press, 1988.

Hemingway, Ernest. *Across the River and into the Trees*. 1950. New York: Scribners, 1970.

———. *Ernest Hemingway: Selected Letters, 1917–1961*. Ed. Carlos Baker. New York: Scribners, 1981.

———. *A Farewell to Arms*. 1929. New York: Scribners, 1969.

———. *Green Hills of Africa*. 1935. New York: Scribners, 1963.

———. *In Our Time*. 1925. New York: Scribners, 1958.

———. *The Old Man and the Sea*. New York: Scribners, 1952.

———. *The Short Stories of Ernest Hemingway*. 1938. New York: Scribners, 1966.

———. *The Sun Also Rises*. 1926. New York: Scribners, 1954.

———. *To Have and Have Not*. 1937. New York: Scribners, 1965.

Meyers, Jeffrey. *Hemingway: A Biography*. New York: Harper and Row, 1985.

Reynolds, Michael S. *Hemingway: The Paris Years*. New York: Blackwell, 1989.

Viertel, Peter. *Dangerous Friends: At Large with Huston and Hemingway in the Fifties*. New York: Doubleday, 1992.

24

Hemingway's Late-Life Relationship with Birds

> "I probably could have been a great ornithologist," Willie said. "Grandma used to raise chickens."
>
> —*Islands In the Stream*

Willie's facetious comment, after he has just observed a Bahamian booby bird on a nearby wreck, presents Ernest Hemingway's apparently mocking but really straight assessment of his *own* interests and abilities. Throughout that novel, the careful and precise observation of birds, their flight and mannerisms and habits, defines and supports action in the book. The studious perception of the flight of birds accompanies the drama. The observation of birds is so intense it resembles that of classical divination to determine the future by reading the patterns of the flight of birds and the entrails of birds.

In 1949, in "The Great Blue River," Hemingway gives an autobiographical basis for his fascination. There, acknowledging that the reason he lives in Cuba is too complicated to explain, he continues, "You do not tell them about the strange and lovely birds that are on the farm the year around, nor about all the migratory birds that come through, nor that quail come in the early mornings to drink at the swimming pool" (*By-Line* 403).

In the remark is his recognition of and love for particular birds and their habits. However, he creates a complication as he goes on in the

368

same essay to observe that he lives in Cuba also because "you can raise your own fighting cocks, train them on the place, and fight them anywhere that you can match them and that this is all legal" (*By-Line* 403), and he remembers with nostalgia his live-pigeon shooting there.

Elsewhere, in *Death in the Afternoon*, his love for and delight in the birds he eats is patent even as he describes their deaths:

> In front of the barn a woman held a duck whose throat she had cut and stroked him gently while a little girl held up a cup to catch the blood for making gravy. The duck seemed very contented and when they put him down (the blood all in the cup) he waddled twice and found that he was dead. We ate him later, stuffed and roasted. (275–76)

He deliberately shocks us with the gentle stroking of the "throat she had cut," the little girl who, like an acolyte, holds up the cup "to catch the blood," the "contented" duck himself who is surprised to discover his own death, and the almost brutal delight of "we ate him later, stuffed and roasted." All that empathy and all that accepted process! Passages like that teach deeply the *un*sentimental meaning of life.

I doubt that there is a more beautiful beginning to any short story than that to "In Another Country," where Hemingway looks carefully and lovingly at the landscape of hunters of animals, birds, and men:

> In the fall the war was always there, but we did not go to it any more. It was cold in the fall in Milan and the dark came very early. Then the electric lights came on, and it was pleasant along the streets looking in the windows. There was much game hanging outside the shops, and the snow powdered in the fur of the foxes and the wind blew their tails. The deer hung stiff and heavy and empty, and small birds blew in the wind and the wind turned their feathers. It was a cold fall and the wind came down from the mountains. (*Short Stories* 267)

The tenderness and precision and hardness are all there, life seen clearly amidst death that is seen clearly, and all of that in the midst of painfully intense sensation and love. There is the acceptance of process in the midst of an undercurrent and tone of lament, for the necessary deaths in life that support the intense delights of life. In another remarkable passage, he writes, "Do you know the sin it would be to ruffle the arrangement of the feathers on a hawk's neck if they could never be replaced as they were?" (*Death in the Afternoon* 159). In "A Christmas Gift," he describes "a string of mallard ducks hung out of reach of cats" and "also hung up Hungarian partridges, different varieties of quail and other fine eating birds" (*By-Line* 466). Such an observation records pursuit that goes beyond death, just as the memory of taste remains beyond the fact of consumed delight. Such moments of fascinated observation underwrote his ornithological knowledge.

In "A Situation Report," in 1956, he writes:

> The sea birds huddled in the lee of the cliffs, coming out in clouds to dive wildly when a scouting bird would sight schoolfish moving along the shore, and the condors ate dead pelicans on the beaches. The pelicans usually died from bursting their food pouches diving and a condor would walk backwards along the beach lifting a large dead pelican as though it weighed nothing. (*By-Line* 473)

This later Hemingway is a writer who not only sees where the driven birds hide but who empathically, feelingly understands their dilemma in the wind and cold, who sees the pattern of their grouped flight, the prey they pursue and how it is pursued. He knows what eats what, what bird can lift what, and how birds die and return through their deaths back into the cycle of life. In "There She Breaches: Or Moby Dick off the Morro" (1936), he writes:

> So we drifted like that all morning, and in the fall, the small birds that are going south are deadly tired sometimes as they near the coast of Cuba where the hawks come out to meet them, and the birds light on the boat to rest and sometimes we would have as many as twenty on board at a time in the cabin, on the deck, perched on the fishing chairs or resting on the floor of the cockpit. Their great fatigue makes them so tame that you can pick them up and they show no fear at all. There were three warblers and a thrush in the cockpit when Enrique poked his head out to get some air from working in the galley and Lopez Mendez said, "Don't let him see the birds. He would eat them."
> "No," said Enrique. "I am a great lover of birds." (*By-Line* 247)

Passages like that can be written only by someone who understands the weariness, the desperation, the fear, and the dangers of these small creatures and who also places his awareness helplessly in the great enveloping process that includes their coevally desperate and beautiful lives. He not only participates in their struggle but brings the great undercurrents of nature and time to visibility through them. This sympathetic aware-ness of their lives and desperations Hemingway gave fine expression to in *The Old Man and the Sea*, where Santiago binds himself to the crea-tures of the air as he will later bind himself to the great fish of the sea:

> He was sorry for the birds, especially the small delicate dark terns that were always flying and looking and almost never finding, and he thought, the birds have a harder life than we do except for the robber birds and the heavy strong ones. Why did they make birds so delicate and fine as those sea swallows when the ocean can be so cruel? She is kind and very beautiful. But she can be so cruel and it comes so suddenly and such birds that fly, dipping and hunting, with their small sad voices are made too delicately for the sea. (29)

Such a passage lets the reader close into Hemingway's love. We infer it from the qualities he projects upon his characters—here, as we em-pathize with Santiago in his feeling perceptions, his reflection upon, and his measurement of man and the birds. He uses the birds as ways to see more deeply the ironies of beauty and kindness within rapacity and destruction. Letting the birds help him as he labors and suffers, and alive to their suffering, he is able to acknowledge his participation with the bird and see that "the bird is a great help" (38).

The depth at which birds inhabit Hemingway's unconscious life is recognized in the frequent association between the flight of birds in his work and the orgasmic moment of fully completed love, when the soul seems, in the ecstasy of loving, to have been released from and therefore apprehended through the body, so that infinitely heightened life and death become one and the same. It is this love/death, attainment of spirit through flesh, of paradise on earth, that the flight of the bird records—whether for Cantwell with Renata, or for Robert Jordan's "ris-ing" and "sailing" and "wheeling" and "soaring" (*For Whom the Bell Tolls* 379) as he and Maria sexually become one, or for Nick Adams with Trudy. Late in his life, Hemingway describes the aged Cantwell's response after his lovemaking in the gondola with Renata: "She said nothing, and neither did he, and when the great bird had flown far out of the closed window of the gondola, and was lost and gone, neither of them said anything" (*Across the River* 154). As Hemingway earlier in

"Fathers and Sons" reached for an image of a boy's first introduction to the mystery and wonder of sex, he wrote:

> Could you say she did first what no one has ever done better and mention plump brown legs, flat belly, hard little breasts, well holding arms, quick searching tongue, the flat eyes, the good taste of mouth, then uncomfortably, tightly, sweetly, moistly, lovely, tightly, achingly, fully, finally, unendingly, never-endingly, never-to-endingly, suddenly ended, the great bird flown like an owl in the twilight, only it daylight in the woods and hemlock needles stuck against your belly. (*Short Stories* 497)

What the passage records is the night bird in the double light as the unending and the suddenly ended are joined: *that* moment. So that the relations between love and death are not lost, Hemingway in that story belabors the association. Nick's father has given him shells to go hunting black squirrels, only three shells a day because "it wasn't good for a boy to go banging around" (497). The black squirrel hunting is associated with sex, pure and simple, and when Nick, at the end of "The Doctor and the Doctor's Wife," offers himself as guide to take his sexually defeated, masturbatory father to where the black squirrels are, the overtones are strong that this love/death experience that he leads him toward, which goes by way of the hemlock woods—remember the hemlock needles stuck to Nick's belly as the great bird has flown—is a way achieved by a death journey through sex. The experience binds together birth, death, birds, and the feminine: "When you have shot one bird flying you have shot all birds flying. They are all different and they fly in different ways but the sensation is the same and the last one is as good as the first" (*Short Stories* 498).

My point here is that Hemingway has invested birds and their beauty and their flight, and their role as mediators between the earth and the heavens, with mythological and psychic significance. They are related to the ecstatic love moment of orgasmic transcendence, even as they are related to the polar experiences of heightened life and death. Although he usually carefully distinguishes birds as either male or female, they are metaphorically established as avatars of and the means whereby the male may enter the primal experience of the feminine.[1]

Hemingway's interest in birds has its scientific, aesthetic, and religious components. He increasingly gives ritualistic and mythological significance to birds. Late in *Across the River and into the Trees*, he has Cantwell imagine the gift he would most wish to give to his beloved:

> I'd like to give her a vest made of the whole plumage the way the old Mexicans used to ornament their gods, he thought. But I suppose these ducks have to go to the market and no one would know how to skin and cure the skins anyway. It could be beautiful, though, with Mallard drake skins for the back and sprig for the front with two longitudinal stripes of teal. One coming down over each breast. Be a hell of a vest. I'm pretty sure she'd like it. (282)

The vest he describes is really, as he suggests, an investiture for her still to be ritualized adoration-enthronement. Conceived in "the way the old Mexicans used to ornament their gods," the vest he describes barely conceals the way it as costume transforms his beloved into a bird goddess. The sexual and ritual transformations and investments with power that *Across the River* records are further enunciated as this man, who wears a small eagle with wings outstretched on each shoulder (283), finds himself later imagining a real down jacket that he would additionally like to have made for Renata: "I could find out how they are quilted and make one with duck down from here. . . . I'd get a good tailor to cut it and we would make it double-breasted" (289), he continues.

Across the River is filled with the many gifts that Cantwell brings to Renata to lay at her feet: his love, his sense of the past and its meaning, his usually defended prerogatives and command, and, ultimately, his life. It is with an imagery of birds that this level of meaning is enunciated in the novel, which progresses from the first scene and its shooting of the birds to the last scenes, in which the guns are put away and the killing of birds is abjured. It is a novel studying the ritualized self-overthrow of the male who in ritual self-castration divests himself of the signs of his authority and power and transfers them to his female consort. It is a studied examination of a shift from the patriarchal to the matriarchal mode, an understanding that the time has come culturally for that shift, and it is told to an extent in "bird language." Lest the reader miss the meaning of his treatise, Hemingway etches the movement to the future iconographically. Following the last words of the preceding chapter, "The shooting's over" (294), the new chapter begins as "the boatman placed the ducks carefully, breasts up, on the bow of the boat and the Colonel handed [up] his guns" (295). As the transference of power ends, Cantwell looks at the injured mallard drake, a "cripple" whose beating heart and "captured hopeless eyes" he observes. He asks the boatman to "put him in the sack with the hen" (298). That metaphor is historical and profound.

In "The Last Good Country," an incest story that was written late and never completed for publication, Hemingway deals, as he does in so many of his later works, with the sexual inversions and sexual transformations necessary for a transference of power. As Littless says, she is "practicing being a boy" (*Complete Short Stories* 533), and this should remind us of Catherine's metamorphoses in *The Garden of Eden*. In this story again, as Nick enthrones/invests Littless with power, he brings to her as gift the bird totems that belong to her. Nick and Littless have gone into fresh and virgin territory, where they come on the "last really wild stream there is" (541), and there they observe cedar waxwings "calm and gentle and distinguished moving in their lovely elegance with the magic wax touches on their wing coverts and their tails" (540). Littless says, "They're the most beautiful, Nickie. There couldn't be more simply beautiful birds" (540). "They're built like your face" (540), he says. The birds make her so proud and happy that she cries. Nick then brings to her three grouse that he has shot for her and lays them out on the moss at her feet. She feels them "warm and full-breasted and beautifully feathered" (540). Such ritualized moments in which the male brings the bird costume or the bird beauty or the bird experience to the woman he loves should recall to the reader the many moments in Hemingway where the bird is equated with orgasmic transcendence. As he sees bird beauty and fashions it for his beloved, it is not only adoration but service, self-abnegation in the interest of her empowerment.

Since the dimensions of my subject are large, in the remainder of this essay I will confine myself to and focus primarily on the third book of *Islands in the Stream*, "At Sea," and there look at Hemingway's remarkable descriptive passages that define the role of birds in the lives of men.

Within a page of its beginning, with the discovery of the bodies of the executed villagers, Ara remarks that "birds haven't worked on them but the land crabs are working on them" (333). Instantly the birds are related to the inescapable voracious food cycle, identified with and related to the lives and deaths of men; but the point is made that that which descends from the skies and that which emerges from the land both feed upon life in its life/death cycles. Shortly after the gruesome discovery of the deaths, which will call Hudson and his men into pursuit and lead some toward their own deaths, Hemingway describes the terns:

The sand was high like new-made graves and over the island sooty terns were flying in the wind. They nested in the rocks up at the windward end and a few nested in the grass of the lee. They were flying now, falling off with the wind, cutting sharply into it, and dipping down toward the grass and the rocks. They were calling, sadly and desperately. (351)

The birds are invested with the sorrow and the prescience and duties of harbingers and heralds. Sooty and calling their lament, they are precisely seen in their customary and exact flight movements and nesting habits and are never allowed to escape in their beautiful release in the wind from inescapable descent into death: the neutral sand already suggests the graves awaiting. That chapter concludes as Thomas Hudson discusses with the lieutenant at the radio shack what he needs to know that he has not seen and must know. "I saw the birds moving," he says. "'The poor birds,' the Lieutenant said" (354), and the chapter ends. Later, it will be the movement of the birds that reveals and tells and leads and determines for Hudson the movement of the Germans and foretells Hudson's fate.

As they pursue and search, Thomas Hudson sees "a tall white heron standing looking down in the shallow water with his head, neck, and beak poised. . . . Then the heron rose and flew further up the beach. Braking widely with his great white wings, and then taking a few awkward steps, he landed. I am sorry I disturbed him, Thomas Hudson thought" (376–77). Only one who has observed with exquisite care could note the triply poised heron, with its braking action and its "awkward" steps; but, more, only one empathically inside the world of birds could feel the sorrow for having disturbed the heron. Later, he notes "one turtle with a sea gull flying around him. I thought he was going to perch on his back. But he didn't" (387). Again, he enters with empathy into the decisions and choices of the bird, wondering about that incidental life. The birds usurp much of his attention. Going behind the lagoon, he had found

the place where the flamingoes came at high tide and he had seen many wood ibis, the *cocos* that gave the key its name, and a pair of roseate spoon-bills working in the marl of the edge of the lagoon. They were beautiful with the sharp rose of their color against the gray marl and their delicate, quick, forward-running movements, and they had the dreadful, hunger-ridden impersonality of certain wading birds. (399)

These observations are ornithological wonders: the recognized "hunger-ridden impersonality" is not only remarkably acute but is used to establish relationship to other birds similarly driven. As the painter he is, Hudson carefully notes colors and contrasts. The "roseate" and then the "sharp rose" identify his different observations, while his "delicate" and "quick" establish the birds as he has seen them.[2]

Later, "in the morning light they could see four terns and two gulls working around the shoal. They had found something and were diving. The terns were crying and the gulls were screaming." Willie, sympathizing like Santiago with the birds, notes that "those poor bastard birds have to get up earlier in the morning than we do to make a living. . . . People don't appreciate the work they put in" (406). Again the appreciation, based on empathy and comparison, is there, while the crying and screaming dramatically orchestrate the drama. The struggle and pursuit of the birds is allied with the mission of Hudson's men as irregular troops, and it is Willie again who sees the booby bird as "probably come to reinforce us" (407). Hudson studies the "flocks of shore birds wheeling and settling on the banks to feed" (415), and these predatory cycles echo against their own hungers and pursuit. Throughout this book, the patterns of natural hunger and life and death are the background to the *unnatural* dying and diving—this is, after all, a submarine crew they pursue.

Hudson, alone on his *flying* bridge,

> watched the shore birds working on the flats and he remembered what they had meant to him when he was a boy. He could not feel the same about them now and he had no wish to kill them ever. But he remembered the early days with his father in a blind on some sand-spit with tin decoys out and how they would come in as the tide lowered and bared the flats and how he would whistle the flock in as they were circling. It was a sad whistle and he made it now and turned one flock. But they veered off from the stranded ship and went far out to feed. (417)

Because his memories are thoroughly grounded in his pursuit of birds, Hudson finds his nostalgia come up on him, raised by the birds, bringing together both innocence and guilt, and the sense of senseless slaughter together with the strategies of war. The memory of the birds thoroughly structures the drama unfolding between himself and the German submarine crew. Then, quick on the heels of this recognition,

> he saw a flight of flamingoes coming from the left. They were flying
> low over the water, lovely to see in the sunlight. Their long necks
> were slanted down and their incongruous legs were straight out;
> immobile while their pink and black wings beat. . . . [Hudson] mar-
> veled at their downswept black and white bills and the rose color
> they made in the sky, which made their strange individual structures
> unimportant and still each one was an excitement to him. (418)

The flamingoes relate him to himself as an artist, their color and form
being aesthetically related in his mind as he simultaneously recognizes
through them the loss of the individual in the group, the solitary insignificance in the larger pattern. Even as he understands this, he, as an artist
and a significant man, knows that he puts together the universal and the
particular, the larger meaning resting on the unique fact, for "each . . .
was an excitement to him." The relationship between individual anger
and justification for murder and group rage and the accepted monstrosi-
ties of war is debated through the recognized flamingo patterns. The birds
themselves are marvelously seen in their precise neck slant, with "incon-
gruous" legs and "downswept" black and white bills. Their choice for the
mud bank to the right and their feeding there tell Hudson that they had
been "spooked flying over the key"(419). They have given him an index
to the prey he seeks. But the flamingoes are still more important to him.
He dismisses his crew because, as he says, "I want to watch the flamingoes
for a little while" (420):

> He stood on the flying bridge and watched the flamingoes. It is not
> just their color, he thought. It's not just the black on that rose pink.
> It is their size and that they are ugly in detail and yet perversely
> beautiful. They must be a very old bird from the earliest times. He
> did not watch them through the glasses because he did not want
> details now. He wanted the roseate mass on the gray brown flat.
> Two other flocks had come in now and the banks were colored in a
> way that he would not have dared to paint. Or I would have dared
> to paint and would have painted, he thought. It is nice to see
> flamingoes before you make this trip. (420)

The quasi-prehistoric flamingoes bring to him a reconciliation of opposites, of now and then, of beauty and ugliness, of color against the gray
brown flat of things. They establish for him the limits of daring between
the real and the fictional, the surreal colors and grotesque forms and the

incredible actual beauty. He is fully aware of "the details" that support the abstractions, the way "the roseate mass" and the "flocks" take their origin in each fact that gives him the ability to extrapolate, as artist or hunter of men. They assure him and get him to define his own aesthetic daring and courage—this, now, for a soldier going into physical battle—how real or great it is. The trip looms larger than just an exploration behind the keys: surely, "this trip" will be into death.

As they journey further inwards toward the center of darkness where lies their fatal encounter, Hudson sees "a night heron rise from the trees in the center and fly away. Then he saw two wood ibis rise and wheel and fly off with quick-flapping, then coasting, then quick-flapping wing beats downwind toward the little key" (432–33). The described flight of the wood ibis is the sort of exact ornithological description Hemingway exhibits in his later years, after he has established his home in Cuba. These birds, exactly described in their manner of flight, pinpoint the movements of Willie and the others, who are scouting for Hudson. But the flight of birds also increasingly establishes the tension. "Occasionally a bird, or a pair of birds would fly up, and they knew these birds had been frightened either by Willie or the others" (434). Ara knows that the birds must make Willie angry, and Hudson remarks, "He might as well be sending up balloons" (434). Hudson suddenly does "not like any of it now. There were too many birds getting up from the key. . . . It does not look good with so many birds getting up," and just then, "Another pair of wood ibis rose not far from the shore" (434). The birds are signals and omens:

> A bittern came out from the mangroves and Thomas Hudson heard it squawk and watched its nervous swooping flight downwind. Then he settled down to trace Willie's progress along the mangroves by the rising and the flight of the birds. When the birds stopped rising he was sure he was headed back. Then after a time they were being put up again and he knew Willie was working out the windward curve of the key. After three-quarters of an hour he saw a great white heron rise in panic and start its slow heavy wing-beats to windward and he said to Ara, "He'll be out now." (435)

How carefully Hemingway distinguishes the "nervous swooping flight" of the bittern from the "slow heavy wing-beats" of the heron, and how intricately he ties the movements of the men to the flight of the birds, so that their danger or safety is read in the skies.

In the later afternoon, the flamingoes are gone from the flat, though there is a flock of willets working over it. The willets fly up finally, but Hudson notes that there are no flamingoes and that the other birds are nearly all the same except for the flocks of golden plover.

> He remembered the seasons when the plover were gray and the others when the black feathers had the golden tinge and he remembered young Tom's pride at the first one he had ever brought home. . . . He remembered how Tom had stroked the plump white breast and touched the lovely black under markings and how he had found the boy asleep that night in his bed with his arms around the bird. He had taken the bird away very softly hoping he would not wake the boy. . . . As he had taken the golden plover into the back room where the icebox was, he felt he had robbed the boy of it. But he had smoothed its plumage carefully and laid it on one of the grilled shelves of the icebox. The next day he had painted young Tom a picture of the golden plover and the boy had taken it with him when he went off to school that year. In the picture he had tried to get the fast, running quality of the bird and the background was a long beach with coconut palms. (445–46)

This memory triggers another memory in Hudson of when he painted his sleeping son when he "lay on his back with his arms crossed and he looked like the sculpture of a young knight lying on his tomb" (446). The two associated memories link the death of Hudson's beloved son, which he already suffered earlier in the novel, with the death of the golden plover and with his own approaching death. It also establishes the relations between life, dream, and art and time and immortality, the attempt to preserve in time that which is devoured by time, which has been Hudson's dilemma. The boy and the bird are now linked in their fates, the icebox being the preservation of the bird otherwise devoured in process, even as the painting is a similar preservation of that beloved son, and even as memory itself is another variety of suspension-preservation of the timelessness of life in time. The delicacy of Hudson's touch and his son's touch of the delicate markings and plumage of the dead bird reveals Hemingway's sense of the delicacy of life in nature in the midst of its deaths. Imagining his son in his Spitfire that he flew in combat to his death, Hudson places him like the bird in the air out of which he will, like the birds, descend. He remembers his son as having said that the only thing he really worried about was the second coming of the ice age, "That and the extinction of the passenger pigeon" (447).[3] With the remark Hemingway again ties together the bird, the state of suspension that both art and the refrigerator had expressed, and the dead son and his soon-to-be-slain father. We know that it was Hemingway's own father, Dr. Clarence Hemingway, who lamented the passing of the carrier pigeon. How incredibly memory, implicitly the memory of the artist, unites life and lives and living context despite time.

Islands in the Stream has used the birds throughout as harbingers and prophets. Their flight has signaled both safety and danger, but the book ends with Hudson's probably fatal wounding. He suffers it in an ambush that is signaled not by the rising flight of birds but rather by the fact that "there were no birds rising from the mangroves" (454): there "were no birds at all and since the tide was high he knew that the birds had to be in the mangroves" (455). Since the birds have already flown, the mangroves are already stripped of their birds by the forces of death that wait for Hudson there; he has entered the place where no birds sing, where no birds are, where only silence and darkness wait for him.

Notes

1. My belief is that this is because Hemingway prejudices either/or and both/and experiences as male and female: the boundaries, oppositions, definitions, and delineations of war or civilization tend to be the terrain of masculine commitment; those of love or joining or reconciling or of unaided nature itself, where the spirit and flesh inextricably cohabit, tend to be the country of the feminine. The bias is toward heterosexual love, in which the male, unlike Jake Barnes, phallically equipped to enter the "other" undiscovered land, gains in immersion in otherness the compassionate and individuated psyche to enable him to live fully. The flown bird, here and not here, of the earth and then of the sky, in song and flight transcending but not escaping itself, is the emblem of the orgasmic reconciliation.

2. "As he has seen them" is the point. Hemingway sees as a painter sees: in "The Strange Country" (in *The Complete Short Stories of Ernest Hemingway*, 605–50), excerpts from an early version of *Islands in the Stream*, he writes:

> That was the year they shot the wild turkey as he crossed the road that early morning coming out of the mist that was just thinning with the first sun, the cypresses showing black in the silver mist and the turkey brown-bronze and lovely as he stepped onto the road, stepping high-headed, then crouching to run, then flopping on the road. (608)

Hemingway not only records the colors and movements of birds and their beauty and its impact but directs others how to observe. He describes an incoming flight of birds:

> They showed white in the cypress hammock . . . the sun shining on them in the dark foliage and as the sun lowered more came flying across the sky, flying white and slow, their long legs stretched behind them.
> "They're coming in for the night. They've been feeding out in the marsh. Watch the way they brake with their wings and the long legs slant forward to land." (611–12)

There is a similar scene, where one cradles lovingly a dead bird, in "The Strange Country." In those early version notes for *Islands in the Stream*, Hemingway wrote:

> They had put the wild turkey in the back of the seat and he had been so heavy, warm and beautiful with the shining bronze plumage, so different from the blues and blacks of a domestic turkey, and David's mother was so excited she could hardly speak. And then she had said, "No, let me hold him. I want to see him again. We can put him away later." And he had put a newspaper on her lap and she had tucked the bird's bloodied head under his wing, folding the wing carefully over it, and sat there stroking and smoothing his breast feathers while he, Roger, drove. Finally she said, "He's cold now" and had wrapped him in the paper and put him in the back of the seat again and said, "Thank you for letting me keep him when I wanted him so much." (609)

3. The memory of this appears in Hemingway's older sister's reminiscence of her childhood home. She remembers their father reacting to the thought of the extinction of the passenger pigeons: "'And to think they are extinct now,' Daddy said. 'It's wicked!'" (Sanford 11).

Works Cited

Hemingway, Ernest. *Across the River and into the Trees*. New York: Scribners, 1950.

———. *By-Line: Ernest Hemingway*. Ed. William White. New York: Scribners, 1967.

———. *The Complete Short Stories of Ernest Hemingway*. New York: Scribners, 1987.

————. *Death in the Afternoon*. 1932. New York: Scribners, 1950.

————. *For Whom the Bell Tolls*. 1940. New York: Scribners, 1968.

————. *Islands in the Stream*. New York: Scribners, 1970.

————. *The Old Man and the Sea*. New York: Scribners, 1952.

————. *The Short Stories of Ernest Hemingway*. New York: Scribners, 1938.

————. "The Strange Country." *The Complete Short Stories of Ernest Hemingway*. New York: Scribners, 1987.

Sanford, Marcelline Hemingway. *At the Hemingway's: The Years of Innocence*. Boston: Little, Brown, 1962.

25

Androgyny and Individuation in the Work of Ernest Hemingway

Hemingway, whose work generally exhibits a dramatic therapeutic journey from psychic wounds toward healing and psychic wholeness, is superbly versed in and consistently studies both the masks of individuation and the real and necessary stages on the way toward psychic health. To see this, one must first examine what is meant here by androgyny and individuation.

In the *Oxford English Dictionary*, all first-definition meanings of androgyny or its variations focus on physical evidence of characteristics of both sexes, and the term is there scarcely distinguished from hermaphroditism. Only in secondary meanings does the dictionary consider internal exemplifications of sexual crossover. Individuation, on the other hand, is so fully associated with the terminology of Carl Jung that its major meaning in our time seems to derive from him: it defines the process whereby contents of the unconscious are finally consciously incorporated to become parts at last of the whole personality, which has ultimate uniqueness and individuality and maturity through and by means of this process of integration and absorption.

To quote briefly from Hall and Nordby's restating of Jung:

> Let us illustrate transcendence by considering the integration of the anima with the masculine side of man's personality. At the same time that each of these components is being permitted to individuate by being expressed (rather than repressed) in conscious

acts, they are also tending to form an amalgam. That is, each conscious act comes to express both sides of a man's nature. Instead of opposition or separation, there is a harmonious blend. The man who has integrated his anima with his maleness is not one whose behavior is sometimes in the masculine mode and sometimes in the feminine mode. He is not part man and part woman. Rather, a true synthesis between opposites has been achieved so that it may be said transcendence has abolished gender except in a biological sense. (Hall and Nordby, *A Primer of Jungian Psychology*)

The quotation well illustrates by contrast the prevailing focus upon gender that exists in bisexual stages of androgyny and the tendency of individuation to move toward the ideal state of genderless being. That is almost all I here wish to take from these terms. My thesis is that Hemingway not only made a comparable distinction but also made it a focal point for meaning in his novels. It is possible to say that Hemingway created novels that are with few exceptions ritually based on rites of inversion and crossover into the territory of the other, rites that closely resemble the individuation process at work, observed in its fulfillment and failure. Frequently in his works, a protagonist, disdainful of the masks of sexual crossover, undergoes a major psychic integrative sexual evolution.

Close readers of Hemingway know that androgynous imagery is plentiful in his work; they also know that women dressed or coiffured as men, or men assuming feminine characteristics, are not necessarily sexually integrated, certainly not in the work of a writer who plays with and uses masks as astutely as Ernest Hemingway. Similarly, critics would no more assume a male/female balance in the transvestite than assume that Frederic Henry in *A Farewell to Arms* is Italian because of the uniform he wears. The homosexual and lesbian, in drag, inversion, or role playing, are not necessarily effeminized or masculinized by their assumptions or nature. Jake's attitude toward the homosexuals in *The Sun Also Rises* is meant to be read not as simplistic bias but rather as Jake's revulsion, that of a uniquely sexually incapacitated man offended by their mockery of genuine heterosexual bonding, the act he seems excluded from. And David's late attitude toward Catherine's lesbian experiments in *The Garden of Eden* is meant to be read not as exasperation but rather as his firm recognition that her inversion misses any profound assumption of the nature of the other sex. These attitudes express a contempt for the mask of integration, for the substanceless image, for a fiction that is not participating in truth. Hemingway was always intent on fiction as a mode of access to fundamental truth, and upon genuine solutions to complex psychosexual problems, and he scorned simplistic and self-deceptive alternatives.

Although Hemingway focused throughout his work on role reversal, sex shifting, costuming, masking, and intricate inversions, he well understood the distance between external adoption of characteristics of the other sex and a fully realized psychic synthesis based on complex rites of integration. That is one reason why in A Farewell to Arms he gives us what seems to be Frederic's assumption of morning sickness and mock pregnancy at the beginning of the very next chapter after Frederic learns from Catherine of her pregnancy: partly the better to highlight the absurd nature and the impossibility of fulfillment of a desire to take the place of another. (We should remember that The Sun Also Rises derided scapegoat psychology, in which the scapegoat is made to take the place of others and suffer for their sins. Frederic can no more take Catherine's place—she will die alone—than he can finally really be her lost boy lover or than the soldier whom he sends to try to hold his place for him on the train will be allowed to possess what is not his to possess.) Nevertheless, the scene metaphorically announces an unconscious male desire to, at that moment, assume feminine identity. Whatever the reasons for Frederic's sickness, and however bad the lovers' relationship may then be, the reader is meant to recognize that the two lovers are, finally in Milan, implicated in one another. Catherine's subsequently expressed desire in Switzerland to become more like the male and to make Frederic more like the woman, through hair styling, a desire reinvoked by heroines in other Hemingway novels, and her simultaneously expressed desire to have had his gonorrhea and to have stayed with his girls, reveal a psychic yearning to take unto herself male identity, for several implied reasons. By assuming his male identity, she would better understand other women's behavior toward men, as well as male expectation and performance and desire. The soldiers in chapter 1 who, carrying bulky equipment, go to war looking as if they are six months pregnant, early establish the image for bisexual androgyny.

In For Whom the Bell Tolls, we vividly see that Pilar's assumption of what was patriarchal authority in the cave is an inversion of order, one in which she is described as cowing Pablo as she inverts the cycling stirring spoon to make it a phallic, masculine baton of authority with which she now commands. This sexual inversion is carefully orchestrated by a woman who acknowledges a seeming lesbian attraction toward Maria and whose masculine characteristics are carefully defined. The reader is meant to hear against the Pablo/Pilar inversion the history of Robert Jordan's parents, where his "bully" of a mother similarly unmanned his father, who subsequently became the *cow*ardly suicide. The reader is not spared the full psychic effect of the woman's effeminization of the man: Jordan tells us that after he dropped the gun that had killed his father into a high mountain lake, his horse, old Bess, *bucked and bucked* while he *swung* on this old "rocking horse" (337). The cycling of the masculine and the masculinization of the feminine (upon the immersion of the father's gun in the feminine lake) are Hemingway's meanings.

The major scene of the novel, the execution of the fascists in Pablo's town, a tale told by Pilar, ritually and mythically studies the replacement of the solar by the lunar principle and the systematic overthrow/extinction of patriarchal, Apollonian attributes and their replacement by Dionysian/feminine alternatives. (See my essay "Pilar's Tale: The Myth of the Message" included in this volume.) A vital vision of the novel is that the river is rising and that under such a historical imperative there is a necessity for the male principle to adapt if it is going to survive: Pablo's reversal, or change, paralleled with Paul's on the road to Damascus, is the miracle of the novel. Hemingway here studies, as he has in "The Snows of Kilimanjaro," *To Have and Have Not*, and *Green Hills of Africa*, the need for an effeminization of the masculine psyche in our time.

In *Across the River and into the Trees*, there is a moment when Cantwell, after learning that Renata has her menstrual period, is kissed by her hard, so that he can then taste his own blood in his own mouth, which he enjoys as he watches her make her mouth new with lipstick. Her moon-related cycles become momentarily his. It is important to note that she is the agent of his transformation while he is the one to meaningfully accept it: she brings the blood to his mouth, and he understands and likes its meaning as sexual inversion. This metaphoric experience of menstruation in the midst of his sympathy for the woman's unique biological situation finds a corollary in *The Garden of Eden* in David's acknowledgment of his own enjoyment of the inversion that Catherine presses upon him, as it does also in the moment in *Across the River* when the green emeralds that have been passed down matrilinearly through Renata's family are placed in his own pocket. Feeling them there, his reflections become speculations on the lot of a woman, who goes through each day with the danger and dilemma of that feminine fertility in her "pocket." We are not to overlook the fact that it is she who has slipped them into his pocket like a thief, and that she is therefore, like the Catherine of *The Garden of Eden* or the Pilar of *For Whom the Bell Tolls*, the agent of his effeminization. Just what she has stolen from him is not hard to guess. Such empathic projection, like that of Frederic with his morning sickness, is not a mere external appropriation of characteristics of the other sex, not merely costume and masking, but a genuine psychological and physical attempt at internalization of the feminine.

Readers of Hemingway need to be alert to the difference between the portrayal of Brett as "a chap" (*Sun Also Rises*, 22, 32) and of the homosexuals in heterosexual parody and the portrayal of Frederic Henry's genuine nausea and Cantwell's real blood in his mouth to recognize that Hemingway is here describing another order of crossover projection into "the other." Neither of the protagonists in these *A Farewell to Arms* and *Across the River and into the Trees* scenes is merely playing: though Frederic's nausea is related to his jaundice and Cantwell's blood is not menstrual, the associations are genuine and rest on a sense of genuine empathic projection. When Cantwell, in spectatorial detachment, says, "My poor Daughter!" (110) upon learning that Renata has her monthly period, he at once pities and suffers *for* her, and then, as he assumes a metaphor of menstruation within himself, he suffers *with* her. This suffering *with* rather than *for* shifts the basis of attention from sacrificial suffering *for* another to incorporation of the other *within* the self. Such acts are no more meant to make these protagonists into the woman than Nick's empathy as he watches the trout in "Big Two-Hearted River" is meant to make him become the fish he observes. But we have seen that as Nick sees the trout tighten as he faces into and against the current, his own heart tightens, and we learn throughout that story that such projective transcendence of the egocentric self in acts of *Einfühlung* or self-transcendent empathy are a part of genuine therapy, the way to Nick's healing: that he moves toward a whole self as he similarly takes external nature within himself, as he psychologically witnesses the shadow and internalizes it. The moment when Cantwell identifies with Renata in her cyclical nature, acknowledging the wheel from which she cannot be detached, like Catherine's Catherine wheel on which she is martyred, is but one of an elaborate series of moments of love in which Cantwell comes to accept and inhabit and take within himself the cyclical base of her being, as such moments systematically replace the dialectical either/or dynamics of his warrior mode. Other moments, like those in the gondola when

Renata gives the commands to the gondolier and assumes command of the mode of loving in the gondola, or when the craft itself is laid on its other side or the lovers in that craft "change over"—moments like those other, larger inversions when Cantwell, in seizing his love and abandoning his métier to court his death, places himself in the realm of "the other," that Great Goddess whose avatar is Renata—compel a psychic transformation.

If androgyny may suggest merely the mask of adaptation rather than the state of holistic synthesis, masturbation may similarly suggest false because merely abstract integration while remaining firmly egocentrically centered. Its mode implies avoidance or ignorance of the other, and therefore masturbation and onanistic alternatives to full heterosexual exploration or inhabitation of "the other" are frequent in Hemingway's works and are judged with contempt. In *The Sun Also Rises*, *To Have and Have Not*, *For Whom the Bell Tolls*, and *The Garden of Eden*, masturbation is studied as a device guaranteed to develop egocentric imagination at the expense of the true or genuine knowledge of "the other" that is necessary to mature development. "Continence is the foe of heresy" (164) is one of the messages of *For Whom the Bell Tolls* because one cannot inhabit or cross over to the other side without gaining a knowledge and sympathy that make political slogans absurd. Chapter 31 of that novel studies the egocentric license that the imagination purchases through continence and drives the lesson home that to be "there" without the other is unacceptable: one cannot accept fulfillment at another's hands (climax induced by another who himself/herself is not coevally fulfilled) or spill one's seed on the ground and remain a significant human being: "How did Onan turn out? . . . I don't remember ever hearing any more about Onan" (342).

The supreme example of extrication from (because of fear of) the other is found in "The End of Something," and there is a good example of it in *Across the River and into the Trees*, when the cowardly soldiers who wish to avoid the line and to live forever incapacitate themselves for duty by infecting themselves with gonnorheal pus collected in a matchbox. The poetry of the image suggests a fear of the feminine that is equivalent to a fear of death, and it suggests that the only contact or "match" the coward is able to make is one that avoids the cycle, one that would insist upon avoiding immersion—by recourse to a spurious mask of synthesis based on a *square* that will help one avoid the *line*. How to lose the masculine through fear of the feminine is part of the message.

Frequently Hemingway's male/female relations are examples of the error of those who look for solution to personal inadequacy in mutual fulfillment, who try to solve the problem of personal psychic immaturity through an external bonding: Catherine in *A Farewell to Arms* is not mad, but her desire that the two should become "one" is a form of madness. This desire, shared by subsequent heroines, is for Hemingway the false logic that aborts a necessary individuation process. Francis Macomber and the Hemingway of *Green Hills of Africa* become truly whole only when they abandon their mates and go off to establish within the self the rituals and devices by which they become complete. Also, Frederic fishing with the barman and playing billiards with Count Greffi is becoming in those carefully structured rituals shared with other men—both of which are based on rites of crossover reversal, as were the rites of Jake and Bill at Burguete in *The Sun Also Rises*—more a whole human being whom Catherine can love, one more in tune with the other side of his own nature than he obviously has ever yet become in bed with Catherine.

That Hemingway's works are often focused on men without women only underscores his accurate belief that the individuation process is one that has to be accomplished inside the self and has little to do with bonding with another, though it obviously has everything to do with knowledge of "the other." Men and women find maturity through an accepting acknowledgment of the other sex within themselves, which they explore or give expression to within the self. This experience is essentially a private ritualistic acceptance and acknowledgment of the anima or animus. Cantwell's almost ritualized explorations of his softer side, a journey on which he is conducted by Renata, are typical, as are those of Catherine in *The Garden of Eden*, who tries to discover her own masculine nature. Renata is indeed so much the principle rather than the woman who reconciles birth and death and love and war—the paradigm of the functioning of the anima within the individuation process itself, which humanizes and completes the old warrior Cantwell—that she somewhat fails to emerge as a character. Nevertheless, although there are only men aboard Harry Morgan's chartered fishing boat in *To Have and Have Not*, we need not have a woman aboard to know that when Mr. Johnson loses the great fish of the sea through failing to keep the butt of the fishing rod in the socket and subsequently when he decamps by plane with the money he owes Harry—thereby becoming the abandoning father figure who disappears into the skies after having betrayed the sea and lost

Harry's, his surrogate son's, "equipment"—we are reading an intricate paradigm of sexual injury sustained by the son whose father fails to establish the terms of proper male/female integration. Johnson is a man who fails to properly respect or relate to the moon-driven sea beneath him, the sea that Harry will ritually accept as he lies dying and where, unlike Mr. Johnson, he will take "the roll." As Harry hangs on the wheel and accepts the roll, we are witness not only to an emblematic effeminization of the man who will soon announce that "a *man alone* ain't got no bloody fucking chance" (225) but also to the creation of the image of a man who is sacrificially dying for the sake of others and in his death is acknowledging and accepting the feminine cyclical base of nature in whose terms and for which he dies. By the time Hemingway writes *For Whom the Bell Tolls*, this image will be magnificently orchestrated: Jordan, though split into a nonresponsive, crushed left side and a responsive right side by his wound, will get himself at last turned over into firing position, and he will die on those absolute evergreen yet brown (fallen because necessarily deciduous) pine needles, die acknowledging and accepting the integrative rites that have made him at last whole.

The missing feminine world, in most of the early stories, exists on another side, across a boundary, in the realm of unconsciousness, darkness and/or death, and the men often, in what is judged to be a censurable cowardice, try to hold off this dark, threatening other half that they are forced at last to inhabit. When Hemingway in "The End of Something" has Nick break his contact with Marjorie, avatar of that dangerous because complicating reproductive world, he carefully codes this feminine world that Nick turns from as the physical woman, the dark moon-driven waters, and instinctive and intuitive rather than rational controls. These are precisely not the terms that Nick and Bill of "The Three-Day Blow" confront in the dry, logical, interior world of the father that endorses light, spirit, and abstraction. These stories, like others of Hemingway's youth, including his high school stories, establish an unremitting dialectical opposition between two antithetical forces that are finally placed in interactive relations so that an immature protagonist is made to recognize and finally inhabit the country of "the other."

Jake Barnes in *The Sun Also Rises* is remarkably given as a de-phallused protagonist so that Hemingway may clearly argue for a thesis he pursues throughout his career, that the development of the feminine side of a man's nature, or his acceptance of his anima, is not dependent upon his being able to physically enter a woman, any more than a woman's development of her masculine nature, or her animus, is dependent upon her being able to be entered by a man. Though Brett, who has curves like a racing yacht, may bob her hair to be more like one of "the chaps," she remains at the end essentially immature, while Romero, who knows how to enter into the terrain of the bull and to become one with his adversary, succeeds. Jake, who learns from Romero how this bonding with the other can take place at no vital expense to the self, has also crossed over and in that alien country found himself at last. It is only after Jake has learned Romero's lesson, and after his own therapeutic ordering and cleansing at San Sebastian, that he is prepared as a more whole man to again meet Brett. Hemingway brings Jake to the sea with a description of the beach sand that is precisely taken from the earlier description of the rolled level yellow sand of the arena prepared for Romero's corrida. At five o'clock, *a las cinco de la tarde*, the moment of the corrida, Jake approaches his own bull of the sea in his own suit of lights; and there he reconciles, as methodically as did the younger Nick Adams in "Big Two-Hearted River," sun and sea (or water), shadow and brightness, watery depths and airy heights, and both sides of himself. The reconciliation of antitheses within himself absolves him of a pursuit of completion in external bonding: he need no longer reach beyond himself to be completed by Brett. Bumping against her in the taxi at the novel's end, as he was at the beginning, he finally knows what their individual limits are, and he is able to recognize that the image of a wholeness with Brett is merely spurious "pretty" thought. Throughout the book the masculine names implicit in the names Hemingway's women bear—Brett, Jo, Frances, Georgette, Edna—as well as Brett's attitude and attire, and the urgency in the homosexual crowd to dance with Georgette, all express false or fraudulent masks and signs of a deeply needed genuine sexual synthesis.

In *A Farewell to Arms*, the novel repudiates Catherine's desire that she and Frederic should become one, or each like the other, at a cost to the self that the novel has constantly accurately measured. To her fantasy are opposed the realistic pragmatic necessities that Frederic gradually determines are inescapable, and the need for each, in his or her uniquely separate self, to become whole. This is the Frederic who has experienced death and then returned to life; who has been both soldier and deserter; apparent Italian and apparent Austrian infiltrator; who has fathered a child and then, upon learning of that fact, assumed in his own body the attributes and semblance of a mother's pregnancy. Such attempts at physical fusion with one's opposite, albeit impelled by a psychic need for fusion, teach one of the harder lessons of the book, the impossibility of externally becoming the "other" and the need instead to come to terms with it inside the self. In *Green Hills of Africa*, Hemingway can at last uncompetitively be joined to Karl, and rejoin Poor Old Mama and Pop, only after he has crossed over without them to the other side. It is to the rolling country on the far side that Francis Macomber must go to gain *his* victory—where in virgin, new and unexplored, unhunted country he goes through intricate rituals of brotherhood that bind him to his black trackers and guides. The thumb-jerking ritual at the base of the reconciliation process is one in which Hemingway assumes both the male and female roles. Before the hunt is over he has acknowledged his "Black Chinaman" Mama-worshipping tracker M'Cola, who is throughout identified with the feminine, as "immeasurably the better *man*" (*Green Hills* 269). In both *For Whom the Bell Tolls* and *The Fifth Column*, the protagonist is a man approaching his successful apotheosis by having become an operator behind enemy lines. Operation "behind the lines" is a covert explanation of the writer's, Hemingway's, technique, and it also places each of his protagonists (in a Jungian sense) in the feared and dangerous territory of "the other," where, indeed, a writer empathically must place himself. It is there that Robert Jordan is able to coevally have the realities of love and war, to experience the immaculately conceptive Maria (Mary) as the potentially biologically reproductive Rabbit as in one sleeping bag they bond male hardness to feminine softness and discover the coevality of now and forever. Santiago of *The Old Man and the Sea*, Colonel Cantwell of *Across the River and into the Trees*, and Robert Jordan of *For Whom the Bell Tolls* are all split men who come to terms with the other halves of their warring selves. Santiago's "betraying" and seemingly dead side must be made to come alive and cooperate with his good side, and Cantwell's split hand, that he considers insensate and dead, must, by Renata—whose very name speaks of the rebirth she oversees— be resurrected to feeling and function. She convinces him that "there is very much sensation in that hand" (85). Jordan, before he dies, gets turned over and at the end is "completely integrated now" (471). Cantwell's observant doctor has noted the increased intraocular and intracranial pressure between the two halves of this dialectically split old warrior. As this hard veteran of many battles awakens the "other" part of the self, crossing the many bridges of Venice and the psychic bridge he must cross to get to his other side, to bind himself to the goodness and kindness he at last accepts, he simultaneously accepts in the hands of the Goddess of Love the fact of death that he has always as a man of war held off. Cantwell's journey from the front seat to the back seat of his car, as though to there accept his death on wheels, is one of many such psychic journeys in Hemingway toward the realized individuated state.

That the Hemingway protagonist achieves at last a genderless individuated state most often goes unseen, for he achieves his psychic goal only *at* or just before his death, through what seem to be masculine modes and means. His death, however, acknowledges the cyclical terms he has finally accepted. There is an additional pattern to be noted: in Hemingway, bisexual experimentation seems to compel and provide the paradigm for individuation—the artificially androgynous woman in "Cat in the Rain," *The Sun Also Rises, For Whom the Bell Tolls,* and *The Garden of Eden* acts as a catalyst to expose the need for integrative wholeness in her male counterpart. Jake, Jordan, and David, as well as Francis Macomber, *in reaction* learn necessary rites of individuated wholeness. Behind this aesthetic pattern we might choose to see the desperate strategies of survival that Hemingway was fashioning for someone in his father's dilemma (the dilemma of not accepting one's "other" side in an integrated, individuated way) and that he needed to discover for his own fulfillment as man and artist.

I have glanced at these several works to make a point: that the constant dramatic direction of Hemingway's work is toward the realized individuated state. My corollary is that androgyny in his novels is often merely an appropriated mask, worn by one who has not achieved the desired state. Hemingway was not driven to his imagery by his particular and incidental history but was led to it, as any artist always is, by the need to find in his art the externalized exemplification of wholeness and whole organic being. The works of art that Hemingway fashioned are consistently and sequentially studies in the psychic possession of integrity and a completely individuated state, as are all works of art. If their imagery seems obsessively fixed upon role or gender reversal, I would judge that this has more to do with the historical situation he witnessed and evaluated in his time than with his personal situation. He well understood that it was becoming more and more necessary that radical measures be taken to adjust the sexual and psychic imbalance of his age.

Works Cited

Hall, Calvin S., and Vernon J. Nordby. *A Primer of Jungian Psychology*. New York: New American Library, 1973.

Hemingway, Ernest. *Across the River and into the Trees*. New York: Scribners, 1950.

———. *For Whom the Bell Tolls*. 1940. New York: Scribners, 1968.

———. *Green Hills of Africa*. 1935. New York: Scribners, 1963.

———. *The Sun Also Rises*. 1926. New York: Scribners, 1954.

———. *To Have and Have Not*. 1937. New York: Scribners, 1965.

26

Gentlemen's Agreement

The Ernest Hemingway–Carlos Baker
Correspondence in the Charles B. Field Collection
of the Stanford University Library

In 1985 the Stanford University Libraries received a large and extraordinary gift in the Charles D. Field Collection of Ernest Hemingway. Together with an additional gift in 1986, the collection has become a bonanza for Hemingway scholars. It includes first editions, galley proofs of Hemingway's fiction, articles, scripts, poems, translations of his work into thirteen different languages, photographs, and letters that Hemingway wrote to and received from nearly forty correspondents. Among these letters is the extensive and rich exchange between Hemingway and his important critic and biographer Carlos Baker.

The Hemingway-Baker correspondence takes place largely during the years 1951 to 1954, when Hemingway is living at the Finca Vigía outside Havana. Mary Welsh Hemingway, the last of his four wives, skilled at guarding him from a too-intrusive public, is with him. When Baker first contacts him, Hemingway is fifty—the same age as Colonel Cantwell of *Across the River and into the Trees*, his latest book, which has been unconscionably savaged by the critics. He is at once smarting from the wounds of that cruel reception and already completing *The Old Man and the Sea*, which, after publication in 1952, will lead him to the Nobel Prize in 1954. Ironically, Baker, who is to become Hemingway's definitive biographer, first writes to him on February 15, 1951, two days before Hemingway is to reputedly complete his most celebrated work.

Carlos Baker, then a professor of English at Princeton University, is at work on a large-scale, critical study, *Hemingway: The Writer as Artist*, and his first letter is an appeal to the author for help in getting the facts straight. Hemingway's response, initially to this appeal, rapidly creates a friendly exchange to which Baker's book becomes almost secondary. Their correspondence continues well after the publication of *The Writer as Artist*.

To read these letters is an experience at once poignant and refreshing, for what emerges is not the "established" image of Hemingway as a man caught in a world of violent rites and rituals, where love is never far from war, and war, psychic or actual, is constant. Rather, we find a reflective figure, a man at home, writing, reminiscing, and speculating about that nightmare world he has known as reporter, correspondent, soldier, and passionate adventurer. He bears on his body and deep in his psyche the multiple wounds of those encounters. In these letters, however, he seems to want to put aside that life, which belongs to nobody but the artist himself, and to guard what measure of peace he has. This very different man from the one who begot the myth seems to ask for understanding, even to yearn for it.

The difference, I think, is in part due to the depth to which he has been hurt—something that also shows in his other published letters (*Ernest Hemingway: Selected Letters*) and in part to a carefulness uniquely elicited by his new correspondent, whose delicacy of introduction and evident code of values Hemingway quickly respects and warms to. With Baker he remarkably *does* become confidential, but he remains mannered with this stranger and only rarely and then with quick apology brings in any roughness or sparring. He apologizes repeatedly to Baker: for hastiness of reaction, for tardiness of reply, for any imagined hint that he might wish to lead, control, or limit Baker's evaluations or judgments.

As Hemingway seeks in Baker someone who can share his perceptions and recognize the increasing hostility of the world about him, he becomes confessional and vulnerable. He tries to explain the values by which he has lived, and he looks to Baker for an understanding of certain apparently vanishing attitudes. Fortunately, this new, younger correspondent can hear his lament and share his point of view.

Baker's initial February letter may have been fortuitous indeed, for it catches Hemingway at a high point after completing *The Old Man and the Sea*; it is an appeal for help from the younger man to the master craftsman—offering the teacher-acolyte situation that Hemingway repeatedly created in his life and in his literature; and it declares Baker's respect for truth, Hemingway's greatest desideratum. Baker wants his critical study (which was to become one of the first books on Hemingway to look systematically at the consistent and deep patterning and structuring of Hemingway's works) to be a "true book. . . . I would like to destroy the legend, puncture the windbags, clear the air a little, and show your achievement in something like its true dimensions. There has been enough malice and lying and misunderstanding. My motive is to straighten out and make right." He assures Hemingway, "Mainly I want to tell you that you can trust me. I don't want to invade what is private."

That careful definition of the limits of his inquiry brings from Hemingway, two days later, a candid and even confessional three-page letter, illustrating at once the fundamental generosity and kindness and goodness of the man (qualities that have been downplayed or obscured by many biographers who have chosen instead to focus on his apparent machismo or violence). The letter also suggests his loneliness and his desire to find a confidante capable of a disinterested honesty, someone who can share the artist's agony with him.

Who would dream that a single-page letter from a stranger could elicit from this major artist such a confessional and reflective outpouring? Several times in it he says that a writer has a right to his private life "while [he is] alive," and that his art matters but not his life. "If I denied every lie that is written about me," he writes, "I would have no time to do anything else. You could not set the record straight in a hundred years." Accepting Baker as "an honorable man," he pleads, "Couldn't you just write about what I've written. I would help you on that in any way I could. That is all that matters."

Baker's answer a few days later assures Hemingway that his focus of concern is indeed the work, that his motives are "entirely honorable," and that he would "sooner cut off an arm than limit your freedom as writer." The four-page letter establishes explicitly the boundaries of his concern: in his book there is "nothing private or personal"; his job is one of interpretation and does "not aim to gossip at all"; he will avoid anything even remotely scandalous, and biographical material will be kept to "an absolute minimum." He offers to clear any part of his book at any time with Hemingway.

The contract that underlies the book and the correspondence is established: it rests on the sort of men they are, their mutual sense of honor, and an attempt to be honest without injuring Hemingway's privacy and freedom. Baker wants Hemingway to know "as thoroughly as possible what I am up to and what my motives are."

398   Gentlemen's Agreement

Reassurances continue throughout their correspondence. Baker tells Hemingway repeatedly that he may trust his discretion, good will, and honesty and that Baker would never "attempt to pull a fast one on an honest man whose writing I like and respect." Hemingway in turn refuses to intrude upon Baker's "reading" of his life or work, although he admits there are places where he would disagree with the interpretations. He acknowledges that his *own* vision may be "completely prejudiced and wrong" and that every man should have his free judgment.

Their exchange becomes a little like a conversation between two gentlemen reflecting on the decline of an established order. Like Jefferson's *veritable aristoi*, both are aristocrats by taste and inclination, by their sense of responsibility and service—something instilled in Hemingway by his father and grandfather in Oak Park—and both are beset by a world that doesn't seem to understand, or hasn't educated itself to understand, certain fundamental rules of honor among men. Discovering their common code of behavior, Hemingway makes himself more accessible to Baker.

In a much later letter of "June II 1953" (*sic*) to Baker, in which he is decrying the "mumbo-jumbo" of a self-styled psychoanalytic critic, Hemingway places Jefferson first on a list of "prophets" he would rather "believe in" than Freud, Jung, or Adler. This reaction is predictable, for Hemingway had Jefferson's physiocratic and democratic bias and therefore also a quick contempt for the easy rhetorics of those who fail to back their abstractions with knowledge or commitment. (In *Across the River*, Colonel Cantwell partly defines a "jerk" as "a man who has never worked at his trade . . . truly" (97). Like Jefferson, Hemingway believed in values taken from knowledge firmly related to, being gained through, experience. Talent and craft and expertise are, for him, finally moral.

The unimportance of his life compared to the primacy of his art is a major theme in Hemingway's letters. In a four-page handwritten note, he reveals that it makes him "truly sick at the stomach" to talk about himself. "I care so damned much about my work and my life is no more important than my body will be when I am dead." His life, he declares, "is as pleasant a subject as the quick of the end of a finger with the nail torn off (other parts of it are fine and sound and clear. But who knows about them?)." Speaking of his work, he describes the reality of fiction when measured by the unreality of fact: "People do not know what happens when you write i.e. how it makes everything else: life, death or green bananas seem completely without importance." Becoming confidential: "But Carlos, you have to invent from *something* when you write fiction. If you describe it is flat. If you make it up it is round and you walk clear around it; or if it is a forest you can walk into it."

As Hemingway attempts to answer Baker's questions, he discusses the writing he is doing and his plans and hopes. He also reflects upon the education he gave himself in languages and cultures; his years in Paris in the twenties (Stein, Pound, McAlmon, Ford) and in Spain before and during the Spanish Civil War (his lack of politics, though being an "anti-fascist from the murder of Matteotti" and one who "had no Stalinist period"); other writers (Conrad, Anderson, Crane, James—"It's hard to write about James because people are for him or against him like politics [or the church]"); and literary critics.

The pain of betrayal by critics flows through Hemingway's letters. He increasingly views his attackers as men of little candor and no conscience or honor, men who do things "no human being could do." He documents their "blackmail" and their pettiness: "I think Dante might have made a special circle for some of these characters."

His own conscience rules his behavior. It drives him to work; it forces him to amend hasty, intemperate reactions with kindness, "trying to make up for being a bastard." He hates his own faults, labors to discipline his temper, and suffers deeply when he feels he has been unfair.

At one point Hemingway was put upon by a critic he felt had been seriously injuring and maligning him. Yet when the critic confessed that the publication of his interpretative book meant his "academic future and whether he and his wife [ate] or not," Hemingway gave him previously blocked permission rights to quote and also turned over his own expected share of reprint rights to the critic. "But it is a new approach to have someone want you to help them destroy the value of your work, your peace of mind and your happiness in working because they need money." To Baker he exclaims, "Carlos, what kind of ethics do these people have?" Of another critic, whose intrusive research Hemingway felt was destructive, interfering with his writing, compromising him with friends, and muddying up creative waters Hemingway had carefully kept clear for eventual "fishing," he exclaims: "Are there no morals nor standards nor ethics in this metier?"

Acknowledging that he has aided the very critics who are trying to do him in, he writes: "I have many times had a fighter say to me, 'Don't knock me out, Ernie. Let me stay.' You should always knock them out because they will knock you out. . . . It isn't much of an epitaph to say, 'He never put his thumb in a one-eyed man's good eye.' But I will settle for that."

His love of writing and his dedication to his craft are constantly revealed in the letters, but also his art's function as a means toward a state of grace, and his own need to rediscover nature in its pristine state. "But let's us [sic] always write so we can wake up clean in the morning with the same feeling as a desert morning." He sees the loss of a pure nature to a society filled with greed: Milan was ruined for him, "not from bombing; from cupidity," and Oak Park, Illinois, where he grew up, had been subdivided into cheap housing developments and gas stations. "This isn't complaint. It is just comment. But where the hell does a man go now?" Of course, for him, the "sea is still ok." At the death of his mother, whom he had come to hate, he remembers "how beautiful she was when she was young before everything went to hell in our family and . . . how happy we all were as children before it all broke up."

Hemingway recognized the distance between his own awareness of his art and the general critical unperceptiveness. He was continually caught between his need for genuine response and the malice he accurately saw in the world; he knew his own competence, trusted his own judgments, and astutely gauged the limitations of his critics.

> I love to have people care for my stuff and understand it. The trouble is that I get truly embarrassed (that looks like bare-assed) at praise and the embarrassed thing makes me seem surly. We all need to [be] spoken well of sometimes if we've done anything really well (and you spend your life trying to do things as well as they possibly can be done and better) but I have never learned yet not to be made shy by praise even when I need it the most.

> If I didn't know what was good when I write it they ought to ground me as a writer. But when you know how good something is and say so in a natural way, as impersonally as you would discuss a horse or the merits and demerits of the Red Sea or different rifles or the speed attained by birds in flight or the good and bad points of a good aircraft, then you are supposed to be concerned and bragging. If you don't want to discuss it then you are churlish.

For the casual reader, the letters between the two men are important for what they reveal of Hemingway, but for the Hemingway scholar they matter additionally for what they explain of the sources and the nature of the Baker/Hemingway relation. Their eventual general publication should do much to answer the questions that repeatedly rise with respect to Carlos Baker's yet-definitive biography, *Ernest Hemingway: A Life Story*.

To many—to Malcolm Cowley, to Truman Capote, to William Seward, to Hemingway's son Jack—the biography gave a radically distorted picture of the man, which could be explained only as a mistake or as the result of an unspecifiable but contaminating bias. Many questioned why Mary had given the role of official biographer to a man who had never met her husband. A. E. Hotchner justified his own biography, *Papa Hemingway*, as an attempt to rectify what he felt was the false image provided by Baker's book. And both books, in their polar opposition, are probably in part responsible for the spate of biographies that have, each in turn, sought to describe the true lineaments of the man.

I think that anyone reading the Baker-Hemingway correspondence of 1951 to 1954 will grant that Mary Hemingway had at least two good reasons for the choice she made: no other major Hemingway critic had as intimate and understanding a relation with her husband as Carlos Baker had, albeit by correspondence, and *The Writer as Artist* was one of the very few large-scale attempts to get beneath the surface of Hemingway's art.

Yet for many who knew Hemingway—as well as for some who knew him only from his work—the tone of the biography was wrong, the sense of the man they knew or knew about was absent. I ran into the problem regularly with my Hemingway students at San Francisco State University, and one day in 1980 I wrote to Carlos Baker, who had been my teacher at Princeton, asking him if he could help me understand why the tone existed. (I had described to Mary Hemingway the precise nature of this disturbing "prejudice" as a factor of verbs—pejorative descriptive verbs like *lumber, glower,* and *glare* might be part of the portrait of an action none had witnessed—and she had replied, suggesting I should notice "the adverbs.") Baker's answer to me, however, was remarkably generous and candid:

> The point you raise about my attitude towards EH in the biography is not new to me. The feelings of those readers who find between the lines a slightly acerbic tone may be founded on something. It might have been different if I had set out to write a "critical" biography in the other sense, analyzing and discussing his works in connection with his life. Since I care very much for his work, even after

half a century of reading and rereading it, the presence in the biography of that kind of enthusiasm might have served to change the impression of cool objectivity (which was what I aimed at) that now either bothers or interests your students. . . . I don't really think that a "negative tone" predominates in the biography. No man can be in all respects a doubledyed hero to his valet or his biographer.

I quote this material at length to suggest that neither the several guesses of many critics nor Baker's own statement explains the seeming bias adequately but that the letters in the Charles Field collection come closer. They were written during a period when Hemingway felt unusually beset by hyenas, sycophants, and hostile critics (he even suggests a conspiracy of viciousness to put him out of business). These letters set careful limits beyond which a critic had no right to go if he respected a writer.

It is my guess that, when Baker later assumed the role of biographer, the limits he had agreed to in 1951—limits he had seen others abuse with painful results—trapped him unconsciously in a double bind: a promise to Hemingway to leave his private life alone and a promise to posterity and scholarship to reveal the truth insofar as he could find it. Though Baker apparently believed in his own integrity, this split in loyalties may have led to an unconscious hostility toward his role and his subject. The result, I feel, was a tendency for him to accent the negative aspects of the man to which he felt access was denied. This disapproving tone might never have existed had he been spared the assurances he so lavishly gave at the beginning of the relationship. Hemingway was harder on himself, always, than any one else could ever be: writing, for him, was a lonely, solitary activity that took him far out and deeply into himself. He was seldom self-deceived. He didn't need strangers inaccurately and uncomprehendingly speculating about moral faults that he had already carefully confronted in his work. Therefore, he could write to Baker on April 1, 1951: "The writing of a book is sort of like pitching a one hit game, on a cold and windy day, with a sore arm and in front of empty stands. Afterwards you read about it in the papers and you say, 'Oh shit. I don't have to read about it. I pitched the son of a bitch.'"

NOTE

There has been much glib criticism referring to Hemingway's paranoia, but any close critic of Hemingway sees that his pain was very real and the cause of it very real: I know of no American artist of Hemingway's stature who has been subjected to any comparable censure. He was always thin-skinned, though he tried to hide this vulnerability, and however much he was a counterpuncher, or however much he may have invited the attacks that were launched against him—most frequently he did not!—he was as one flayed under the malicious and sustained personal criticism he received. The *Selected Letters* reveal that twice in the 1930s Hemingway was pushed toward suicide by the pressure of the unrelenting critical attack, and the Baker letters reveal that he was, in the 1950s, desperately trying to survive such onslaughts again. What seems Hemingway's own mistreatment of men like Anderson and Fitzgerald and Lewis and Ford is another highly complex matter in no way germane to the issue here, which is a study of not the cause but the effect of such attacks on Hemingway himself.

Works Cited

Baker, Carlos. *Ernest Hemingway: A Life Story*. New York: Scribners, 1969.

———. *Hemingway: The Writer as Artist*. Princeton, NJ: Princeton UP, 1952.

Hemingway, Ernest. *Across the River and into the Trees*. New York: Scribners, 1950.

———. *Ernest Hemingway: Selected Letters, 1917–1961*. Ed. Carlos Baker. New York: Scribners, 1981.

Hotchner, A. E. *Papa Hemingway*. New York: Random House, 1966.

Acknowledgments

Many of the essays in this volume have appeared in a previously published form. The editor and publishers thank the owners of copyright for their permission to include selections in this volume.

"Set Piece." *The Hemingway Review* 14, no. 2 (spring 1995): 127. © 1995 The Ernest Hemingway Foundation. All Rights Reserved.

"Introduction." Sections presented at the Hemingway Society's Hemingway Centennial Conference, "Literary and Historical Perspectives at 100," Oak Park, Ill., 18–21 July 1999. To be published in the forthcoming proceedings.

Chapter 1. "Hemingway and Joyce: A Study in Debt and Payment," published as a monograph (Corte Madera, Calif.: Square Circle Press, 1984). Presented in an earlier version at the annual meeting of the Philological Association of the Pacific Coast, Stanford University, 1981. Sections presented at the Hemingway Society's "Ernest Heminway: The Writer in Context" program hosted by Northeastern University and Wellesley College, Spring 1982.

Chapter 2. "A Brief Safari into the Religious Terrain of *Green Hills of Africa*." *The North Dakota Quarterly* 60, no. 3 (summer 1992): 26–40. Paper presented at the Fourth International Hemingway Conference, Boston, Mass., 7–12 July 1990.

Chapter 3. "The Ritualization of Death and Rebirth: The Reconstruction of Frederic Henry." *Hemingway in Italy, and Other Essays*, ed. Robert W. Lewis (New York: Praeger, 1990), 133–42. Paper presented as "*A Farewell to Arms*: The Dynamics of Birth and Death" at the Second International Hemingway Conference, Lignano, Italy, June 1986.

Chapter 4. "The Suspended Woman in the Work of Ernest Hemingway." *Hemingway: Up in Michigan Perspectives*, ed. Joseph Waldmeir and Frederic Svoboda (East Lansing: Michigan State University Press, 1995), 265–74. Reprinted with permission of the publisher. Paper presented at the Second Up in Michigan Hemingway Conference, Petoskey, Mich., 17–20 October 1991.

Chapter 5. "Artists in Their Art: Hemingway and Velásquez—The Shared Worlds of *For Whom the Bell Tolls* and *Las Meninas*." *Hemingway Repossessed*, ed. Ken Rosen (London and Westport, Conn.: Praeger, 1994), 17–27. Reprinted with permission of the publisher. Paper presented as "The Artist in His Art: Hemingway in *For Whom the Bell Tolls*—A Comparison of Velásquez's *Las Meninas* and the Work of Ernest Hemingway" at the Fifth International Hemingway Conference, Pamplona, Spain, 15–21 July 1992.

Chapter 6. "'An Alpine Idyll': The Sunstruck Mountain Vision and the Necessary Valley Journey." *Hemingway's Neglected Short Fiction: New Perspectives*, ed. Susan Beegel (Tuscaloosa, Ala.: University of Alabama Press, 1992), 163–83.

Chapter 7. "Pilar's Tale: The Myth and the Message." *The Hemingway Review* 10, no. 1 (fall 1990): 19–33. © 1990 Ohio Northern University. Presented as "The Start of the Movement in Pablo's Town: The Complex Mythology of Pilar's Narrative in *For Whom the Bell Tolls*" at the Hemingway in Idaho Conference, Boise, Ketchum, and Sun Valley, Idaho, 9–11 June 1989.

Chapter 8. "*The Torrents of Spring*: Hemingway's Application for Membership in the Club." *North Dakota Quarterly* 66, no. 2 (spring 1999): 20–34. Presented at the Up in Michigan Hemingway Conference, Petoskey, Mich., 16–18 October 1998.

Chapter 9. "The Cost of Sin in the Garden: A Study of an Amended Theme in *The Garden of Eden*." *Resources for American Literary Study* 19, no. 1 (1993): 1–21. © 1993 by The Pennsylvania State University. Reproduced by permission of the publisher. Paper presented as "The Cost of Sin in Ernest Hemingway's *The Garden of Eden*" at the Third International Hemingway Conference, Schruns, Austria, June 1988.

Chapter 10. "On the Definition of a Definitive Text: Hemingway." *The Hemingway Review* 1, no. 1 (fall 1981): 18–22. © 1981 Ohio Northern University.

Chapter 11. "Dubliners in Michigan: Joyce's Presence in Hemingway's *In Our Time*." *The Hemingway Review* 2, no. 1 (fall 1982): 48–61. © 1982 Ohio Northern University. Sections presented at the annual meeting of the Philological Association of the Pacific Coast, Stanford, Calif., fall 1981.

Chapter 12. "Sacrifice and Redemption: The Meaning of the Boy/Son and Man/Father Dialectic in the Work of Ernest Hemingway." *North Dakota Quarterly* 62, no. 2 (spring 1994–95): 166–80. Paper presented as "The Isaac Syndrome: The Sacrificed Son and the Redeemed Father in the Work of Ernest Hemingway" at the American Literature Association Conference, San Diego, Calif., 28–31 May 1992.

Chapter 13. "'Is He Building a Bridge or Blowing One?': The Repossession of Text by the Author in *For Whom the Bell Tolls.*" *The Hemingway Review* 11, no. 2 (spring 1992): 45–51. © 1992 Ohio Northern University. Paper presented at the Southern Atlantic Modern Language Association meeting in Tampa, Fla., November 1990.

Chapter 14. "False Fathers, Doctors, and the Caesarean Dilemma: Metaphor as Structure in Hemingway's *In Our Time.*" *North Dakota Quarterly* 65, no. 3 (summer 1998): 53–61. Paper presented as "Craftsman at Work: The First Three *In Our Time* Stories and Their Intimate Relations—Metaphor as Structure in *In Our Time*" at the American Literature Association Conference on the Short Story, Cabo San Luca, Mexico, 7–10 November 1996.

Chapter 15. "*A Farewell to Arms*: The Psychodynamics of Integrity." *The Hemingway Review* 9, no. 1 (fall 1989): 26–32. © 1989 Ohio Northern University.

Chapter 16. "'Where Did Uncle George Go?': A Study of Debridement and Purgation Rituals in the Works of Ernest Hemingway." Published as "Purgation/Debridement as Therapy/Aesthetics" in *The Hemingway Review* 4, no. 2 (spring 1985): 12–17. © 1985 Ohio Northern University. Paper presented at the annual meeting of the Modern Language Association, New York, December 1983.

Chapter 17. "Gender and Role Reversal in Fitzgerald and Hemingway: Dick Diver's Metamorphosis and Its Hemingway Analogues." Published as "The Metamorphosis of Fitzgerald's Dick Diver and its Hemingway Analogues" in *French Connections: Hemingway and Fitzgerald Abroad*, ed. J. Gerald Kennedy and Jackson Bryer (New York: St. Martin's Press, 1998), 297–316. Reprinted with permission of St. Martin's Press, LLC. Paper presented at the Sixth International Hemingway and Fitzgerald Conference, Paris, France, July 1994.

Chapter 18. "Elephant Hunt in Eden: A Study of New and Old Myths and Other Strange Beasts in Hemingway's Garden." *The Hemingway Review* 7, no. 1 (fall 1987): 14–19. © 1987 Ohio Northern University. Paper presented at the annual meeting of the Modern Language Association, New York, December 1986.

Chapter 19. "The Oxymoronic Compound and the Ambiguous Noun: Paradox as Paradigm in Hemingway's A Farewell to Arms." North Dakota Quarterly 63, no. 3 (summer 1996): 40–49. Paper presented at the American Literature Association Studies in American Fiction Conference, Cabo San Luca, Mexico, 7–10 November 1991.

Chapter 20. "'Road to Hell Paved with Unbought Stuffed Dogs': Prefigurations of David Bourne in Hemingway's Earlier Work." Paper presented at the Eighth International Hemingway Conference, Les Saintes-Maries-de-la-Mer, France, 25–31 May 1998. To be published in the forthcoming proceedings.

Chapter 21. "The Mad Sad Bad Misreading of Hemingway's Gender Politics/ Aesthetics." North Dakota Quarterly 64, no. 3 (summer 1997): 36–47. Paper presented at the South Atlantic Modern Language Association meeting, Savannah, Ga., 11 November 1996.

Chapter 22. "Bridges: Their Creation and Destruction in the Works of Ernest Hemingway." Up in Michigan: Proceedings of the First National Conference of the Hemingway Society, ed. Joseph Waldmeir (Traverse City, Mich., 1983). Paper presented at the First National Conference of the Hemingway Society, Traverse City, Mich., 20–22 October 1983.

Chapter 23. "Harder on Himself Than Most: A Study of Hemingway's Self-Evaluation and Self-Projection in His Work." Paper presented at the Conference on American Literature at the American Literature Association meeting, Baltimore, Md., 28–30 May 1993.

Chapter 24. "Hemingway's Late-Life Relationship with Birds." Hemingway and the Natural World, ed. Robert E. Fleming (Moscow, Idaho: University of Idaho Press, 1999), 175–87. Paper presented at the Seventh International Hemingway Conference, Ketchum and Sun Valley, Idaho, 22–27 July 1996.

Chapter 25. "Androgyny and Individuation in the Work of Ernest Hemingway." Paper presented at the annual meeting of the Modern Language Association, New Orleans, La., 27–30 December 1988.

Chapter 26. "Gentlemen's Agreement: The Ernest Hemingway–Carlos Baker Correspondence in the Charles B. Field Collection of the Stanford University Library." IMPRINT (Spring 1987). Reprinted with permission of the Associates of the Stanford University Libraries and Stanford University Libraries Department of Special Collections.

Index

Numbers in **bold** indicate an entire chapter.

AEE-7036